IMPERILED WHITENESS

IMPERILED WHITENESS

How Hollywood and Media Make Race in "Postracial" America

PENELOPE INGRAM

University Press of Mississippi / Jackson

The University Press of Mississippi is the scholarly publishing agency of
the Mississippi Institutions of Higher Learning: Alcorn State University,
Delta State University, Jackson State University, Mississippi State University,
Mississippi University for Women, Mississippi Valley State University,
University of Mississippi, and University of Southern Mississippi.

www.upress.state.ms.us

The University Press of Mississippi is a member of
the Association of University Presses.

Any discriminatory or derogatory language or hate speech regarding race, ethnicity,
religion, sex, gender, class, national origin, age, or disability that has been retained or
appears in elided form is in no way an endorsement of the use of such language outside
a scholarly context.

Portions of chapters 3, 5, and 7 appeared in "Obama, Trump, and the Politics
of an Ape Planet," *Jump Cut: A Review of Contemporary Media* 58 (Spring), 2018.
https://www.ejumpcut.org/archive/jc58.2018/index.html
Reprinted by permission.

Portions of chapter 6 appeared in "Race, the Final Frontier: Star Trek, Trump and
Hollywood's Diversity Problem" from *The Kelvin Timeline of Star Trek: Essays on
J. J. Abrams's Final Frontier*, ed. Matthew Wilhelm Kapell and Ace G. Pilkington
(Jefferson, NC: McFarland © 2019): 39–57. Reprinted by permission of McFarland
& Company, Inc., Box 611, Jefferson, NC 28640. www.mcfarlandbooks.com.

Copyright © 2023 by Penelope Ingram
All rights reserved
Manufactured in the United States of America

First printing 2023

∞

Library of Congress Control Number: 2023012315
Hardback ISBN 978-1-4968-4549-8
Paperback ISBN 978-1-4968-4550-4
Epub single ISBN 978-1-4968-4551-1
Epub institutional ISBN 978-1-4968-4552-8
PDF single ISBN 978-1-4968-4553-5
PDF institutional ISBN 978-1-4968-4554-2

British Library Cataloging-in-Publication Data available

*To William and Thomas,
with hope for a better future*

CONTENTS

Acknowledgments ix
Introduction: Media Events, "Pandemic TV," and
    the Ruse of the Postracial 3
Chapter 1: White Identity Politics. 28

PART I: CONTAGION

Chapter 2: We're All Infected 75
Chapter 3: Simian Flu or Ebola Redux. 101

PART II: ANIMALITY

Chapter 4: When the Looting Starts, the Shooting Starts 127
Chapter 5: "Animals" with Guns 155

PART III: MONSTROSITY

Chapter 6: Bioengineered Monsters 203
Chapter 7: Of Chimeras and Men 227

PART IV: POSTRACIAL RESISTANCE

Interlude 255
Chapter 8: Black Horror. 260
Chapter 9: Animals with Technology 290
Conclusion: Media Matters. 309

Notes 331
References. 339
Index 374

ACKNOWLEDGMENTS

I started writing this book in the fall of 2016, during the campaign and election of Donald Trump, and I completed it a few months after the inauguration of Joe Biden in 2021 when the coronavirus pandemic was still rampant and new variants were springing up with alarming rapidity. From a research perspective, investigating media's role in racism and social extremism in the age of Trump proved to be a moving target. Occasions for analysis piled up daily: the White House careened from scandal to scandal (including two impeachment trials), and rallies celebrating white hate (Charlottesville, Capitol riots) and protests mourning Black death (Ahmaud Arbery, Breonna Taylor, George Floyd, and so many others) unfolded in real time.

Researching white supremacist and neo-Nazi movements is a depressing and degrading experience, and the support of family, friends, and colleagues has been invaluable during this long process. Peggy Kulesz, Amy Tigner, Tricia Jenkins, Bethany Shaffer, and Jennie Lawrence Hoffman provided many recreational escapes and opportunities to vent. Stacy Alaimo extended exceptional guidance and friendship over the years and was always available to talk through a question or a problem. In the deserted summer corridors of Carlisle Hall, Ken Roemer was a welcome friend and interlocutor whose patience, solicitude, wit, and conversation brightened some very long and solitary writing days. The College of Liberal Arts at the University of Texas at Arlington offered financial support in the form of a Faculty Development Leave and an Endowment for Faculty Research Grant. The Department of English offered supplemental funds for the purchase of media and other materials. Margie Jackymack was particularly helpful in securing funding for me and explaining to various university officials that *The Walking Dead* comics and DVDs and other assorted zombie miscellany were legitimate research expenses. I am extremely grateful to Rodney Dunning for allowing me to use, gratis, several of his photographs of the Charlottesville "Unite the Right" rally. I would also like to thank my students at UTA for their interest in this project over the years and their enthusiasm for my classes on "Race and Science Fiction,"

"'Postracial' Horror," and "Diversity on the Big and Small Screen in the Age of 'Colorblindness.'"

My family was an unfailing source of encouragement throughout the writing of this book. Although my mother did not live to see me finish it, I know she would have been proud of the work accomplished herein and happy that I finally "got my life back"! My dad's love and support and his constant question, "Are you finished yet?" kept me going at times when I wanted to quit. He offered valuable guidance and mentoring during the research, writing, and editing stages. I owe a big thank you to my sister, Louisa, who was always available for a quickish chat about politics and the state of the world and supported me during some very sad times.

Finally, I wish to thank my loving and patient husband, Cedrick May, for reading every single word of the manuscript and offering invaluable commentary and critique. It was in and through our many conversations about race and representation that I was able to clarify, amend, and hone my arguments. Finally, I dedicate this book with love to my sons, William and Thomas, who deserve a better world than the one they've got.

IMPERILED WHITENESS

Introduction

MEDIA EVENTS, "PANDEMIC TV," AND THE RUSE OF THE POSTRACIAL

On March 11, 2020, the World Health Organization declared COVID-19 a pandemic. The term is employed for those viruses that are "able to infect people easily and spread from person to person in an efficient and sustained way" (CDC 2020). While many Americans expected and feared such a declaration, Donald Trump's administration repeatedly downplayed the severity of the virus and its likely impact on Americans, likening it to the flu and asserting in January 2020 that the US had "very little problem" and the virus was "well under control," a sentiment he would repeat through February and March as the number of American deaths rivaled and eventually surpassed those in China and Europe (Watson 2020). By July 19, 2020, US deaths accounted for 142,926 of the 606,481 deaths recorded worldwide. By July 6, 2021, the number of US deaths had risen to 621,346 of a total worldwide toll of 4,003,549 (Worldometer, n.d.). Dahlia Schweitzer argues that "[h]ow a society responds to disease, especially epidemic disease, can illuminate its relationship not only to science and medicine, but also to illness, fear, death, and identity" (Schweitzer 2018, 33). The partisan response of the US reveals deep fissures in a cultural landscape riddled with competing truth claims. On February 28, Trump accused the Democrats of politicizing the coronavirus and called it "their new hoax" (Egan 2020). This talking point was quickly taken up by Fox News, with commentators like Sean Hannity repeatedly calling the Democrats' assessment of the virus's threat "hysterical" and the latest political cudgel in their war against Trump (Narea 2020). Rush Limbaugh, for his part, suggested the virus was a "deep state" plot (Grynbaum 2020; Henderson 2020). The pandemic became a global media event. As Hepp and Couldry make clear, "media events are intended—by the media or by other social actors who have interest in constructing reality in specific, perhaps conflicting ways—to establish certain discursive positions and to maintain those actors' power" (Hepp and Couldry 2010, 12). In a time of extreme physical isolation, Americans were bombarded with messaging about the virus. From broadcast news to narrowcast cable shows to streaming entertainment, the pandemic was not so much endured as it was *consumed*.

In April 2020, when most Americans were bound by their states' mandatory "stay-at-home" orders, *Vulture* magazine published a list of "The 79 Best Pandemic Movies to Binge in Quarantine" (Crucchiola and Ebiri 2020). Classic virus movies that mirrored the current situation like *The Andromeda Strain* (1971), *Outbreak* (1995), and *Contagion* (2011), which involve stories of airborne viruses infecting large swaths of the population, were popular, but the majority of films in this genre were zombie movies such as *Dawn of the Dead* (1978), *28 Days Later* (2002), *I am Legend* (2007), *World War Z* (2013), *Quarantine* (2008), and *Train to Busan* (2016), where "good" people must defend themselves against murderous, rapacious, undead "bad" people. The ubiquity and popularity of "Pandemic TV" (by which I mean not just pandemic/infection movies but highly popular entertainment content streamed in high volume during the 2020 coronavirus lockdown) is an instructive example of how entertainment media products assume new meanings in changed contexts and how "other discourses will set some of the terms in which any particular text is engaged and evaluated." As Dave Morley has argued, "[O]ther discourses are always in play besides those of the particular text in focus—discourses which depend on other discursive formations, brought into play through 'the subject's' placing in other practices—cultural, educational, institutional" (Morley 1980, 154). Along with the text, the consumer, too, is positioned in a web of discourses that shape and intervene in their reception of the text. Recognizing the pandemic as a media event is a productive way to think about the ways that "Pandemic TV" fed into other media discourses surrounding the pandemic. In the context of the coronavirus, the lockdowns, the rising death toll, and the growing partisan politicization of the virus, these seemingly anodyne escapist programs helped shape our views of and response to the pandemic in real time. As Udo Göttlich argues, media events are *"produced realities"* that "play a special role in *the dramatization of everyday life*" (Göttlich 2010, 172). The hybrid media platforms of news, entertainment, and social media produced the pandemic as a kind of "reality commodity" defined and circulated in a myriad of ways. Along with debates about real vs. fake science, partisan branding was a key output of audience/consumer/voter engagement with the competing stories of the pandemic.

Programs in the "Pandemic TV" cycle created, shaped, and helped to reinforce prevailing fears of "us" and "them." As Priscilla Wald notes, the "outbreak narrative . . . accrues contradictions: the obsolescence and tenacity of borders, the attraction and threat of strangers, and especially the destructive and formative power of contagion. It both acknowledges and obscures interactions and global formations that challenge national belonging" (Wald 2008, 33). Narratives of "us" and "them" are central to infection discourse, but also to populism, as the appeal of another "Pandemic TV" breakout hit, *Tiger King*, demonstrates. The "true crime documentary," riddled with murder, misogyny, gay and straight polygamy, as well as extortion, is at its core a story about a white working-class hero's struggle to secure his Oklahoma small business (a roadside zoo) from the rich animal-activist woman who wants to take him down. The narcissistic, delusional egomania of Joseph Maldonado-Passage, better known as Joe Exotic, and his obsession with painting his female rival, Carole Baskin, as a criminal, have prompted some commentators to draw comparisons between Joe Exotic and Trump (Sharf 2020). As one critic puts it, "They are both compulsive liars, misogynists, and business cheats with a penchant for bitter grudges against perceived enemies."[1] Despite such a comparison, or perhaps because of it, Joe Exotic was enormously popular. Netflix data reveals that *Tiger King* was watched by more than thirty-four million viewers in the first ten days of its release and is Netflix's most popular US Original of 2020 (Hersko 2020).

Tiger King was pushed out of its top spot in April 2020 by *Waco*, a limited series that dramatizes the 1993 standoff between the Branch Davidians, followers of cult leader David Koresh, and officers from the ATF and FBI. Although the FBI suspected the self-proclaimed messiah of practicing polygamy and child sexual abuse, it was the suspicion that the compound possessed a large stockpile of illegal weapons that precipitated the raid. The fifty-one-day siege in Waco, Texas, which resulted in the death of over seventy-six people, has long been considered proof by those on the far right that the federal government was seeking to limit the Second Amendment rights of citizens to bear arms. Waco was the event that prompted Timothy McVeigh to blow up an Oklahoma federal building in 1995, two years to the day after the Waco siege, and it was the memory of Waco that animated the 2014 armed-citizen defense of anti-government activist and cattle rancher Cliven Bundy in his standoff with federal and state law enforcement in Nevada. In other words, "Waco," in its myriad permutations, represents a consistent and effective rallying cry to the right. During the pandemic, the populist David and Goliath message of *Tiger King* and *Waco* was consumed alongside news stories about fracases related to masking, government overreach, Chinese bioterrorism, and "fake science," and helped to shape the way consumers of that media responded to the lockdown and reinforced their perspective on the role of the government in securing or restricting liberties. These media narratives constitute a form of cultural convergence wherein technology, politics, entertainment, and "the event" combine in a "matrix of processes," which is not external to the user but "occurs within the brains of individual consumers and through their social interactions with others" (Jenkins 2006, 3).

Obviously, we cannot ignore the commercial interests of media providers and the marketing strategies that inform programming decisions; however, profit aside, in the context of an international viral pandemic, we need to consider how these fictional texts construct our reaction to and perception not just of pandemics in general, or of Joe Exotic's guilt or innocence, or of the David and Goliath narrative proffered in *Waco*, but of the coronavirus crisis *as it is taking place*. We should consider how the discourse, dogma, scapegoating, and xenophobia inherent in the COVID-19 media event, because it functions as a shared reference point for many Americans, affect the way we understand and respond to the world around us. In other words, we should take note of how the sudden proliferation of narratives of "us" and "them," whether in the guise of a zombie outbreak, a gun-toting tiger tamer, or a defiant cult leader primes our real-time response to the social, political, and economic dynamics of *this* pandemic. As Stuart Hall notes, "Though the production structures of television originate the television discourse, they do not constitute a closed system. They draw topics, treatments, agendas, events, personnel, images of the audience, 'definitions of the situation' from other sources and other discursive formations within the wider socio-cultural and political structure of which they are a differentiated part" (Hall 1980, 118–19). A media event doesn't simply operate on a fictional plane to represent or remark upon something that happened in the past. Rather, it is so closely connected with the real that we can no longer find markers by which to distinguish the real from its representation, for it "gathers up into itself the reality of the event that may or may not have preceded it" (Fiske [1996] 2016, 2). In the communication/dissemination circuit of a hybrid media environment, media events produce a corollary "event culture" (Göttlich 2010, 173) that influences our perception of the pandemic—whether we see the virus as a natural pathogen or a foreign person, or whether we consider the closing of non-essential businesses as crucial to flattening the curve and keeping us safe or a dangerous restriction of our civil liberties.

CONVERGENCE CULTURE

Media events become part of the collective public consciousness in times of social crisis, indirectly interposing between and commenting upon real events, and priming our response to them. In a networked mediascape, the political cannot be divorced from the commercial and questions of power cannot be separated from industry concerns, even in the news. Film and television are consumed alongside their paratexts (blogs, zines, wikis, fan conventions, fan fiction, merchandise, spinoffs, etc.), and in the age of SVOD (Subscription Video on Demand), YouTube, and social media, these paratexts include news media. The versatility and myriad availability of entertainment and news programming produce a blurring of boundaries of each. Media studies scholars' attention to convergence, transmedia, paratextuality, complexity, "produsage,"[2] and flow are attempts to analyze and make sense of "new media" and how they foster both personal and public engagement while acknowledging their simultaneous containment by and resistance to free market neoliberalism. Certainly, the kind of interactivity that takes place between shows and audiences in "Pandemic TV" is part of this circuit of communication. Entertainment media texts are complex and dynamic, and consumers derive enjoyment from them in a variety of ways. However, recognizing media's pleasures and capacity to engage in contestatory discourse need not inhibit analyses of the cultural work entertainment can do. Producers and consumers of media are both constrained and enabled by larger social, economic, and political forces, and those constraints affect the way we receive and interpret media texts. As Harsin and Hayward recognize, "Politics rarely happens without popular culture because culture is one of the modalities where the popular, as a constitutive site of political actors and actions, is made material" (Harsin and Hayward 2013, 203). Because media are accessible on a number of platforms and devices, and generic boundaries are slipping partially as a result of modes of distribution and reception, the slipperiness between the real and the fictional and the effect of that slippage on consumers' views about issues relating to cultural and national topics, as well as their conception of their place in culture, is worth examining further. This is especially true because, as Herman Gray notes, these "crowded cultural and social spaces like [i]nternet-based social network sites (Twitter, Facebook) and user-generated content sites and distribution platforms (Instagram and YouTube)" fulfill consumers' "desire for recognition and the quest for individual distinction" (Gray 2013, 771).

In his extensive work on the relationship between culture and media, Gray has consistently and persuasively argued that "popular and commercial culture" has the "power to organize, articulate, and disarticulate feelings and understandings that move people, enlisting and positioning them in different political and social configurations." Recognizing that entertainment media is the place where consumers make sense of real-world social, economic, and political struggles, Gray examines how media both contribute to and provide counterpoints to hegemonic meanings (Gray 1995, 7). Apocalyptic pandemic movies and programs like *Tiger King* and *Waco* provide an insightful window into how fictional[3] narratives operate as forms of discourse, which *make*, rather than merely reflect or comment upon, social meaning. John Fiske argues that "the most significant relations of any piece of discourse are to the social conditions of its use . . . [and] its function in deploying power within those conditions." Like Gray, he recognizes that "[d]iscourses work to repress, marginalize, and invalidate others . . . and fight to promote and defend the interests of their respective social formations" (Fiske 2016, 4). *Tiger King*'s extensive popularity among all segments of the viewing audience at a time of national economic anxiety brought about by a "foreign" virus illustrates how popular entertainment television operates as both a carrier and a *producer* of political and cultural messaging. In a similar vein, the re-release of *Waco*, which had originally aired in 2018 and recounts an event that many on the right consider the ultimate symbol of federal overreach during a time when most state governments closed businesses and ordered citizens to stay at home, magnifies and dramatizes the isolation and threat that were prevalent in some communities.

In their portrayal of sympathetic outsiders led by compulsive, strong-willed white men who will not capitulate to social dictates or norms, *Tiger King* and *Waco* operate discursively to support and reignite white working-class people's perception of their marginality vis-a-vis prevailing systems of power. According to media and social media narratives that proliferated during lockdown, many (white) Americans shared this sentiment and railed against the intrusive power of government to regulate their freedom, even for the larger goal of keeping people safe. George Lipsitz observes that "culture exists as a form of politics, as a means of reshaping individual and collective practice for specified interests, and as long as individuals perceive their interest is unfilled, culture retains an oppositional potential" (Lipsitz 1990, 16–17). *Imperiled Whiteness* explores this negotiation between culture and politics, particularly the culture industries' capacity to shape the interests of diverse publics for political ends, and the oppositional potential individuals in the culture industry can leverage against such practices.

IMPERILED WHITENESS

Obviously, entertainment programs in the "Pandemic TV" cycle don't all elicit the same response among the viewing populace, but I contend that these shows do represent a carefully curated cluster of themes that target white audiences specifically and magnify a sense of perceived threat from an outside entity. Although the coronavirus has the capacity to infect all Americans and indeed disproportionately affects Blacks and Hispanics, "Pandemic TV" is a predominately white affair. White people are its victims and heroes; foreigners and outsiders contaminate and kill. "Pandemic TV" is the latest example in a cycle of programming explored in this book that buttresses and exploits an affective experience among a white populace, a feeling or sense of white vulnerability or loss that I call "imperiled whiteness." Rather than identifying this sentiment in entertainment media alone, I utilize a convergence/transmedia approach, examining how entertainment media work in tandem with other forms of media, including news media and social media, as well as political discourse on the left and right to circulate meanings around race, culture, and differences in society at large. As Gavan Titley has argued, the idea that racism is "debatable," which is to say it is open for contestation among different groups, is a result of the way public cultures are "shaped by dense transnational networks of media flow and communicative connectivity that provide unprecedented possibilities to both extend and challenge racializing discourses, images, frameworks and information" (Titley 2019, 3).

Reading fictional narratives through political ones, I argue that during the eight years of Obama's presidency, 2008–2016, and beyond, a variety of media platforms, including film, television, news, and social media, turned whiteness into a commodity that was packaged and disseminated to a white populace. These outlets propagated a narrative of whiteness under attack and did so in the context and under the guise of progressive "postracial" film and television, including the most prominent postracial ruse of all—Obama's presidency. Numerous scholars have noted that the concept of the postracial enables racism to "proliferate in the wake of the supposed death of race" (Goldberg 2015, 152) and has brought renewed attention to racism and who can define it (Titley 2019). Turner and Nilsen argue that postracial rhetoric employs colorblind ideology "to celebrate an image of a multicultural society while simultaneously disregarding the systemic and institutionalized racism impacting minority communities" (Turner and Nilsen 2019, 4). Similarly, Catherine Squires argues that postracial discourses "obfuscate institutional racism and blame continuing racial inequalities on individuals who make poor choices for themselves or their families" (Squires 2014).

While fully recognizing the covert centrality of whiteness to postracial discourses, I take a slightly different approach to argue that discourses of the postracial, in addition to reinforcing colorblind racism, enabled the rise of white identity politics among whites of different political leanings. In ways not possible in the late twentieth century, in climates where overt mainstream attention to white identity raised the specter of Nazism or the KKK, the rhetoric of postracialism allows for a celebration of white identity precisely because it disseminates the notion that racism and indeed, race itself, are seemingly obsolete. In the "Obama-to-Trump era,"[4] this renewed attention to "mainstream whiteness" has enabled a resurgence of the rabid white nationalism previously confined to racist dog whistles and legislative actions that restricted minority rights. As the editors of a recent collection called *Racism Postrace* observe, postracial mythology is "productive and generative, profound in its affective grasp on the cultural imaginary and dangerous in its capacities to confound and stymie struggles for racial justice and equality" (Mukherjee et al. 2019, 4). I argue that it was the discourse of postracialism, perversely, that made way for expressions of white identity and for movements advocating "racial justice" for whites.

Michael Omi and Howard Winant argue that colorblindness is just the latest in a long line of reactionary discourses meant to contain and constrain racial groups not part of the white majority (Omi and Winant 2014). The "e-racing" of race that colorblindness purportedly delivers results in "strategic 're-racings'" of non-white people "especially in the context of workplace tokenism, criminality, and national security" (Mukherjee et al. 2019, 7; see also Crenshaw 2012; Alexander 2010). I argue that white people, too, were subject to a discursive "re-racing" under the logic of colorblindness. Newly visible representations of whiteness surfaced in the context of narratives about Blackness and Brownness circulating on the airwaves. Images of whites in peril and under attack by an encroaching wave of otherness, forced to "fight back" and "take back" what is rightfully theirs, emblematized and reinforced the racialization of the social order.

WHITE IDENTITY POLITICS

Racial commodification is "a way of managing the production of racial epistemologies as embodied in media representations" (Saha 2018, 66). Typically, the commodification of racial identity in advertising and entertainment media occurs to non-white "others," to whom diversity is sold with the promise of recognition and access (Gray 2013; Squires 2014; Harper 1998; Mukherjee et al. 2019). Herman Gray has argued that, in the 1980s, commercial culture "produced, circulated and enacted" Blackness as a site of struggle open to rearticulation (Gray 1995, 2). I argue that in the Obama-to-Trump era, entertainment media seized upon and exploited the disaffection, fear, and anxiety in the white populace. Politicians on the right stoked anxieties about "losing ground" and "being left behind," and a form of commodified racialized whiteness was proffered to whites in a variety of forms. In this partisan postracial landscape, whiteness became an identity open to exploitation and definition. In a neoliberal marketplace, postracial mythology depends upon the leveraging of groups against one another. The magnification of white grievances has long been central to this calculus. What I identify in these media texts certainly participates in and reinforces this trope of victimization as privilege; however, much of that white affect arises from the hypervisibility of Blackness and Brownness (Knowles and Tropp 2016), as well as a proliferation of the ethnically "ambiguous" person as a symbol of "melting" and "mixing" that animates whites who fear being "replaced" or having their blood "diluted." The commodification of whiteness builds on this emotional base through a shoring up of white identity politics, whereby white privilege arises not from its unmarked value but through its newly marked status.

Social scientists observe that the rise of identity politics on the right is viewed by whites as analogous to the kind of racial/ethnic/sexual pride practiced on the left, including an embrace of intersectional identities (Kaufmann 2019; Jardina 2019; Knowles and Peng 2005; Knowles and Tropp 2016). To many whites, a demonstration of white pride or solidarity is merely an expression of pride in their Western, white, European heritage, a sense of belonging to which all groups are entitled. In his 2019 book *Whiteshift*, Eric Kaufmann argues that "ethno-cultural reference points dear to whites" should be celebrated and embraced in the same way as minority group symbols and identities are. Otherwise, he cautions, we end up with "'asymmetrical multiculturalism,' where minority identities are lauded while white majority ones are denigrated" (Kaufmann 2019, 519). However, as C. Richard King warns, "[T]hese rhetorical counterpoints are meant to reframe and normalize, allowing white power discourse to thrive in a colorblind, multicultural milieu" (King 2014, 222).

PERFORMING WHITE WITH THE ALT-RIGHT

Numerous scholars have demonstrated that internet platforms and social media sites like Parler and 4chan have contributed to a racial radicalization among certain groups of whites and have stoked the flames of white supremacy (Phillips 2012; De Cook 2018; Johnson 2018), what sociologists call "out-group hostility," but far less attention has been given to the way that white identity not linked to extremism has been cultivated in mainstream media, both the news media and in films and television. I suggest that the rise of the alt-right during the Obama administration not only gave a political, rather than merely cultural, meaning to white racial identity, it also turned whiteness into a performance that could be demonstrated and enacted. Indeed, it was the public performance of that whiteness, which was covered exhaustively by the media (by pundits on the left and the right) and in Trump's tweets, that turned whiteness into a saleable commodity exploited by the news and entertainment media. Importantly, this kind of "white identity activism" originates in mediated narratives of racial tensions during the Obama years, which were packaged and framed in ways that conjured white fears and stoked white pride. While the framing and agenda-setting perspectives of news outlets emphasized white group threat and stoked out-group hostility among whites, film and television depicted a white identity consistent with the postracial rhetoric of the time. How the media, in its myriad forms, co-opted the narrative around the postracial, making whiteness a disenfranchised commodity, and vivified white nationalist and neo-Nazi movements on the alt-right is central to my argument. So, too, is the part played by networked hybrid transmedia platforms and the blurring of the roles of consumers and producers of media texts. In the last few years, scholars have linked the rise of white supremacy to a networked media ecology where actors can mobilize and radicalize large groups at low cost and in a short period of time. As critics have shown, trolling and meme culture (Phillips 2016; Titley 2019; Johnson 2018) and the media's response to these online behaviors have contributed to the popularity and even "mainstreaming" of these groups (Winter 2017). While "dark" social media sites do figure into my analysis, I am primarily concerned with mainstream news and entertainment franchises that also relayed race messaging, albeit in a postracial, colorblind package.

Anamik Saha notes that "cultural industries shape the media products that we consume and, in turn, ideas about racial and ethnic difference as embodied in these texts" (Saha 2018, 6). It is vital, then, that we move from analyses that examine how media *represent* race to an analysis of how they *make* race (Saha 2018, 11). And this kind of race-making occurs in and on a variety of networked platforms, including news, entertainment, and social media. In a networked convergent media landscape, infotainment and journalism utilize the same kinds of cinematic sensationalism and are accessed in the same way as cinematic productions (Downing and Husband 2005; Sim 2016). Audiences consume entertainment media in the context of the social moment and the discourses produced in that moment. In the Obama presidency, this convergence of politics and media was instrumental in establishing a heightened sense of racial identity among whites. However, these media events weren't the sole construct of traditional media outlets. Because "[c]rises, breaking news situations, and in general, instances when news changes too quickly for mainstream media to develop a coherent and fully sourced narrative, bring ambient, always-on news platforms to the fore of news reporting" (Papacharissi 2015, 31), individual actors, too, participated in the narrativization and curation of these highly charged politicized events. In a twenty-four-hour "always-on" news environment, individuals "can not only influence but instigate a media event" (Fox 2016, 18). This convergence of broadcast, narrowcast, and consumer "prodused" content, along with a diverse range of TV shows and films released during Obama's presidency, directly impacted and regulated America's perception of and reaction to hot-button topics of his administration, including immigration, racial activism, and gun control. When viewed alongside the narrativization by the media of cultural flashpoints like DACA, #BLM, and debates over gun control and Second Amendment rights, these productions did more than entertain us; they intervened in and altered our understanding of the events taking place in real time.

SPECULATIVE FICTIONS

The fictional texts I examine in this project belong to the speculative fiction (SF) genre encompassing fantasy, science fiction, and horror. Numerous scholars and critics have acknowledged SF's long tradition of political and social allegory. The genre, whether through literature or film, has utilized aliens with advanced technology to comment on everything from atomic warfare to the war on terror. Representations of "imperiled whiteness" find a fitting home in white science fiction and fantasy because the genre has long navigated race in a doubled fashion, being simultaneously accused of reactionary and progressive postures in its depiction of racial difference. I've chosen to examine white SF texts here because I see distinct parallels between the postracial rhetoric of colorblindness that claims not to see race and the tropes employed by white SF to represent racial otherness and make racial meaning through metaphor and allegory. Both rhetorical modes advance white concerns, be it white fragility or white heroism, through racial obfuscation. Alien difference is an oft-used metaphor for racial difference, and conservative ideologies of gender and race frequently get reproduced in SF, attesting to their seeming natural inevitability. Indeed, the history of SF betrays culture's obsession with race and racial hierarchy and its efforts to conceal it. As Dominique Johnson observes, the "uncritical historicity of many dystopian fantasies encourages its creators and consumers to reassert hegemonic divisions when convenient, and thus reproduce racial subordination while encouraging hostilities under the guise of harmless artistic interpretation" (Johnson 2015, 261).

At the same time, white SF is frequently heralded as progressive and groundbreaking in its treatment of racial, ethnic, and gender differences. *Star Trek*, in particular, has defined itself through the philosophy of "Infinite Diversity in Infinite Combinations," and many fans see in the franchise the promise of world(s) without divisions. *Star Trek* has long been lauded for its liberal vision in part due to the well-documented politics of its creator, Gene Roddenberry. Several scholars have disputed this easy characterization, recognizing in the series' numerous spinoffs and iterations a contradictory and, at times, traditional ideology stemming from the liberal humanism of its creators and note that subsequent texts reflect the more conservative militaristic vision of global American dominance prevalent in the 1980s and '90s (Bernardi 1999; O'Connor 2012).

As a genre, then, white SF serves as a precursor to the colorblind fantasies peddled by the postracial, and at the same time, continues to enact and embody latent racial tensions still extant in American life. I include the modifier "white" in front of SF because, as numerous scholars have argued, the genre is permeated with racial assumptions, hierarchies, and anxieties. By contrast, Black SF creatives, like early pioneers George Schuyler, Samuel Delany, and Octavia Butler, and more recently Afrofuturists like Nnedi Okorafor, Nalo Hopkinson, and N. K. Jemisin, consistently foreground questions of race in innovative and provocative ways. Their texts frequently challenge white SF through direct engagement with racialized/racist metaphors or through racial world-building that ignores the tropes used in white SF altogether. Part four of *Imperiled Whiteness* will examine the challenge that two Black SF creatives (Jordan Peele and Ryan Coogler) present to white SF. While it may seem odd to include the work of Black filmmakers in a book titled *Imperiled Whiteness*, I do so as a means of pointing to the potential in the genre to rewrite and reimagine racial representations in SF. Adilifu Nama argues that:

> At its best, science fiction cinema challenges the audience to envision a world beyond our current conditions, for better or for worse. Whether or not the genre openly confronts the issue of black racial formation, American SF cinema still reflects the nation's struggle to confront and resolve the nagging problem of race, if for no other reason than that the ideological impulses, premises, possibilities, and limitations of black representation in American SF cinema have been and will continue to be a function of the oscillating state of race relations in American society. (Nama 2008, 41)

In utilizing the tropes and allegories central to white SF of contagion, animality, and monstrosity in ways that disrupt a white racial imaginary, Peele and Coogler offer a different kind of cultural race-making, what Ralina Joseph calls "postracial resistance," which has the capacity to re-form the genre in important and necessary ways.

Instead of presenting an extended list of SF films from 2008–2016 that represent race as simply progressive or regressive, I examine three highly rated, profitable, and popular film and television franchises produced during Obama's presidency—*The Walking Dead* (2010–2022), *The Planet of the Apes'* prequels (2011–2017), and the *Star Trek* reboots (2009–2016). The popular impact of these programs can be measured by their profitability and longevity. *Star Trek* and *Planet of the Apes* are two of the most lucrative and longest-running film and television franchises of all time. *The Walking Dead* has just wrapped its eleventh season and, at the nadir of its popularity in 2014, was one of the most-watched TV series in history. *Rise of the Planet of the Apes*, *Dawn of the Planet of the Apes*, and *War for the Planet of the Apes* have together earned over two and a half billion dollars worldwide, and the three *Star Trek* films have earned just over a billion. Eric King Watts notes that "colonial ventures, slave economies, concerns over widespread disease transmission, and global commercial traffic involving bodies and other consumables provide affective investments for the repetition and enjoyment of postracial fantasies" (Watts 2017, 321). I'm interested in the way these popular twenty-first-century stories reproduce, refashion, and maintain the well-traveled and well-interrogated colonial tropes of contagion, monstrosity, and animality in progressive postracial vehicles. I have chosen to examine SF texts because of the covert race-work that they do. The stories they tell seem innocuous because they're fantastic and unreal; yet these speculative texts, because they offer alternate realities, or, rather, because they transpose our reality into a fictional world, have considerable power to structure and guide our response to the social landscape. These programs are written and produced in a purportedly "postracial" space where diverse identities and cultures are foregrounded yet consistently feature white people under attack and the heroic, galvanizing measures they must take in order to retaliate in the face of encroaching danger.

FRANCHISES AND PARATEXTS

I've selected franchises rather than individual films because analyzing a movie franchise or serial franchise allows for a reading of racial meaning across texts and, in the case of *Star Trek* and *Planet of the Apes*, across decades. Both *Star Trek* and *The Planet of the Apes* have extensive paratexts, which include films, books, television shows, comics, and other media. As Jonathan Gray argues, "[A] filmic or televisual text and its cultural impact, value, and meaning cannot be adequately analyzed without taking into account the film or program's many proliferations." Each of these proliferations "holds the potential to change the meaning of the text, even if only slightly" (Gray 2010, 2). This transmedia approach enables a consideration of the role played by prequels, sequels, and paratexts in the construction of the narratives being presented.

In the case of *Star Trek* and *Planet of the Apes*, for example, an understanding of the original 1960–70s productions and their overt engagement with the politics of their own eras enhances our understanding of the franchises' later films. The early texts emerged during a period of racial turmoil at the waning of civil rights activism and the rise of Black Power movements. *Star Trek: The Original Series* (*TOS*) and the original film in *The Planet of the Apes* (1968) cycle both have been read as racially recuperative and inclusive of gender and cultural differences. As Daniel Bernardi has argued, race and racial differences are an integral part of *Star Trek* and its paratexts. The *Star Trek* "mega-text" is "both implicitly and explicitly about the meaning of race: about integrated casts and crew; about anthropomorphic aliens and intergalactic half-breeds; about the discovery and exploration of extraterrestrial worlds and cultures; about space colonies, colonizers, and dissident movements; about a utopian [E]arth where there is no poverty, no crime, and . . . no racial discrimination" (Bernardi 1999, 3). In these productions, Black characters are no longer structurally absent but instead have speaking roles—in the case of *Star Trek*'s Lt. Uhura (Nichelle Nichols), ongoing significant ones.

But, as Nama notes, "[B]y the mid-to-late 1970s, Black Power politics was almost completely extinguished, the blaxploitation film craze was in a precipitous decline, and a white cultural backlash against the perceived excesses of the struggle for racial justice was gathering a full head of steam" (Nama 2008, 22). The later films in the original *Apes* franchise (*Beneath*, *Conquest*, and *Battle*) reflect this reversal. Just as I demonstrate the current *Apes* reboot draws from racial tensions surrounding Black Lives Matter activism and the rise of white nationalism, these earlier films are part of their own historical media event. Paratexts, whether prequels, sequels or reboots, are always in dialogue, whether intended by the filmmakers or not, with the original representation. Analyzing these current franchises through their earlier intertexts, in addition to the media discourses that surround them, offers a perspective on the cultural race-work being undertaken in these newer iterations, particularly the two-pronged representation of whiteness in peril and in power.

The Walking Dead franchise, which is so large AMC calls it *The Walking Dead Universe*, includes the original comic series by Robert Kirkman, the AMC network television program *The Walking Dead* (*TWD*), two spinoff series: *Fear the Walking Dead* and *The Walking Dead World Beyond*, a live aftershow featuring *TWD* actors called *Talking Dead*, numerous video games based around plots from various seasons, as well as *The Walking Dead Universe* Twitch Stream, multiple fan blogs, and a variety of merchandise including clothing, mugs, wine glasses, Funko Pops, toys, posters, etc. Significantly, AMC was one of the first networks to target fan participation through its live-tweeting "Story Sync" experience, which allowed fans to take polls, answer trivia questions, and access exclusive content while watching the broadcast. An analysis of *TWD*'s extensive range of paratexts is clearly beyond the scope of this book,[5] but an examination of aspects of fan engagement with the show on social media is relevant, especially in relation to two racially polarizing (from a fan perspective) characters: white Merle, an explicitly racist "redneck," and Black Michonne, an intelligent, skilled fighter. As Angie Fazekas argues, "[F]andom has an ongoing and overwhelming problem with race . . . [D]espite claims of progressives, there is a significant tension in transformative fandom between its unmet potential to be a space of gender subversion and radical sexual politics and the way it often ends up falling short and falling back on racist narratives" (Fazekas 2020, 95). Fan interaction should be understood as another kind of produsage and, when read in the context of the cultural and political climate of the program's production, forms part of the show's media event. SF is critical to this examination of how cultural tastes of diverse publics are shaped in and through media texts, for no other form of entertainment produces as vast a transmedia consumption as SF. Although fans engage with different genres in myriad ways, the capacity of SF texts to generate extensive paratextual universes has had a more profound impact on culture than any other literary, dramatic, or comedic genre.

While speculative fiction has a long history of fashioning public perceptions of the "other," I would argue that a key component of this allegorical power is SF's secure distance from reality. "By absorbing real-world issues into the relatively 'safe' realm of fantasy, . . . [the] relatively marginal status [of SF] frees the genre to express ideas suppressed in the political public sphere" (Takacs 2012, 176). Indeed, the futurity of events depicted in speculative texts can "obscure racialist meaning . . . and often masks the presence of race and racism" (Lavender 2011, 30). Although the three franchises belong to the SF genre, they are quite different in tone and scope. It is possible, however, to identify trends across the franchises, specifically the kinds of storylines that are foregrounded: whites under attack by monstrous others—others that, in every case, are not human but can be seen to stand in for humans of color. These representations are two-pronged, both depicting white people in peril and the courageous measures they employ to combat the incipient threat. These programs are written and produced in a purportedly postracial space where diverse identities and cultures are central to the story. However, despite the inclusive casting and the depiction of multiracial resistance to global threats, whiteness prevails. The effect is a fostering of in-group solidarity without overtly stoking out-group hostility. As Ashley Jardina notes, however, the two sentiments are connected: "[H]istory is replete with examples of how in-group favoritism can be a source or component of group hostility, oppression, and violence . . . [for] the same factors that have led to the increased salience of white identity among the general white American population have energized pro-white movements across the country" (Jardina 2019, 275).

IMPERILED WHITENESS PROGRAMMING CYCLE

In their book *Horrible White People*, Taylor Nygaard and Jorie Lagerwey examine a cycle of programming comprising thirty-plus-minute comedies featuring "Horrible White People" (HWP), whom the authors define as "well-intentioned, self-identified liberal White characters who are floundering and who emphasize their own precarity" (Nygaard and Lagerwey 2020, loc. 247).

Nygaard and Lagerwey note the impact of the Great Recession (2007–2009) and its cultural aftermath (2014–2016) on popular media representations of whiteness in comedies like *Louie, Casual, Fleabag, Broad City, Girls, Transparent*, and many others. This "period of dramatic cultural change," they argue, "continues to disproportionally centralize affluent Whiteness and White suffering in an era of growing income inequality, highly visible racial inequality and violence, rampant anti-immigration rhetoric, and persistent gender and sexual discrimination against marginalized communities" (Nygaard and Lagerwey 2020, loc. 239). The SF shows I examine here certainly form part of the same cycle of programming as the comedies analyzed in *HWP*. My book attempts to understand and theorize the factors that *animate* and *perpetuate* this cycle, specifically the role played by the convergence of entertainment, news, and social media in a digital, networked environment.

The centering of whiteness across genres in television and film during this period is worthy of note. However, the differences in genre also yield variances in the representation of that whiteness. Nygaard and Lagerwey argue that white social and economic precarity is highlighted in these comedies in order to "recenter liberal White failure and victimhood while usurping attention from the plight of minorities whom these liberal and progressive White people supposedly seek to help" (Nygaard and Lagerwey 2020, loc. 270). Whereas *HWP* shows take liberal white people and "white people problems" as their primary focus, my programs, consistent with the generic attributes of SF, at first glance, decenter whiteness through overt incorporations of diverse races and species in characters and worlds. However, because these representations rely on tropes that have historically reinforced racist attitudes and practices that have justified slavery, lynching, disenfranchisement, disproportionate rates of incarceration, and violence by police on the streets and at the border, in speculative fiction programming of this era it is not liberal whiteness that is being recentered, but an older, more familiar form of whiteness. This is the whiteness that provokes KKK rallies and Jim Crow laws, redlining, and One Strike laws. It acquits police killers and puts immigrant children in cages. It is the same kind of whiteness, in other words, that revitalized white supremacy movements in the so-called postracial age.

Certainly, zombie films and postapocalyptic films are always popular movie fare and frequently feature white families in peril. The shows I examine here are clearly not the only programs in the speculative genre with a capacity to construct and shape new forms of whiteness or evoke anxiety about the security of white identity. Rather than offer an exhaustive list of programs that do function in this way, I offer these franchises as highly popular and profitable examples of how SF is able to disguise white racist fantasies about the monstrosity of the other and foster the simultaneous and opposing feelings of white precarity and white supremacy. Paul Elliott Johnson argues that "[a]llegories create connections between audience members in which the *substitutive* rather than *representative* character of the narrative effectively conceals how the allegory might unite audiences at the level of shared assumptions" (Johnson 2016). Released at a time of purported white "wokeness," these representations appear to do postracial work of inclusion and diversity but, instead, package race in ways that reinforce white norms and at the same time gesture to white loss. Informed by the rhetoric of colorblindness, which "justifies and perpetuates systemic racial differences," these programs "galvanize" a "multiplicity of white identities" (Turner and Nilsen 2019, 4), representing widespread feelings of white precarity and the white machismo required to combat it.

METHODOLOGY

I employ a diverse methodology and draw on a variety of disciplines: cultural studies, media studies, postcolonial and race studies, philosophy, and film studies, and endeavor to contribute insights about the production and consumption of race in culture industries beyond just the analyses of the entertainment franchises offered in the book. In other words, I recognize that analyses of fictional representations of race can be something of a closed circuit. Studies that attend only to the accuracy or inaccuracy of representations or good and bad depictions of minorities risk falling into "representational correctness" (Schiappa 2008) and neglect the complexity of representations and the diversity of experiences and backgrounds of groups being represented (Harper 1998). Beyond a simple recognition that they are made in a nexus of relations of economic, social, and political power and of the cultural work that such representations facilitate in maintaining structural inequality, the value in this kind of work, then, is to shed light not just on the fact that they're made or why they're made, but *how* they're made and how they continue to be made and endure through the centuries.

Twenty-first-century representations of racial otherness are remarkably unchanged from their colonial iterations, but their repurposing in techno-progressive "colorblind" vehicles of contemporary film and TV is worthy of examination for the way they seemingly attempt to undo the race-work of those earlier texts. In relation to a proliferation of positive media representations of Muslim Americans after 9/11, Evelyn Alsultany has argued that such progressive depictions constitute a "new kind of racism, one that projects antiracism and multiculturalism on the surface but simultaneously produces the logics and affects necessary to legitimize racist policies and practices" (Alsultany 2013, 162). Examining the politics of representation today means recognizing how race is made in an assemblage of technological practices individually and collectively. Digital technologies are instrumental in reinforcing racial views as well as constructing and shaping new ideas about race and how actors construct racial identities online. As Lisa Nakamura and Peter Chow-White note, "the digital is altering our understanding of what race is as well as nurturing new types of inequality along racial lines" (Nakamura and Chow-White 2012, 2).

Using a transmedia lens to analyze media representations of race during Obama's presidency reveals a renewed attention to whiteness, not as a transparent universalizing norm, but as a marked, beleaguered identity in a struggle for its existence. While that narrative, as I will discuss, was often cultivated and disseminated on right-wing talk shows and websites, it was frequently masked in cultural and creative texts by and through the rhetoric of the "postracial"—including, but not limited to, an increase in the number of people of color cast in supporting roles and storylines that attended to various forms of difference. This is a form of what Catherine Squires calls "post-racial mystique," a cultural effect "conjured by the disjuncture between the entrenched effects of institutional racism and the media texts that deny—or purport to resolve—racial inequalities" (Squires 2014, 129). Eduardo Bonilla-Silva and Austin Ashe observe that "diversity in its symbolic form is a part of the abstract liberal agenda" (Bonilla-Silva and Ashe 2014, 68); at the same time, as I will argue in this book, expressions of diversity can reinforce a more openly conservative agenda, sending a message of white dispossession and or irrelevance. Part of the appeal of speculative fiction texts is that they represent events "that could never happen." But this is the reason why we should attend closely to how our consumption of these forms of media can produce that seeming impossible reality. Because "the media is directly involved in the production of racial ideology, specifically colorblind racism" (Bonilla-Silva and Ashe 2014, 68), viewing fictional texts in and through the social conditions of their production and through the paratexts and intertexts that surround them reveals how forms of discourse can project particular kinds of knowledge that serve prevailing systems of power.[6] As Titley explains, "The 'politics of representation' today, therefore, is more than an academic field of textual research. It is a distributed practice increasingly integrated into everyday media engagements with the flow of symbolic content, and honed to contest or accentuate, however ephemerally, the register of representations of race" (Titley 2019, 37). Reading these franchises within the context of the surrounding cultural events and media analyses of those events in the Obama-to-Trump era, I argue that these major franchises reproduced well-established colonial and racist stereotypes of contagion, animality, and monstrosity in a postracial, progressive package. Further, I argue that such representations contributed to a prevailing anxiety, documented by sociologists and political scientists, among "mainstream" non-radicalized whites about "race mixing" and the ceding of cultural and economic power to surging minority populations and prompted renewed attention to white identity politics.

POSTRACIAL RESISTANCE

Media interpret cultural and historical moments as we experience them; therefore, they can also represent contested sites of social struggle. The toxic racial environment circulating around Trump gave rise to a variety of film and TV shows drawing attention to anti-Black racism. Comedy-dramas like *Insecure* (2016–2021), *Atlanta* (2016–2022), *Dear White People* (2017–2021), and *She's Gotta Have It* (2017–2019), and dramatic films like *Birth of a Nation* (2016), *BlacKkKlansman* (2018), *If Beale Street Could Talk* (2018), and *Blindspotting* (2018), helmed by Black creatives, are just a few examples from different genres that represent another cycle of programming arising from the environment of virulent racism on display in the Trump era. As a way of understanding how mediated race-work operates in counter-hegemonic ways and can be generative of alternative political capital, I devote part 4 of this book to an examination of select films of Jordan Peele and Ryan Coogler, specifically *Get Out* (2017), *Black Panther* (2018), and *Us* (2019). Produced and released in the Trump era, these films respond creatively to the current racial landscape by employing the genres of horror and fantasy to satirize white fears of empowered minorities and to refashion representations of racial difference in philosophical and generically formal ways. These highly popular, lucrative films engage in a form of "postracial resistance" (Joseph 2018, 2). I argue that the genre of speculative fiction allows Peele and Coogler to "trouble" the visual field in which Black life has been presented as knowable and consumable (Fleetwood 2011). In doing so, Black SF alleviates the demand placed on realist filmmakers to produce the "truth" of Black life. Herman Gray reminds us that "commercial culture operates as a site of and a resource for black cultural politics" and "African Americans continually appropriate images and representations from commercial culture in order to reconstitute themselves and therefore transgress the cultural and social locations that constantly attempt to contain and police them" (Gray 1995, 4–5). Just as white SF productions maintain and uphold white space through postracial rhetoric, Black SF offers Black filmmakers a means of interceding in and disrupting colorblind racism.

Get Out was released in the US just three days after Trump's inauguration and inspired later efforts in the speculative genre like 2019's reboot of *The Watchmen* and 2020's *Lovecraft Country*. Peele's success with *Get Out* and *Us* enabled him to produce other racially progressive horror films, such as Nia de

Costa's *Candyman*, a remake of Bernard Rose's 1992 film starring Tony Todd, and paved the way for other Black horror productions like *Ma* (2019) and *Antebellum* (2020).[7] The significance of *Black Panther* as both a commercial and creative success cannot be overstated. *Black Panther*'s membership in the MCU, a franchise that routinely centers whiteness and white strength, makes Coogler's achievement even more remarkable. Not only is Coogler the first African American to direct a film in the Marvel franchise, but (at this writing) *Black Panther* is the highest-grossing film of all time by an African American director. In his critically successful first film, *Fruitvale Station* (2013), Coogler brought issues of racial justice to the big screen in the harrowing depiction of the 2009 killing of Oscar Grant at the hands of a BART police officer in Oakland, California. His second film, the seventh installment in the *Rocky* series, was a commercial and critical success focusing on the son of Apollo Creed. But it is his adaptation of the story of the lesser-known superhero Black Panther and his creation of a vibrant, evocative Wakanda that brought Black and white filmgoers to the cinema in droves and in costumes, which illustrates the power of narratives of contestation. Heeding Zakiyyah Jackson's call to reimagine Black life beyond the scope of animalized abjection and "denied humanity," I explore the ontological possibilities that *Black Panther* and Afrofuturism offer for disrupting, subverting, and rewriting the association of Black people as animals (Jackson 2020, 3).

Like the shows in the "Imperiled Whiteness" cycle examined in the first part of the book, this Black cultural work, when interpreted through a transmedia lens (that is to say, through the narrativization by the media of resurgent white nationalism, ongoing incidents of racially motivated police violence, and the birth of "zombie Republicans" [Krugman 2020]), constitutes a media event with the capacity to contest media narratives of white precarity. I am not suggesting that the increase in production and popularity of films engaging with anti-Black racism necessarily represents a marked shift in American racial attitudes or even a significant Hollywood trend in filmmaking. And we should not discount how the increase in this kind of programming reflects the desire of Hollywood to capitalize on emerging white support on the left for #BLM after the murder of George Floyd. Herman Gray, Anamik Saha, MaryAnn Erigha, and Nancy Wang Yuen have argued for a greater understanding of the role Black creatives can play in the mediascape and also how they are constrained by neoliberal forces that require concessions and capitulations to Black creative visions. While the popularity of *Get Out, Us,* and *Black Panther* with white moviegoers is important and can certainly indicate white interest in entertainment that disrupts the racial status quo, there are many science fiction/fantasy/horror franchises not engaged in race-work or that actively traffic in racist stereotypes, which are equally popular with white moviegoers and audiences of all races. Entertainment media dealing with racial themes have the capacity to produce complex, ambivalent, and contested responses among audiences (Gray 1995; Saha 75); I offer the work of Peele and Coogler here not to represent a sea change in Hollywood but rather to demonstrate how two high-profile Black filmmakers are redeploying classic SF tropes of contagion, monstrosity, and animality—tropes that do significant race-work in the "Imperiled Whiteness" cycle—in order to expose the anti-Black racism that is foundational to the fabric of the United States and the national cannibalism that an American nativism produces.

POSTRACIAL POSTURING

My goal in this book is twofold: first, to demonstrate how three SF franchises during this period offered seemingly progressive narratives while at the same time consistently reproduced historically racist imagery in the utilization of the tropes of contagion, monstrosity, and animality; and second, to illuminate how the race messages (the sense of whiteness in peril) in these popular franchises are reinforced by concomitant political and social media narratives concerning race and race relations that stoke out-group hostility. Racial tensions became increasingly inflamed during the Obama era and are reflected in the polarization of the American populace regarding the Deferred Action for Childhood Arrivals (DACA), the Black Lives Matter movement (BLM), and debates over gun control. I read the popular culture texts through these three political flashpoints as a way of demonstrating how entertainment media cannot be divorced from the cultural and political locus in which it is produced and as a means of interpreting the resurgence of a toxic, deadly white nationalism, and the popular, and at least initially unexpected, appeal of Donald Trump to a white populace. We cannot understand the fiction of the postracial and its cultural and systemic effects without understanding how "public policies and practices geared to state repression and violence, the material impacts of populist white anger, as well as those of social movements and alliances geared to racial and social justice" interact with cultural products in a commercial marketplace (Mukherjee et al. 2019, 5).

Although I take whiteness as my subject, it is not my intention to draw attention to whiteness in order to reaffirm its centrality or to validate its perceived precarity; rather, my aim is to demonstrate how Hollywood, in the guise of decentering whiteness through diverse and multiethnic stories and casting, which is to say in its "postracial" posturing, has been centering whiteness through transmedia racial "storytelling" targeting and appealing to white fragility and its cousin white supremacy. As a white woman, who, at the onset of this project, belonged to the key eighteen-to-forty-nine-year-old viewing demographic, I represent the ideal consumer of this kind of programming. Interestingly, my identity as a feminist and antiracist theorist and activist, drawn to the progressive genres of fantasy and science fiction, also positions me as part of the ideal viewership for this kind of entertainment. The science fiction and fantasy franchises that belong to the cluster of "Imperiled Whiteness" programming exhibit a doubleness—an ability to appeal to racist *and* antiracist communities. These programs utilize "racial symbolic capital" that animates white desire and "depends less on appropriation or impersonation than on the theatricalization of race itself, the production of a kind of fantasy zone amenable to racial phantasmagoria" (Lott 2017, 7). But these well-traveled racial fantasies, masked by the cover of postracial colorblind rhetoric (including diverse casting and seemingly racially sensitive narratives), evoke white vulnerability, whether as a result of economic, viral, or monstrous calamity and a galvanized white response to that fear. Elements that fuel colorblind ideologies, or what we might also call "postracial posturing," mask overt racism through the employment of tropes of contagion, monstrosity, and animality, while at the same time recentering whiteness and its perceived loss of status and fading economic power. I attempt here to offer a framework by which fictional representations of white peril can be read and understood alongside political events and the reporting of those events in news and social media. It is my hope that this analysis will provide another lens by which to interpret twenty-first century's toxic racism and can be taken up by other scholars and applied to other franchises and genres.

In chapter 1, I set up the parameters of the book's argument, explaining in more detail how the convergence of digital platforms, networked media, and twenty-four-hour "always on" news cycles results in forms of race-making. I then examine the contours and meaning of whiteness in the Obama and Trump eras, particularly how analyses of colorblind racism have obscured our understanding of the ways that white identity politics was being curated not just on the far right but in mainstream media narratives during this time. Then I will turn to media analysis, specifically the concept of transmedia and convergence culture, to show how media narratives about the three political flashpoints (DACA, BLM, and gun control) I examine in later chapters were read in terms of the stories about vulnerable whiteness being represented in entertainment media. Specifically, I outline the concept of the media event and convergence culture and how popular entertainment media operates as both a carrier and producer of political and cultural messaging.

In the chapters that follow, I will demonstrate how the racial, cultural, and political flashpoints of Obama's presidency operated as shared reference points for the nation, regardless of their political orientation, and shaped the way the viewing public would receive the fictional stories they consumed. Part one, "Contagion," examines the connection between racial or foreign otherness and contagion. I explore how the discourse of pollution, infestation, or infection is repeatedly utilized to figure the threat that Hispanics and African Americans are considered to pose to the nation and its people. In chapter 2, "We're All Infected," through a reading of the zombies in *The Walking Dead*, I argue that the language of pathology and disease is used in news and entertainment media in discourse about the immigrant/refugee/asylum seeker and examine the potential impact of that association on the attitudes and voting practices of Americans. In chapter 3, "Simian Flu or Ebola Redux," through an examination of *Rise of the Planet of the Apes*, I analyze how white fear of African American advancement and the myth of African American exceptionalism is represented as an uncontainable (simian) virus with the capacity to destroy the (white) human population or render it mute.

In part two, "Animality," I explore the association of African Americans with criminality and lawlessness and how that association has justified and authorized excessive policing and impacted legislative and policy conversations regarding gun control. In chapter 4, "When the Looting Starts, the Shooting Starts," I look at the political and cultural context surrounding the release of 2014's *Dawn of the Planet of the Apes*, which included an unprecedented number of racially incited police murders of Black people and the ensuing protests, including those over the deaths of Eric Garner, Michael Brown, and Tamir Rice. I argue that the timing of the franchise's release and its representation of violent, lawless apes, who seek revenge on humans for injustices done to them, cement a long-standing racist association of Blackness with animality and criminality and justify and naturalize the incarceration of African Americans. In chapter 5, "'Animals' with Guns," I examine how guns and their valorization and use in *The Walking Dead* work to uphold white racial politics and underscore a prevailing narrative in white America, exploited by Trump, that white culture is vulnerable to attacks from non-white others, and must be defended. I argue here that the overt and constant scenes of violence against zombies occlude the racial violence that takes place on an intra group level between white and Black survivors. In the first five seasons of the show, *The Walking Dead* promotes a survivalist, doomsday prepper culture that glorifies white masculinity at the same time as representing white men as victims that need to "take back" their country.

Part three, "Monstrosity," explores how the dissolution of species boundaries can be seen to be entwined with fears about the dissolution of racial boundaries and national boundaries, as well as the social and cultural hierarchies that keep those boundaries in place. In chapter 6, "Bioengineered Monsters," I argue through a reading of *Star Trek Into Darkness* and *Star Trek: Beyond* that Brown and Black people are represented as instruments of biological terror with the capacity to destroy the purity and superiority of whiteness. In chapter 7, "Of Chimeras and Men," I demonstrate through a reading of *Rise of the Planet of the Apes* how the racial monster trope gets articulated through anxieties related to science and eugenics, specifically the fear that advanced biotechnology will not only eradicate human dominance over animals but will potentially eradicate white dominance over non-whites. Drawing on the work of social scientists, geneticists, bioethicists, journalists, and cultural studies scholars, I argue that monstrous themes and imagery in popular science fiction productions are racialized in the context of the resurgence of white supremacy and neo-Nazi movements.

Part 4, "Postracial Resistance," turns away from media representations of whiteness and looks at the ways Jordan Peele and Ryan Coogler use SF to contest and trouble the depiction of Black life as it is represented in realist films. In chapter 8, "Black Horror," I argue that in addition to exposing the hypocrisy of white progressives and their fetishization of Blackness, *Get Out* plays on white fears of miscegenation by depicting an aging, anemic whiteness that quite literally requires the vitality of Black life to sustain itself. In *Us*, I suggest that Peele broadens his critique of America, implicating all of "us" in the horrors of the political environment of the Obama-to-Trump era. In our divisive insularity and partisanship, we are all tethered to a shadow world of our own making. Contagion resides not outside our borders but within ourselves. This section also examines the social and cultural work that Black horror can do. While recognizing the political and cultural importance of the films' narratives, my reading extends our understanding of their significance by attending more closely to the generic elements of the films and the underexamined role that form can play in an analysis of the politics of Black film. Chapter 9, "Animals with Technology," returns to the persistent trope of bestialization in anti-Black racism, arguing that *Black Panther* asks us to consider how the kind of world-making central to the fantastic offers new possibilities for Black identity at both a political and *ontological* level, and what cultural difference it might make. I argue that Coogler's Wakanda forces viewers to wrangle with the promise of American democracy, as well as offering possibilities for interrogating and undermining the colonial logic which has excluded people of African descent from the category "human" since the transatlantic slave trade and produced an ontological crisis for the Black subject.

In the conclusion, "Media Matters," I return to two of the series discussed in the book, *The Walking Dead* and *Planet of the Apes*, as both franchises continue into the Trump era, yet the recent installments differ in significant ways from the earlier iterations produced in the Obama years. I argue that seasons 7–10 of *TWD* and the last film of the *Apes* franchise, *War for the Planet of the*

Apes (2017), respond to the racial backlash they helped to produce, offering an alternative to the fears they stoked during the Obama era in the persons of Negan and The Colonel, respectively. Instead of glorifying the violent, oppressive tactics both men deploy, I argue that each character functions as a portent of what awaits an America supportive of and manipulated by the oppressive tyranny of leaders like Trump.

Chapter 1

WHITE IDENTITY POLITICS

On January 6, 2021, a riotous, violent pro-Trump mob stormed the US Capitol with the intent of disrupting the joint session of Congress convened for the purpose of formalizing the election of Joe Biden as the forty-sixth president of the United States. The siege, which lasted nearly three hours and resulted in the death of five people, including a Capitol police officer, was undertaken by a throng of people bearing an assortment of weapons (including stun guns, pepper spray, and baseball bats). They broke through barricades, smashed windows with police shields, looted offices, and rifled through sensitive material left on the House floor as members of Congress fled in fear for their lives (Dreisbach and Mak 2021). The group, summoned to Washington by Trump (Barry and Frenkel 2021), attended a "Rally to Save America" on the evening of January 5 as speakers who believed that Trump was the real victor in the 2020 election, fabricated claims of election fraud engineered by a cabal of Democrats, communists, and left-leaning media outlets. The frenzy continued the next day when Trump held his own "Stop the Steal" rally where he repeated the false narrative of a stolen election, which he called "an egregious assault on our democracy," berated his heretofore loyal Vice President Mike Pence for his refusal to overturn the results of the electoral college, and encouraged his supporters to walk to the Capitol and "show strength" because "you'll never take back our country with weakness" (Chavez 2021). As of November 2022, the FBI had charged more than nine hundred people with crimes related to the riots, including charges of conspiracy, criminal acts of violence, property damage, theft, and unlawful entering of a restricted building. Trump himself faced an unprecedented second impeachment charge of inciting the insurrection.[1]

Many Americans, still bound by COVID-19 lockdown restrictions, watched the violence and mayhem from their living rooms and expressed incredulity at the unfolding melee. Not only was the act of insurrection itself shocking to many, so too were the size and fervor of the crowd, as well as the delayed response by law enforcement to the criminal and violent acts being performed. Numerous commentators noted the vast difference between the

"Stop the Steal" insurrectionists loyal to Donald Trump scale the walls of the US Capitol during the January 6, 2021, riot. (Jose Luis Magana, Associated Press)

lack of police presence at the Capitol on January 6 and the swift, excessive, heavily militarized (assault rifles, tear gas, shields) preemptive display and use of force employed against Black Lives Matter protestors in the aftermath of the death of George Floyd in May of 2020. By contrast, the mob on January 6 itself deployed tear gas, metal pipes, and shields to repel officers and invade the Capitol. Video of the attack reveals some members of the Capitol police taking selfies with rioters and others standing aside to let them enter the building (Chason and Schmidt 2021; Chavez 2021; Brantley-Jones et al. 2021). It was several hours before the National Guard was activated, even though the attack had been largely organized, orchestrated, and telegraphed for months on social media (Marcotte 2021). While the scope of the attack on the Capitol was shocking and surprising, the zeal of the insurrectionists and their blind devotion to Trump were not. The presence of Confederate flags, QAnon shirts, Proud Boys hats, white supremacist banners, and a variety of other hate symbols reflected the specific form of pro-Trump extremism cultivated by Trump and the right-wing media.

Throughout his presidency, Trump courted the support of the alt-right. He deliberately avoided denouncing neo-Nazis and white nationalists after a "Unite the Right" rally organized to protest the removal of a statue of Confederate General Robert E. Lee in Charlottesville, VA on August 12, 2017, ended in deadly violence and prompted the governor to call for a state of emergency. Although the neo-Nazis had marched the night before bearing torches and shouting

QAnon followers and other Trump supporters seeking to overturn 2020's election results confront US Capitol police outside the Senate chamber of the Capitol Building on January 6, 2021. (Manuel Balce Ceneta, Associated Press)

"Jews/You will not replace us" (Chia 2017) and the protest itself ended with an avowed Nazi supporter plowing his car into a street of peaceful protestors, killing one woman and injuring nineteen more, Trump asserted that there was hatred, bigotry, and violence on "both sides." His failure to repudiate Nazis and the KKK shocked and angered Democrats and Republicans but thrilled the white supremacists, who wrote on the neo-Nazi website the Daily Stormer: "He didn't attack us. . . . No condemnation at all. When asked to condemn, he just walked out of the room. Really, really good. God bless him" (*New York Times* 2017; Wang 2017). Former Grand Wizard of the KKK, David Duke, tweeted "Thank you President Trump for your honesty and courage to tell the truth about #Charlottesville & condemn the leftist terrorists in BLM/Antifa" (Kunzelman 2017).[2] While those who marched in Charlottesville did so under the banner of white supremacy, the most striking thing about the Capitol rioters is the number of Americans participating who did not identify with the alt-right (*NPR* 2021). Insurrections and protests like the ones taking place at the Capitol and in Charlottesville represent an "emerging form of white male identity politics that far exceed[s] the boundaries of white nationalism" and represent a "cataclysmic remaking of the social order that would restore white men to their entitled place in society" (Kelly 2020, 2). Interestingly, and perhaps surprising to many is the fact that, of the rioters charged, only 16 percent have ties to far-right, extremist, hate, or conspiracy groups, including the Proud Boys, the Oath Keepers, and QAnon. Unsettling to many government officials

Armed militia groups converged on Charlottesville, Virginia, August 11 and 12, 2017, to protest the removal of Confederate statues and monuments. (Rodney Dunning)

is the fact that 13 percent of those arrested and charged in the riots are current or former law enforcement officers and military members, including one of the casualties, Ashli Babbit, a fourteen-year Air Force veteran, who ran a pool supply company with her husband and had formerly supported Obama.

Scholars who track the rise of hate groups have noted that the "soft barriers" separating support for Trump from support for conspiracy theorists or hate groups have collapsed. Michael Hayden, an investigator at the Southern Poverty Law Center, notes the "degree to which your bread-and-butter GOP supporter, who fills out rallies and events, seem to be intermingling with extreme far-right factions: accelerationists, neo-Nazis, white nationalists, people who believe there is no political solution at all" (Bergengruen 2021). The cause for this creep of white identitarian politics into mainstream white culture, particularly those whites who do not identify as supremacists, is the subject of this book. The majority of whites who are "high on racial solidarity," meaning whites who have a strong sense of racial identity and who express a "sense of commonality, attachment, and solidarity with their racial group," argues Ashley Jardina in her book *White Identity Politics*, eschew the white supremacy moniker and are "primarily concerned with their in-group and desire to protect its status" (Jardina 2019, 3, 8). Historically, white supremacy has flourished both through legally enacted forms of racial discrimination, including slavery and Jim Crow, and also through covert racist practices that limited opportunities for minority advancement through redlining, gerrymandering, police brutality,

Member of the far-right, anti-government militia group "Three Percenters" at "Unite the Right" rally in Charlottesville, Virginia, 2017. (Rodney Dunning)

disproportionate rates of incarceration, and other systemic forms of oppression. However, scholars note that white supremacy in its current form is pervasive and extends well beyond easily identifiable modes of discrimination (Wise 2010; Bonilla-Silva 2014). Rather, it is better understood as a collective "operation of forces that saturate the everyday, mundane actions and policies that shape the world in the interest of white people" (Gillborn 2006). "Whiteness, then," as Eduardo Bonilla-Silva argues, "in all of its manifestations, is embodied racial power [w]hether expressed in militant (e.g., the Klan) or tranquil fashion (e.g., most members of the white middle class) and whether actors deemed 'white' are cognizant of it" (Bonilla-Silva 2003, 271).

In its modern iteration, white supremacy as a philosophy may characterize the racist views and vitriolic actions of groups like the Proud Boys, Oath Keepers, Minutemen, and Patriot Prayer, but it also includes those whites who do not consider themselves racist and who do not align with specific ideologies of racial inferiority. In research conducted after Obama's election, Jardina finds that 30–40 percent of whites express strong in-group identification, but those views are not necessarily synonymous with prejudice against and racial hatred for non-whites. However, she argues that those feelings of in-group solidarity do arise from a sense of cultural and racial displacement due to the imminent future where whites will no longer constitute the majority group in America. As Eric Kaufmann argues in his book *Whiteshift*, "Demography and culture... hold the key to understanding the populist movement. Immigration is central.

Donald Trump supporters contesting the 2020 election of Joe Biden as president advance on the Capitol Building, Washington, DC, January 6, 2021. (Jose Luis Magana, Associated Press)

Ethnic change—the size and nature of the immigrant inflow and its capacity to challenge ethnic boundaries—is the story" (Kaufmann 2019, 7).

This chapter will examine the rise of this arguably "softer" form of white identity politics: where it comes from and how it is cultivated and feeds into the more virulent, rabid forms expressed by avowed neo-Nazi white supremacist groups. Indeed, the argument of this book is that in a networked media ecology, a variety of actors, including news media, entertainment media, and users of social media, construct racial meanings (particularly a racialization of white identity) on both sides of the spectrum (in-group solidarity and out-group animus). Agenda-setting and framing by news outlets on immigration reform, BLM, and issues of gun control from 2008–2016 stoked racial resentment and out-group hostility (and certainly, we can argue that that was the deliberate intention of shock jocks like Limbaugh and O'Reilly [Jardina 2019] and later Hannity and Carlson); however, entertainment media work in tandem with news media and social media to cultivate feelings of white vulnerability and potential weakening of white identity, which effectively promote and foster feelings of white solidarity among all white people, even those who espouse liberal or progressive political views. Social scientists surveying racial attitudes among whites during the period Obama was in office found that a large number of whites believed anti-white bias was more prevalent than anti-Black bias (Norton and Sommers 2011, 215). Researchers note that "[i]ntergroup hostility does not come solely from 'realistic' conflict over power or material resources, but is also influenced by psychological responses to economic and physical duress" (Oliver and Mendelberg 2000, 575). Jardina's research shows that white identity is tied to American identity: "[T]he construction of whiteness is based largely around three themes: its relationship with a particular conception of American identity, the adoption of a sense of pride and entitlement, and the prevalence of a sense of grievance and deprivation" (Jardina 2019, 119). All three of these themes are on display in the three "Imperiled Whiteness" franchises I examine in this book. And these two sides of the spectrum (white vulnerability and white solidarity) help to explain the doubleness of these narratives—how they appear to be progressive and inclusive, appealing to a diverse viewership while at the same time bolstering white racial solidarity through appeals to its vulnerability. This two-sidedness is also reflected in the story Americans tell themselves about what the election of Obama represented, what it purportedly said about America as postracial. It gave the illusion that racism was a thing of the past, that white Americans were "off the hook" with regard to social and economic inequities that fracture along racial lines. As conservative commentators argued after Obama's win, the election demonstrated that "the myth of racism as a barrier to achievement in this splendid country" could finally be put to rest, and they called on Obama to lead the effort to do so (Feagin 2013, vii).

Henry Jenkins uses the term "convergence" to describe "the flow of content across multiple media platforms, the cooperation between multiple media industries, and the migratory behavior of media audiences who will go almost anywhere in search of the kinds of entertainment experience they want" (Jenkins 2006, 2). In an age of purported postracial colorblindness, and at a time when media outlets inform and entertain in frequently indistinguishable ways, I explore the role played by the news media and entertainment media in the construction of a *newly visible* white identity shaped by a sense of white vulnerability and white pride. Because "convergence alters the logic by which media industries operate and by which media consumers process news and entertainment" (Jenkins 2006, 16), I'm interested in the way race and racial meanings were "produced," circulated, and consumed across these digital platforms. I argue that strategies of fandom (including performance and brand identification, which are cultivated in entertainment franchises) were utilized by different kinds of media outlets, including mainstream news and social media platforms, as well as more fringe, niche, alt-right partisan news programming (Breitbart, Infowars) and that they crossed over and became operable in political and racial identity movements. The effect of these strategies was to develop and reinforce a collective white identity among whites of different backgrounds and political leanings—both "racially resentful" whites, i.e., white nationalists and others on alt-right who embrace a whiteness steeped in "Western Chauvinism," and "racially conscious" whites, i.e., whites who don't tie racial identity with the in-group to racial hostility against an out-group (Jardina 2019).

After the Capitol riots of January 6, Mark Pitcavage, a Senior Research Fellow at the Anti-Defamation League, noted that, "one can't just simply say there are mainstream Trump supporters and then there are these extremists, white supremacists or whatever, because some of those Trump supporters are no longer mainstream, they have become an extreme movement of themselves" (Trianni n.d.). Conversely, we might say not that the mainstream has become extremist, but the extremists have become mainstream (Knowles and Tropp 2016; Winter 2017). Indeed, as the results of the 2020 election, where Trump received 57 percent of the white male vote and 47 percent of the white female vote reveal (Igielnik et al. 2021), white support for Trump far exceeds those who identify with the alt-right. Indeed, while many white voters openly embrace his brazenly racist and sexist language, other whites are drawn to his appeals to racial identity, even if they themselves don't couch that identification in terms of racial hostility.[3] As researchers polling white attitudes in 2011 noted, whites believed that anti-Black bias was on a sharp decline, whereas anti-white bias was increasing. And this perception, researchers argue, stems not from a difference in racial disparity but rather from "recent changes in how bias is conceptualized" (Norton and Sommers 2011, 216). In other words, there is no demonstrable change in racial prejudice itself, just the way people are encouraged to think about it. A study published in 2021 noted that the perception of bias was in large part due to the way the media "exacerbate perceived differences between racial and ethnic groups, political parties, religions," contributing to "increasing tensions and the gaps between 'us' and 'them'" (Isom et al. 2021, 213).

AFFECTIVE RACISM

The genesis and articulation of this specific "Trumpian Whiteness" (both its hard [racially resentful] and soft [racially conscious] forms) can, in part, be seen in a cycle of programming, both mainstream news and entertainment media narratives, produced during Obama's presidency.[4] More than ever in the age of convergence culture, consumers of media are not isolated but always situated in political, cultural, and institutional discourses (Hall 1978, 2004, 2019; Lipsitz 2006; H. Gray 1995, 2013; Couldry 2010; Fiske 2016). Media texts influence the way people understand and interpret cultural events, but they also play a consequential role in the structuring of attitudes and perceptions around race; they serve "as a barometer of race relations and a potential accelerator either to racial cohesion or to cultural separation and political conflict" (Entman and Rojecki 2000, 2). In his influential work *Policing the Crisis*, Stuart Hall ties the rise of authoritarian populism of 1970s–'80s Britain to the ideological and discursive construction by the press of the crime of mugging, a crime which Hall notes in the intervening period had become associated with Black youth (Hall et al. 1978). Hall et al. show how the media's production of a crisis legitimized the encroaching coercive power of the State, smoothing the way for Thatcherism. In a similar vein, Herman Gray (1995) documents how right-wing, anti-Black sentiment was disseminated in and through both news and entertainment media in the Reagan and Bush years through repeated and frequent depictions of Blacks and Latinos as monstrous and violent. "Crack whores," "super predators," "terrorists," and "other threats to the American way of life" were reproduced and repackaged in order to reinforce in whites a sense of group threat on economic and identity levels. In a similar vein, postcolonial scholars examine the ways that minority, indigenous, and other subalterns are represented in the literature of the dominant classes. Such work demonstrates how certain representations reproduce or challenge power relations, as well as other differences of race, class, and gender. Scholarship that attends to representations of whiteness as a racial category typically understands it as transcendent or unmarked (Dyer 1997; Frankenberg 1993; Morrison 1992). And though there has been renewed attention to whiteness studies (Winddance Twine and Gallagher 2008), especially in the so-called postracial era where whiteness enjoys greater privilege as a result of colorblind racism, analyses of the specific ways that whiteness is represented in the Trump era are only just beginning (Johnson 2017; Kelly 2020; Nygaard and Lagerwey 2020). Most scholarly attention to colorblindness has assessed how colorblind rhetorics serve neoliberalist agendas and "reify and legitimize racism . . . by denying and minimizing the effects of systematic and institutionalized racism on racial and ethnic minorities" (Nilsen and Turner 2014, 4). I fully concur with these analyses of how colorblindness perpetuates *structural* racism but am interested in how it also perpetuates *affective* racism.

Jardina notes that identity, "a psychological, internalized sense of attachment to a group . . . can provide an important cognitive structure through which individuals navigate and participate in the political and social world" (Jardina 2019, 4). Postracialism and colorblindness clearly function as accommodating fictions to a white majority and reinforce white privilege, but how does postracial rhetoric in its negation of the importance of the role race plays in regulating social structures produce a corollary experience of white anxiety among certain whites that they are losing their *identity*, which is tied to their status, their place atop the racial hierarchy? Although many of the whites Jardina interviewed did not express overt racial animus toward other groups, 30–40 percent of them expressed a desire to "reassert a racial order in which their group is firmly at the top" (Jardina 2019, 5). Woody Doane makes clear that "colorblind racial ideology is *not* about the inability to see color or

"Unite the Right" rally in Charlottesville, Virginia, 2017. (Rodney Dunning)

the lack of awareness of race," but rather the perception that "race is most often (but not always) defined as a characteristic of *individuals* in a world where racism is no longer a major factor and race plays no meaningful role in the distribution of resources" (Doane 2014, 17). If racism is no longer a *system* that regulates racial relations, whites might perceive themselves as having as much to lose as minorities supposedly have to gain. As Jardina notes, "white identity is sometimes latent, but it is also *reactive*—made salient by threats to the dominance of whites as a group" (23).

Through an examination of the cultural production of race in news, social, and entertainment media, I argue that white people were depicted as a casualty in a mediascape where race purportedly no longer mattered, provoking feelings among whites of "imperiled whiteness." Obviously, as I will argue, the feeling of a loss of status among whites is itself a form of affective racism; my point here is that postracialism fostered different kinds of racial appeals to whites. Take, for example, the following quote from Rush Limbaugh:

> How do you get promoted in a Barack Obama administration? By hating white people, or even saying you do, or that they are not good, or whatever. Make white people the new oppressed minority and they are going along with it, because they're shutting up. They are moving to the back of the bus. They are saying I can't use that drinking fountain, OK. I can't use that restroom, OK. That's the modern day Republican Party, the equivalent of the old South, the new oppressed minority. (Quoted in Jardina 2019, 219)

If a sense of racial solidarity among whites impacts how they engage with political and social issues and is a "pivotal factor in contemporary electoral politics" (Jardina 2019, 4), then we should look to the way that whiteness became racialized during the Obama era and contributed to white support for Trump, who deliberately and effectively mobilized whites around their racial identity (Jardina 2019; Kaufmann 2019; Coates 2018; Belcher 2016; Knowles and Tropp 2016). In the context of Obama's presidency, including the announcement of right-wing pundits that Obama was a Muslim working for ISIS, that his election signaled the end of the white race or a Black takeover, where racial violence by police was met with protest and civil unrest, and where stories about Obama's failure to secure the US/Mexican border led to a belief about an imminent Mexican takeover, whiteness became a commodity ripe for "reclaiming" in a postracial marketplace. In a media landscape saturated by stories of otherness, a specific kind of programming curated a particular form of white identity consumed by white audiences. Beyond race-baiting and debased, stereotypical representations of minorities, certain media narratives during the Obama years capitalized on and made a commodity of white identity. In a "postracial" media landscape that was already suffused with a variety of non-white content, "whiteness" became a site of contestation and struggle.

MEDIA FRAMING AND RACE-MAKING

Rush Limbaugh's 2009 statement, quoted above, is an example of an overt appeal to whites about the status threat that Obama represented. However, cultural representation is a complex phenomenon with competing claims, and it would be reductive and determinist to suggest that all media in the Obama era facilitated representations of Black and Brown threat and whites in peril. On the contrary, as I demonstrate below, 2008–2016 saw a considerable number of movies and television shows featuring Black leads and "Black stories" in a positive, progressive light. Certainly, the film and television franchises examined in this book appeal as much to progressives as to conservatives. It is the "doubleness" of these purported postracial entertainment narratives that interests me most, especially when read alongside stories in the news about immigration, racial activism, and gun control. I analyze how these seemingly contradictory representations work together to deepen our understanding of the way "cultural industries *make* race" (Saha 2018, viii). Although news media purportedly value impartial and objective reporting and telling stories from "both sides," often the effect of such proclaimed balance is to reinforce extant majority white views. As Stuart Hall explains, news media frequently assume the role of "making comprehensible what we would term 'problematic reality.'"

In addition to selecting which stories they deem newsworthy or commercially appealing, news media frame those stories in ways that repeatedly shape and reinforce cultural presumptions "through a variety of 'explanations,' images and discourses which articulate what the audience is assumed to think and know about the society" (Hall 1978, 56).

Through agenda-setting and framing and a twenty-four-hour news cycle where journalists are forced to produce an ongoing supply of material and keep current stories trending, news media draw on outrage and buzz. And much of this buzz is generated on social media platforms where "motivated and strategically oriented actors" influence "the resulting agenda of issues" (Papacharissi 2015, 29). Rather than ascribe motive, prejudice, or even a broader agenda on the part of the media or Hollywood or to argue that all whites responded the same way to these stories, I demonstrate a media environment ripe for white identity race-making. Specifically, I argue that multiple modes of "storytelling" (Papacharissi 2015)—news media, social media (including image boards like 4chan and 8kun), television programs, and film franchises—create the discursive field in which and over which competing claims and struggles as to what constitutes "American" identity are waged, and that, in a putatively colorblind postracial age, this struggle is tied to the meaning of white identity. How, then, did media narratives, including progressive Hollywood fare, circulating during the presidency of Barack Obama produce, enable, and encourage expressions of white identity that simultaneously depicted white people as victims and victors? How do these media outlets contribute to a sense among whites that whiteness itself is imperiled? And how has this narrative of white precarity precipitated the entry into American circles of inflammatory and discredited beliefs like the Great Replacement Theory, which is fueling populist movements on the European far right?

RACE ON THE BIG AND SMALL SCREEN

In the eight years of Obama's presidency, there was an increase in the kind and number of African American representations onscreen. Indeed, not since the 1980s and '90s, the era of Spike Lee and John Singleton, have we seen such an emphasis on African American storylines and characters (Caffrey 2013). On the eve of the inauguration of Obama's second term in 2013, *New York Times* film critics A. O. Scott and Manohla Dargis wrote:

> Four years ago, on the historic occasion of Barack Obama's first inauguration, we took a look at the good, bad and outrageous movie characters who helped make his election possible. The road to the White House,

we wrote, hadn't just been paved by Mr. Obama's speeches, innovative campaign strategies and the hopefulness of a majority of voters, but also by decades of African-American men in movies.... Now, on the eve of a second Obama term, the images are more complex, and in some ways blurrier. Politically and personally this president functions as a screen onto which different Americans project their fears and fantasies. (Scott and Dargis 2013)

In the same vein, Sarah Turner and Sarah Nilsen note that "during a time of unprecedented social discord and division," which is to say in our so-called postracial moment, the "film industry has been engaged in a discursive battle over the articulation of current racial relations" (Turner and Nilsen 2019, 6). David Izzo notes that movies in the Obama era used "race" as context and subtext, whether through overt racial narratives like *Twelve Years a Slave* or covert ones likes *The Hunger Games* "that are about outsiders seeking to get inside and influence the status quo" (Izzo 2015, viii). Many of the films produced during Obama's first term exploited old stereotypes. *The Blind Side* (2009) and *The Help* (2011) are two examples that use the worn trope of the powerless Black character as a foil for the growth and development of the open-minded white who "rescues" them. In Obama's second term, however, there were more nuanced, progressive offerings featuring Black actors and Black storylines that were big at the box office and prompted conversations about slavery, oppression, Blackness, and retribution. In 2012, *Django Unchained*, Tarantino's violent epic of slave revenge, or as Scott puts it, "a wild and bloody live-action cartoon" (Scott 2012), was nominated for five Academy Awards, including Best Picture (it won Best Original Screenplay and Best Supporting Actor) and grossed over $425 million at the box office. In 2013, Steve McQueen's *12 Years a Slave* also earned adulation with nine Oscar nominations and three wins, including Best Picture, and grossed $188 million worldwide. Though different in temperament and style—*Django* is a biting satire and *12 Years* a harrowing drama—and helmed by a white and Black director, respectively, both of these movies expose the violent, dehumanizing degradations of slavery and the culpability of whites in the process. As *Rolling Stone*'s Peter Travers makes clear, "[Y]ou don't just watch *12 Years a Slave*. You bleed with it, share its immediacy and feel the wounds that may be beyond healing.... McQueen basically makes slaves of us all. It hurts to watch it" (Travers 2013). The year 2013 alone saw at least six movies produced that featured African Americans: *The Butler, Fruitvale Station, The Inevitable Death of Mister and Pete, Blue Caprice,* and *42*. These films deal with issues as various as civil rights reform, gun violence, homelessness, and discrimination in sports. Indeed, critics have dubbed this period as marking the beginning of "Hollywood's African-American film renaissance" and penned articles assessing "Why the Black Image is Dominating Contemporary Film" (Caffrey 2013; Davis 2016; Rose 2013). One reviewer opined that Lee Daniels's *The Butler* "promised to be a kind of cultural signpost, an occasion for still more soul-searching and commemoration leading to this month's 50th anniversary of the March on Washington" (Seymour 2013).

The small screen played its part, too. From 2010 to 2018, Shonda Rhimes, an African American writer and producer, dominated the coveted Thursday night primetime lineup on ABC with three shows featuring strong Black characters: *Grey's Anatomy*, *Scandal*, and *How to Get Away with Murder*. *Scandal* (2012), which ran for seven seasons, had consistently high ratings and won several awards, including being named "Television Program of the Year" by the American Film Institute in 2013, as well as numerous Emmy and Golden Globe awards. The drama stars African American actress Kerry Washington, whose character, Olivia Pope, is a "fixer" initially working exclusively for the White House and the white president, with whom she is having an affair. Olivia Pope was instrumental in rigging the election win for the president and, in the first few seasons, essentially runs the day-to-day operations of the White House. Another Shonda Rhimes production, *How to Get Away with Murder* (2014), stars Emmy, Tony, and Academy Award-winning actress Viola Davis, playing a Black female law professor and criminal defense attorney involved in investigating and, at times, covering up murders. These programs, although wildly popular among fans, have prompted at least one prominent white critic to read Rhimes's powerful, intelligent female characters as versions of the "angry Black woman" (Stanley 2014).

Black men have also enjoyed the spotlight. Lee Daniels's award-winning *Empire* exploded onto TV screens in 2015 as the only broadcast series in twenty-three years to increase its viewership in each of the televised first five episodes (*NewsOne* 2015). Looking to capitalize on *Empire*'s success, in 2016, Fox also aired the comedy-drama *Atlanta*, starring Donald Glover, which follows two cousins trying to make their way in the rap scene of Atlanta. Both productions focus on the music industry and drug culture and are viewed as "authentic" Black shows by some critics.[5] In the case of *Scandal*, *How to Get Away with Murder*, *Empire*, and *Atlanta*, the popularity of "Black shows" and the visibility of Black faces on TV seems to produce racial anxiety among certain viewers and critics about whites getting equal time. According to a writer for *Deadline*, some critics suggest that "the pendulum might have swung a bit too far in the opposite direction. Instead of opening the field for actors of any race to compete for any role in a colorblind manner, there has been a significant number of parts designated as ethnic this year [2015], making them off-limits for Caucasian actors" (Andreeva 2015). Ironically, Rhimes's production company does employ colorblind casting, which critics argue obscures rather than enables minority representation and frequently depicts Black characters devoid of Black experiences. Kristen Warner argues that because "[f]ixed racial identities operate at the level of skin color . . . Rhimes builds characters that occupy a more universal normative appeal." Shondaland shows, Warner argues, "appeal to mainstream (White) audiences who do not want to 'see' race" (Warner 2015, 42; Bonilla-Silva and Ashe 2014).[6] In an example that reveals the way fans interact with story-worlds, Warner demonstrates how Black female fans of *Scandal* interrogate the colorblind racial politics of the show through a clever composition of memes and GIFs that allow them to "fill the gaps" left in the show's attempt to "mainstream" Olivia, while at the same time expressing their affection for the characters (Warner 2015).

RACE IN THE REAL WORLD

It wasn't just at the movies that Black lives and Black history were being foregrounded. As one critic argued of 2013, "[Y]ou could not escape the matter of race if you tried" (Respers 2013). Frequently, it was white people who were accused of racial improprieties: lifestyle maven Paula Deen's use of the "N-word"; the scandal of the white NAACP Spokane chapter president, Rachel Dolezal, passing as Black; the outing of numerous politicians and celebrities for past or current wearing of blackface; and the Supreme Court's overturning of a portion of the Voting Rights Act. In 2013, three Black women, Opal Tometi, Alicia Garza, and Patrisse Cullors, founded the grassroots movement Black Lives Matter (#BLM) in response to the acquittal of George Zimmerman in the murder of unarmed seventeen-year-old Trayvon Martin. Although Obama was frequently criticized by the Black community for not taking a deliberate stand on racial issues, he personalized Martin's death—"Trayvon Martin could have been me 35 years ago"—and addressed the unequal treatment of African Americans in the legal system: "[T]here is a history of racial disparities in the application of our criminal laws, everything from the death penalty to enforcement of our drug laws" (*Washington Post* 2013). His statement angered conservative commentators and voters, who accused him of being a "racial agitator" and of letting his race interfere with his judgment and the good of the country (Thernstrom 2013). BLM's organizational strength and mobility have continued to grow through protests against the ongoing violence of police toward African Americans, most notably the 2014 killings of Michael Brown and Eric Garner, most recently, the 2020 murder of George Floyd; Black deaths in custody; and the disproportionate rate of Black male incarceration, more generally.[7] In 2016, the San Francisco 49ers' quarterback Colin Kaepernick made headlines and infuriated many whites for refusing to stand for the National Anthem at the start of his games in protest against police brutality. Beyoncé did her part, too. Her half-time show at the 2016 Super Bowl inflamed police officers who called the show anti-law-enforcement and urged police to boycott the security detail for her upcoming concerts. Donned in outfits reminiscent of those worn by Black Panthers and evoking images of recent police shootings of unarmed Black people, Beyoncé used the national platform to make a political statement about the importance of Black lives (France 2016). It's not surprising that a *New York Times* poll taken in July 2016 found that racial discord among Blacks and whites was at its highest level since the 1992 acquittal of Los Angeles police officers for the beating of Rodney King and the riots that ensued in its wake (Russonello 2016).

These cultural flashpoints, the growing cultural presence of Black Lives Matter activism against police violence, and Obama's response to this violence, in addition to the proliferation of Black characters on TV and film, all formed a media event that contributed to the growing sense of "imperiled whiteness," that is, a sense that white issues and white lives had been pushed aside, and whites risked being "replaced"[8] by growing minority groups and concerns. Media events operate as forms of discourse, the primary function of which is to produce forms of knowledge that support prevailing systems of power.[9] These feelings of white precarity were fueled by both news and entertainment media, furthering a racial divide in American culture and politics. As Blackness became more visible and a general sense of anti-white discrimination (Norton and Sommers 2011; Knowles and Tropp 2016; Winter 2017; Jardina 2018) pervaded the white mainstream, white supremacist and neo-Nazi groups seized on this affective trend, recruiting on social media and voicing their opinions and views on mainstream media platforms.

COMMODIFYING WHITENESS IN ENTERTAINMENT MEDIA

Recognizing that commercial media is a site of cultural politics, Herman Gray has argued that in the 1980s, "the sign of blackness was constructed, produced, claimed, performed, and struggled over" in political, social, and cultural arenas (Gray 1995, 2). Conservatives, he argues, successfully deployed popular media images of Black and Latinx people in order to "disturb and reconfigure the symbolic chain of association through which 'America' came to be represented and defined ... Together with these racialized images of the 'immigration problem,' news footage of drug- and violence-ravaged urban communities made it seem as if (white) America were being attacked from within and without" (Gray 1995, 20). If Reaganism was the dominant discourse around which representations of race were organized in the 1980s, Trumpism is that discourse for the 2010s.

However, this shift takes place well before Trump in the Obama years. The election of Obama had a profound effect on the cultural representation of Blackness, and film and television reflected this change, constituting part of the discursive field in which competing claims and struggles over representations of Blackness occurred (Izzo 2015; Turner and Nilsen 2019; McCollum 2019). While there are significant similarities in the way images of Blackness were produced and circulated in media during the Reagan and Obama years, there is a marked difference in the way whiteness is represented. Indeed, although associations of minority groups with criminal behavior effectively serve the same purpose in both eras—instilling in whites a sense of fear and vulnerability and pushing them further to the right of the political spectrum—there is no attempt to redefine or reclaim whiteness in the Reagan/Bush era, suggesting that definitions of whiteness were not contested. Indeed, scholars writing in the 1990s about white identity, such as Toni Morrison (1992), Ruth Frankenberg (1993), and Richard Dyer (1997), have argued that, historically, whites have viewed themselves as unmarked and unraced, transcendent, and omnipresent. Many of the people interviewed by Frankenberg, while acknowledging the privilege of universality that whiteness conferred on them, lamented the lack of identity or ethnicity that other groups possess and can rally around. "If I had an ethnic base to identify from, if I was even Irish American, that would have been something formed. . . . But to be a Heinz 57 American, a white, class-confused American, land of the Kleenex[-]type American, is so formless in and of itself. It only takes shape in relation to other people" (Frankenberg 1993, 196).[10] As Kaufmann notes, "White majorities in the West are every bit as ethnic as minorities are, but, for many, their sense of ethnicity and nationhood is blurred" (2019, 8).

In the same way that the media has historically marketed and commodified "ethnic" diversity in advertising and has glamorized racial difference, seducing the "Other into thinking that this represents an opportunity for cultural economic recognition" (Saha 67), new media technologies, including news, entertainment, and social media platforms, in the Obama-to-Trump era, have curated a brand of whiteness that offers visibility to white people as white people, not just as the mainstream norm. This "alliance of social, technological, and cultural fields constitutes a new racial regime—the shift from race to difference—and this recognition and visibility on which it depends is a form of power" (Gray 2013, 771). In the ubiquity of its presentation and its engagement with rapacious, encroaching others (whether in an allegorized form in speculative fiction or in news-framing of cultural "crises"), whiteness was presented to whites as something that needed articulating and defining and a means through which to "reclaim" power. At the same time, renewed attention to whiteness offered an alternative to seemingly "race-neutral" programming (which employed colorblind casting practices, featured symbolic inclusion of actors of color or ethnically ambiguous actors in formerly white roles, and did not draw attention to minority issues) and a way to differentiate and distinguish them from more marked minority racial content in the media (Bonilla-Silva 2014; Nilsen and Turner 2014; Warner 2015). Because "symbols of race and ethnicity, especially when tapping into the fears and desires bound up in imperial nostalgia or postcolonial melancholia, are able to give commodities a competitive advantage" (Saha 2018, 67), white identity previously unmarked was now accessible and visible as *both beleaguered and heroic*. In an era where identity is tied to visual and public activism, whether racial, sexual, environmental, or disabled, these two poles of white identity gave whites, regardless of political orientation, a cultural and political visibility that many felt had been lacking (Norton and Sommers 2011; Plaut 2010; Oliver and Mendelberg 2000).

This is part of a process that Eric Kaufmann, an advocate of "soft" white identity politics, calls "Whiteshift," and he considers it essential to maintaining the coherence and political stability of white ethnic-majority nations. Kaufmann argues that when governments motivated by inclusivity and multiculturalism "sidelin[e] symbols many whites cherish" and "minorities challenge aspects of the national narrative like empire or Western settlement" at the same time that immigration prompts demographic change, whites begin to develop a strong sense of "ethno-traditional nationhood." He argues that the solution to racial extremism *on both sides* is to gradually "assimilate" minority groups "into the ethnic majority, [thus] maintaining the white ethno-tradition" (2019, 11). How this "soft" (in-group solidarity) identity politics fed into and buttressed the "hard" (out-group animus) identity politics of the neo-Nazi/white nationalist groups that resurfaced in the Trump administration and the media's role in it need further examination. I suggest that transmedia platforms were instrumental in the facilitating of race production and race-making, particularly in the creation of hard white identity politics; however, mainstream news and entertainment media were priming the idea of white fragility before the militant form became mainstream.

ECONOMIC PRECARITY AND THE WHITE WORKING CLASS

In the months after Trump's upset win in the 2016 election, the seemingly overwhelming consensus on both the right and the left was that the Democrats had become a party of East Coast elites/elitists who had left the working class behind. Articles and books were published that attempted to uncover the plight of the underclass, for the prevailing opinion was that this was the group fueling Trump's rise. David Brooks, in an op-ed piece for the *New York Times* titled "Dignity and Sadness in the Working Class," concluded that "I can't help feeling that society is failing them in some major way, and not just economically" (2016). Eventually, it became apparent that when journalists referenced the disenfranchised working class, they were referring to the *white* working class. In what felt like an attempt to assuage the guilt of their own purported demonizing of the "Trump supporter," reporters from left-leaning publications like *The Atlantic, Salon, Vox, The Nation,* the *New Yorker,* the *New York Times,* and *The Guardian* analyzed the failures of the Democratic Party and, most pointedly, of Hillary Clinton's campaign to attend to issues of class, particularly among whites.[11] The email scandal and FBI Director James Comey's handling of it were acknowledged to have played a role, but a cursory look at the titles of many of these pieces make it clear that ignoring the white working class was the reason the pundits believed the Democrats would and did lose the 2016 election. And considerable self-flagellation ensued.

Several books were published in 2016, before and after the election, which sought to address the thorny issue of class exposed by Bernie Sanders first, before it became the rallying cry of Trump. Titles such as *The New Minority: White Working Class Politics in an Age of Immigration and Inequality*; *Strangers in their Own Land: Anger and Mourning on the American Right*; *Hillbilly Elegy: A Memoir of a Family and Culture in Crisis*; and *Listen, Liberal: Or Whatever Happened to the Party of the People?* all more or less concurred. A sense of widespread white economic precarity was fueled by media sensationalism as journalists sought a scapegoat in the racial rhetoric of whiteness. As Kaufmann notes, "numerous media 'safaris' into Trumpland . . . simply confirm reporters' biases. Journalists have been mesmerized by election maps" (2019, 6). This is not to discount the reality of those made economically vulnerable by the Great Recession; however, by attributing Trump's win solely to economic forces and characterizing that economic vulnerability in terms of whiteness, specifically white loss, the media created and inflated feelings of "imperiled whiteness." The predicament of white economic vulnerability relayed in a constant barrage of articles, books, and op-eds came to stand for white precarity in general and reflected a sense of outrage about that racial displacement.

Motivated by similar presumptions, sociologists and political scientists polled a variety of 2016 Trump voters in order to assess their motivations. Some people did voice concerns about the economy, the closing of industrial plants, and the gutting of communities as people moved away to find work. Robert Wuthnow attributes Republican support among these communities to a sense of displacement and loss, a feeling of being "left behind." Washington is "*distant* and at the same time *intrusive*" and is perceived to cater to urban interests. These communities, he argues, "feel threatened and misunderstood" (Wuthnow 2018).

Economic precarity is not unique to rural communities, however, and we cannot overlook the dependence and popularity in these communities on news outlets like Fox and conservative talk radio, which frequently and consistently tied these feelings of rural alienation to white alienation (Bittle 2020). As Wuthnow acknowledges, when discussing their feelings of displacement, interviewees also expressed comments "with blatant racist overtones" about Obama (2018). The feelings of economic loss and cultural isolation might seem separate from racial animus; however, because they are tied to anti-Washington sentiment and Obama was a metonym for Washington, feeling "threatened" takes on racial overtones. As Jardina's research reveals, "many white voters saw [Trump] as restoring and protecting their group's power and resources" (2019, 234).

Interestingly, Jardina's data show that whites' anxiety about Obama does not correlate seamlessly to economic vulnerability.

> Whites high on identity and consciousness are not, for the most part, objectively economically vulnerable. Most own houses, have average incomes similar to most whites in the United States, are employed, and identify as middle class.... The evidence presented here suggests that the pervasive narrative about class is not a story about realistic group conflict, in which the most objectively economically vulnerable whites are aggrieved and now politically conscious, uniquely airing their grievances at the ballot box. Indeed, there are many whites who possess high levels of racial consciousness who are financially secure and situated in white-collar jobs. (Jardina 2019, 116)

That there is a "tendency among those high on racial consciousness to report a greater degree of financial despair" than is actually reflected in their economic reality suggests that this group of whites was influenced by the media reporting of white precarity so that the *perception* of whites losing economic ground is tied to heightened white racial consciousness. Systemic racism has long impacted the economic security and advancement of Americans of color; however, when white Americans experience economic vulnerability, it results in a reckoning about white identity and finds its scapegoat in the Obama administration's perceived elevation of minority concerns. This is particularly ironic as the Obama administration reversed the recession that the Bush administration created (including bailouts of the banking and auto industries that many argue saved the US economy from sliding into a depression) (Reed 2017). Kaufmann's research supports this, also. As he notes, "next to immigration, 'left behind' issues are a busted flush.... Ethnic change is central to explaining Trump's victory" (2019, 126–27).

REARTICULATING RACE

Like other racial categories, "whiteness" is formed in and through social relations that change over time. The extending of white identity to "ethnic" minorities in the US and elsewhere was an extension of privilege and a means of distinguishing certain minority groups from others whose enslavement or dispossession by the capitalist, colonial power structure became inexorably tied to their racialization and justified exclusionary policies (Du Bois ([1903] 2016; Roediger [1991] 2007; Ignatiev 1995; Lipsitz 2006; Bonilla-Silva 2022). As Omi and Winant have argued, renewed attention to dominant identity politics is cyclical and frequently coincides with threats to the security of that dominance. The concept of "disenfranchised whiteness," the idea that whites were being "left behind" touted by the media as an explanation for Trump's rise, is a form of "racial rearticulation" (Omi and Winant 2014). Racial ideology is rearticulated by the dominant racial hegemony as a means of both containing efforts of activists to mobilize at the level of race and to further the interests of the dominant group. In the decades following World War II:

> Rearticulation proved far more effective than repression in containing the radical thrust of the Black movement, and of its allied movements as well. A clear sequence of ideological tropes deepened and extended "post-civil rights" era rearticulations of racism: first code words, then reverse racism, and finally colorblindness. At each stage of its development, the racial reaction carried out what we might call cumulative "latent functions." Code words channeled white shame, fear, and rage; reverse racism deracialized discrimination, effectively absolving whites; and colorblindness reasserted American nationalism and the "unity" of "the American people" across supposedly disappearing boundaries of race. (Omi and Winant 2014, 255–56)

According to Omi and Winant, "racial rearticulation" usually follows advances and gains won by progressive movements. Code words are employed to redirect the language of complaint and accommodate it. This is evident in the right's corruption of the phrase "Black Lives Matter" to "All Lives Matter" or "Blue Lives Matter." It serves both to deflect attention away from the legitimate complaint voiced in the original slogan—the unlawful killing of Black people—and to claim the position of victim instead of perpetrator. To be effective, racial rearticulation must "recast themes of racial equality and justice in ways that would serve to rationalize and reinforce persistent patterns of racial inequality" (Omi and Winant 2014, 190).

The election of Barack Obama and the many socially progressive policies that his administration implemented, including reforms in the areas of health, energy, education, gender equality, and the military, required a racial rearticulation of a greater degree than those previously. Obama was no longer a community organizer whose policies impacted a few hundred people; he was president of the United States, and his policies impacted everyone. Ta-Nehisi Coates has argued that Trump is "the first president whose entire political existence hinges on the fact of a Black president." "Ostensibly assaulted by campus protests, battered by theories of intersectionality, throttled by bathroom rights, a blameless white working class did the only thing that any reasonable polity might," elect a man who denounced these cultural firestorms not merely as products of a liberal agenda but of a Black liberal agenda (Coates 2018, 345, 344). While Trump's overt race-baiting is new, his methodology is not. Faced with a desire to turn back progressive reforms of the Kennedy/Johnson administration, Richard Nixon's campaign was deliberate in its efforts to rearticulate the map of race relations in the US. It recognized that "Republican victory and long-term electoral realignment were possible on racial grounds . . . that a great majority of southern white voters had abandoned the Democratic Party, and that Negrophobia was alive and well, not only in the South but nationally. In fact, what was 'emerging' had been there all along: a massive racist complex of white resentment, dread, and shame that went back to slavery, the 'lost cause,' and reactionary political resentment" (Omi and Winant 2014, 194). The political/social/racial climate today bears an eerie resemblance to that faced by Nixon. But there is one crucial difference: "These were the early days of racial rearticulation, when white supremacy was in the process of 'going underground.' In later stages of the process, the new right would *adopt* Black demands, claiming that civil rights enforcement and efforts at racial redistribution constituted 'racism in reverse.' Still later, efforts at rearticulation would involve the wholesale denial of racial discrimination and indeed of racial identity itself" (Omi and Winant 2014, 197).

Numerous critics have noted how the concept of "postrace" enabled a return to a more regressive racism that David Theo Goldberg calls "born-again racism" (2009), but at the same time, developed new and distinct expressions of white identity and anti-Black racism. The Tea Party, Birtherism, and anti-immigrant activism all constitute part of this white backlash against Obama. The media's consistent and unyielding examination of the white working-class recuperated and reactivated a virulent form of whiteness that animated the alt-right neo-Nazi mediascape. While it is evident that Obama's election produced a white backlash at social and political levels, how that backlash was cultivated in entertainment media, especially in progressive "colorblind" media, is of interest to me. The commodification of white racial identity, i.e. the production of whiteness as a sign open to reinterpretation or branding, occurred in seemingly anodyne ways in entertainment media but contributed in fundamental ways to the rise of the alt-right during the Obama administration.

Certainly, Trump's appeal to those who are "anti-expertise, anti-elitism, and pronationalist" (Oliver and Rahn 2016, 189) depends upon the fostering of white in-group solidarity, which has historically "fanned the flames of white supremacy, homophobia, and anti-immigrant hatred." As Lipsitz makes clear, whites are encouraged to "inves[t] their identities in these narratives of the nation that depend on the demonization of others" (2006, 98–99). But because a whiteness that elevates the bearer above non-whites is itself the commodity that is sought, certain whites become invested in their whiteness and status and are satisfied and placated when that elevation of whiteness is achieved, even at the cost of other political or economic benefits that might demonstrably change their lives for the better. The alt-right is particularly adept at these kinds of ideological appeals, articulating "those values and institutions that it sees as key to the identity of a people (e.g., race/ethnicity, culture rooted in fixed narratives and symbols, history, masculinity, etc.) but it also seeks to erase and obscure those other qualities—notably the socio-economic—that are, arguably, central to the material and lived reality of concrete individuals within capitalist societies" (Saull et al. quoted in Titley 2019, 104). Indeed, a 2011 study revealed that, to many whites, racism is a zero-sum game in which "Whites have replaced Blacks as the primary victims of discrimination" (Norton and Sommers 2011, 215). Trump's stoking of white identity politics by emphasizing group threat operates as an obvious clarion call to groups like The Proud Boys, who know to "stand back and stand by,"[12] but it also rouses those whites who seek to protect the interests and privileges of their group's collective interests. Executive orders like the one banning federal contractors from conducting implicit bias workplace training that purportedly promotes "divisive concepts" or perpetuates the belief that "America is an irredeemably racist and sexist country" (EO 13950, September 2020)[13] or the ban on the teaching of critical race theory or any discussion of racism or white privilege in classrooms around the country[14] are clear examples of how the rhetoric of in-group solidarity has political appeal that extends beyond the explicit torch-wielding, Confederate flag-waving actions of alt-right extremists. As Jardina makes clear, "Out-group attitudes are not the only factor, or even necessarily the primary factor, motivating voters. Many whites in 2012 also seem[ed] especially concerned with protecting their racial group's status" (224). In other words, you don't have to express deliberate racial animus toward the out-group to want to protect the in-group. Yet, in the context of heightened racial conflict of the Trump era where racial violence in the streets and verbal racist rants comprised the twenty-four-hour news cycle, it becomes hard to distinguish one from the other.

WHITE RACIAL FRAME

Social scientists note that the "social environment can influence racial attitudes in ways that have little to do with racial composition or with interracial competition for resources" (Oliver and Mendelberg 2000, 575) and have demonstrated an increase among whites of feelings of economic, social, and cultural/racial precarity in the period from 2008–2020 (Jardina 2019; Kaufmann 2019; Oliver and Rahn 2016; Norton and Sommers 2011). How does the frame of "imperiled whiteness" and white working-class precarity, produced by the media after the election of Trump, overlap with and, in many ways, issue from news, entertainment, and social media narratives surrounding white identity during the Obama administration? At the same time, how does the commodification of whiteness in these kinds of media stem from the more traditional racial framing around Black and Brown bodies as inherently dangerous and/or rapacious? How do these two kinds of framing generate and promote a notion of whiteness "under attack"? What do these portrayals of "imperiled whiteness" in media and news accounts tell us about the racial climate during Obama's presidency, and what might they suggest about white identity politics in the Trump era?

Joe Feagin has argued that whites' racial views and prejudice, which are often at odds with racial realities, and their "collective denial" about racial disparity and inequity can be interpreted through the "white racial frame." Feagin suggests that this "dominant frame is an overarching white worldview that encompasses a broad and persisting set of racial stereotypes, prejudices, ideologies, images, interpretations and narratives, emotions, and reactions to language accents, as well as racialized inclinations to discriminate" (Feagin 2013, 3). But such beliefs and inclinations don't spontaneously generate; rather, they are cultivated and perpetuated by narratives—historical, cultural, scientific, and political understandings of the dominant white culture, the sole purpose of which is the maintenance of whites' superior economic and social position. Eduardo Bonilla-Silva argues that de facto white racial segregation produces a "'white habitus,' a racialized, uninterrupted socialization process that *conditions* and *creates* Whites' racial taste, perceptions, feelings, and emotions and their views on racial matters" (Bonilla-Silva 2022, 152). Bonilla-Silva contends that the white habitus produces in whites generally positive feelings about their race and their status while at the same time constructing a generally negative sense about minorities and their attributes. However, he also points out that "Whites construct their accounts with the frames, style, and stories available in color-blind America in a mostly unconscious fashion" (2022, 106). In the twentieth and twenty-first centuries, the media has contributed significantly to these kinds of racial frames.

Movies, television, and other forms of popular media extend "the intergenerational transmission" of the white racial frame, helping to bolster and sustain systemic racism (Feagin 2013, 129). Bonilla-Silva, Feagin, and others note how these media frames have historically represented minorities in a debased light, where whites have typically been accorded noble and virtuous characteristics. As Susan Courtney observes, "Hollywood cinema has contributed to the cultural production and dissemination not only of particular racial fictions—the wide array of types and stereotypes—but of an entire racial epistemology, a system of knowledge that deems 'race' to be a visible fact" (Courtney 2005, 142). These reductive representations, although repackaged, endure and are constantly made and remade according to the dictates of a neoliberal marketplace that draws from and perpetuates colonialist logics around race. In a hybrid media environment where racial meanings are constructed and consumed through a variety of platforms, it is important to go beyond an analysis of representations that attends solely to the binary logic of positive/negative, authentic/stereotypical. As Herman Gray has noted, representations are contingent and racial meanings and counter-meanings are produced by media industries "for differently situated publics" (Gray 1995, 36). What is needed, as Saha has argued, is to interrogate how race is made and governed through "industrial or semi-industrial forms of symbol creation and circulation in modern societies that relate directly to the media" (2018, 22). It's my argument that this commercial "race-making" extends to whiteness as white people emerged as a profitable target market during Obama's presidency.

FRAMING AND "PRODUSING" RACE IN HYBRID MEDIA SYSTEMS

The decentralization of the three main networks in 1987 as a result of the Reagan Administration's repeal of the Fairness Doctrine of 1949 has had a profound impact on the way consumers acquire information and entertainment.[15] Obviously, a networked media environment, including the interactivity of social media platforms, has dramatically altered how consumers access information; from broadcast to narrowcast to SVOD, "'the media' has given way to a fragmented, niche-oriented, interactive, digitalized and increasingly polarized mediascape" (Ouellette and Banet-Weiser 2018, 2). While talkback radio programs like pioneer Rush Limbaugh's have long provided forums for sensational and hyperbolic political commentary, such venues were largely limited to the AM dial. With the advent of Fox News in 1996 and its cadre of polished anchors and commentators like O'Reilly, Hannity, and Carlson, who present right-wing partisan talking points alongside broader news content presented as "fair and balanced," ideological material with an overt political bias proliferated in the media landscape (Jones 2012, 178). Indeed, thanks to its inclusion in basic cable packages, Fox had a broad reach into American households, resulting in "a small bump in Republican vote share and a major increase of as much as 28 per cent in turnout among registered Republicans" (Vigna and Kaplan 2007, quoted in Kaufmann 2019, 114). Media outlets like Fox and MSNBC became brands that deliberately cultivated and curated partisan political content for their targeted consumers. "These competing media brands do not attempt to constitute a universal, unquestionable understanding of 'the ways things are,' as much as they package and sell competing vantage points, political punditry and commentators, contributing to the polarization of discourse in which the extreme right has thrived" (Ouellette and Banet-Weiser 2018, 2). Consumer identification with a media brand produces political and ideological silos among the populace. Audiences seek platforms where their views are reflected; at the same time, those views become shaped through the polarizing discourse essential to the media brand's survival. Mainstream social media platforms like Facebook, Twitter, Reddit, and Tumblr provide consumers even more opportunities to seek out and engage in partisan echo chambers (Isom et al. 2021).

Popular media play a central role in not just reflecting but directing the views and values of the citizenry. Media-framing analysis focuses on the way public attitudes about current events or policy debates are shaped by framing, priming, and agenda-setting practices utilized by media. As D'Angelo and Kuypers explain, "Politicians, issue advocates, and stakeholders use journalists and other news professionals to communicate their preferred meanings of events and issues." These stakeholders frame events according to the way they'd like them to be reported, and journalists, in turn, "cannot not frame topics because they need sources' frames to make news" (2010, 1). Framing thus has a profound effect on the dissemination, reception, and circulation of media events across diverse publics. "Frames influence media audiences to recall, evaluate, condense, and interpret an issue in particular ways" and are a tool, along with agenda-setting and priming, "used to benefit those who create, control, and maintain the society's dominant economic, political, and other social frames" (Ortega and Feagin 2016, 20). In light of the agenda-setting intentions of informing stakeholders, framing renders certain issues or causes more salient than others, has the capacity to shape, form, and change public opinion on issues, and "activate[s] emotional responses" in consumers of media (D'Angelo and Kuypers 2010, 2). However, as Goffman argues in his original work on the subject, framing is also a cognitive process utilized by individuals to make sense of both natural and social occurrences in their worlds (Goffman 1974).

In his influential essay, "Notes on Deconstructing the Popular," Stuart Hall warns against conceiving of an audience that is wholly passive, something of a "cultural dope" in the hands of the media's manipulative agenda-setting discourse. As he points out, this presumes that audiences themselves collude with that agenda or are living in a state of perpetual "false consciousness" (1981, 352). Similarly, Fiske reminds us that "audience" is not a social category and "people constitute themselves quite differently as audience members at different times" (Fiske 2013, 56). Hall cautions against setting up a true authentic popular culture, one that speaks to and is embraced by the "real" working class, who would not be taken in by the neoliberal motives of the commercial media. Rather, he reminds us that there is no popular culture outside the "relations of cultural power and domination." While that cultural power is concentrated in the hands of the few, there is always a doubleness to popular culture, a perpetual oscillation from containment to resistance (1981, 348). In the context of twenty-first-century new media ecology where infotainment traverses platforms and mediums, and "popular culture" in all its forms can be created, accessed, altered, and redistributed on a plethora of devices in a range of places at any time of the day, we should take account of the ways that cultural texts are formed through participatory exchanges between producers and consumers of media content. Axel Bruns defines "produsage" as the creation of shared content "in a networked, participatory environment which breaks down the boundaries between producers and consumers and instead enables all participants to be users as well as producers of information and knowledge" (http://produsage.org/produsage; Bruns 2008). The question is to what extent produsers also employ framing techniques to manipulate and manufacture consent in their respective circles of influence.

Henry Jenkins has argued that grassroots activism, such as the kind that manifested on the left during the 2004 election, sprung from web-based media platforms that facilitated this kind of produsage and enabled a "shift in the public's role in the political process," enabling them "to mobilize collective intelligence to transform governance" (Jenkins 2006, 208). Most of Jenkins's analysis relates to the progressive democratic possibilities of convergence culture, how consumers' capacity to co-create media content affords them a kind of political capital. Critics of his approach have noted how his and others' celebration of the participatory and revolutionary anti-capitalist, anti-fascist nature of new media technologies fails to take into account how the tools provided to the people for their revolution are produced and curated by the same media marketplace against whom the revolution is directed (Verstraete 2011; Hay 2011; Andrejevic 2011; Harsin and Hayward 2013). Audiences are targeted, branded, incentivized, and directed into the communities from which their agency springs. Much of the consumer engagement with media events occurs through outrage and public demonstration of political stance, which social media engines capitalize on and exploit by inviting users to add frames or filters to their profiles, be it BLM, French flags, Pride flags, voting, masking, or vaccinating. Facebook, for example, argues that "profile frames are a great way to inspire the world around you ... [and] can enable government, political and nonprofit organizations to creatively make a statement, celebrate important moments, show support for special causes or rally people around important public service announcements" (Meta 2021). Users of these filters have been dubbed "slactivists" for their passive endorsement of causes. Critics argue that these performative displays of allegiance to a cause have no real political effect or influence other than a circulatory exchange among a self-selected group of followers/friends eager to demonstrate their progressive capital (Lee 2015; Mulvaney 2015).[16] Obviously, social media activism can and has facilitated democratic resistance, protest, and mobilization (Arab Spring, Occupy Movement, #BLM, #SayHerName, #TakeAKnee, #MeToo). But such counter rhetoric doesn't contradict the fact that the technology enables and anticipates consumers' interaction with it and profits from it (and frequently coopts it for opposing ends). Such public "incitements to discourse" (Couldry 2012) are particularly prevalent in race/anti-race discourses which, as Titley argues, are "driven by the unexpected circulation of digital objects, or the capacity of ubiquitous digital technologies to make 'hidden racism' public, or the opportunities for publicity provided to racist groups by the 'always on' prerogatives of content production in a hybrid media system" (17). Hence tags like #whitegenocide, #maga, #trump, #qanon are used to amplify far-right content and direct traffic to specific publics.

Less discussed is the fact that the use of and response to these kinds of technologies are not always liberal or progressive, and the kind of organizing and branding can occur just as easily and in as grand sweeping a manner on the right as it can on the left. James Hay demonstrates how the Tea Party's co-option of the phrase "grassroots activism" obscured the ways the group was less a leaderless assemblage of patriots than a highly networked and mediated organization, which utilized and relied on the networking capacities of entities like FreedomWorks and media personalities like Glenn Beck, who worked together to target, incentivize, and cross-market to consumers on convergent media platforms like Facebook and Twitter (Hay 2011; White 2018). Though this kind of partisan engagement occurs on both sides of the political divide, researchers note that it's more prevalent in conservative circles (Benkler et al. 2017).

On Facebook alone, despite the right's claim that the social media engine is policing conservative speech, researchers note a "parallel media universe" that has been "stunningly effective in shaping its own version of reality" (Roose 2020). During Trump's presidency, shares and likes of conservative news stories or opinions tripled those of mainstream news pages combined. "Pro-Trump political influencers have spent years building a well-oiled machine that swarms around every major news story, creating a torrent of viral commentary that reliably drowns out the mainstream media and the liberal opposition" (Roose

2020). Further, the capacity of hackers and trolls, homegrown or foreign, to intervene in the transmedia exchange by produsing "fake news" as they did in great numbers during the 2016 and 2020 election cycles demonstrates how stories get built, altered, and sensationalized through their dispersal across platforms. "Recognizing a meme, remixing a meme, referencing a meme—these actions establish a set of subculture borders, thus providing a 'meaningful whole' to which additional signifiers may cohere [Hebdige 1979, 103, 113]. Within the trollspace, these seemingly chaotic signs—whether expressed through language or artifacts—do something. In the context of trolling, they build worlds" (Phillips 2012, 503). "Digital objects" (text, GIFs, memes, videos) can be combined and recombined in an iterative loop and shared inside and outside discourse communities. "[N]ews streams generated by users reporting and conversing about what is happening blend various perspectives on space and place and, in doing so, frequently emerge as the primary alternative for information sharing and news dissemination" (Papacharissi 2015, 31).

Attention by media watchdogs to the disinformation problem of fake news and the circulation of tools to detect such news themselves become open to debate and parody among certain groups, producing a proliferation of "facts" and contested claims of what is real and fake.[17] Part of the problem is that the accessibility of social media and its user-friendly interfaces encourage phatic, not analytic, engagement. As Jessica Johnson notes, "[L]ikes, retweets, and emoji have become arbiters of authenticity and audience reception on Facebook and Twitter, influencing news feed algorithms and the policing of user-generated content" (Johnson 2018, 102). A recent analysis found that consumers engaged (liked, tweeted, or shared) with "unreliable news sites" in 2020 twice as frequently as they did in 2019, with *The Daily Wire*, a conservative news outlet founded by Ben Shapiro, receiving 2.5 times the traffic it did in the previous year. Alignment with one's party has produced a form of political identitarianism that shapes how we think about policy issues like military withdrawals, national debt, immigration, and gun control, but also about ethical questions like racism, unemployment, and human trafficking (and immigration and gun control). As Mark Andrejevic notes, "audience fragmentation and mass customization" are facilitated by a proliferation of information across digital platforms and "threaten a shared public understanding of current events underwritten by common reference points provided by the mass media" (2011, 605). In the hyperpartisan Obama-to-Trump mediascape, this form of political identitarianism has become aligned with racial identity, and a networked digital ecology has emerged as a central mobilizing tool for white supremacist actors on the right to consolidate and further their aims.

TRANSMEDIA IDEOLOGIES

The concept of transmedia storytelling provides a useful lens for studying the visibility and popularity of newly empowered alt-right movements. Transmedia storytelling, as Jenkins explains, "represents a process where integral elements of a fiction get dispersed systematically across multiple delivery channels for the purpose of creating a unified and coordinated entertainment experience. Ideally, each medium makes its own unique contribution to the unfolding of the story" (Jenkins 2011). While Jenkins is talking about fictional narratives that traverse platforms and can involve branding, franchising, adaptation, etc., I want to consider the role transmedia plays in the dissemination of ideology, which, highly narrativized, takes on its own fictional dimensions. Scholars have noted the role played by internet and social media platforms such as 4chan, 8chan, The Daily Stormer, and social messaging apps like Kik, and, more recently, Telegram, in the radicalization of (predominantly) young white men (Guhl and Davey 2020); scholars have also noted how mainstream media outlets have bolstered and legitimized the claims made in online spaces extending access to these ideas and further disseminating them to general audiences (Phillips 2012; Khallis 2015; Hawley 2017). Other right-wing political outlets like One America News, The Drudge Report, The Daily Wire, Infowars, and Breitbart represent clearly defined partisan platforms, which, in a hybrid media ecosystem, are often party to or originators of the dissemination of "fringe" news. As Gavan Titley explains, the digital media environment allows far-right groups to "circulate misinformation and 'alternative' facts; integrate into news flows and public discourse dynamics, and build media operations that often skillfully navigate media space provided by the accelerated and extended contemporary news cycle" (Titley 2019, 103). In this mediated environment, individuals have become co-creators of news content, utilizing modes of storytelling to "develop their own takes on what makes a news story, and what counts as journalism." The capacity of individuals to engage with digital affordances in ways that permit certain stories to go viral and trend is an example of how "storytelling becomes an exercise in power" (Papacharissi 2015, 28).

Jenkins notes that transmedia is how convergence, the "layering, diversification, and interconnectivity of media" (Jenkins 2011), is practiced. Transmedia narratives can be expressed in a number of different ways: storytelling, branding, performance, ritual, play, activism, and spectacle. Frequently, a transmedia narrative utilizes a number of those modes, but the story has to develop or change across media—co-creation and collaboration are central to transmedia value. In other words, each iteration of the text adds something or consolidates elements of the narrative and the affordance of the specific medium, the unique way that a specific medium functions (passively, interactively, visually, textually, etc.), affects the mode of story transmission. When thinking about transmedia in relation to real events, as opposed to fictional ones, it is useful to consider how such events are only accessible to (most of) us through their narrativization by the media and that consumers' curation of different media sites and modes changes the story they receive and pass on to others. As Papacharissi notes, "[S]ocial news climates like Reddit, Digg, and Twitter, in particular, generate collective news intelligence through a blend of social practices that include voting, filtering, and commenting on news. They generate news streams that blend cursory references to news with deeply personal and mostly affective reactions to how this news is covered" (2015, 30–31). The aggregation and consolidation of niche news and partisan branding create "information bubbles" that are nevertheless networked transmedially across different platforms within the partisan mediascape. "[P]latforms like Twitter, Reddit, and a variety of blog and microblog services sustain collaborative storytelling, co-creation, and curation of news content. These pluralized and collectively prodused news feeds, generated by citizens committing independent or coordinated acts of journalism, present an important alternative to the dominant news economy" (Papacharissi 2015, 30).

However, these forms of produsage can be locked in partisan echo chambers, too. In analyzing the role right-wing sites like Breitbart played in social media users' trafficking of news items, Benkler et al. (2017) analyzed social sharing patterns on Facebook and Twitter and found that media sharing was utilized in different ways by right- and left-leaning users. Whereas pro-Clinton audiences engaged with traditional media, "pro-Trump audiences paid the majority of their attention to polarized outlets that have developed recently, many of them only since the 2008 election season." Breitbart surfaced as the center of this distinct right-wing media system, with outlets like Fox, Infowars, the *Washington Examiner*, and other lesser-known ones contributing to the mix. What's most relevant here is that the stories that were retweeted or reposted by right-wing consumers were not so much "fake" as they were deliberately misleading in their use of "true or partly true bits of information." The result, Benkler et al. argue, is a "network of mutually-reinforcing hyper-partisan sites ...combining decontextualized truths, repeated falsehoods, and leaps of logic to create a fundamentally misleading view of the world" (2017).

PERFORMING WHITENESS IN A DIGITAL AGE

Whitney Phillips argues that while virtual spaces are usually thought to free participants from race, gender, and class markers, typically, trolls' "terrestrial" experiences, including political views, education levels, and racial identities, inform their attitudes and responses to topics discussed on the boards. Importantly, the posters on the /b/ board, which is 4chan's most popular board and "pumps out some of the Internet's most recognizable, not to mention offensive, viral content," do so anonymously. However, based on an analysis of the content and language of postings, Phillips has determined that the majority of trolls are between eighteen and thirty, are middle-class sub/urban Americans, and are men. She also notes that "trolling behaviors are strongly indicative of whiteness." In fact, white racial identity is so much the default that the culture of the board dictates that any non-white anon should "flag himself or herself as racially other" (2012, 497). By 2006, anon trolls on 4chan adopted the collective identity, "Anonymous," which harnessed the "rhetorical power of the faceless collective as well as its behavioral effects" (Phillips 2012, 499) and started to infiltrate other web spaces, hacking users on Myspace and other social media sites. Fox and other news outlets' reporting on Anonymous gave the trolls a national platform. "What once had been an underground site, known only to the few thousand active participants, had become a household name," driving more traffic to 4chan and the repulsive racist, sexist, homophobic content found there. By "March of 2010, the *New York Times* reported that the daily page view total had climbed to 800,000 and that the site boasts 8.2 million unique monthly visitors [Bilton 2010]" (Phillips 2012, 501).

It is worth considering how the popularity of boards like 4chan, 8chan/kun, and the collective hate behavior of groups like Anonymous fit into the wider media ecology and the kind of race-making that takes place there. In alt-right circles, as Julia DeCook notes, memes enable the "spreading of propaganda, and are bite-sized nuggets of political ideology and culture that are easily digestible and spread" (DeCook 2018, 485). The saliency of a specific "news" item's trafficability is its outrageousness—the more shocking or emotive the language in a post, the greater the likelihood of its circulation (Stewart 2020). In meme form, outrage is entertainment—the more appalling or grotesque an item is, the more value it provides to the topic and to the poster. Meme culture, particularly, is a way for individuals to express a social and political identity. Indeed, while the content being circulated does significant cultural work in shaping attitudes and directing opinions, we shouldn't overlook the cultural capital (or anti-capital) that is derived by the poster, tweeter, or troll; how much of their identity is tied not just to the message being disseminated but to how being a participant in the exchange consolidates and affirms their identity in the group. As Roger Silverstone makes clear, "communities have always been symbolic as well as material in their composition.... They are acted on and acted out. Yet without their symbolic dimension, they are nothing. Without their meanings, without belief, without identity and identification there is nothing: nothing in which to belong, in which to participate; nothing to share; nothing to promote, and nothing to defend" (quoted in Jones 2012, 180–81). So, while produsage can offer empowering spaces for liminal viewpoints (Jenkins 2006; Papacharissi 2015), it also facilitates and extends hyperpartisan niche markets and contributes to the erosion of consumers' ability to discern the factual from the fictional. This erosion was particularly fraught in the Obama-to-Trump era, creating a space wherein white identity politics could flourish. Produsage enabled forms of "storytelling" that provided a curious mix of racial Armageddon ("white genocide," "replacement theory") and Western Chauvinism ("practiced" by Proud Boys and Boogaloo Bois).

Jessica Johnson argues that the radicalization of white men occurs through a "social process of affective networking" (2018, 101) rather than by a specific issue or cause, such as the case of individuals who are radicalized by Islamic extremism. By contrast, she notes that white extremists are motivated by a generalized sense of paranoia that their power is being taken away from them. Importantly, this paranoia "materializ[es] in the process of digital communication" (Johnson 2018, 100) through alt-right networks that have "no head or center but rel[y] on human and nonhuman actors to bodily move and digitally connect men across the country as they enjoy lolz online" (2018, 102). As journalist Joseph Bernstein, who joined a white supremacist group called "White Pride World Wide" on the private app-based messaging group, Kik, observes:

> Yes, there were the requisite repugnant jokes about the intelligence of African-Americans and the work habits of Mexican-Americans, and yes, there were the requisite conspiracy theories about Jewish dominance of finance and the media. But much more common were discussions about the relative racial purity of different white nations and the dissolution of white European culture. (Bernstein 2015)

Neo-Nazi activists like Dylann Roof (Charleston), James Alex Fields (Charlottesville), Robert Bowers (Pittsburgh), Brenton Tarrant (Christchurch), and Patrick Crusius (El Paso) did not simply perform violent acts; they telegraphed them on message boards and, in some cases, livestreamed them on Facebook. The networked mediation of these acts is central to recognizing the performative nature of this form of racial hate. Whether utilizing one's own website (Roof), niche platforms like Gab (Bowers), 8chan (Crusius), social messaging apps like Kik or Telegram, or more mainstream ones like Facebook (Field, Tarrant), the perpetrators invariably post about the act before performing it, and frequently the final post follows heightened posting activity about various forms of threats to white status—white genocide, replacement theory, etc. While the posts certainly include racist, bigoted screeds against the target population, the motivation appears to be less about the group being attacked (Jews, Blacks, Muslims, etc.) than the perceived effect of that group on the poster's group (whites). And in many cases, the final post is a declaration that the poster has had enough of posting and wants to take action. Dylann Roof's final post declares that "I can't sit by and watch my people get slaughtered. Screw your optics, I'm going in" (Robles 2015). Similarly, Robert Bowers, who murdered eleven people at the Tree of Life synagogue in Pittsburgh in October 2018, wrote in his final post, "I have no choice. . . . We have no skinheads, no real KKK, no one doing anything but talking on the internet. Well someone has to have the bravery to take it to the real world, and I guess that has to be me" (Beckett 2018). These final media posts are examples of how "the affective networking of paranoia is also critical to the political mobilization of white bodies" (Johnson 2018, 104). Without the public echo chamber of the web, without the witnesses and the phatic engagement of like-minded "fans," the act itself lacks meaning. Part of this performance perhaps stems from the anonymity of original forums like 4chan. Anonymity provides a freedom to reinvent oneself but, at the same time, it produces anxiety about being misrepresented. Overt and outward displays of identity politics allow for a specific identification of a poster's identity with the content being posted. As Titley makes clear, for those "dispersed or clustered individuals in small and fragmented movements, the increased variety of participative venues provide[s] not only information, but also forms of belonging and negotiated collective identity" (Titley 2019, 116).

It's not simply the fact that digital platforms contribute to the radicalization of white men (which numerous scholars have shown they clearly do); rather, the question here is how the kind of produsage that originates out of a networked ecology offers an environment in which whites can *perform* their whiteness and how those online performances eventually manifest in real-life displays of racial aggression. As Hay notes, "[c]ollectively, or as a nexus of interactive networks of membership," digital platforms "offer a glimpse of the technology of participation through which democracy is performed for a *particular* and technically *specific* population (rather than a general state of democracy that has been restored through a media revolution" (Hay 2011, 664). It's important, then, to recognize the ends to which these digital acts of performative patriotism are directed. The behavior of white "Unite the Right" protestors in Charlottesville and white "Stop the Steal" rioters at the Capitol cannot be understood merely as extreme singular events or actions by organized and motivated far-right political groups; rather, these actions constitute a series of performative behaviors which stem from cultivated representations of whiteness in mainstream and niche media, the repetition of which in public marches, rallies, and riots produce and cement white identity.

Members of the far-right hate group Vanguard America, marching to protest the removal of Confederate statues in Charlottesville, Virginia, on August 12, 2017. (Rodney Dunning)

The ubiquity of khaki pants and white polo shirts worn by protestors at "Unite the Right" and the trademark Fred Perry black and yellow polos co-opted by the Proud Boys are important signifiers of group identity and the desire of members to pass themselves off as mainstream, but they also signify these groups' yearning to be visible, to be seen, and to be identified with the ideology of the group (Sheppard 2017). The robing and masking of Klan members in years past was intended to hide their identities, but that hiding also betrayed the fact that they needed to hide.[18] By contrast, if today's white supremacists "believe their purpose is around a promotion of whiteness and the goodness of whiteness . . . [Y]ou could make the case that there's no shame or fear that comes from that, that you should be willing to own that and be willing to be public with it" (Turner quoted in Wolf 2017). It was precisely this desire to be visibly and militantly white that motivated and inspired militia groups like the Wolverine Watchmen to occupy the Michigan capitol and plot the kidnapping of the Democratic governor, Gretchen Whitmer, because she had dared to implement and enforce COVID lockdown protocols, as well as regular citizens like Mark and Patricia McCloskey, a St. Louis couple, who in June 2020 brandished weapons from their front porch at BLM demonstrators who had entered their private street on the way to a protest at the governor's mansion.

The McCloskeys' actions, which were captured by the cellphone camera of a protestor, immediately went viral in both conservative and progressive circles. What to the left looked like an outrageous display of force and racial aggression

James Alex Fields Jr. (center) at the Charlottesville "Unite the Right" rally in 2017. In 2019, Fields, a member of Vanguard America, received two life sentences without parole for ramming his car into a crowd of peaceful counterprotesters, killing one woman, Heather Heyer, and injuring others. (Rodney Dunning)

Clergy and other antiracist groups assemble peacefully in the streets of Charlottesville, Virginia, on August 12, 2017, in response to the violence and vitriol expressed by neo-Nazi and far-right militia groups at the "Unite the Right" rally on the evening of August 11, 2017. (Rodney Dunning)

Antiracist activists take to the streets to protest "Unite the Right" rally in Charlottesville, Virginia, August 12, 2017. (Rodney Dunning)

Chaos and violence in the streets in Charlottesville, Virginia, August 12, 2017, as white supremacists, antiracist demonstrators, and police face off during the "Unite the Right" rally. (Rodney Dunning)

Mark and Patricia McCloskey threaten BLM demonstrators passing by their St. Louis, Missouri, home on June 28, 2020. (Bill Greenblatt/UPI)

read to the right like a legitimate defense of private property. The McCloskeys' actions catapulted them into instant right-wing stardom. The couple became the face of "white America under attack" as Trump utilized the incident to foster fading support for him among white middle-class voters and to cultivate fears about low-income housing "invading" the suburbs. As the Capitol insurgents, Wolverine militia, and Charlottesville neo-Nazis represent the fringe of white nationalism, the McCloskeys, along with the thousands of other "regular" Americans who turned up to Washington on January 5th and 6th to protest Joe Biden's election win, represent the mainstreaming of white identity politics. Indeed, the McCloskeys appeared so mainstream to the Republican establishment that they were invited to speak at the 2020 Republican National Convention. In May 2021, Mark McCloskey announced his campaign for the US Senate seat vacated by Republican Roy Blunt (Green 2020).

MAINSTREAMING WHITE NATIONALISM

Social media is a highly effective tool primarily because of its capacity for amplification. Sharing, reposting, and retweeting are efficient means to spread conspiracies and ideologies by both advocates and detractors. In September 2016, when Hillary Clinton called those Trump supporters with connections to the alt-right and ethno-nationalist factions in the Republican Party a "basket of deplorables," she provoked multiple memes and counter memes which were circulated by numerous users, not just extremists, on social media. Eric Trump's Instagram post of a photoshopped image of himself, Donald Trump, Mike Pence, Pepe the Frog, and a telling mix of media and political advisors captioned "The Deplorables" prompted the Clinton Campaign to re-post Trump's meme for the purpose of offering an explanation of the Pepe the Frog symbol and its connection to the alt-right. As Whitney Phillips notes, not only did this explanation result in derision and scorn from media outlets on the left and the right, but it also amplified the presence and importance of the alt-right (Phillips 2018).

In her analysis of trolling culture on 4chan and the toxic spread of online hatred in the 2000s, Phillips demonstrates the symbiotic relationship between online trolling culture and mainstream media, particularly Fox News. Phillips argues that "trolling behaviors are homologous to mainstream media output, not diametrically opposed to" and "the motivations of each group might diverge, but their respective rhetorical strategies are often indistinguishable" (Phillips 2012, 495). As Phillips makes clear, trolls don't invent content; rather, they are "cultural scavengers, fashioning amusement from that which already exists. And, more often than not, what already exists first passes through the mainstream media filter. The relationship between trolls and the media, then, isn't just unsurprising, it's close to definitional—forcing us to rethink our framing not just of trolls but of the media itself" (2012, 503). And while extensive opportunities for alt-right messaging were being created by the proliferation of message boards and blogs, we should not overlook the ways in which the "phenomenon" of the alt-right is perpetuated by the media's reporting on it, providing a further amplification of and legitimacy to the "movement." While Fox, Breitbart, One America News, and others have political and economic stakes in the growing of a right-wing consumer base and the dissemination of right-wing propaganda, the broadcast news outlets, too, have helped magnify extreme political movements in the name of news, as well as relying on the agenda-setting of a variety of stakeholders interested in perpetuating specific political agendas (Hay 2011; Phillips 2016; White 2018).

WHITE BRANDING AND FANDOM IN A TRANSMEDIA ECOLOGY

Entertainment, both how it's distributed by producers and how it's received by audiences (consumers), is a key facet in theorizations of transmedia, specifically, how fans respond to such content and what those responses engender and reproduce in other spaces. When applied to an analysis of alt-right ideologies, a transmedia paradigm is useful, especially when understood in relation to fan culture and its associated behaviors. In what ways do the kinds of overt displays of white nationalism witnessed in the Trump era dovetail with the kind of performative identifications fans and other "engaged" (Evans 2020) consumers display in and around popular media franchises? And, if we can interpret rabid nationalism in terms of engaged fandom, how might situating this behavior within the discourse of transmedia storytelling allow us to analyze how popular entertainment media franchises form a part of the transmedia ecology? As Jonathan Gray, following Jenkins and Fiske, has noted, fandom is "a collective strategy, a communal effort to form interpretive communities that in their subcultural cohesion evaded the preferred and intended meanings of the 'power bloc'" (Gray et al. 2007, 2). Fans style themselves against the "culture vultures" and embrace low-brow, anti-elite subcultures; however, the stakes of those allegiances vary depending on the fandom. Typically, political participation differs from fandom—barracking for a team is different from voting for a political party. Germane to this difference is the belief that political allegiance is a function of citizenry, an obligation conferred upon us by the social contract: political partisanship is not subcultural. These distinctions have become increasingly indistinct in the twentieth and twenty-first centuries because of the optics of broadcasting and the need for candidates running for office to be televisual and charismatic. However, these lines became irretrievably blurred with the candidacy and election of Donald Trump, who cultivated his following by styling himself as a low-brow, anti-elite Washington outsider and tapping into an audience base already established by his hit TV show *The Apprentice*.

In a commercial mediascape in which candidates for office vie for airtime and constant coverage in the news cycle, cultivating fans is a smart marketing strategy, especially as fan fervor extends a brand's marketing for free. As Ouellette and Banet-Weiser and others note, the digital proliferation of news and entertainment content means that frequently "political participation bleeds into consumption and electoral politics can become a type of fandom" (2018, 2). Trump cultivated a toxic brand of fandom grounded in prejudice toward out-groups of all kinds. Bigotry, racism, sexism, and xenophobia were all celebrated in "Trump world" because, as he implied over and again, these are the tools required to "Make American Great Again." Gray notes that "emotion, and particularly emotive forms of political communication, refeudalizes the public sphere, acting as an obstacle to a meaningful and active deliberative democracy" (Gray 2007, 77). Candidate/President Trump offers an instructive example of how in a transmedia landscape the distinction between political participation motivated by reason and fandom motivated by emotion collapses. Trump's already cultivated TV fan base became his political base as he crossed over to the political sphere.

THE DIGITAL MATERIALITY OF RACE AND THE POLITICAL COLOR OF WHITENESS

Fandom is a performance, and, in alt-right fandom, whiteness is a mode of that performance—it's how to do alt-right properly. However, non-white men are also attracted to the alt-right movement. The former leader of the Proud Boys, Enrique Tarrio, is an Afro-Cuban, who is just as vocal in his support of white nationalism as his white counterparts. Proud Boys, in particular, call themselves Western Chauvinists, and don't restrict membership to whites only. As Gavin McInnes, the group's founder, notes, "[T]he only requirements for membership are that a person must be biologically male and believe the West is the best" (Gupta 2018). However, this form of Western Chauvinism is heavily tied to white privilege and exclusionary belief systems that have produced genocide, slavery, and other forms of racial violence and exclusion. Cristina Beltrán argues that many non-white members join far-right groups because they don't want to identify or align with politics of difference and the 'niche' interests of ethnic minorities. Instead, they seek "freedom from the politics of diversity and recognition" and pursue inclusion in the mainstream fabric of American society and the privileges that are conferred upon whites. Beltrán calls this phenomenon "multiracial whiteness [which] reflects an understanding of whiteness as a political color and not simply a racial identity." As long as non-white members embrace white supremacist views and participate in the denigration and persecution of minority groups, they are welcomed into the fold. As Beltrán notes, "[I]n the politics of multiracial whiteness, anyone can join the MAGA movement and engage in the wild freedom of unbridled rage and conspiracy theories." Multiracial whiteness consolidates and affirms the concept of white racial performance. You don't have to *be* white to *perform* white; you just have to support and defend the ideology of whiteness, which is increasingly defined by being anti-everything else. "America's racial divide is not simply between Whites and non-Whites . . . it is a division between those who are drawn to and remain invested in a politics of whiteness and those who seek something better" (Beltrán 2021). David Neiwert notes that minority American men are radicalized in the same way white men are: through social media, video game culture, trolling, and conspiracy theories (Gupta 2018; Neiwert 2018). The story that crosses the media in the transmedia paradigm is the story of whiteness. Just like any other narrative, it is produced, disseminated, curated, consumed, and then spread across other platforms.

Sanjay Sharma has examined the production of "ethno-racial collective behaviors" like the use of Blacktags on "Black Twitter" to argue for the digital materiality of race. He suggests that race (and racial ordering) is transformed through its encounter with digital networks, so that online identities move beyond the ethno-racial into the space of the "technosocial." Like Jessica Johnson (2018), Sharma recognizes the affective relations at play on social media platforms and argues that the "contagious effects of networked relations" produce "emergent racial aggregations" and "digital-race assemblages," which go beyond a simple representation of the lived raced identity of the user. Sharma's analysis is helpful in thinking about whiteness as a performance that is available to whites and non-whites. The "political color" of whiteness is a form of "ethno-racial" behavior that spreads across platforms and is "materialized through the contagious social relations produced by the networked propagation" of white meme culture (Sharma 2013, 46, 2). In this sense, "white identity" is curated and disseminated in transmedia racial assemblages and is performed online in and through its engagement with transmedia textuality. "Memes, then, serve as the vehicle to express either an individual or a collective voice. They are a reflection of the cultural spaces from which they emerge, even resulting in 'meme culture wars' originating from 4 Chan [sic] and other digital communities to construct and reinforce group identity" (DeCook 2018, 486).

Following Arun Saldanha, Sharma notes, "Rather than only as a problem of representation or embodied difference, race is discovered in its emergence through *connections* between bodies, and other entities and processes. 'From a machinic perspective, race is not something inscribed upon or referring to bodies, but a particularly spatiotemporal disciplining and charging of those bodies themselves. Bodies collectively start behaving like situationally distinct aggregates —racial formations, racial clusters'" (2013, 54). The racialized assemblages of online platforms where race and racial identity are discursively produced get carried over into real-world performances of racial identity, such as we saw in Charlottesville in 2017 and Washington in 2021. Trump fandom, as expressed in the alt-right mediascape, is a modality for the expression of white racial identity.

CLEARING A SPACE OF RECOGNITION

It is here, particularly in this moment of convergence culture, that Hall's insights from the vastly different media landscape of 1981 can still be applied. Forging a path between audience as passive dupe and ever-active resister, Hall notes that the power of the cultural industries is not in their ability to imprint us as if we were "blank screens"; rather, it is how they construct our own conception of self. In a receptive populace, Hall argues, the culture industries "find or clear a space of recognition" in which to "impose and implant such definitions of ourselves as fit more easily the descriptions of the dominant or preferred culture" (Hall [1981] 2019, 353). And these definitions are frequently "reworked

Racist graffiti on the side of a dugout in Wellsville, New York, November 2016. (© Brian Quinn/USA Today Network)

and reshaped" as required by the changing dynamics of the dominant group. In today's networked culture, these cleared spaces of recognition are top-down and bottom-up as audiences both consume and produce content. Passive consumption of entertainment programming is juxtaposed with active participation as consumers make use of the affordances of various technologies as well as the variety of platforms open to engagement. DeCook notes that "since social media are serving as socializing spaces for youth and young adults, these platforms and the subcultures they support are pieces in the construction of ideological sense[-]making and as larger learning spaces for civic engagement" (DeCook 2018, 486). Social media are also the primary site for self-branding, which Alison Hearn defines as the "self-conscious construction of a meta-narrative and meta-image of self through the use of cultural meanings and images drawn from the narrative and visual codes of the mainstream culture industries" (Hearn 2008, 198). The commodified identity of "imperiled whiteness" feeds into the performative display of white identity, particularly white masculinity, and found expression in Trump's campaign and release during his presidency.

After the 2016 election, the hate speech that was seemingly contained by the hangars, auditoriums, and amphitheaters escaped like a noxious gas, contaminating cities and towns across America. Whites demonstrated their fealty to whiteness (and, by extension, Trump) through a performance of white identity. "Day 1 in Trump's America" saw a spate of hate crimes worse than those seen after Obama's election. On a college campus in Louisiana, graffiti appeared bearing hate speech such as "BUILD THE WALL" and "FUCK YOUR SAFE SPACE"; in North Carolina, the words "BLACK LIVES DON'T MATTER AND NEITHER DOES [sic] YOUR VOTES" were spray-painted on a wall in Durham. There were numerous reports of Muslim women all over the country having their hijabs ripped off; in New York, swastikas were painted in playgrounds and on the side of a building with the words "MAKE AMERICA WHITE AGAIN"; and a Black doll was found hanging by a rope with a noose around its neck in a college in upstate New York (O'Kane 2016).

The Southern Poverty Law Center counted 867 cases of harassment and intimidation in the days following the election (Southern Poverty Law Center 2016). While outrage and panic gripped communities of color and their allies, it became clear that the so-called fringe had overtaken the center. While Trump himself told his supporters to "stop it" in an interview with CBS "60 Minutes," Paul Ryan stated on CNN's "State of the Union" that "real Republicans" were not responsible for the attacks (Easley 2016). However, it became obvious that Trump's firm support among whites was due to a backlash (or "Blacklash") against Obama and the feeling that previously white-only spaces, like the White House, had been usurped and that minorities were disproportionally advantaged by Obama's presidency.

These iterative, performative, collective, and, most importantly, public repetitions initially produce and then, through subsequent performances, reinforce this new whiteness—a highly militarized and masculinized identity that cannot and will not be cowed by traditional forms of power. Each public presentation of white identity, whether the 2020 occupation of the Michigan Capitol, the private militias patrolling BLM marches or "securing" polling places during the 2020 election season, or the brazen entitled behavior of rioters at the Capitol in 2021, contributes to the performance. These stylized and repeated identity acts manage to both telegraph and reinforce this form of whiteness, and at the same time, recruit and radicalize others. Indeed, this performative white identity found new purchase during the pandemic and the lockdowns that ensued. The perception that masking and lockdowns were a symptom and symbol of government overreach and control of the "little man" further galvanized this white identity.

Hall's "spaces of recognition" offer a productive way to understand white responses to the reporting on and representation of a changing racial landscape. These contested and commodified narratives of race and race-making, proliferating in a digital, networked mediascape, provided a space of recognition in which whites could identify and name their whiteness. Media systems are "comprised of actors and institutions that have material, social and ideological relations with vested interests and elite power, that regularly reproduce hegemonic forms of 'common sense,' but that are nevertheless 'not immune from the movements and ideas that circulate in society at any one time and that seek to challenge these power structures'" (Titley 2019, 26). In a digital economy, where race and race meanings were commodified and exchanged by both media produsers and prosumers, and as the harder forms of alt-right recruitment on social media offered an affective network for white nationalists, entertainment media also interpellated a white viewership, offering them a brand of white identity reworked and reshaped according to the preferred dictates of a white majority group. Central to this reworking is the battle over "tradition" and how it gets defined. "Not only can the elements of 'tradition' be rearranged, so that they articulate with different practices and positions, and take on a new meaning and relevance. It is also often the case that cultural struggle arises just at the point where different, opposed traditions, intersect" (Hall [1981] 2019, 357–58). Obama's election and its attendant discourse of postracialism offered a counter-tradition to white America's conception of itself and what it means to be American. It is in the realm of the popular that the contest over the "traditional" meaning of Americanness is articulated. As Hall makes clear, there is a "continuous and necessarily uneven and unequal struggle, by the dominant culture, constantly to disorganize and reorganize popular culture; to enclose and confine its definitions and forms within a more inclusive range of dominant forms" (Hall [1981] 2019, 354). White identity politics, then, arises not only as a way to counter the visibility of Blackness but just as importantly as a reclamation and redefinition of the meaning of whiteness and, by extension, Americanness.

The success of media depends upon consumer engagement, particularly its capacity to elicit "recognition and identification, something approaching a re-creation of recognizable experiences and attitudes" (Hall [1981] 2019, 354). But as Hall notes, these representations are deeply contradictory. And this contradictory nature accounts for the doublespeak, the having it both ways that colorblind postracial "quality programming," such as I examine in the following chapters, exhibits. The media industries clear spaces of recognition in their representations of racial conflict in the news and in "race fantasies" in film and television; I would argue that the diverse social, cultural, and political locations of the audience result in different spaces of recognition being "cleared" in relation to race relations, but that the ordering of identity in terms of the dominant group occurs to both. In the following chapters, I will explore these contested, contradictory expressions of racial meaning in *The Planet of the Apes*, *The Walking Dead*, and the newest films in the *Star Trek* movie franchise.

Part I
CONTAGION

Chapter 2

WE'RE ALL INFECTED

On June 16, 2015, Donald J. Trump announced his candidacy for the presidency. It was a rambling speech that set America against its enemies who "are getting stronger and stronger," while America, under Obama, "is in serious trouble." Trump's bellicose discourse claimed he would "beat" China and Japan in trade deals, but his most shocking statements related to Mexican immigrants and his claim that "[t]hey're bringing drugs. They're bringing crime. They're rapists" (*Washington Post* 2015). In July 2015, he asserted that "tremendous infectious disease is pouring across the border" in the body of immigrants. Along with the ongoing "build a wall" rhetoric, during his time in office, Trump repeatedly pursued opportunities to restrict immigration and limit the number of refugees entering the country and sought authority to deport undocumented workers and repeal DACA. He used his nomination speech at the Republican National Convention in 2016 to incite fear and panic among his supporters. America, he declared, was in a "moment of crisis" with "violence and chaos running rampant in our communities." Illegal immigrants were "roaming free to threaten peaceful citizens," and children were being "sacrifice[d] on the order and the altar of open borders." He proclaimed that America, under Obama, had endured "one international humiliation after another," but under Trump, "Americanism, not globalism, will be our credo" (Beckwith n.d.). In May of 2018, Trump stated that immigrants "aren't people. These are animals," and in the following June of 2018, in response to criticism of his policy of separating families at the US-Mexico border, he accused immigrants of "infesting" the country (Graham 2018).

In their book, *White Backlash, Immigration, Racism, and American Politics*, Marisa Abrajano and Zoltan Hajnal demonstrate that the views of white Americans toward immigration have a direct bearing on their political views and voting practices. Opponents of immigration skillfully deploy a "threat narrative," which "emphasizes cultural decline, immigrants' use of welfare, health, and educational services, their propensity to turn to crime, and their tendency to displace native citizens from jobs" (Abrajano and Hajnal 2015, 18). The discourse on immigration operates on two levels. One is an economic appeal—they're taking our jobs, they're using up our social services, and the other is more nebulous but potentially more effective. It relies on an appeal to an implicit American identity, who "we" are and what "we" believe. Now, as has been the case throughout history, this definition of Americanness is understood as a white Christian identity. Results of a survey taken in 2017 after Trump's presidential victory reveal that "[n]o other factor predicted changes in white partisanship during Obama's presidency as powerfully and as consistently as racial attitudes. This alignment between partisanship and racial attitudes extended far beyond attitudes toward Black people. By 2012, white Democrats and white Republicans diverged over whether they evaluated Muslims favorably and whether immigration should be restricted" (Sides 2017). White Republican voters were more likely to favor restricting immigration and had more negative views toward Muslims, and as Abrajano and Hajnal note, these attitudes were shaped in part by media stories on immigration. In fact, the proportion of campaign news coverage that mentioned immigration increased more than three-fold between 2011 and 2016. Abrajano and Hajnal argue that "how whites perceive immigration, whether they think it is a widespread problem, and ultimately whether they buy into an immigrant threat narrative" relates to media reporting on the issue. Their research demonstrates that a staggering 66 percent of network news coverage connects immigration with crime or terrorism, helping to "generate fear and anxiety among the public regarding the presence of immigrants, and specifically Latinos" (2015, 25, 43, 150).

Research finds that Trump's views on immigration and terrorism align with those of his base of primary supporters and account for the wide-scale defection of whites to the Republican Party (Haynes et al. 2016; Abrajano et al. 2017).[1] Ted Cruz and Marco Rubio also addressed the need for immigration reform and for tightening the southern border in their campaigns, but it was Trump's personalization of the issue—the people themselves were bad, not just the policies—that cultivated white Americans' fears of being "overrun" and "infected" by immigrant hordes. When polled on their attitudes to "concerns about rising diversity"—the likelihood that America will be majority minority by 2043—those who voted for Trump interpreted rising diversity as a drain on government services and were most concerned about immigrants taking jobs. The pollsters note that "[v]oters who held views of immigrants, Muslims, minorities, and feminist women as the undeserving 'other' were particularly susceptible to Trump's appeal" (Griffin and Teixeira 2017). Furthermore, as Abrajano and Hajnal demonstrate, "unskilled, native-born Americans whose jobs and wages are most in jeopardy tend to be most strongly opposed to immigration" (Abrajano and Hajnal 2015, 56).

Despite the fact that immigration from Mexico had declined in the period from 2009–2014, as more Americans headed to Mexico than the other way around, these polls reveal that the Trump supporter attributed economic stagnation in the white working class to the supposed influx of immigrants to the United States. Moreover, the perceived threat that the immigrant represents is racialized: immigrants "soil" the purity of white American identity. As Eric King Watts notes, "Such flows across borders put tremendous pressures on the nation-state as a dwelling place, which is always already a place of imagined kinship and racial identification" (Watts 2018, 443). It's no coincidence that Trump's continued talk of border walls, drug mules, and rapists is reminiscent of an earlier time in American politics, "hearkening back to both a different demographic moment in US immigration history (1990s and early 2000s) *and* a different political era in US Immigration policy ("Operation Wetback"), as well as the perceived innocence of the 1950s, where American workers faced less competition for jobs and there was less racial and ethnic diversity" (Winders 2016, 292). The voters polled in 2016, including those who switched from Obama to Trump, had also been polled in 2012, and those with strong views about restricting immigration in 2012 were twenty-six points more likely to support Trump in 2016. While there is no question that Trump's rhetoric contributed to a growing anxiety about these issues, and pollsters do note the tendency of voters to change their positions on issues to match those of their candidate, these polarizing views on race and immigration were developing during the Obama administration. "In Pew surveys from 2007, white people were just as likely to call themselves Democrats as Republicans (44 percent to 44 percent). By 2010, white people were 12 points more likely to be Republicans than Democrats (51 percent to 39 percent). By 2016 that gap had widened to 15 points (54 percent to 39 percent)" (Sides 2017). This data reveals that Trump didn't create the xenophobia and racism he continually expressed on the campaign trail; rather, he tapped into and exploited existing sentiment among voters. But where did these views arise? How have immigration, disease, and infection become connected in the popular imagination? What role have film and television played in constructing cultural scripts that teach us whom and what to fear? And how is this tied to the rise of white identity politics?

In this chapter, I will examine how racial or foreign otherness has become associated with disease in a white imaginary. I will examine why the biggest threats to America's conception of itself as a white nation are believed to come from Brown and Black people and how that threat is characterized as a form of contagion in both the news media and in popular entertainment media. Politicians and media have frequently utilized the discourse of pollution, infestation, or contagion to figure the threat that Hispanics, African Americans, and (especially after 9/11) Muslims are considered to pose to a white nation (Bloodsworth-Lugo and Lugo-Lugo 2010; 2011). I want to revisit some of these tropes in terms of the emergent discourses of white supremacy surfacing in the Obama-to-Trump era. Through a reading of *The Walking Dead*, and by way of the 2013 film *Elysium*, I will explore how such representations contribute to a sense of "imperiled whiteness" and reinforce and magnify more extreme right-wing views like Replacement Theory and "white genocide." Released in 2013 on the heels of Obamacare and vocal Republican resistance to it, *Elysium* offers an instructive example of how entertainment media and news media combine to create media events that shape public views about political policy. These national debates about policy reflect a polarized partisan landscape, which is frequently racialized. *Elysium* and *The Walking Dead* are examples of progressive, postracial programming, which, in their depiction of whiteness imperiled by invasion/contagion of the nation-state, re-race whiteness in ways that develop and reinforce white identity politics.

DISEASE, DEATH PANELS, AND THE UNDOCUMENTED

Set in the year 2154, the 2013 science fiction film *Elysium* depicts a world of wealthy elites who live on a pristine, utopian space station called Elysium. The rest of the largely Brown population lives on the "diseased, polluted and overpopulated" Earth where resources are scarce. The citizens of Elysium have pure air and high-tech medical care: "no poverty, no war, no sickness"; they have unlimited leisure time and endless recreational opportunities. By contrast, the citizens of Earth live in an environmental wasteland policed by aggressive, militant robot droids who regulate and control the factory-line work done on Earth. The film's critique of US policies related to immigration is obvious. In a black-market economy, Hispanic mules pilot "undocumented ships" in order to smuggle inhabitants of Earth across the border of Elysium. The ships seldom make the journey and are frequently shot down before they arrive. Apart from the promise of a better life, a key motivation of the undocumented to seek entry into Elysium is to gain access to its high-tech medical care—machines that, in one quick scan of the body, can mend broken bones and cure cancer. Elysium represents a hyperbolic version of the health care situation in the United States, where the privileged few, by virtue of personal wealth or employer subsidy, have access to affordable, good quality medicine, but the vast majority of people amass enormous debt to cover even basic procedures and are forced to prioritize medications based on the cost of a prescription or forego treatment altogether.

The Affordable Care Act (ACA), popularly known as Obamacare, passed in 2010 during Obama's first term[2] and extended coverage to all Americans by implementing a tax on the wealthiest 1 percent in order to fund benefits to those in the bottom 40 percent of income distribution. The ACA faced strong opposition from Republicans who dubbed it "socialized medicine" and fanned media narratives about extended waiting times for critical surgeries and government rationing of medical care. Sarah Palin, former governor of Alaska and 2008 vice presidential candidate, galvanized opposition to the bill in 2009 when she provocatively and falsely claimed that government "death panels" would determine who among the sick and elderly was most deserving of medical care. A 2009 editorial published by the *Wall Street Journal* echoed this view, stating, "Once health care is a 'free good' that government pays for, demand will soar and government costs will soar too . . . Yes, the U.S. 'rations' by ability to pay (though in the end no one is denied actual care). This is true of every good or service in a free economy and a world of finite resources but infinite wants" (*Wall Street Journal* 2009). Neill Blomkamp's *Elysium* magnifies this conflict between *finite resources* and *infinite wants* by offering a broad critique of global capitalism and the way neoliberalism perpetuates social and economic inequality along racial lines. *Elysium* reveals how resource scarcity, overpopulation, climate change, immigration, globalization, and affordable health care are underwritten by racial disparities and how neoliberal responses to these problems exacerbate rather than ameliorate those divisions.

At the same time, this progressive critique is undermined by linking health care to immigration. Although the medical disparities shown in *Elysium* mirror the unequal distribution of health care in the United States, Blomkamp frames this resource inequality in and through an immigration narrative; everyone within the nation-state has access to medical treatment, it's those outside Elysium's borders who are denied care. This framing is interesting because it reorients the health care debate from the obligation of government to extend care to its own citizens to demanding that it provide for citizens of other countries/regions. Indeed, the idea that Obamacare would offer insurance to undocumented people was a key talking point in the Tea Party's vocal opposition to the ACA and prompted Republican congressman from South Carolina, Joe Wilson, to accuse Obama loudly and publicly of lying during Obama's 2009 speech to a joint session of Congress. Although Wilson was reprimanded and later apologized, the accusation had enough traction in the news media that the Obama Administration released a statement assuring the public that provisions of the ACA would not extend to undocumented immigrants.

In Blomkamp's film, the elites on Elysium hoard medicine and medical care not simply because they constitute a luxurious Elysian commodity but because they offer much-needed protection against the disease that the illegal immigrants are presumed to carry. A citizen code is required for medical care on Elysium, thus underscoring the point that infection is a defining marker between "us" and "them." If "immunitary concerns basically drive many modern nation states into erecting both juridical and physical walls around their borders" (Andersen and Nielsen 2018, 625), the film makes apparent the metaphorical contagion that the immigrant is believed to represent to the home country. Elysium's scheming secretary of defense, Delacourt (Jodie Foster), is acutely aware of this dilemma and seeks to fortify Elysium by increasing military force and preventing the illegals from entering her airspace. In order to do this, she stages a coup against the current president, Patel, one of the few brown-skinned people on Elysium, whose more humane views set him at odds with Delacourt. Though Delacourt is a two-dimensional, predictable villain, who is taken down by our white hero, Max (Matt Damon), and his Hispanic buddy, Spider (Wagner Moura), she also serves as a mouthpiece for the kind of nativist, populist white identity politics that was emerging in the US in 2013. Although the film clearly intends a critique of the US health care system, the immigration frame, along with other visual and narrative elements of the film, works to undermine the progressive message and reinforce white precarity. At the same time, the film rekindles fears extant since 9/11 about the nation-state's ability to secure its borders against diseased and lawless outsiders.

When the film opens, little Max, a white, blond-haired child, runs ragged and unkempt on the dirty, polluted streets of a dystopian city. In a community of brown-skinned people, Max's whiteness stands out. He has no family other than the Hispanic nun who raised him and his best friend, Frey. In dress and habitat, the film works hard not to make Max seem different from his friends and co-workers, but he is visually out of place. There is something uncanny about Max's belonging. By contrast, the Elysium elite is predominately white, apart from the Asian Indian president, Patel, and a few "model minority" Asians. Because Max is one of very few whites in his community, the film feeds into fears of "demographic replacement," a key conviction of anti-immigration proponents, who believe that white Americans are steadily being "replaced" by Brown and Black people, whether through immigration or intermarriage.[3] At the same time, because the rich white elites live on Elysium with their Brown president, Max seems "left behind" by an economy and politics that don't support him or his needs. An ex-con, Max works for Armadyne, the company that supplies arms and weapons to Elysium. Working the assembly line, producing the very robots that police him, Max epitomizes white working-class alienation in the twenty-first century. When he gets pushed into the radiation chamber that will lead to his eventual death, it's clear that he's expendable, a literal and figurative casualty of techno-globalization.

On the one hand, the film seems to offer a critique of policies that closely align with Republican positions on immigration and health care. However, the depiction of a brown-skinned president, whose concern for human life is represented as a failure to police the borders, countered by the strong, militant Delacourt, who shows no hesitation in shooting down illegal ships and the refugees within, echoes Republican critiques of the Obama administration as "soft on terrorism." When Patel reprimands Delacourt for her aggressive use of the military to police the border, her retort closely mirrors the immigration rhetoric that was gaining traction in Republican circles during Obama's second term. "I understand that it is not the fashion to think and act as I do. I understand that perfectly. But when they come for your house or the house you built for your children and your children's children, it won't be PR and campaign promises that keep them out. It will be me" (Blomkamp 2013). The speech reads like an eerie foreshadowing of the "Midnight in America" convention speech Trump would deliver in 2016:

> The attacks on our police, and the terrorism in our cities, threaten our very way of life. Any politician who does not grasp this danger is not fit to lead our country... Tonight, I want every American whose demands for immigration security have been denied—and every politician who has denied them—to listen very, very closely to the words I am about to say. On January 20th of 2017, the day I take the oath of office, Americans will finally wake up in a country where the laws of the United States are enforced. (*Los Angeles Times* 2016)

Delacourt then justifies her overthrowing of Patel by claiming that, under his leadership, Elysium is dying: "There is a political sickness inside of it. A tumor that needs to be removed" (Blomkamp 2013). Max, now empowered by an exoskeleton, finds his purpose by smuggling data from the brain of Carlyle, the owner of Armadyne. Although Spider intended Max to steal financial data, it turns out the information contained on the brain chip is a reboot of Elysium's computer system that would enable residents of Earth to become citizens of Elysium. Unfortunately, the activation of the data will result in Max's death. Where Spider's motivation is financial, Max's is altruistic. Predictably, Max sacrifices himself for his disadvantaged brothers and sisters on Earth, ensuring that everyone will have access to the bounties of Elysium. But in doing so, the film effectively reintroduces the problem that the creation of Elysium sought to correct, that of limited resources and infinite wants. When the Brown citizens of a diseased and dying Earth enter Elysium at the cost of our white hero Max's life, the conceptual elements in place depict them not so much as fleeing disease as embodying it and bringing it to the pristine shores of their new home.

THE AESTHETICS OF "BIOINSECURITY"

As *Elysium* reveals, the discourse of "diseased outsider" operates as a larger metaphor for the security of the nation state. Steven Pokornowski argues that the "rhetorics of global health and global security, like the 'civilizing' colonial rhetorics before them, attempt to normativize Western identity across cultures, revising and reinforcing imperialist notions of alterity and pathology" (2013, 217). History provides numerous examples, from persecuted religious minorities to asylum seekers, of states seeking to keep the foreign, ethnically distinct other out; indeed, increasingly, anti-immigration rhetoric suggests that it is the foreigner's very "ethnic-ness," whether racial or religious, their capacity to taint or pollute through incursion the purity of the state, that is the reason for their exclusion.[4] Popular culture, too, frequently utilizes the insider/outsider trope, often couching the threat to a nation-state's security through the metaphor of contagion. These cultural products constitute what Pokornowski calls a "bioinsecurity aesthetic," which typically features "desolated cities, states of emergency, and an ambivalent privileging of the medical and the military, where biomedical and political vulnerabilities are conflated in an embodied dual threat" (2013, 217–18).

Here I consider how this trope is utilized in film and television produced during the Obama administration and how it worked to frame and prime white perceptions of immigrants and the seeming menace they represent to the health of the country in cultural, social, and demographic terms. In other words, I will examine how the immigrant narrative in America has gone from being one of inclusion, of an understanding of ourselves as a "land of immigrants," to one where the immigrant is viewed as contagion, a parasite draining the body of the nation.[5] This is not to imply that all, or even the majority of, Americans perceive immigrants this way, but recent polls indicate that a majority of Republicans do. According to a 2019 survey undertaken by the Public Policy Research Institute (PPRI), 89 percent of Republicans support restrictive immigration policies, compared to 55 percent of Independents and 32 percent of Democrats. The poll found that Americans who support Trump are twelve times more likely to favor stricter immigration laws and ten times more likely to believe that "immigrants are invading our country and replacing our cultural and ethnic background" (PRRI 2020). How did media industries in the Obama-to-Trump era, including film and television, contribute to the rise of these beliefs, and how did campaign-trail Trump and his xenophobic architects, Steve Bannon and Steven Miller, propagate and exploit fears about immigrants within the American populace?[6] How, in other words, did media narratives (whether in an allegorized form in speculative fiction or in the news framing of the immigration "crisis") clear "a space of recognition" (Hall [1981] 2019) in which whites could articulate and define their whiteness in a postracial landscape that they perceived to have at best sidelined them and at worse vilified them?

FRAMING THE GREAT REPLACEMENT

Media scholars, sociologists, and political scientists have demonstrated how public opinions about immigration during Obama's presidency were driven by media reporting on immigration and particularly by the negative framing of much of the coverage. Robert Entman notes that "framing works to shape and alter audience members' interpretations and preferences through priming. That is, frames introduce or raise the salience or apparent importance of certain ideas, activating schemas that encourage target audiences to think, feel, and decide in a particular way" (Entman 2007, 164). In their analysis of media framing about immigration from 2007–2014, Haynes et al. note that frames are highly partisan and reflect the biases of the media outlets producing them. Lou Dobbs, for example, who was ousted (with a severance package of $8 million) from CNN in 2009 because of complaints by viewers and unfavorable publicity from lawsuits mounted by immigration groups and the Southern Poverty Law Center, was a vocal opponent of immigration and on two occasions broadcast his nightly show live from the convention held by the Federation for American Immigration Reform (FAIR) (Kaufmann 2019, 103). Immigration-related news drives salience and, as Kaufmann notes, "[S]alience is critical because only then do political parties take notice and begin to campaign on an issue, shifting policy" (2019, 100). Media framing has a significant impact on shaping public opinion in terms of the language used to describe immigrants—"illegal aliens" versus "undocumented immigrants"—as does the narrative used to prime the story. "Threat" narratives, not surprisingly, prime audiences to think negatively about racial and ethnic minorities. As Abrajano et al. note, "[M]edia overwhelmingly focus on an 'immigrant threat' narrative that links immigration to economic costs, social dysfunction, illegality, and cultural decline" (2017, 9). Several researchers note the associations made between "criminal," "Latino," and "illegal" and how these associations inhere in news coverage and in the attitudes of poll respondents (Haynes et al. 2016; Abrajano et al. 2017). Further, in their research on the correlation between media frames and political identification from 1980–2011, Abrajano and Hajnal found that most media frames represented immigrants negatively and that media framing of immigrants in an unfavorable light resulted in an increase in white alignment with the Republican Party and reduced support for immigration reform.

Historically, both Republicans and Democrats have made implicit racial appeals to white voters utilizing code words like "welfare reform," "law and order," and "immigration reform" to signal to their base their support (or lack of support) of policies targeting specific minority groups (Omi and Winant 2014; Tesler and O'Sears 2010; Belcher 2016; Anderson 2017). But in 2016, Donald Trump showed not only that racial and ethnic groups could be talked about explicitly and derogatorily but that such invective would be welcomed by large swaths of the voting public (Tesler 2016b; Beauchamp 2017; Osnos 2015). Many studies correlating voters' degree of racial resentment with support for Republican candidates have found that "Republicans who scored highest on racial resentment were about 30 percentage points more likely to support Trump than their more moderate counterparts" (Tesler 2016a; see also Tesler 2016b; Belcher 2016). Whereas Black/white relations have often been the subtext for Republican race-baiting, such as George H. W. Bush's successful deployment of African American convicted murderer Willie Horton in an ad implying Michael Dukakis was "soft on crime," Trump targeted a variety of racial and ethnic minorities and nationalities. By attacking Mexicans, Muslims, Jews, and Chinese, Trump could tap into a range of current national concerns, including immigration, terrorism, and the economy, and by citing bogus statistics about "Black on white crime"—in reality, 15 percent, not the 81 percent cited by Trump—and criminal justice reform, or rather, in the parlance of the right, the "war on cops" (Taylor 2015; Lynch 2016). By expressing his racism in terms of a national and/or economic threat to "us," he deftly segregated the country into whites and non-whites, Christians and non-Christians. From New Hampshire voters who believe that illegal immigrants "are sucking our economy dry" to neo-Nazis who believe that they have found "the one man who actually represents our interests" (Osnos 2015), his politically incorrect speech became the patriot's playbook and appealed to both hard and soft white identity politics. In closing borders, banning Muslims, deporting "illegals," and ending scrutiny of police departments with a record of civil rights abuses (Lichtblau 2017), Trump made very clear that America's economic and national security, as well as its very identity, required a racial and ethnic purge. As Trump supporter Pat Buchanan made clear in a 2016 interview, "Anybody that believes that a country can be maintained that has no ethnic core to it or no linguistic core to it, I believe is naïve in the extreme" (*NPR* 2016).

Buchanan's comments highlight that Trump's nationalist, racist rhetoric is not spontaneous nor merely a reflection of his anti-PC "tough talk"; rather, Trump's talking points dovetail in content and tone with a well-defined and well-known doctrine originating from the French *Nouvelle Droite* and increasingly embraced by white nationalist groups in the US—the Great Replacement Theory. The theory, outlined by French identitarian author Renaud Camus in his book *Le Grand Replacement*, argues that European whites are being culturally and demographically replaced by non-white immigrants and blames interracial marriage and (feminist) women choosing to delay or forego pregnancy for a falling white birth rate. The theory is related to another right-wing conspiracy, "white genocide," which argues that Jews and other elites are plotting the extinction of the white "race" through their support of miscegenation, immigration, and abortion. Kaufmann argues that these more extreme views spring from the same anxieties expressed by Tea Party Republicans and their constituencies. The Tea Party "reflected a whole new right-wing ecosystem . . . nourished by activists linked via Fox News, talk radio and the right-wing internet," with immigration being one of the movement's "top priorities" (2019, 109). Immigration reform, including amnesty for DREAMERS and DACA, he notes, failed because there was a "70 per cent overlap between the Congressional Immigration Reform caucus . . . and congressmen supported by the Tea Party" (Kaufmann 2019, 109).

It was this same right-wing ecosystem and its fears over immigration and white replacement that Trump exploited in his campaign, especially when polls demonstrated that it resonated with voters. Immigration quickly became a signature issue for Trump. Calling himself the "law and order candidate" (L. Nelson 2016), he vowed to immediately deport two to three million undocumented immigrants and promised a "total and complete shutdown of Muslims entering the United States" (Taylor 2015).

IMMIGRANTS AND ZOMBIES

Arguably, the most controversial action related to immigration was the Trump administration's family separation policy at the US-Mexico border, which was implemented officially from April to June 2018 but was in effect as early as 2017 and as late as July 2019 (US House of Representatives 2019). Consistent with his "zero tolerance" policy toward undocumented people, children were removed from their parents or guardians and placed in detention facilities, while the accompanying adults were prosecuted and sent to jail or placed in other detention camps awaiting trial. Facing national and international condemnation, Trump reversed the policy through an executive order in June 2018 but enacted no provisions to reunite the families. The administration faced further criticism once conditions at the detention centers were made known by several attorneys who, investigating whether the minors' human rights were being violated, visited a camp in McAllen, Texas. In the centers, described variously as "concentration camps" and "torture facilities," the children faced extremely cold temperatures, constant artificial light, lack of medical care, and an absence of basic sanitation (no soap or toothpaste) and adequate food. At another camp in Clint, Texas, one doctor described conditions where children, covered in mucus and feces, were being "cared for" by children as young as nine. Detainees were told to drink from the toilet if they wanted water (Stieb 2019). An internal investigation by the Department of Homeland Security found conditions in the camp to be "squalid" and that "serious" overcrowding represented "an immediate risk to the health and safety of DHS agents and officers, and to those detained" (Montoya-Galvez 2019).

Giorgio Agamben has characterized Nazi concentration camps and detention centers like Guantanamo Bay as "states of exception" wherein individuals are reduced to "bare life," a state of existence (*zoê*) that, because absent the protection of human or civil law, is distinguished from a particular mode of life (*bios*). Bare life is not to be confused with "simple natural life" but is, rather, "life exposed to death." The state of exception occurs when governments aggregate to themselves the ability to suspend the rights of citizens in cases of emergency or presumed threat by an outside force. The Patriot Act of 2001 and The Homeland Security Act of 2002, instituted by the Bush administration after the attacks of 9/11, which allowed for infinite detention of immigrants and the capacity to search a home or business without the owner's consent or a court order, are examples of the employment of a state of exception. Prisoners in Guantanamo, titled "enemy combatants," were robbed of their human rights under the Geneva Convention, denied legal or moral rights (*bios*) and were rendered bare life through the sovereign (nation-state) exercise of power. As *zoê*, these individuals can be killed but not sacrificed (a sanctioned or ritualized form of execution) because they exist beyond the legal protection of the state that *bios* would afford them, yet, according to Agamben, they are the exception that allows the law to function normally. They are included in the law as an exclusion. Notably, Agamben includes refugees in his criteria of bare life, arguing that they represent "such a disquieting element in the order of the modern nation-state" because "by breaking the continuity between man and citizen, *nativity and nationality*, they put the originary fiction of modern sovereignty in crisis. Bringing to light the difference between birth and nation, the refugee causes the secret presupposition of the political domain—bare life—to appear for an instant within that domain" (Agamben 1998, 131). One Border Patrol agent described the conditions at the family detention center in McAllen as like a "scene from a zombie apocalypse movie." With "sickness and filth everywhere[, it] looked like a walled-off compound where the government had the last safe zone and was taking in refugees fleeing the deadly zombie virus" (Thompson 2019).

Numerous critics have noted the association between contagious zombies and displaced peoples, immigrants, refugees, and asylum seekers. Jon Stratton has argued that in the modern world, the zombie represents an example of bare life. "The zombie apocalypse is the fantastic representation of the modern state being overwhelmed by the bare life that underpins its existence; the bare life that is lived by those people excluded from the privileges of citizenship and rights" (Stratton 2011, 203). Following Foucault's observation that "in a normalizing society, race or racism is the precondition that makes killing acceptable," Gerry Canavan argues that the state requires this kind of racial division "in order to retain its power to kill" (Canavan 2010, 438). Zombies function as particularly salient metaphors for exploring cultural anxieties about nuclear war, terrorism, viral pandemics, and rapacious capitalism, and many attribute the proliferation of zombie narratives in the last two decades to artistic attempts to make sense of life in the aftermath of 9/11 (Bishop 2009; Lauro and Embry 2008; Schweitzer 2018). Zombies resonated with audiences after 9/11 in part because they signified death and destruction in the context of borders that failed to hold. In this formulation, terrorism is an infection arising from an "other" that cannot be contained. Pokornowski has argued that cultural texts frequently express biomedical and political insecurities of the state in the figure of the zombie, and those discourses work to reinstate colonial and imperial ideologies which require an assimilation or annihilation of difference (2013). Kyle Bishop argues that "historically, zombie cinema had always represented a stylized reaction to cultural consciousness and particularly to social and political injustices." But he notes that America in the 1990s was too complacent and stable for "zombie movies to fit the national mood" (Bishop 2009).

While most contemporary zombie narratives like *I am Legend* (2007), *28 Days Later* (2002), *World War Z* (2013), and *Train to Busan* (2016) associate the zombie with the threat of infection, the history of the zombie is tied to racial oppression. Originating in Haiti, the "zombi" first entered the American imaginary through W. B. Seabrook's sensationalist journalistic account of Haitian vodou in *The Magic Island* (1929) and the Halperin brothers' film *White Zombie* (1932). In the Haitian context, a zombie is a "mindless slave risen from the dead by evil magic" (Moreman and Rushton 2011) to toil endlessly in the fields. Existing at the intersection of slavery, colonial occupation, and capitalist exploitation, the zombie is "a manifestation of collective unconscious fears and taboos." The ultimate border-crosser, the zombie is liminal in life, race, and statehood. This is not to imply that it exists beyond or outside the categories of race and nation, but always between, threatening contamination (Bishop 2010, 37). Eric King Watts argues that Seabrook's narrative captivated and frightened readers in the West because it reordered racial hierarchies. On the one hand, it presented possibilities as to how "postcolonial domination of black bodies" might be sustained, but at the same time, the Haitian zombie aggravated white fears of "extraordinary black biopower that might challenge white mastery" (2018, 449).

The figuration of the zombie as a foreigner, an immigrant, and an outsider who represents a biopolitical threat to the state redefines and reframes white identity. Indeed, the zombie's frequent representation as a postracial, posthuman entity obscures the political race-work that zombies perform in popular entertainment narratives.[7] Such representations enable and justify violence against and exclusion of those Others who, seeking resources and sanctuary from "us," are perceived to threaten the security of the homeland. As Schweitzer makes clear, "There is no ambiguity about who the zombie is or whether it is acceptable to attack it" (Schweitzer 2018, 151). If the zombie trope becomes operable in times of political and cultural crisis, how might we understand its deployment in our colorblind postracial moment? And how is the zombie trope called upon "to manage felt emergencies regarding a loss of white privilege and place" (Watts 2018, 444)?

WALKING WHITE

Set in the southern state of Georgia where, in the absence of any viable laws or government, the survivors "take back" their country and fight the invading hordes of undead, *The Walking Dead* (*TWD*), an adaptation of Robert Kirkman's popular comic book of the same name, thematizes and articulates a discourse of "imperiled whiteness." In its survivalist end-of-days narrative, where social safety nets are ripped away and replaced by a backwoods country code, the series valorizes white working-class masculinity, ridicules liberals, and promulgates a narrative of "us" and "them"—the strong who must fight for survival and defend their territory and the parasites (humans and zombies) that bleed us dry. If, as Stratton argues, the proliferation of zombie narratives in the late twentieth and early twenty-first centuries should be understood as a formulation, or working through in a popular realm, of the threat that displaced people—immigrants, refugees, asylum seekers—are thought to represent to the neoliberal Western nation-state, we might consider what function the zombies of *The Walking Dead* serve in this cultural and political age. Specifically, it is worth examining how these zombies are fashioned and interpreted against the backdrop of Obama's and Trump's America and how they contribute to the divisive racial politics of our age.

Airing just two days before the midterm election of 2010, in which the ruling Democratic Party suffered massive losses at the federal and state levels, the storylines of the initial seasons of *The Walking Dead* reflect the political and cultural zeitgeist of conservative white America. According to a CNN poll, 52 percent of midterm voters polled identified the economy and the unemployment rate as their top concerns, followed closely by health care and illegal immigration (CNN 2010). Prior to this election, immigration had largely been taken off the political table following the failure of the passage of the Comprehensive Immigration Reform Act of 2007, which included a version of the DREAM Act in addition to funding for increased border security. However, in 2010, both sides of the debate became energized when Arizona passed its controversial Senate Bill 1070, known as the "Support Our Law Enforcement and Safe Neighborhood Act." The law required immigrants to carry their immigration papers with them at all times or face misdemeanor charges and granted Arizona's law enforcement agencies increased power to investigate the immigration status of those suspected of having illegal status, as well as to enforce state and federal immigration laws. Amid widespread protests and claims of racial profiling, the United States Justice Department under Obama sued, claiming that the law usurped the power of the Federal Government to regulate immigration. Several states joined in an amicus brief in support of Arizona's bill, defending the state's authority to enforce federal immigration law "in light of the selective and even lack of enforcement of those laws by the Obama administration" (Center for Security Policy 2010). Reviewing the case in 2012, the US Supreme Court overturned parts of the Arizona law but granted Arizona police the authority to check the immigration status of people who are suspected of being in the country illegally only when making lawful stops. At the center of the controversy was Joe Arpaio, the sheriff of Arizona's Maricopa County. A colorful figure, Arpaio was notorious for racial profiling and the unlawful enforcement of immigration law. He was a staunch advocate of Trump and a vocal supporter of his immigration policies during the 2016 campaign. In July 2017, Arpaio was served with a criminal contempt of court charge for continuing to detain people suspected of being in the country illegally after being barred from doing so in a 2007 lawsuit brought by defendants claiming racial profiling. In a controversial move, on August 28, 2017, Trump pardoned Arpaio, who claimed that his conviction was a "political witch hunt by holdovers in the Obama justice department" (Lee 2017b).

MICROTARGETING REPUBLICAN VIEWERS

These clashes over immigration offer an important context for interpreting the politics of "us" and "them," which is central to the world of *The Walking Dead* (*TWD*). In 2016, the year of Trump's election, "*TWD* was the single most-watched TV show among the sought-after 18–49-year-old age group" (Turner and Perks 2019). Overall, it is the most-watched cable show in history, beating out even *The Sopranos* and *Game of Thrones* (Lang 2014). While the show's popularity crosses regional divides, a recent poll revealed that *The Walking*

Dead is more popular with Republicans than Democrats and particularly with Republicans living in rural border states. In fact, so popular is the show with conservatives that the Trump campaign microtargeted *Walking Dead* audiences in the lead-up to the 2016 election. In an interview with Forbes in 2017, Jared Kushner explained how the campaign employed Cambridge Analytica and utilized tools like Deep Root to identify shows popular with specific voter blocks in specific regions. The data revealed that people who watched *The Walking Dead* were more likely to be sympathetic to Trump's views on immigration than those who didn't watch the program (Bertoni 2016).

With its "postapocalyptic backdrop, the collapse of societal infrastructures, the indulgence of survivalist fantasies, and the fear of other surviving humans" (Bishop 2009, 20), *The Walking Dead* offers the perfect canvas on which to project contemporary anxieties about the Other and to validate a form of American whiteness believed displaced by the claims of immigrants and "home-grown" minorities. I would argue that *TWD* follows the traditional zombie formula in working through cultural fears of pandemic and apocalypse but expresses its anxiety and instability by shoring up a conservative defense of the fear of the outsider, largely through validation of white masculinity, generally, and white working-class identity, more specifically (Kunyosying and Soles 2018; Ho 2016; Turner and Perks 2019; Dunaway 2018). "Because zombies mark the demarcation between life (that is worth living) and unlife (that needs killing), the evocation of the zombie conjures not solidarity but racial panic" (Canavan 2010, 433). While the zombie "walkers" are obviously the perennial outsider, as the show progresses the surviving band of humans is threatened as much by other human groups as non-human ones. Because the Trump campaign identified the show as appealing to audiences who had conservative views related to immigration and because Trump himself has repeatedly used the discourse of infection and infestation in relation to immigrants, I want to consider how *The Walking Dead* has shaped audience views on immigrants and has colluded with and exploited Americans' perceptions of immigrants as parasites in the media. As Canavan makes clear:

> [O]ne of the ways that State apparatus builds the sorts of "preaccomplished" subjects it needs is precisely through the construction of a racial binary in which the (white) citizen-subject is opposed against nonwhite life, bare life, *zombie* life—that anti-life which is always inimically and hopelessly Other, which must always be kept quarantined if not actively eradicated and destroyed. (Canavan 2010, 433)

Certainly, the one consistent message of the show is the fear of the outsider. Every season, the characters have to negotiate borders and boundaries and decide whom to let in and whom to keep out. As Rick's group encounters more and more survivors, each community negotiates the cost of trusting the stranger, erecting walls, surveilling, and patrolling to keep invaders out. When read in relation to its political timeframe, which over ten seasons includes intense partisan debates over DACA and the rights of dreamers; media stories about undocumented people purportedly attacking, raping, and killing innocent Americans; legislation aimed at restricting "Sanctuary Cities"; and Trump's constant call to build a border wall, *TWD* functions as more than entertainment, it constitutes part of a media event. Because news media and entertainment media are consumed in the same way and often deploy the same rhetorical and cinematic tools, we must recognize how fictional representations, like *TWD*, even when employing metaphor, destabilize the relationship between the real and its representation, which in turn affects how we read and respond to the real events that correlate with them.

"YOU PEOPLE ARE LIKE A PLAGUE!"

In season 1, episode 1, "Days Gone Bye," Sheriff's Deputy Rick Grimes (Andrew Lincoln) awakes from a gunshot-induced coma to a world overrun by zombies known as "walkers." Eventually reunited with his family, Rick and a small posse of other survivors head to the CDC in Atlanta, where they hope to find an explanation and a cure for the virus. There Rick learns that everyone carries the virus that results in reanimation upon death. You don't need to be bitten by a walker to get infected; "we're all infected." Interestingly, so as not to cause panic among the survivors, Rick keeps this information from the group and the audience until late in season 2. This allows plenty of opportunities for the survivors to establish the "us" and "them" dynamic, both with the zombies and other groups they encounter along the way. In the beginning, as Rick and his group fight for survival and seek shelter and asylum in a variety of communities, they appear like immigrants. When Dr. Jenner at the CDC asks, "Why are you here? What do you want?" Rick answers that they want "a chance." Rick wants Jenner, who has been garrisoned since the outbreak, to understand how hard it has been for his group. "You don't know what it's like out there. You may think you do, but you don't. We'd have died out there. It was only a matter of time" (Darabont et al. 2010, 1:1). This is the first, but not the last, time that Rick's group will seek entry into a fortified safe haven. Sometimes they bargain and cajole (Hershel's Farm, Alexandria), and other times they use violence to gain admission (the prison, Woodbury). In the early seasons, the group effectively functions as a roving band of refugees, seeking shelter from place to place. But they are rarely given a handout; instead, they contribute to, and eventually either take control of the society or renounce it. The walkers, by contrast, are rambling hordes without aim or purpose, contaminating everything they come into contact with. In this way, the show acknowledges the American "land of immigrants" story but works hard to separate good people from bad.

In episode 11 of season 2, "Judge, Jury, Executioner," Hershel (Scott Wilson) asks Glenn (Steven Yeun), who is Korean American and has recently begun a relationship with Hershel's daughter, Maggie (Lauren Cohan), where his family is from. Glenn, clearly uncomfortable, answers, "Michigan, but before that, Korea." Hershel reminds Glenn that "immigrants built this country. Never forget that" (Darabont et al. 2012, 2:11). He then proceeds to give Glenn the watch his Irish grandfather had passed down through the generations. But the same Hershel, just a few episodes before, angered and upset by the discovery and elimination of the zombies he was keeping in the barn, which included his wife and stepson, lets loose on Rick: "You people are like a plague! I do the Christian thing, give you shelter, and you destroy it all!" (Darabont et al. 2012, 2:8). In this way, the series employs its double voice in relation to the immigration question. It shows how displaced people all need the same things but then carefully sets up a narrative that reinforces the view that not all those who seek asylum are equal, are worthy. When Hershel disparages Rick's group in this way, the viewer knows it's not true, knows they're mostly good people, or, rather, recognizes them as people who are mostly flawed but okay. However, the statement lingers and resonates beyond Rick, reinforcing views already extant in the viewing audience that immigrants take and destroy.

In season 2, episode 8, "Nebraska," Rick, Hershel, and Glenn encounter two brash, rough guys from Philadelphia who seek refuge at Hershel's farm; our group has only recently been accepted there, having at first been denied shelter. One of the men, Dave, pleads to be included: "We got some buddies back at camp, been having a real hard time. I don't see why you can't make room for a few more. We can pool our resources, our manpower." Rick tells him that it's "not an option." Using the same language that Rick himself employed at the CDC and at the farm, Dave tells Rick, "You don't know what we've had to go through out there, the things we've had to do." "You've got to understand," he explains, "we can't stay out there." Rick maintains that there is no room at the farm and to "keep looking," and then, suspecting Dave is about to draw his gun, Rick shoots both men dead (Darabont et al. 2012, 2:8). This exchange is notable for the way it is colored by class and regional differences. One the one hand, the two men, with their city accents and uncouth ways (one urinates in the corner of the bar), seem suspicious or threatening because they're different. But on the other hand, everyone is desperate, and Rick's group has seen and committed its own fair share of heinous acts. Yet the judgment is made quickly, without any real provocation, in part because of the difference these two men represent to the southern gentleman, upstanding lawman, and model minority characters represented respectively by Hershel, Rick, and Glenn. In this example and numerous others, we see how the show fills in the zombie/immigrant outsider metaphor to include real people whose claims on the group's finite resources make them unviable. Consistent with its colorblind logic, the racialist politics of the show are obscured by the fact that these outsiders, just like most of the zombies who are routinely and efficiently slaughtered, are white.

"REALLY BIG WALLS"

In season 3 of *TWD*, we are introduced to a new group of survivors who live in the fortified town of Woodbury, run by a slick confidence man called "The Governor" (David Morrissey). Woodbury has high makeshift walls, patrolled by armed guards who keep the "creepers" away and allow the residents to continue on with life as usual. When Andrea (Laurie Holden) and Michonne (Danai Gurira) are given a tour of Woodbury, their guide tells them that their "walls haven't been breached in well over a month." She refers to the town as "inside" and tells them about the "curfews" that are enforced for their safety. She reminds the women that the armed guards "put their lives at risk every day to protect this town" (Darabont et al. 2012, 3:3). The lines between inside and outside, "us" and "them," couldn't be drawn more clearly than in Woodbury, which, with its perfectly manicured lawns, colonial style buildings, quaint storefronts, and white pristine folksiness, is a stereotypical Mayberry. This self-fashioning becomes particularly marked in the town's varied degrees of comfort with and acceptance of Andrea and Michonne. Andrea, who is white, is visibly enamored of Woodbury and is quickly taken in by the smooth-talking, suave Governor. Michonne, who is Black, is suspicious of The Governor from the beginning, angering Andrea and prompting her to question whether Michonne has "ever trusted anybody." In obvious ways, the show aligns Andrea's openness and naivety with her whiteness and Michonne's reserve and skepticism with her Blackness. Andrea tells Michonne, who, nursing her back to health from a deadly infection, saved Andrea's life, "I still feel like I hardly know you." By contrast, Andrea styles herself as an "open book" (Darabont et al. 2012, 3:3). Michonne's distrust of The Governor and his operation and her unwillingness to follow his rules create tension between the newly romantic Andrea and The Governor. He tells Andrea that Michonne "makes people uncomfortable. . . . some people want her to leave," reminding her and the viewing audience that "what works out there doesn't work in here. We are not barbarians" (Darabont et al. 2012, 3:5). When Michonne finally leaves, without Andrea, who has been persuaded to stay, The Governor sends Merle on a (failed) mission to kill her.

The Governor makes clear that what makes Woodbury different, safer, and better than other places is the wall. When Andrea asks him how he maintains the bucolic order of Woodbury, he says, "really big walls," but he makes clear that "the real secret is what goes on within these walls. It's about getting back to who we were. Who we really are.... And men willing to risk everything to defend them. Compromise our safety, destroy our community, I'll die before I let that happen" (Darabont et al. 2012, 3:3). Walls are central to maintaining the distinction between "us" and "them," healthy and diseased, friend and stranger. In season 3, episode 3, The Governor saves a soldier from a helicopter crash for the sole purpose of establishing the whereabouts of his group and their ammunition. Killing all the soldiers, The Governor returns to Woodbury and, standing atop the tank, tells his people that the soldiers died because "they didn't have our walls or our fences" (Darabont et al. 2012, 3:3).

ANGELS AND DREAMERS

Season 3 aired between October 2012 and March 2013 and, although the talk of "walls" as a preferred means of keeping out others certainly predates Trump's oft-promised border defense, it coincides with the immigration debates taking place in Congress, specifically the controversy over DACA, the executive order signed by Obama in June 2012. DACA—Deferred Action for Childhood Arrivals—originated from the Obama administration's frustration with the failure to pass the DREAM (Development, Relief, and Education for Alien Minors) Act. The DREAM Act sought to grant temporary residency and included provisions for work and study, and a conditional path to citizenship for immigrants who were brought to the United States illegally as minors. The act was first introduced in the United States Senate in 2001 but did not garner enough votes to pass. It was included in the Comprehensive Immigration Reform Act of 2006 and the Comprehensive Immigration Reform Act of 2007, but both bills failed. A priority of the Obama administration, a version of the bill was passed by the Democrat-controlled House in 2010 but did not reach the sixty-vote threshold needed in the Senate. Following the failure of Congress to pass the bill, Obama announced in June 2012 that his administration would stop deporting immigrants who fit the criteria proposed in the Dream Act, effectively creating his own state of exception by assuming the discretionary power granted to him by the Constitution to circumvent existing immigration law. Obama signed an executive order applicable to those individuals who were younger than thirty-one as of June 15, 2012 (the program's starting date), and have lived in the US continuously since June 2007, granting them the right to work, live, and study in the US providing they stay free of criminal activity. DACA allows for the deferment of deportation to be renewed every two years; unlike the DREAM Act, DACA does not provide a path to legal citizenship. The Pew Research Center estimated that approximately 800,000 undocumented immigrants had received work permits and deferred deportation under DACA. Ninety percent of DACA recipients are from Latin America, and, of that number, Mexico represents 79.4 percent (López and Krogstad 2017). On the campaign trail, Trump promised to terminate DACA. In June 2017, he said he would keep the program, continuing to grant work permits to eligible recipients, but then reversed course again in September 2017, directing the Department of Homeland Security to stop processing any new applications. In November 2019, the Supreme Court reviewed the legality of the program and, in June 2020, in a 5–4 vote, blocked the Trump administration's plan to end the program. Writing for the majority, Chief Justice Roberts called the proposed ban "arbitrary and capricious" and noted that the administration failed to provide, as required by law, "a reasoned explanation for its action" (Totenberg 2020).

When polled, a majority of Americans expressed support for a path to citizenship for "dreamers" (Krogstad 2020). Just as in the case of children separated at the border, most Americans don't want to assign culpability to children for the actions of their parents. And research demonstrates that Dreamers are less likely than native-born Americans to commit crimes and are well integrated into the social fabric of the country (Nowrasteh 2018). In order not to alienate these voters but to advance their agenda with regard to immigration reform, Republicans made a rhetorical separation between the Dreamers and other undocumented immigrants, who, those on the right claim, disproportionally engage in criminal and violent behavior. To that end, the term "Angel," referring to citizens killed by undocumented people, started to be used by the right-wing media. In an attempt to extricate compassion for the Dreamers from his larger immigration agenda and, particularly, to deflect attention from what he called "phony stories of sadness and grief" coming from families separated at the border, in June 2018, Trump hosted several "Angel families" at the White House. It was these families, not the ones in detention on the border, which he claimed were the true victims of family separation: "They're not separated for a day or two days. These are permanently separated, because they were killed by criminal illegal aliens." To these so-called Angel families, Trump promised, "I hear you, I see you, and I will never let you down.... Your loss will not be in vain. We will secure our borders" (Trump White House 2018). He then invited the families to recount in graphic and lurid detail the crimes (including rape, sodomy, immolation, and torture) endured by their mostly grown children at the hands of undocumented people. When Democrats accused Trump of manufacturing a crisis at the border to justify his wall (Norman 2019), Trump ramped up his rhetoric, stating, "To those who refuse to compromise in the name of border security, I would ask, imagine if it was your child, your husband or your wife whose life was so cruelly shattered and totally broken.... To every member of Congress, pass a bill that ends this crisis. To every citizen, call Congress and tell them to finally, after all of these decades, secure our border" (Trump White House 2019).

Although Trump wasn't yet using the rhetoric of the wall to talk about immigration in 2012, the concept and the security a wall was presumed to provide was already established in cultural discourse through popular and entertainment media vehicles like *TWD*. The Governor's manic authoritarianism, though ultimately shown as destructive and dangerous, does not take away from the security and sanctity of the haven that the wall provided. Woodbury, just like Trump's soon-to-be made great again America, "is about getting back to who we were. Who we really are." The Governor's appeal, like Trump's, rests on the fantasy of lost wholeness that can be reclaimed: "We're going out there and we're taking back what's ours. Civilization. We will rise again" (Darabont et al. 2012, 3:3). The citizens of Woodbury bought into the rhetoric in the same way Trump's electorate did. This ideology of bioinsecurity depends on creating divisions between people: those whose lives are worthy of saving and those who threaten that salvation. "To foster life most efficiently may require the deaths of those who pose a 'risk' to the population's health and well-being. As risks are always only potential, however, this means individuals may be punished for what they *might* do or what they *represent*. It is about probabilities and risk minimization, rather than 'punishment' or 'correction'" (Schweitzer 2018, 177).

The convergence of the racial and infection zombie narratives in *The Walking Dead* raises questions about the show's longevity and popularity with both conservative and progressive viewing publics and critics. Recognizing the importance of the zombie metaphor and its applicability to a variety of situations, it's useful to go beyond the meanings attending the zombie as immigrant and its capacity to destabilize social order and examine how the zombie narrative in *TWD* enables renewed attention to whiteness and white identity politics. How does this contemporary, highly popular "postracial" series utilize zombies to reinforce fears of "white genocide"?

SPECULATIVE FICTION, ZOMBIES, AND "WHITE GENOCIDE"

Contemporary far-right theories of "white genocide" find their roots in genetic racism of the nineteenth and twentieth centuries as well as in bioscientific anxieties about germs and contagion. Speculative fiction frequently expresses these two discrete fears as convergent, as Blomkamp's *Elysium* reveals. The *overlap* between these anxieties offers a useful starting point to interrogate the way contemporary SF productions, like *The Walking Dead*, tie anxieties about immigration and outsiders to the potential for contagion and infection of the white body. Laura Diehl notes that early twentieth-century science fiction writers were animated by the same narratives of contagion and border permeability as were "anti-immigration activists, eugenicists, and microbe hunters." Diehl notes that:

> As the concept of a microbial parasite was extended to a race parasite, the language of bacteriology—bad blood, infection, invasion—converged with the language of national defense—border patrols, resistance, immunity—to militarize the fight against foreign agents that penetrated the body, took up permanent residence, and transformed the host into a killer by subverting the body's/nation's security defenses. (Diehl 2013, 85)

Just as the news media employ framing that includes "threat" narratives and draw associations between criminality and Hispanic people by utilizing negative terms like "illegal" and "unauthorized," speculative fiction has historically employed frames related to science and race. As Diehl and others have shown in SF, the "fight for racial survival" is frequently depicted as virological in nature. Invasion novels of the 1950s increasingly portrayed white men in combat with a "biological/ideological virus that contaminates and transforms the human into a soulless simulacrum." Cultural and demographic shifts brought about by unrestricted immigration policies after World War II manifested in fictional anxieties about the racial future of the country and were symbolized by aliens' "excessive breeding." As Diehl notes, "[W]hether parasites, slugs, or communists, foreign bodies bred rapidly and were deadly" (2013, 96–97).

How do these convergent racial/virological fears hold up in SF today and particularly in *The Walking Dead*? In his reading of Kirkman's comic, Kyle Bishop argues that *TWD*, like other zombie fare, shifts the monstrous identity from the zombie to the humans and depicts the "potential devolution of humanity." Humans become "chaotic creatures of selfishness, violence, and unchecked aggression who do more damage to ourselves and the world around us than any reanimated corpse ever could." Bishop suggests that this kind of reversal provides audiences with "ethical guideposts and a sober warning against atavistic barbarism" (2015, 74). The aggressive and preemptive strike by the US on Afghanistan and Iraq after 9/11, the holding of "enemy combatants" in Guantanamo Bay, and the use of "enhanced interrogation techniques" like waterboarding reveal the "moral and ethical decline of a fearful U.S. population desperately seeking an Other they may scapegoat and blame." This human failure, Bishop argues, is mirrored in Kirkman's comic as the survivors experience a "slow, tragic loss of humanity" (2015, 78).

Bishop's reading can certainly be supported and applied to the AMC show and might explain its appeal to more liberal audiences. But like other franchises examined here, *TWD* employs a doubleness—engaging in both progressive and conservative messaging, fostering its appeal among diverse and polarized viewing publics. The audience, Stuart Hall reminds us, is both "the source and the receiver of the television message." However, "[b]efore this message can have an 'effect' (however defined), satisfy a 'need' or be put to a 'use' it must first be appropriated as a meaningful discourse and be meaningfully decoded." And it is "this set of decoded meanings which 'have an effect,' influence, entertain, instruct or persuade, with very complex perceptual, cognitive, emotional, ideological or behavioural consequences" (Hall [1980] 2004, 119). Because audiences are not monolithic, the decoded meanings of a program will vary depending on the viewer's location and position in a network of social, cultural, and political discourses. While it is the case that after 9/11 many on the left considered the US government to have violated human rights and international law, millions of Americans supported Bush and Cheney's "War on Terror" and happily relinquished their domestic civil rights in the interests of the nation.

At the same time, we should not discount the way that fictional vehicles allow audiences of different political leanings to derive pleasure from terrible people doing terrible things, thus providing audiences the opportunity to "maintain *plausible deniability* regarding their own morally suspect ideological investments" (Johnson 2017, 15). Because media in all its forms "clear a space of recognition," in which and by which consumers define themselves in relation to the dominant culture (Hall [1981] 2019, 353), we should attend to the ways shows like *TWD* affirm and celebrate white American identity, crossing partisan lines to reveal that the investment in American whiteness is as salient on the left as it is on the right. In his discussion of toxic white masculinity in *Breaking Bad*, Paul Elliott Johnson argues that being American requires white citizens to ignore the genocide and enslavement that founded the nation and instead embrace the myth of American exceptionalism and progress. Shows like *Breaking Bad* and, I would add, *The Walking Dead*, "attempt to compensate for this dual instability, offering moral alibis for the exceptional violence of America while simultaneously figuring white men as marginalized in their own right" (Johnson 2017, 15). Rather than viewing Rick and his survivalist posse as tragically broken or irredeemably altered by the zombie apocalypse, many fans see him as a strong, virile patriot who is doing what's necessary to protect and survive. Fan support of the "Ricktatorship," discussed in chapter 5, is a clear example of this.

AMC'S WHITE NICHE MARKET

In her analysis of the impact of cable and streaming services on television, Amanda Lotz notes that networks like AMC contributed to the rise of quality programming that rivaled and eventually surpassed, in popularity and profitability, offerings on main broadcast networks. *The Walking Dead* was central to AMC's success because it was consistently ranked as the "most watched show of the week" among all demographic groups for the first several seasons of its run. *TWD* proved a profitable vehicle for AMC, not just because of its wide popularity and attendant advertising revenue, but because it was also the first program that was produced by AMC's own production company, AMC Productions. This allowed the network to maintain ownership and profit from creation through distribution rather than outsourcing shows to larger studios that would benefit financially when the shows were then sold to Netflix and other secondary buyers. Apart from the profitability of this new business model, it also gave AMC the flexibility to produce targeted programming that catered to specific markets. Unlike the broadcast studios that "developed series targeting a broad cross section of the audience," cable studios "created distinctive content designed to resonate with a niche audience and establish a channel brand" (Lotz 2018, 89). *Breaking Bad* (*BB*), whose ordinary everyman Walter White turns to a life of crime to support his family after a terminal cancer diagnosis, is another of AMC's most popular and commercially successful shows. And both *TWD* and *BB* overlapped with another drama showcasing powerful and precarious white masculinity, *Mad Men*. As Sarah Nilsen notes, part of the appeal among white audiences of *Mad Men*, which is set in the 1960s, "can be explained in terms of a sentimental nostalgia for an era of uncontested white privilege" (Nilsen 2014, 191). If we take primary campaigning into account, all three shows span the Obama-to-Trump era: *Mad Men* aired in 2007, ending its run in 2015, *Breaking Bad* ran from 2008 to 2013, and *The Walking Dead* began in 2010 and aired its final episode in 2022. In a diversified model, money comes from audiences, not studios, so it's important to appeal to those audiences through niche marketing. AMC further catered to this new market through its interactive platform, Story Sync. Story Sync was launched during season 2 of *TWD* and allowed fans the opportunity to interact with episodes as they were broadcast. Using a variety of digital mediums, fans were encouraged to participate in polls, answer trivia questions, predict outcomes, and rate scenes. "The timing of each nugget of interactive content is designed to complement the natural flow of each broadcast, not compete with it. By syncing the two, AMC allows fans to actively engage with the intense, emotional moment in the show, without having to worry about keeping one eye on the TV and one eye on a computer screen" (Graham 2012).

Viewed alone, we might read the popularity of *TWD* as extending from a more pervasive and recent cultural fascination with zombies. However, when taken together, these three popular AMC shows comprise another niche market that focuses on "white masculine victimage, and the gendered racialism of neoliberalism" (Johnson 2017, 15). If we consider that *Mad Men*, *Breaking Bad*, and *The Walking Dead* were all produced in the Obama-to-Trump era, AMC bought and produced scripts that foregrounded white men laid low by new cultural norms relating to gender, class, and race. The appeal of these shows among a cross-section of viewers and the critical acclaim each show has garnered suggest that white stories, specifically stories about whites battling and overcoming the threats to their privilege and cultural primacy, not only resonated with audiences but also with writers, producers, and other creatives in the mediascape who cultivated and profited from this new "white market."

Taking into account the most recent data on race and ethnicity from the 2020 census, which revealed that the multiracial population (people identifying as belonging to two or more races) in the United States increased by 276 percent from 2010 and the "white alone" population decreased by 8.6 percent, whatever anxiety white Americans might have about demographic "replacement" was primed for manipulation (Jones et al. 2021). In this context, the discourse of zombies and the rhetoric of infection in the eleven-season run of *TWD* constructs, rather than merely reflects, Americans' views about issues related to immigration and border security and reinforces an "us versus them" narrative in the context of "finite resources and infinite wants." Agamben makes clear that "[h]e who has been banned is not, in fact, simply set outside the law and made indifferent to it but rather *abandoned* by it, that is, exposed and threatened on the threshold in which life and law, outside and inside, become indistinguishable. It is literally not possible to say whether the one who has been banned is outside or inside the juridical order" (Agamben 1998, 28). The immigrant's exclusion becomes a necessary, even qualifying, condition of the citizen's inclusion. In the cultural politics of the twenty-first century, these forms of inclusion/exclusion are starkly racialized: inclusion equates to whiteness. White supremacist theories about "white genocide" and the Great Replacement reflect this logic. Just as the law/sovereign requires the exclusion that bare life represents, so too do citizens need the refugee/immigrant/person of color's non-belonging as a way to delimit and define American identity as white identity. *TWD* exemplifies this in its entanglement of the living and the dead. If "we" are all infected, then at any moment, "our" status—which is to say, a status that conflates Americanness with whiteness—could be revoked or rendered invalid. As Dr. Jenner (Noah Emmerich) warns Rick in the final episode of season 1: "You know what's out there. A short, brutal life and an agonizing death ... This is what takes us down; this is our extinction event" (Darabont et al. 2010, 1:6).

Chapter 3

SIMIAN FLU OR EBOLA REDUX

Dahlia Schweitzer argues that "the way infectious viruses are appropriated by Hollywood may provide the greatest insight into the viruses themselves and the world we live in" (Schweitzer 2018, 21). Fans of *TWD* have their own theories about how the zombie virus started: genetic mutation, government bioweapon, SARS-like virus, a flu epidemic, etc. A popular fan theory is that the virus originated from the meth lab of Walter White, a character from *Breaking Bad*, another AMC show (Otterson 2016). When Rick and his group enter the CDC for answers, they are appalled that Dr. Jenner doesn't have any. Andrea challenges Jenner: "You have no idea what it is, do you?" He says, "It could be microbial, viral, parasitic, fungal." Rick picks up the charge: "But you don't know. How can you not know?" (Darabont et al. 2010, 1:6). It's interesting to read the failure of the CDC here in light of its numerous missteps in handling the outbreak of COVID-19.[1] Rick and his group have to escape the CDC in order to survive—the government is useless; it can't protect us; we must take matters into our own hands. The intertwining of actual pandemic events, the viruses that produce them, and the imagined response of real government agencies like the CDC are common devices in contagion narratives and highlight the way mediated narratives construct global crises and our reactions to them. In the age of globalization, these stories assert, the government cannot protect us from infection.

Functioning as "entryway paratexts," which attempt to control and frame a viewer's entry to the text (Gray 2010, 23), the advertising media for *Dawn of the Planet of the Apes* similarly employ real-world anxieties about pandemics and government control. One of the ads incorporates actual footage of Obama and his Homeland Security Secretary Janet Napolitano, discussing the 2009 H1N1 pandemic, as well as footage of sick Asian men and children, and migrants massing on the border. Images of police in riot gear are juxtaposed with clips from the film and posters advertising Simian Flu screenings. Assembled in a fast montage, the real and the fictional are deliberately blurred. In the same fashion, another of the ads for *Dawn* is styled as a public service announcement highlighting the

Real footage of Barack Obama's Secretary of Homeland Security Janet Napolitano discussing the H1N1 epidemic in 2009 in a trailer for *Dawn of the Planet of the Apes*. (*Dawn of the Planet of the Apes*, 2014)

rapidity of the spread of the virus. The text-based ad utilizes a red drop graphic on a white screen, which falls and spreads, simulating the reach of the disease and its deadly toll. Connecting the racist discourse of the "one-drop rule" to virological contamination, the ad warns, "One drop can change your life, one drop can take your life," noting that "every nine seconds someone in the world is infected with the Simian Flu" (Movieclips Trailers 2013).

Infection narratives like *Outbreak* and *Contagion* frequently depict viral pandemics arising from zoonotic (animal-to-human) transmission. These diseases typically originate in Asia or Africa and contaminate the "West" via the extreme rapidity of global communication and contact. The threat, as Marina Levina makes clear, is depicted as a "direct result of globalization, both in the origin of the disease and its mode of transmission" (2015, 80). If outbreak storylines foreground the threat of permeable borders, inefficient governments, and faulty science, they also situate the main threat in the body of the Other, the outsider who contaminates and pollutes the sanctity of the national (American) body and its metonym, the white body. Although the virus in *Rise of the Planet of the Apes* is created in an American lab, not an African jungle, the name of the virus, "Simian Flu," retains and reinforces the association of apes as carriers of the virus. In this chapter, I will examine how the implied zoonotic transmission from ape to human in 2011's *Rise* draws on the long-standing racist association of Africans and apes to portray the Black body as a biothreat. Via an analysis of the 1995 film *Outbreak* and the 2014 Ebola crisis, I will argue that Black intellectual superiority is represented as an uncontainable (simian) virus with the capacity to destroy the (white) human population or render it mute. Consistent with its location in the "postracial" space of Obama's presidency,

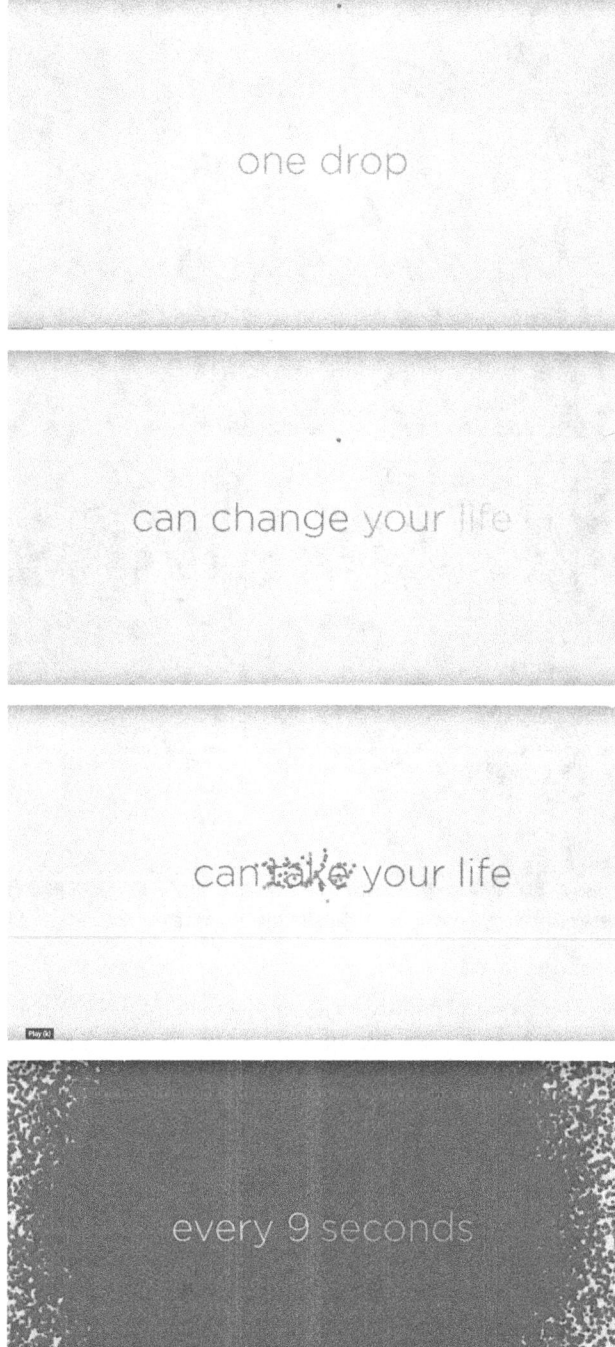

Promotional advertisement for *Dawn of the Planet of the Apes* styled as a Public Service Announcement connects racist "one-drop" rhetoric to virological contamination.

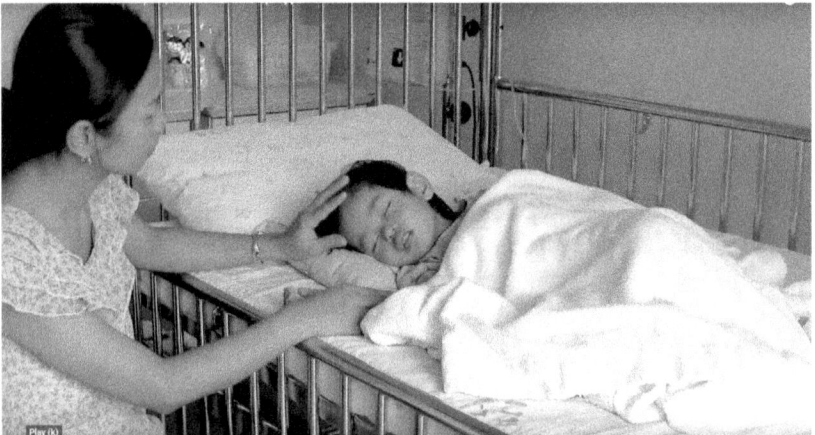

One official trailer for *Dawn of the Planet of the Apes* links infection to Asian populations.

the film obscures its racial politics by its employment of the familiar formulaic conventions of the contagion narrative and its clever, sympathetic imagining of the backstory to the original *Apes* movies.

OUTBREAK OBAMA

In March 2020, when the Trump administration was being challenged for its handling of the coronavirus, Republicans, including minority whip Steve Scalise, resurrected the Ebola crisis of 2014 and Obama's supposed mishandling of it for the purpose of deflecting attention away from Trump's mismanagement of COVID-19. At the same time, as most Americans were in lockdown, the 1995 blockbuster film *Outbreak* was trending in Netflix's top 10 (Maas

2020). Starring Dustin Hoffman and Renee Russo, *Outbreak* is loosely based[2] on Richard Preston's 1992 *New Yorker* article, "Crisis in the Hot Zone," and subsequent 1994 nonfiction book, *The Hot Zone: The Terrifying True Story of the Origins of the Ebola Virus*, which details the 1989 outbreak of an airborne strain of Ebola, not transmittable to humans, in a primate quarantine facility in Reston, Virginia. The monkeys responsible for the outbreak in Reston were crab-eating monkeys from the Philippines. As the virus rapidly spread among the animals, all 450 were euthanized and had their carcasses incinerated (Paugh 2014). Consistent with its fictionalization of the real outbreak and as a way to simplify or cement the association of Ebola with Africa and to appropriately prime fears among theatergoers that Ebola was an imminent threat to humans, the monkey responsible for the spread in *Outbreak* is brought to California from Africa, not Asia, and the rapid dissemination of the airborne disease quickly puts the whole town in jeopardy. Although there were no human cases in the US in 1995, the culture of fear around Ebola was inflamed by media and popular culture and centered on America's vulnerability to foreign agents carrying disease and death to its shores.

It is quite curious to watch *Outbreak* in the context of 2020's coronavirus pandemic. The film opens in a mercenary camp in Zaire in 1967, with rows of dying white soldiers, and a Black, seemingly immune physician standing over them. When the Americans in hazmat suits arrive, one of the soldiers begs them to "get me out of this shithole." They don't; they bomb the whole place. In the film, Washington clearly agrees with the soldier's sentiments: an African town is expendable, American citizens notwithstanding. Viewers in 2020 are quite likely to believe the American government is capable of the same actions, especially when Trump in 2018 referred to countries in Africa, as well as Haiti and El Salvador, as "shithole countries." Consistent with his "us vs. them" rhetoric, Trump tapped into the long-standing formula of Africa as dirty and diseased and, in doing so, effectively deployed the kind of race-baiting, dog-whistle language that was politically effective in the 1980s and '90s. Trump's twenty-first-century version echoes and reinforces colonialist and eugenicist rhetoric of race as contagion.

The discourse of infection is frequently articulated as foreign, invading the sanctity of home space (Wald 2008; Levina 2015; Booth 2015; Schweitzer 2018). Central to the mediated political and fictional narratives of the Ebola outbreak is the pervasive subtext of an unclean Africa. When Ebola resurfaced in 2014, during Obama's presidency, Republicans seized on the conceptual associations of Ebola and Africa not only to question Obama's handling of the crisis but Obama himself.[3] Obama, the son of an African-born father, was "read" against the narrative of foreign contagion. Though not yet a candidate for office, in 2014, Trump was an outspoken critic of Obama's handling of Ebola, accusing him of failing to close borders and of following CDC guidelines that were perceived to be inadequate. Throughout the lead-up to the 2014 midterm elections, citizen Trump repeatedly railed against the Obama administration's management of the virus and called for a ban on travel to all Ebola-infected countries. When Obama did not close the borders, Trump called him "dumb"[4] and tweeted that his refusal to do so was "almost like saying f— you to [the] U.S. public" (Lahut 2020). Both right-wing and mainstream media picked up on Trump's tweets, and Republican lawmakers echoed his call for a travel ban and tighter border security, stoking fears in the general populace that "the specter of a lethal African virus [was] being spread through the United States by migrants" (Rupar 2020a).

Republicans under Obama used the "Ebola crisis" as an opportunity to rehearse their predictable talking points that the populace faced an imminent threat from Ebola due to the Democrats' "softness" on terrorism, and that Obama himself, his "foreignness," his ties to Africa and his "Muslimness," posed an implicit risk to Americans. Conceptually, fear of Ebola depends on the rhetoric of unclean, "primitive" Africa—a "jungle culture" of bat-eating and unorthodox religious practices. As Frank Wilderson explains, "Africa, in the collective unconscious of the world, is a place of crisis and catastrophe" (Wilderson et al. 2016, 17). The risk that Ebola represented, or was depicted as representing, threatened both the individual and the nation. In this case, the foreign virus was a symbol of the penetrability of our borders and the need to strengthen and protect the homeland from the contagion that the unclean Other threatened. Schweitzer argues that "outbreak narratives—and the anxieties they reflect—feed into larger narratives constructed by government organizations, journalists, and Hollywood to fuel an ever-expanding relationship between fear, power, and money" (2018, 11). Rhetoric deployed by the media and the government during the 2014 Ebola crisis demonstrates that while the threat to individuals and the nation from Ebola was relatively small—it can only be transmitted through contact with bodily fluids, not particulates in the air, and as of 2017 there were only four laboratory-confirmed cases of Ebola diagnosed in all of US history—it was frequently referred to as a bioterrorist threat for which America was vastly underprepared and underfunded (Schweitzer 2018, 12). The popular response to Ebola was largely stoked by media reports and articles that typically exaggerated the capacity of the virus to spread and sensationalized the risk posed to Americans.

What is perhaps most remarkable about the hysteria over Ebola is the fact that it posed a very small danger to the US population. Although the 2014 outbreak resulted in more than 4,500 deaths in Liberia, Sierra Leone, and Guinea, there were only two deaths in the US, and both of those were people who had contracted the disease in Africa. Trump's 2014 framing of Ebola as a border issue—"The U.S. must immediately stop all flights from EBOLA infected countries or the plague will start and spread inside our 'borders.' Act fast!"—established the connection between lax borders and foreign contagion that he would so successfully exploit in his 2016 campaign for president, where he railed against immigrants, Muslims, and refugees (Lahut 2020). It also demonstrated Donald Trump's political value to the Republican Party. Trump's crass hyperbolic untruths were received by a bipartisan electorate as a brand of "straight talk" and had a pivotal effect on the 2014 midterm elections. Those midterms, where Republicans won control of the House with a gain of sixty-three seats and acquired seven seats in the Senate, were essentially a referendum on Obama's bailout of Wall Street, the overhaul of the health care system, but also, to some degree, his perceived incompetence in dealing with Ebola.

The scope of the risk of a given pathogen gets interpreted by the way it is framed by politicians as well as news and entertainment media (Levina 2015; Schweitzer 2018). Discursively, these accounts operate in tandem in an attempt to make sense of the social conditions that give rise to their expression. However, because the meaning we glean from these texts "is never determined by the nature of the experience itself, but always by the social power to give it one set of meaning rather than another" (Fiske [1996] 2016, 4), it is imperative that we situate these narratives of contagion in the context of the power relations of which they form a part. In Trump's rhetorical invective, Africa/monkeys/Blacks/disease have a metaphorical relation; he deployed these associations during his campaign and called on them whenever he needed to shore up the base and remind whites of their disenfranchisement vis-à-vis the Other.

Consistent with this strategy, in 2020, at the peak of social panic over COVID-19, Republicans resurrected Ebola. Trump repeatedly blamed Obama for the coronavirus, even though it occurred a full three years after his departure from office, and Trump's flouting of his own government's guidelines to wear a mask in public turned mask-wearing into a partisan issue and a question of civil liberty (Rupar 2020b; Weissert and Lemire 2020; Yang 2020; Stanley-Becker 2020a). The fact that the Republicans repeatedly turn to Obama as their fall guy and that blaming him for the Trump administration's issues resonates with many voters (in June 2020, the right-wing media was abuzz with "Obamagate" [Wilson 2020]), indicate that racial resentment toward African Americans among conservative whites has lingered and can be successfully called upon at a given moment when Republicans face strife (Allam 2020; Smith 2020). By invoking Obama, Trump was obviously attempting to distance, if not remove, himself from any culpability related to the spread of COVID-19. However, blaming Obama also helped reinforce the idea that the coronavirus is foreign and, like Obama and minorities in general, presents a risk to Americans precisely because of its difference from an implicitly white "us" and a white way of life.

Because "media transformations are generative for the operations of racism and practices of anti-racism," we should not underestimate the way Hollywood capitalizes on these cultural fears, appropriating and repackaging the association among virus, contagion, and the foreign Other (Dreher 2020, 2364). As I demonstrate below, associating Black people with apes is an enduring racist strategy. In this chapter, I'm interested in examining how the metaphor operates in terms of the discourse of contagion and how the rebooted *Planet of the Apes* trilogy (2011–2017), directed by Rupert Wyatt (*Rise of the Planet of the Apes*) and Matt Reeves (*Dawn of the Planet of the Apes, War for the Planet of the Apes*), helped foster a sense of white precarity among a white populace during the presidency of Barack Obama through the representation of empowered intelligent apes that outsmart and outlive their human counterparts.

POST(RACIAL) APOCALYPTIC FILM

As part of a broader system of cultural representations, films both construct and reflect social reality. Hollywood film, in particular, is always a product of the time and social history which informs it, whether the film is challenging or endorsing the prevailing politics of its epoch (Kellner and Ryan 1988; Kellner 2010). Douglas Kellner argues that filmic representations operate as a form of political ideology. Ideology works to "pacify, channel, and neutralize the forces that would invert the social system of inequality were they not controlled." But ideology also "testifies to the power of those forces, of the very thing it seeks to deny" (2010, 14). Films do their ideological work most keenly during times of "social crisis." "Some idealize solutions or alternatives to the distressing actuality, some project the worst fears and anxieties induced by the critical situations into metaphors that allow those fears to be absolved or played out, and some evoke a nihilistic vision of a world without hope or remedy" (Kellner 2010, 168). In its depiction of a postapocalyptic dystopian world where the boundaries of the human are challenged by intelligent apes, the new *Apes* trilogy both stimulates and justifies viewers' fears about the Other and the self.

Just as the promotional materials for the news *Apes* franchise offer a window into the role paratextual material plays in framing textual meaning and viewer interpretation of a primary text, prequels, sequels, and adaptations have a significant impact on the reception of a film or television narrative. As Jonathan Gray makes clear, "such entities change the nature of the text's address, each proliferation either amplifying an aspect of the text through its mass circulation or adding something new and different to the text" (Gray 2010, 2). In his extensive examination of the original series, Eric Greene argues that the creators of *Planet of the Apes* used species difference as an analog for, and a means of working through, prevailing cultural anxieties related to racial difference. In the midst of civil rights activism and anti-war protests of the '60s, "the sense that racial violence abroad and at home was beyond control had shaken the security of white racial hegemony and led to a self-examination by whites of which the *Apes* films were a part" (Greene 1998, 25). In depicting a society where racial power relations are reversed and humans are treated as an inferior species subject to dehumanization at the hands of their ape overlords, Greene argues that the original 1968 film elicits both fear and sympathy from a white audience.[5]

The new franchise, at first glance, seems worlds away from the original in narrative and design. It has enjoyed financial and critical success due in part to the motion capture technology that affords the actors playing the apes a full range of emotions and actions previously constrained by suits and masks. These apes are believable and sympathetic. The films in the reboot are well-acted and offer entertaining and compelling viewing, with each sequel improving on the last. In its depiction of a subordinate group revolting against an oppressive abusive power structure, its emphasis on family and loyalty, and its representation of archetypal villains and heroes on both the human and ape sides, the reboot offers the viewer opportunities to root for and identify with the apes. However, because the storylines of the new franchise follow so closely the narrative trajectory of the original series and function as interpretive intertexts which instruct the "viewer to use previously seen texts to make sense of the one at hand" (Gray 2010, 117), we must examine how the new version couches these themes within the incendiary political and racial framework of the original *Apes* films.

POPULAR CINEMA AS A FORM OF RACIAL REARTICULATION

After the civil rights reforms of the 1960s and legislation of the 1970s, overt political efforts to maintain white supremacy and enforce racist discrimination were harder to sustain. A new strategy that would "recast themes of racial equality and justice in ways that would serve to rationalize and reinforce persistent patterns of racial inequality" was required to shore up white hegemony (Omi and Winant 2014). These kinds of strategies need to be advanced not solely in a political forum but also in the media and popular culture. Whatever the cultural intentions behind the first two films in the original *Planet of the Apes* franchise (1968–1973), the later films, *Conquest* and *Battle*, in their expression of virulent race paranoia, can be seen to be part of such a reactionary strategy as they clearly work to raise questions in the minds of white Americans about their post–civil rights future.

Omi and Winant argue that the ideology and politics of the new right and neo-conservatism stem directly from "the new social movements of the 1960s, and both were centrally concerned with defining the limits of racial democracy" (2014, 190). If the films of the earlier franchise function as a reactionary racial project, then the films of the new franchise operate as a form of racial rearticulation, which redirect the animus inherent in the history of Black/white relations through species antagonism and "scary" science, all the while signaling to a white audience the racial threat before them. Historically, "rearticulation proved far more effective than repression in containing the radical thrust of the Black movement, and of its allied movements as well" (Omi and Winant 2014, 255). The current reboot of the original franchise, centered on bioengineering and species antagonism, attempts to mask, in our so-called postracial, colorblind society, that racial hierarchies are maintained over time by rearticulating the racist ideologies of previous decades. Kellner has argued that "Hollywood cinema can be read as a contest of representations and a contested terrain that reproduces existing social struggles and transcodes the political discourses of the era" (2010, 2). In this way, prevailing sociopolitical movements or struggles get "translated or encoded" in fictional form as means of both reproducing and contesting dominant ideologies (Kellner 2010, 2, 39). Because the phrase "'planet of the apes' has entered reactionary racist discourse as a shorthand for racial apocalypse" (Greene 1998, 177) and because it has been used widely in the media to describe the United States under the presidency of Barack Obama, we do well to question the ideology behind the reboot and the political and social implications of its timing and success.

Certainly, the high production value, nuanced performances, and motion capture technology of the reboot set it apart from the campy and stilted gorilla-suit acting of the films in the original franchise. Viewed in isolation, without the perspective that the history of the original films provides, the new films can be seen as progressive and validating of the experience of the underdog. Most reviewers have praised the films' exploration of the social and emotional consequences of one group usurping power and exercising it over another and have noted the themes of social responsibility, oppression, loyalty, and betrayal, which traverse the films.[6] Nevertheless, when assessed in light of the franchise's history and situated within the social and political moment of their production, which is to say, when read in the context of the media event of which they form a part, these recently rebooted films participate in and actively shape white audience attitudes about race relations in Obama's America. As Nygaard and Lagerwey note, even programming that is "technologically innovative, and generically, representationally, and artistically progressive . . . can function to sustain and perpetuate white people's cultural centrality and power" (loc.151).

THE POLITICS OF AN APE PLANET

> What planet have I landed on? Did I slip through a wormhole in the middle of the night and this looks like America? It's like the damn Planet of the Apes!
> —FOX NEWS COMMENTATOR GLENN BECK IN 2010

In May 2016, the White House issued a press release announcing that Barack Obama's oldest daughter, Malia Obama, would attend Harvard University in the fall of 2017 after taking a "gap year." When Fox News reported the story on its website, readers responded with virulently racist comments, referring to Malia as an "affirmative action parasite" with "Black privilege." One commentator called Malia a "little monkey," and another referred to Michelle Obama as her "man-thing mother, Sasquatch." One reader suggested that the "little ape should go to college in Africa." The responses were so inflammatory that Fox was forced to shut down the comments section (Diaz 2016). Clearly, associating African Americans with apes is a well-worn racist practice, but its brazen public resurgence can be tied to the entry of Barack Obama onto the political scene.

During the 2008 election cycle, t-shirts and buttons depicting monkeys and/or bananas appeared alongside Obama's name or image. The cartoon character Curious George was frequently used as a stand-in for Obama after a woman caller on conservative Rush Limbaugh's radio show stated that her daughter thought Obama looked like the animated monkey (Joseph 2011). One t-shirt captioned "The Evolution of a President" depicted the well-known drawing of the evolutionary scale from ape to human above Obama's image. A cursory internet search reveals hundreds of photoshopped images of Barack and Michelle Obama as chimpanzees, some swinging from trees, with captions like "Primate in Chief." One white supremacist website featuring such pictures of the Obamas is called "chimpout." In 2009, the *New York Post* ran a cartoon that depicted a dead chimpanzee with bullet holes in its chest and two cops standing over it with a smoking gun. The caption read, "They'll have to find someone else to write the next stimulus bill." In 2016, after Trump's election win, the mayor of a small West Virginia town was forced to resign a day after she had commented favorably on the post of another official, which referred to Michelle Obama as an "ape in heels" (Browning and Bever 2016). While George W. Bush was sometimes lampooned as a chimp during his time in office, as critics have noted, depicting Bush as a chimp is not the same as depicting Obama as one because of the historically trenchant racist association of Blacks with apes (James 2011). Abraham Lincoln, too, suffered the association, not because he was Black, but because of his support of African Americans.

Dubbed the "Black Republican" by Southerners, his condemnation of slavery and support for emancipation also earned him the monikers "Ourang-Outang at the White House," "Illinois Ape," "baboon," and the "original gorilla" (Miller 2011; Bowden 2013).

IMPLICIT BIAS/EXPLICIT RACISM

A 2008 study conducted by Phillip Goff and Jennifer Eberhardt tested the resilience of the Black/ape association in the minds of white and non-white subjects by asking participants to identify distorted images of animals (apes and non-apes) after being primed with pictures of Black and white faces. Goff et al. found that exposure to Black faces increased the speed by which participants identified ape images versus the response time when primed with white faces. The study also found that just as participants saw Black faces as a trigger for identifying ape images (versus those of other animals), they also were more likely to identify Black faces after exposure to ape images. Conducting four different studies, including testing for explicit racial biases, Goff et al. argue that the association of Blacks with apes is maintained largely through implicit knowledge, which circulates culturally. Through "metaphors, visual tropes, and through the convergence of other related stereotypes . . . the association has persisted in the minds of Whites and non-Whites alike" (Goff et al. 2008, 294).

The attribution of simian characteristics to those considered racially inferior can be traced back to Darwin's theory of evolution and his claim (now scientifically proved) that humans share a common ancestor with great apes. Hominins, ancestors of modern humans, split from chimpanzees of the Pan genus between five to seven million years ago,[7] with modern humans dispersing from Africa somewhere between 50,000 and 80,000 years ago.[8] The theory of natural selection argues that species adapt to their environments, and the more successful adaptors become altered at the genomic level and can pass these genetic improvements onto their offspring. The "survival of the fittest" maxim refers to the belief that those who adapt the best have a reproductive and evolutionary advantage over other species. Although by the nineteenth century most evolutionists held to the monogenic theory of race, racial ranking was prevalent. Not surprisingly, the rankers, Caucasian Europeans, placed themselves at the top of a racial hierarchy and Africans at the bottom. This led to the belief that in the hierarchy of races, each was "relatively fixed in their place in relation to each other, but each [was] moving forward at its own pace toward greater civilization" (Ross 2004). At the time, as popularly understood, Darwin's evolutionary model was thought to suggest that humans were descended from apes and not that both shared a common ancestor from which two discrete species evolved. Racist ideology held that Africans were closer evolutionarily to the apes than the purportedly more-evolved Europeans. "'Primitive races' were sometimes seen as static, forever left behind in this quick race towards a perfected culture" (Ross 2014, 41). Samuel Morton's cronies, Nott and Giddon, in their book *Types of Mankind* (1854), juxtaposed sketches of Morton's skulls of Europeans with skulls of Africans, chimpanzees, and gorillas, asserting that "[t]he palpable analogies and dissimilitudes between an inferior type of mankind and a superior type of monkey require no comment" (quoted in Gould 1981, 34).

Images of Blacks as monkeys proliferated in the late nineteenth and early twentieth centuries in postcards featuring the "coon" caricature, a lazy, bumbling, inarticulate buffoon or dandy who was routinely drawn with exaggerated chin and lips and protruding ears, suggesting a simian resemblance. The purpose behind these representations was to "cater to the White notion that Black coons are too stupid to understand that their efforts to assimilate into White culture only emphasize their inherent inferiority" (*History on the Net* 2012). Comic strips, musical lyrics, children's books, and toys all furthered the association, which continued into the late twentieth century with athletes like Jackie Robinson, Michael Jordan, and Patrick Ewing enduring "ape" taunts and banana peels thrown at them on and off the field/court.

Black athletes still experience this level of racist offense. In 2017, Brazilian soccer player Everton Luiz, who plays for a Serbian team, was subject to monkey chants and racist epithets by fans of the opposing team. And in May of the same year, Baltimore Orioles star Adam Jones was racially taunted and had peanuts thrown at him during a game at Fenway Park in Boston. In June 2020, Bubba Wallace, the only full-time African American driver at NASCAR, received racist comments from fans after his vocal support of NASCAR's ban of the Confederate flag from their raceways. On June 10, Wallace wore a shirt printed with the phrase "I Can't Breathe" in reference to Floyd's death and raced a black car with a #BlackLivesMatter decal. On June 21, a noose was found in Wallace's team garage at the Talladega Superspeedway in Alabama, prompting an investigation by the FBI. Although the investigation revealed the noose's presence in the garage predated Wallace's use of the space, many critics blamed Wallace for manufacturing the story to play the "victim card" (Sutare 2020). Wallace was booed and crowds cheered when he crashed his car during a race in Tennessee a few days after the FBI completed its investigation (Dsouza 2020). Trump himself seemed to blame Wallace when he tweeted that the driver should apologize to "all of those great NASCAR drivers and officials who came to his aid, stood by his side, & were willing to sacrifice everything for him, only to find out that the whole thing was just another HOAX. That & Flag decision has caused lowest ratings ever" (Smith 2020).

At a time when cartoonists frequently depicted Obama as an ape; when the phrase "Planet of the Apes" was used as shorthand to describe Obama's administration on right-wing talk shows and blogs; and when Africans, apes, and Ebola exist as conceptual metaphors, it is important to ask why the *Planet of the Apes* franchise was resurrected during the tenure of the first African American president. Films function differently in different contexts and can produce variant political readings, but I would argue that the social moment of the release of these films—when Black men were being shot in alarming numbers by police and white supremacists were organizing on college campuses and marching brazenly in the streets—despite or indeed because of the election of Obama, is eerily reminiscent of the racial climate of the late 1960s and '70s. As Jonathan Gray notes, "'Intertextual fields' are created before we even sit down in the cinema or turn on the television" (Gray 2010). Just as the earlier films do, the new franchise, despite its overt message of minority group resistance, engages in a form of racial politics that reflects an implicit white fear of an empowered African American minority and the waning of white privilege. In the next section, I will examine how the recent reboot uses the discourse of infection to do so.

"CAREFUL. HUMAN NO LIKE SMART APE."

> Ignorance is a high virtue in a human chattel; and as the master studies to keep the slave ignorant, the slave is cunning enough to make the master think he succeeds. The slave fully appreciates the saying, "where ignorance is bliss, 'tis folly to be wise."
> —**FREDERICK DOUGLASS,** *MY BONDAGE AND MY FREEDOM*

The three films in the new franchise, *Rise*, *Dawn*, and *War*, follow the life of Caesar (Andy Serkis), who is born to a mother known as "Bright Eyes,"[9] caught in the wild by African traffickers and sent to the labs of Gen-Sys, a pharmaceutical corporation, as a test subject for an experimental Alzheimer's drug ALZ-112. Bright Eyes (Terry Notary) breaks out and attacks her handlers in order to protect her new baby. As a result of her rampage, the other test apes are euthanized. Caesar is rescued by Will (James Franco), the lead researcher of the study, and brought to the home he shares with his father, Charles (John Lithgow), who is suffering from Alzheimer's disease. Affected by the drug in utero, Caesar experiences rapid intellectual development and, after being exposed to a new version of the drug, ALZ-113, a capacity for speech. Later locked away in a primate shelter, having attacked a neighbor while defending Charles, Caesar empowers his fellow ape captives with ALZ-113 and leads them in revolt against their cruel human jailers. After a tense face-off with police on the Golden Gate Bridge, Caesar leads the apes to a life of peaceful self-determination in the woods. Meanwhile, the drug proves deadly to humans and results in a pandemic known as the "simian flu" (*Rise*).

Ten years later, a small band of surviving humans, seeking access to the hydro-electric dam under the ape compound, encounters the intelligent apes. Nefarious actions on both sides result in an armed confrontation between the apes and the humans, causing Caesar and the surviving apes to flee again (*Dawn*). The final film in the trilogy opens fifteen years later, with the apes holed up in a fortified command base awaiting the inevitable war with the humans. Led by a calculating, crazed Colonel (Woody Harrelson), the humans find the apes and murder Caesar's wife and son, causing Caesar to abandon his group and pursue The Colonel to avenge them. When Caesar goes to kill The Colonel, he finds him already infected by the virus mutation now affecting the surviving humans, rendering them mute. Rather than kill him, Caesar watches as The Colonel takes his own life. Caesar again leads his apes, who have been imprisoned in The Colonel's compound, to a new home where he dies as a result of a wound sustained in the recent battle at the compound (*War*).

As I will argue in subsequent chapters, the films can be seen to allegorize several politically charged topics, including racially motivated police violence and the dissolution of species boundaries brought about by bioengineering. However, of relevance here is that these elements are presented in the context of a virus called the "Simian Flu." *Rise of the Planet of the Apes* was released in 2011 in the run-up to the 2012 election, where Obama would succeed in his bid for a second term. The film predates the most recent 2014 Ebola crisis but utilizes tropes consistent with the Africa/ape/contagion paradigm prevalent in Ebola discourse. *Dawn of the Planet of the Apes* (2014) further reinforces the connection in its use of real footage of Obama warning about the (2009 H1N1 virus outbreak) virus.[10] Typically, in Ebola films like *Outbreak*, the virus originates in Africa and travels via primate to America. In *Rise*, the virus is created in an American lab and is spread from human to human, but the virus manifests in an Ebola-like fashion, producing bleeding from the nose and the eyes until the organs shut down. Instead of causing harm to the apes, the virus improves their cognitive ability, making it possible to outsmart and overthrow their human oppressors, for whom the virus is deadly. Furthermore, the enhancements brought about by the virus can be transmitted in utero to the ape offspring. So-called patient zero, Franklin, a lab technician who contracts the aerosolized virus in the lab through a mishap, then unknowingly contaminates an airline pilot who subsequently spreads it around the globe, acknowledges that the apes "are more resilient than I am" (Wyatt 2011). *Rise* reveals that in apes, intelligence is an infection that can spread to other apes and result in the displacement and ultimate death of the human. *Dawn* demonstrates that the surviving humans must fight the apes to reclaim electrical "power," for "power would lead us back to the life we once had" (Reeves 2014), and in *War* we learn that the virus has mutated with the capacity to "turn [humans] into beasts . . . robbing us of those things that make us human, our speech, our higher thinking" (Reeves 2017).

On one level, of course, the current movies are clearly offering a creative account for the events depicted in the future world of the original series. The first movie in the original series, *The Planet of the Apes* (1968), depicts savage, mute humans kept in cages by intelligent, powerful apes; that the virus has mutated, causing muteness in humans, as explored in *War for the Planet of the Apes*, certainly offers such an explanation. Recognizing that many, if not most, viewers of the reboot had little knowledge of the original plot line, I want to consider how the direct correlation between the rise of the apes and the demise of the humans, in the context of an Obama presidency, becomes interpreted and understood as Black empowerment and white disenfranchisement among white audiences. When viewed in the context of the racial anxiety stoked by the media and perpetuated by right-wing journalists and shock jocks, this franchise can be seen to perpetuate existing and construct new perceptions among whites of Obama and African Americans in general. Overall, the new films engage in a conscious form of white race-making, where whiteness is depicted as vulnerable and porous and in need of safeguarding from a virulent, infectious (yet exceptional), Blackness. Specifically, the first installment of the franchise, *Rise of the Planet of the Apes* (Wyatt 2011), perpetuates and underscores the idea that intelligence in African Americans is unnatural and poses a mortal threat to whites and whiteness.

"BUT AS FOR CAESAR, KNEEL DOWN, KNEEL DOWN, AND WONDER"

Before Bright Eyes (the ape that has been treated with the experimental Alzheimer's cure) is shot in the boardroom, Will tells the board of Gen-Sys that the ALZ-112 virus has produced "full cognitive recovery" in her. This is a curious claim because, unlike real human-animal chimeras who are routinely infected with human diseases in order to test cures on the chimera's human tissue, the film never shows that the scientists have sought to diminish the brain of the chimps by introducing Alzheimer's disease. Rather, the assumption seems to be that a chimp brain is a healthy, albeit less intelligent or high-functioning, brain, which presumably *can* be "recovered" with drug therapy. To be clear, Bright Eyes is not a chimera—she has no human tissue at all—but ALZ-112 effectively functions in the way stem cells do because, according to Will, it "allows the brain to create its own cells in order to repair itself," just as pluripotent stem cells can grow tissue and regenerate cellular damage in any organ of the body. The chimp's brain does, for all intents and purposes, function as a human brain, and the effect of the drug is to improve intellectual capacity and make her more human. Furthermore, the drug seems to have genetically altered her offspring. On ALZ-112, Bright Eyes's cognitive ability was subpar to humans; she was smarter but not as smart as we are. By contrast, her infant Caesar, who was subject to the drug in utero, shows cognitive capacity which surpasses humans. As Will makes clear, "By age two, Caesar was completing puzzles and models designed for children eight years and up . . . At age three, Caesar continued to show cognitive skills that far exceeded that of a human counterpart." In his research log, Will hypothesizes that "A, the green in his eyes indicates that the ALZ-112 has passed genetically from mother to son, and B, that in the absence of damaged cells that need replacing, the drug in his system has radically boosted healthy brain functioning."

How Caesar's enhancement affects "natural" hierarchies becomes apparent as soon as he is brought home. In an establishing shot, Charles (John Lithgow), framed by the archway into the living room, raises the infant above his head and, quoting Shakespeare's *Antony and Cleopatra*, anoints him "Caesar": "But as for Caesar, kneel down, kneel down, and wonder." Charles and Caesar are initially obscured by Will in the foreground, but as Charles raises Caesar over his head, Will bends down out of view. The scene foreshadows the gradual transfer of authority that will take place between Charles and Caesar, between man and ape. Rather than domesticating his power, the home environs make Caesar's strength and intelligence, his difference, more apparent. As he grows into an adult, he is routinely shot from a low angle, suggesting his superiority in comparison to the humans. Charles, a former piano teacher now unable to remember his music and confined to his home under a nurse's supervision, is locked in a prison of his mind. An older white man and, judging from the array of diplomas on the wall in his study, a man of some measure, Charles's stature is eroded by the disease. The diminishment that Alzheimer's has wrought on his brain renders him child-like. He needs to be supervised at all times, lest he run out into the street or operate a dangerous appliance. Disoriented by the disease, he becomes aggressive, prompting the nurse to suggest institutionalization. Caesar, too, is a sort of prisoner. As an animal with no natural rights, he remains a smart house pet, occasionally allowed out on walks. But it is clear to everyone around him that cognitively and physically, he exceeds the restraints they try to impose on him.

Once Will recognizes the drug's effect on Caesar, he immediately begins administering it to Charles. With both undergoing treatment, the characters function as analogs of each other, forcing us to see the parallels between them. Both Caesar and Charles are infantilized, but Charles resumes his rightful place of respect when he demonstrates a return to mental functionality. Initially, Charles experiences a cellular repair of his damaged brain tissue and then, like Caesar, enhanced intelligence and cognitive function, playing the piano better than he could before the disease. Gradually, though, Charles's Alzheimer's returns, and it is clear that the enhanced ape is smarter than a diminished human. Caesar is more capable of day-to-day cognition and functioning than Charles. Caesar not only recognizes Charles's lapses but corrects them for him. Where containment for Charles is a necessary measure to ensure his safety, for Caesar, it is shown to be a cruel curtailing of his liberty. This point is emphasized when Caesar, trapped in his upstairs "play" room, handles a model of the Statue of Liberty. Just as in the original film, when Taylor sees the destroyed Statue of Liberty on the ape "planet" and realizes that the humans brought about their own reversal of power, the scene raises questions about the nature of freedom and its fragility and who among us deserves it.[11]

A captive Caesar gazes out the window and plays with "liberty," turning it over in his hands. But when he observes that Charles has escaped the house and, disoriented, is trying to drive off with a neighbor's car, Caesar breaks out of his upstairs room to rescue Charles from the angry man. Despite the refinement that his advanced intelligence has given him, Caesar is shown to revert to "type," violently attacking the neighbor. As a result of his actions, his virtual imprisonment turns into actual imprisonment as he is locked up in a primate shelter, which, for all intents and purposes, functions as a kind of ape prison.

In subsequent chapters, I will examine how *Rise* explores several issues related to animal ethics, including the bioengineering of animals. But even when we consider the animal elements in the films, we cannot view them as separate from their racial framing, especially when the films utilize and magnify elements of the original *Apes* narratives. The character of Caesar played a prominent role in the fourth and fifth films of the original franchise. In the third movie, *Escape from the Planet of the Apes*, the two chimpanzee protagonists from the original movie, Zira and Cornelius, are transported back in time to 1973 Earth. Originally welcomed by the humans, they are killed when it is learned that Zira is pregnant, for they fear that the "progeny of the apes will one day dominate the human race and destroy the world" (22). Their child, who will be known as Caesar, having been switched with a circus chimpanzee, escapes his death. Eighteen years later, *Conquest of the Planet of the Apes* (1972) finds adult Caesar and his human protector, Armando (Ricardo Montalbán), in a world where apes have become pets to humans. Recognizing the apes' ability to follow directions, the humans train them as a domestic labor force. Horrified by the servile state to which the apes have descended, Caesar secretly organizes the apes, who rise up in rebellion against their human captors. It is significant that the filmmakers of the current franchise followed the narrative elements of the original franchise, particularly when the impetus behind those films was to sound an alarm about the potential loss of white privilege that could follow from African Americans seeking "revenge" for their historic and ongoing mistreatment by white Americans. It is hard not to recognize a representation of the same purported threat in the new franchise when Caesar mobilizes his fellow apes and empowers them with advanced intelligence.

In 1972's *Conquest*, the fourth film in the franchise, the racial subtext is transparent, especially as the insurgent apes are all men dressed in what are, essentially, prosthetic versions of blackface. But we might examine why, thirty-nine years later and after the cultural and legislative advances of the civil rights movement, *Rise* returns to these very same themes, raising questions about racial hierarchies and inciting fears about intelligent apes. In *Conquest*, discussing the plight of an ape who was beaten by his master and then killed for retaliating, Governor Breck (Don Murray) asks his Black assistant, MacDonald (Hari Rhodes), "How many more out there are just like that ape, all burning with resentment, all waiting for an ape with enough intelligence, with enough will to lead them, waiting for an ape who can think, who can talk?" Breck's words speak to white fears not just of Black retaliation for oppression at the hands of whites but of Black intelligence, specifically. In one particularly telling scene of *Conquest*, Breck asks to review the IQ tests of chimpanzees and pronounces them "inflated." Breck is convinced that the very presence of an intelligent ape will sound the death knell for the human race. Because species difference has already been mapped onto racial difference in the films, the implication of Breck's species concern is the fear that with education and opportunities equal to that of whites, Black people will overcome the inequality of their social situation and challenge their historical subjugation at the hands of white people. Further, that challenge will reveal the inherent weakness of whites and result in their annihilation. As Breck makes clear: "If we lose this battle, that's the end of the world as we know it! We will have proved ourselves inferior, weak!" It is significant that the power in the apes that the humans fear most is intelligence. It is not the apes' superior strength or concerns about savagery or bestialization that upset the humans in *Conquest*; rather, the underlying fear is that the talking ape from the future will return, free his people, and destroy the human race. In *Rise*, the warning is more pointedly racist, suggesting that humans (whites) are the ones who will "give" the intelligence to the apes (Blacks) and thus engineer their own demise.

SCARY SCIENCE?

When *Rise* was first released, several articles were published assessing the likelihood of ape intelligence and the kinds of consequences that might ensue.

A headline in *The Atlantic* asks, "Could Simians Get Scary Smart?" and concluded that experts believe they "kinda sorta" could. When *Rise*'s sequel *Dawn* was released in 2014, the question surfaced again, with *Time* musing, "Planet of the Apes: That Couldn't Happen . . . Right?" (Lemonick 2014). But scientists increasingly argued that not only could it happen, but the science was already in place to make it happen. In 2001, scientists in Oregon did, in fact, create a transgenic non-human primate, ANDi, a rhesus monkey who was implanted with an extra marker gene, and in 2009 a transgenic marmoset was born carrying a transgene inherited from its genetically modified parents (Trivedi 2001; Olsson and Sandøe 2010). In this culture of genetic modification, it's not surprising that *Rise of the Planet of the Apes* arises to stoke our fear that "our primate kin could transform into angry biological doppelgangers" (Morais 2011). But it is also imperative to examine how our racially charged political climate, where the promise of the postracial presidency of Barack Obama has instead produced a degree of white racial backlash not seen since the unrest following the 1992 acquittal of police officers in the beating of Rodney King (Ross 2015; Russonello 2016), informs the timing and popularity of an *Apes* reboot.

In Shakespeare's *Julius Caesar*, Brutus kills Caesar not because of his actions but because he fears what Caesar might be capable of—that Caesar, like "a serpent's egg / which hatch'd, would, as his kind, grow mischievous, / and kill him in the shell" (William Shakespeare, *Julius Caesar*, act 2, scene 1). Caesar, the enhanced ape, represents a similar threat to humans. And *Rise* offers a warning about science's capacity to overstep and the need to restrain it. After all, Will is illegally testing the unapproved drug on his father, and it is his smuggling home of the ALZ-113 to treat him that results in the catastrophic takeover by the apes. But it quickly becomes apparent that these films are not just dealing with animal testing and anxiety about the fixity of species boundaries, nor do they represent a simple allegory of race relations as the first series did. What is particularly interesting in this new incarnation of the *Apes* saga is how science and race work together. Because the ultimate message of the film is not one of sympathy toward the apes, but fear—which is to say that it's not motivated by exposing what humans did to the apes (scientific testing) but what the apes will do to humans (take over)—and because the films follow the narrative arc of the original franchise so closely with regard to an ape uprising and decline of the human, this representation of the rapid pace of scientific development and genetic modification bolsters already extant fears about race.

While the quality of the CGI and the motion capture technology offer realistic representations of apes and seem to have transported us far away from the latex gorilla masks and hairy suits of the 1960s and '70s films, *Rise* and *Dawn* exist perpetually in the wake of those original films and their allegorizing of apes as African Americans. As Greene reminds us, it was the goal of the original films to depict an "apocalyptic transformation of racial power relations" (Greene 1998, 24). When *Rise* depicts advanced intelligence in apes as a virus with the capacity to wipe out humans, and when those apes are historical analogs for African Americans, the film implicitly evokes long-standing, though discredited, racist genetic views (advanced in the Enlightenment and recurrent in the twentieth century) about the supposed inferior intellectual ability of Black people.[12]

Employing and adapting the racial subtext of the original *Planet of the Apes* franchise, the new *Apes* films (just like *The Walking Dead*) reimagine and repurpose fears that viral contagion comes from the Other and, if allowed to creep into our labs or across our borders, will eventually kill us all. Greene suggests that the *Apes* films, in their time, "rather than offering a symbolic resolution of cultural tensions and fear . . . magnify and extend those tensions to a fearsome conclusion" (Greene 1998, 23). Anxieties about the catastrophic effects of the atomic bomb were cast alongside anxieties about race relations in the original films. In the new franchise, fears that science can bring about a racial apocalypse, potentially enhancing those whom white society deems inferior and subjugating those who've marshaled science and history to bolster their claims to superiority, find fertile ground among whites "anxious" about the "rise" of African Americans, and symbolized by the visibility and popularity of Obama.

SCIENTIFIC RACISM 2.0

Because entertainment vehicles cannot be viewed separately from the culture that produces them and from the concerns that animate the populace at the time of consumption, it is essential to situate the rebooted scientific racism in the new *Apes* films within the prevailing discourse of genomic science, specifically the mapping of the human genome. Operating from the same "postracial" space as the *Apes* films and Obama's presidency, new genomic knowledge is articulated through the discourse of colorblindness which "operates as a rhetorical mask that obscures researchers' racial thinking in genomics" and justifies findings steeped in unnamed racial assumptions (Williams 2015, 1496). Analyzing the newest *Apes* films in the context of their political and scientific intertexts exposes the cultural race-work they enact, particularly the representation of whiteness vulnerable to an empowered Blackness.

The Human Genome Project, which set out to sequence and map the genome of the species, was completed in 2003 and proved that all humans share 99.9 percent of the same genes. To some observers, however, the remaining 0.1 percent offers proof of discrete races and has revitalized a belief in biological essentialism, particularly that race is genetically hard-wired. In an age of so-called colorblindness, genomics offers a new way to talk about race, often masking racist intentions. As Johnny Williams makes clear:

> Genomic knowledge is simply not a reflection of genetic reality in discourse and language, it is a product of both past and current practices performed in specific social conditions of existence. Previous practices constitute a starting point for the construction of a new set of genomic knowledge traditions congruent with the newest racial environment. In this social context, the human genome is "represented in speech and language" to produce meaning generated from racial ideological and theoretical frames. (2015, 1497–98)

New types of "genomic knowledge" are linked in our "newest racial environment" to anxieties about bioengineering and the potential to genetically alter species, thus working to revivify racial ideologies of the past. As Phelan, Link, Zelner, and Yang note, this "repeated exposure to messages linking race and genes gradually increases beliefs in racial difference, which in turn, over time, increases hierarchization and racism" (Phelan et al. 2014, 313).

We don't have to go too far back in time to see the historical underpinnings of such views. Indeed, if we look more closely at the two prevailing concerns against the mixing of species in the chimera debate, that of intelligence and reproduction (discussed in chapter 7), we return quickly to theories about the inequality of the races stemming from the eighteenth and nineteenth century practices of craniology and laws against miscegenation. The legacy of these racist colonial views traverses the *Apes* reboot, even as it employs a progressive animal rights narrative. Paradoxically, the postracial posturing of *Rise* and *Dawn* maintains the pejorative association of Black humans with apes while at the same time elevating the apes from the bestial association with the animal. In these films, the apes both serve as analogs for African-descended peoples and transcend them.

Early scientific understandings of race in the eighteenth century gave way to the scientific racism of the nineteenth, as the material demands and ideological rhetoric of imperialism and slavery required justification and support. Craniology had particularly pernicious effects in the United States, where it was utilized by proponents of slavery to counter arguments for emancipation. In his book *Crania Americana* (1839), American physician and anthropologist Samuel George Morton (1799–1851) followed Blumenbach's conclusions about the existence of five human races,[13] but, unlike Blumenbach, Morton believed in a polygenic theory of race, thus explicitly challenging Linnaeus's and later Darwin's assertions that all races belong to the same species and evolved from a common ancestor. Subscribing to the implicit ranking inherent in Blumenbach's five races, Morton went further and suggested a correlation between cranial capacity and mental capacity. Measuring more than one thousand skulls, Morton's results put Caucasian skulls at the top, followed by Mongolians, Malay, and Americans. Ethiopians were believed to have the lowest cranial capacity, thus attaining the lowest rank on Morton's scale. Morton's findings were instrumental in advancing theories of biologically based racial inferiority and were used by many Southerners opposed to abolition, including John C. Calhoun.

In arguing that Texas should be annexed as a slaveholding state, Calhoun claimed that emancipating the Negro "would not raise the inferior race to the condition of freemen" but "deprive the Negro of the guardian care of his owner" and result in a state of "depression and oppression belonging to his inferior condition" (Stanton 1960). Morton is considered by many to be the father of "scientific racism," and though a firm believer in Caucasian superiority and racial destiny, claims to have been more interested in empiricism than polemics; while he remained mostly out of the political spotlight, he collaborated with others who would actively connect his research to the social conditions and racial politics of the day. English-born George Robbins Gliddon (1809–1857), Swiss-born Louis Agassiz (1807–1873), and American Josiah Clark Nott (1804–873) all converged in nineteenth-century America and used Morton's conclusions about skull size and mental ability to argue for polygenism and to buttress a mid-century defense of slavery.[14]

Eighteenth- and nineteenth-century efforts by white men to classify and rank races according to intellectual ability were linked to the anxiety resulting from Linnaeus's classification of *Africanus niger* as belonging to the human species and not (as Voltaire claimed) a species of monkey (Voltaire [1772] 2009). Here we see how species difference comes to be mapped onto racial difference and the concerted efforts by those of the in-group to guard against claims of membership from those of the out-group. Scientific racism arose from an effort to rank and order humans into races precisely because evolutionary biology had demonstrated that the different races belonged to the same species and because Darwin's evolutionary model asserted a common ancestry for apes and humans.

By the mid to late twentieth century, the belief in discrete biologically based races was debunked by biologists, geneticists, sociologists, and anthropologists. UNESCO's "Statement on Race" in 1950 declared race a "social myth." Race is real only insofar as it creates a culture and identity for discrete groups within a population and to the extent that those groups have experienced genocide, enslavement, and disenfranchisement on the basis of that shared group identity. Contemporary theories of race, then, understand race as a fact grounded in culture and history, not in biology. And while genetic racialist critics argue that similarities in phenotype—skin color, hair texture, etc.—among people in those population groups provide irrefutable evidence of a genetic basis to race, we would do well to remember, as Joshua Glasgow argues:

> [R]acial categories use visible traits, and visible traits can be correlated with genetic material, but this does not guarantee that when we take those traits (and therefore the DNA markers with which they correlate) and assimilate them into categories, we are not creating the categories. We could similarly divide humanity into people 6.4 feet and above, 5.7 to 6.3 feet tall, and so on, and in doing so divide ourselves according to traits which are to some degree biologically heritable. (Glasgow 2009, 90)

In *Mismeasure of Man*, Stephen Jay Gould famously, and later controversially, questioned Morton's crania research, suggesting that he was motivated by implicit bias and found in his skull measurements exactly what he set out to find—Caucasian superiority and African inferiority. Critics have disputed Gould's assertions and others have defended him,[15] but insofar as Gould demonstrates the political value of theories of biological determinism for asserting and maintaining white power, his work helps us understand the recent resurgence of theories of genetically based racial differences.

Not surprisingly, the twenty-first century, too, sees a return to racialist thinking. In 2017, Sam Harris, a well-known neuroscientist and public intellectual, interviewed Charles Murray, controversial co-author of *The Bell Curve*, on his podcast *Making Sense*. Murray and Herrnstein's 1994 book, which essentially repackaged scientific racism for a late twentieth-century audience, created a marked controversy when it was published, as it revivified debates about race and differential intelligence. The author of several books about atheism and free will, Harris is not known for racist commentary or for including racially inflammatory material on his show. However, Harris began the podcast defending Murray and calling critiques against *The Bell Curve* "politically correct moral panic that totally engulfed Murray's career." Harris then allowed Murray a platform to rehash his findings and defend them (Harris 2017). Airing in April 2017, just a few months after Trump's inauguration, the timing of Harris's interview poses troubling questions about the way that news and entertainment media work to buttress and re-package racist and divisive political views under the cover of intellectual conversation. In the context of renewed public interest in genomic science and the uses to which that science is being put to racialize and commodify racial differences as genetic (Roberts 2011; Nelson 2016), the colonial logic of *Rise*'s messaging cannot be underestimated.

Part II
ANIMALITY

Chapter 4

WHEN THE LOOTING STARTS, THE SHOOTING STARTS

> What you should see when you see Black protesters in the age of Trump and coronavirus is people pushed to the edge, not because they want bars and nail salons open, but because they want to live. To breathe.
> —KAREEM ABDUL JABAAR

On May 25, 2020, as many cities in the nation were beginning to ease coronavirus lockdown restrictions, George Floyd, a forty-six-year-old African American man, was killed in Minneapolis by a white police officer. In a striking parallel to the 2014 case of Eric Garner, who was killed when a white police officer subjected Garner to a fatal chokehold for selling cigarettes, Floyd died when Officer Derek Chauvin refused to remove his knee from Floyd's neck, despite Floyd repeatedly stating that he could not breathe. Days of protests erupted in Minneapolis, New York, Los Angeles, DC, Chicago, and other cities around the nation. Along a scale not seen since the Watts riots in 1965 and those following the assassination of Dr. Martin Luther King Jr. in 1968, protests in Minneapolis turned violent and spread nationwide, requiring states to deploy the National Guard in some cities. On May 28, Trump provoked outrage in a tweet, calling protestors "thugs" and quoting the incendiary comment, "when the looting starts, the shooting starts," made by Miami Police Chief Walter Headley about inner city Black communities in 1967 (@realDonaldTrump). Although Trump attempted to walk back his comments the next day, claiming ignorance of the phrase's origin, he inflamed the situation even further that evening when the peaceful riots turned violent as police, dressed in riot gear, threw smoke bombs into the crowd of demonstrators. Blaming the Democratic governor Tim Walz for a "total lack of leadership," Trump threatened to "send in the National Guard and get the job done right" (@realDonaldTrump, May 29, 2020).

This tweet, like the previous one, was seen as yet another example of Trump's racism, especially in light of his encouragement of the armed right-wing protestors who stormed the Michigan capitol building just a few weeks before the Floyd protests in Minneapolis. Even though the group was protesting stay-at-home orders that the Trump administration had encouraged states to adopt, Trump called them "very good people" who just "want their lives back again" (@realDonaldTrump, May 1, 2020). Chauvin was charged with third-degree murder and manslaughter on May 29, 2020.[1] Seen as an insufficient charge, demonstrators continued their protests as more aggressive elements set fire to the 3rd Precinct station that covers the area where Floyd was arrested.[2] Peaceful protestors also converged on the White House on the evening of May 29, prompting Trump to resume his aggressive stance, threatening the protestors with "vicious dogs" and "ominous weapons." The mayor of DC, Muriel Bowser, rebuked Trump for his comments and noted the historical legacy of law enforcement using dogs to attack African Americans (Moreno 2020).

By June 1, as violent protests continued to escalate, many cities around the country had imposed a nighttime curfew. In a brief address to the nation, Trump threatened to "deploy the United States military and quickly solve the problem" (Zapotosky 2020). Moments before his speech and a full thirty minutes prior to the city's 7 p.m. curfew, police fired tear gas and rubber bullets into a crowd of peaceful protestors assembled in Lafayette Square, across from the White House. According to numerous media reports, the crowd was cleared so the president could stage a photo op in front of the historic St. John's Episcopal Church (Parker et al. 2020). Many news stations broadcast the police action in Lafayette Square in split screen alongside the president's remarks, in which he claimed himself "an ally of peaceful protestors" while promising that "organizers of terror" will "face severe criminal penalties and lengthy sentences in jail" (ABC News 2020). The White House suggested that the protests in Minneapolis had been hijacked by Antifa and left-wing groups (Keeley 2020). Meanwhile, the Democratic leadership in Minnesota blamed outside agitators and suggested that 80 percent of those looting and destroying property were from out of state. Local officials in Pittsburgh arrested "white instigators" of violence during the riots there, and Jenny Durkan, the mayor of Seattle, noted that "many of the people who were doing the looting and stealing and the fires over the weekend were young white males" (Stanley-Becker 2020b).

The killing of Floyd followed closely on the heels of the March 2020 murder of Breonna Taylor, an EMT who was killed in her apartment by police officers with a drug warrant for someone else. According to the lawsuit filed by the family, the police attempted to enter without announcing themselves and fired at least twenty rounds into the apartment. Taylor's boyfriend, Kenneth Walker, who returned fire, injuring an officer in the leg, was charged with first-degree assault and attempted murder of a police officer. Only one of the officers involved in the shooting, Det. Brett Hankison, was charged; however, the charges were not for Taylor's murder, but for firing bullets that potentially endangered Taylor's neighbors.[3] On February 23, 2022, Ahmaud Arbery, a twenty-five-year-old African American man jogging in his neighborhood, was pursued and killed by a white father and son, Gregory and Travis McMichael, though prosecutors refused to issue arrest warrants until May when video of the event surfaced. News of the events surrounding Arbery's death resulted in a groundswell of support among the wider populace. #IrunwithAhmaud trended on Twitter as runners all over the country ran a 2.23-mile run on May 8, what would have been Arbery's twenty-sixth birthday.[4]

Trump's inflammatory comments tapped into and deployed historically racist rhetoric in an effort to remind voters not of the history of racial oppression faced by African Americans but rather of a history of violence associated with protests for racial equality. By utilizing discourse associated with terrorism and criminality, promising to "dispatc[h] thousands and thousands of heavily armed soldiers, military personnel and law enforcement officers to stop the rioting, looting, vandalism, assaults and the wanton destruction of property"; in telling governors that they must "dominate" the streets with the National Guard; in reminding Americans that he is the "law and order" president; and then juxtaposing what he deemed to be Black lawlessness with the "Second Amendment rights" of "law-abiding Americans," Trump repeated a pervasive, effective formula of division, not unity.

POLICING THE CRISIS

How this rhetorical formula is rehearsed and restaged over and again by the news and entertainment media is central to understanding the rise of white identity politics in the Obama-to-Trump era and the ongoing racial tension in the United States. Herman Gray, Evelyn Alsultany, Anamik Saha, and others note that "media discourses—both news and entertainment—come together, interact and contribute to a 'hegemonic field of meaning' (Alsultany 2012, 7) through which racist state policies and everyday discrimination take place" (Saha 2018, 15). Hall et al. argue that the press defines and produces a social reality that reflects the interests of the dominant class and "provide[s] a crucial mediating link between the apparatus of social control and the public" (1978, 63). As they argue in their book *Policing the Crisis*, through its framing in the media with a collapse of law and order, race and poverty, lawlessness and violence, "mugging" became a signifier of social crisis in 1970s Britain. Central to the crisis motif surrounding mugging was the racialization of the crime—Blacks were perpetrators and whites its potential victims. The "moral panic" surrounding mugging was less about the offense than the public response to it, which sought to remedy the perceived breakdown of social order fracturing "our way of life," through increased policing of Black urban youth (Hall et al. 1978, 75).

In the same way, heightened media attention to Black death in the Obama era, rather than producing real opportunities for social justice, instead criminalized and sensationalized Black bodies and produced white victim narratives. Media discourse utilizes a form of "racial grammar" that naturalizes racial hierarchies and supports white supremacy (Bonilla-Silva 2012), thus helping to maintain a white racial frame (Feagin). This chapter will examine how the white racial frame, informed by the long-standing racist association of African-descended people with apes, structured media representations of racialized violence during Obama's presidency, specifically by criminalizing Black bodies and representing them as threatening to white ones. Because media discourse is tied to the other social, cultural, and political discourses of which it forms a part, it is important to recognize how these discourses work together to organize and arrange social and cultural meanings. As Morley makes clear, "such texts privilege a certain reading in part by inscribing certain preferred discursive positions from which its discourse appears 'natural,' transparently aligned to 'the real' and credible" (Morley 158).

Media events construct reality in specific and, at times, conflicting ways for the purposes of establishing certain discursive positions and maintaining the power of the dominant group (Hepp and Couldry 2010). Released in a period of intense racial unrest, which includes the murder of Trayvon Martin and the birth of the Black Lives Matter movement as well as the killing of Michael Brown and Freddie Gray, I argue that *Dawn of the Planet of the Apes* formed part of the media event of "Black death." Susana Loza argues that *Dawn* is a "parable about race and racism in the era of Black Lives Matter. It is a contest between those that demand that #ApeLivesMatter and those that insist #NotAllHumans. A contest in which the scales are tipped in favor of white liberal humanism and against bodies of color" (2017, 124). Far from producing analyses of the causes of violence or working to structure police reform, news and entertainment narratives in the Obama-to-Trump era worked together not only to repackage historically racist conceptions of Black bodies but also to remake racial knowledge within the confines of postracial discourses. In its suggestion that "ape-on-ape killing is the real problem. That apes (black) and humans (white) are equally at fault for the racial apocalypse" (Loza 2017, 124), *Rise* and *Dawn* obscure and redirect white culpability for Black death. In its representation of heroic white men like Will (James Franco), who rescues baby Caesar from euthanization, and Malcolm (Jason Clarke), who befriends

Caesar and saves him and the "good" apes from the evil machinations of bad white men like Dreyfus (Gary Oldman), the films suggest that Black death, and racialized violence more generally, is the product of a few bad apples, not a function of systemic racial and class inequities that structure the lives of people of color. The themes explored in the films are not so much racist, then, as they are racialized, disguising the colonial tropes of Black bestialization through a complex characterization of apes who are diversely situated in relation to the human power structure and are agents of their own demise.

"THEY MAY HAVE GOT THEIR HANDS ON SOME OF OUR GUNS, BUT THAT DOES NOT MAKE THEM MEN. THEY ARE ANIMALS."

The action of *Dawn of the Planet of the Apes* (2014) occurs after the "Simian Flu" has wiped out most of the humans on the planet. From the opening news montage, *Dawn* works to establish the binary of "us" and "them," eliciting our sympathies for the humans unjustifiably killed by the virus. At the same time, in its suggestion of riots and chaos and the end of world order, it also quietly evokes ongoing scenes of destruction and disorder, of clashes between protestors and police, which were populating real news segments at the time of the film's release. A disembodied now-dead voice warns, "Those who aren't killed by the virus will probably die in the fighting. Maybe this is it; this is how it ends. Pretty soon there won't be anyone left" (Reeves 2014). Tellingly, the conflict waged in the film has nothing to do with the virus—it's a non-issue for the surviving humans in the film because they are "genetically immune." What is an issue is territory and "power" (accessing the disabled hydroelectric dam to restore electricity is the plot catalyst), leaving the audience to understand that it's really the fighting that will kill "us." Such a message is certainly consistent with the film's overt warnings about power and violence corrupting. But as Foster, one of the surviving Black characters, notes, the "scary thing" about the apes is that "they don't need power, lights, heat. Nothing. That's their advantage. That's what makes them stronger." By contrast, if the humans don't recapture the power, they could "slip back to the way things were." In this world, the humans live in colonies while the apes roam free. Without the resources of energy, civilization is revealed to be a veneer tentatively affixed to the natural.

After the opening voiceover and montage, an extreme close-up of piercing eyes and white skin, illuminated by flashes of lightning and punctuated by rolls of thunder, emerges from the dark background. As the camera pulls away, we recognize the form as Caesar's, made white by war paint, readying his now very large posse of apes for the hunt. The mise-en-scène, scored with tribal drums and a haunting bass flute in a syncopated rhythm, establishes a primitive, tribal atmosphere with a rainy, gloomy darkness.[5] The apes don't live in trees but in treehouses, surrounded by apotropes made from the bones of their prey. Killing deer with spears, riding on horseback, and walking upright, the apes are depicted not as animals but as "primitives." In the ten-year interval since the outbreak that killed most of the human population, they appear to have advanced along a pseudo-evolutionary timeline, bringing them one step closer to the "fully" evolved humans they will encounter. Power is the commodity that the apes possess; in a world stripped of natural resources, it is their postapocalyptic version of gold, oil, or diamonds. It's something to kill for, though they have no need for it.

Establishing the apes' inherent otherness is achieved in large part through the character of Koba, whose inability to be quelled by the rational, measured Caesar marks him as the film's main antagonist as well as the audience's, a pointed change from our sympathies in *Rise*. Indeed, where Koba's killing of the vilified Gen-Sys CEO Jacobs is tacitly justified, even sympathetic (more of a letting go than killing, really), in *Dawn*, Koba is a vicious, vindictive, gun-toting killer who must be stopped at all costs. Though *Rise* works hard to establish Koba's reactions as a *response* to what has been done to him, *Dawn* works harder to naturalize Koba's difference and make a claim for his innate depravity. Koba recognizes early on that "if [humans] get the power, they'll be more dangerous" and encourages Caesar to "destroy them while they're weak." Here he goes beyond revenge on a quest for ultimate power, lying, and manipulating those close to Caesar, breaking the cardinal rule—"ape not kill ape"—by killing Ash and attempting to kill Caesar, and, ultimately, usurping his role as leader (Reeves 2014).

Koba finds his narrative counterpart in Dreyfus (Gary Oldman), who will stop at nothing to protect his armory and restore human dominance. Dreyfus is a mighty opponent, and his desire for "power" is depicted as logical and appropriate. Representative of mainstream America, Dreyfus is a family man, grieving his own losses. He assumes the mantle of looking out for his people, who, with the restoration of power, thanks to Caesar's help, are peacefully celebrating when Koba's apes attack. The renegade dam technician, Carver (Kirk Acevedo), by contrast, represents an alternative (right) white voice. When Ellie (Kerri Russell) tells him that scientists, not apes, are responsible for the outbreak, he calls her view "hippie-dippy bullshit." Believing an attack by the apes to be imminent because "they killed off half the planet already," Carver's perspective is an uneasy reminder of early twenty-first century discourse on race and racial violence. His ape bigotry echoes racist dogma. He hates the apes and doesn't understand why the others "don't get sick to [their] stomach at the sight of them" (Reeves 2014).

Koba ambushes Carver. (*Dawn of the Planet of the Apes*, 2014)

As if to firmly situate Carver within a certain demographic, *Dawn* links Carver's bigoted views to a Second Amendment subtext as he stresses the importance of defending themselves against the apes. Carver is the first to fire a weapon and the first to kill. When told by Malcolm that relinquishing their guns is Caesar's one condition for allowing them access to the dam, Carver secrets his in his bag, resulting in the humans almost being expelled again. Carver is considered an unlikeable "asshole" by his peers and by much of the viewing audience, but when killed, unarmed, by Koba, who is depicted as the epitome of "Black" revenge and concomitant white fear, the film tacitly validates Carver's views.

Koba's first act of treachery is to set fire to the apes' home, shoot Caesar, and frame the humans. Before Caesar is shot, the woods are dark and quiet, with low lighting around the ape house. As Caesar, Maurice, Malcolm, Ellie, and Alexander look down benevolently from high in the trees onto the now-illuminated lights of the city, a peaceful quiet settles over the community, suggesting a hopeful outcome for harmony between apes and humans. But the calm is quickly disrupted by the piercing gunshot and the shrieking ape panic that ensues. The unlawful transfer of power from Caesar to Koba is depicted as the lighting changes from still darkness to burning conflagration. Standing, elevated above the others, and brandishing his gun overhead as the fire he has lit rises, Koba utters a call to arms: "Humans kill Caesar! Burn ape home! Go! Get them! Apes must attack human city. Fight back!" he yells, surrounded by fire (Reeves 2014). As the flames rise, Malcolm and his family run, fleeing the angry, now violent apes. Having scouted out the humans' stockpile of weapons, Koba then leads an ape attack on horseback into the city.

Dawn of the Planet of the Apes depicts a dramatic shift from a community of peaceful, cooperative apes capable of congregation and diplomacy to a violent, angry mob with no moral restraint.

The media's continued sensationalized coverage of the violence in Ferguson, Missouri, and Baltimore, Maryland, works to construct and reinforce the racial polarization of the nation, making us more susceptible to divisive political ideologies. (Lucas Jackson/Reuters Pictures)

Dawn depicts a dramatic shift from a community of peaceful, cooperative apes capable of congregation and diplomacy to a violent, angry mob with no moral restraint. The nighttime cityscape with its dark skies, bursts of machine gun fire, and hordes of marauding black figures looting the armory and attacking the barricaded humans, recalls and, through a variety of formal

One of the millions of media images of Ferguson, Missouri, "on fire" and hands raised in surrender, November 2014. (Christian Gooden/*St. Louis Post-Dispatch*, Associated Press)

Dawn of the Planet of the Apes reproduces images of violence and destruction that resonate with the racial conflicts of Ferguson, Missouri, and Baltimore, Maryland.

elements, reproduces the media spectacle of the clashes between Black protestors and rioters and militarized police. The apes, it seems, have reverted to "type," embracing their wild, savage nature, which no amount of enhanced intelligence can conceal. In depicting racial strife through an ape allegory, the filmmakers undertake a political sleight of hand. With the absence of the noble and rational Caesar, we are coerced into rooting for the humans and not the apes. As Dreyfus makes clear, "They may have got their hands on some of

Ferguson, Missouri, continued to burn after a grand jury returned no indictment in the shooting of Michael Brown, November 2014. (Jim Young/Reuters Pictures)

our guns, but that does not make them men. They are animals. We will push them back. Drive them down!" (Reeves 2014). Koba, by this point, is a crazed vigilante, satiating his own desire for power and primacy. Because of the pervasive media coverage of racial unrest and the film's depiction of visually similar scenes, a white audience is primed to project Koba's rapacious revenge onto twenty-first-century racial conflict.

WHO'S GOT THE POWER?

During the press junkets for *Rise* and *Dawn*, screenwriters Rick Jaffa and Amanda Silver make clear that they had every intention of following the plot of the original films, where the apes come to rule the Earth. They claim to have asked themselves, "What's going on in our world today, that if the right dominoes were to line up, touch each other, it could lead to apes taking over the planet and, perhaps, getting Colonel Taylor on that beach in thirty-nine hundred years?" (Hasan 2011). It seems apparent that in *Rise* they determined the right dominoes were to be found in science, specifically in bioengineering and the threat of talking, intelligent apes. As I will examine in chapter 7, as legislative debates about chimeras and stem cells augur, genomic science might well be a threat to humans, and the film certainly draws out in dramatic, cinematic fashion the potential implications for our species of an "Other" empowered by genetic manipulation.

Had the writers and directors remained within the narrative of threatening science, we might not find quite as trenchant a racial subtext; however, *Rise*'s dramatic climax is one of violent confrontation between unarmed, though nevertheless menacing, apes and police, a plot which *Dawn* draws out and enhances in its narrative of guns and violence and a thinly veiled metaphor about "power." The tipping point in 2014, as in 1965, and indeed in 2020 and beyond, seems to be violent confrontation between an "us" and a "them," leading us right back to the racial tensions that inspired the original franchise. Just as the ape liberation scene in 1972's *Conquest* borrowed heavily from the urban uprisings of Watts and later riots in Boston, Chicago, Detroit, and elsewhere (Greene 1998, 80), *Rise*'s climactic confrontation on the Golden Gate Bridge between the apes and the police, and the scenes of destruction and mayhem in the city that precede it, call to mind the unrest in LA in 1992 after the acquittal of four white police officers in the severe beating of Black motorist Rodney King. In the composition of the images and the framing of the apes smashing windows and aggressively hurling heavy objects into crowds of innocent bystanders, scenes from the films resonate visually with the violence of the King uprising. Further, the use of symbols like the Black Power fist in both *Rise* and *Dawn* and the scenes of apes burning down the forest and looting the armory mirror, in uncanny and uncomfortable ways, representations of racial conflict, generally, and criminalized Blackness, specifically, constructed by the wider mediascape.

In 2011, when *Rise* aired, the "Rodney King riots" (as the protests came to be known in the mainstream white media) were the most recent consequential episode of violence stemming from racist police practice and a judiciary that exonerated white cops.[6] But by 2014, when *Dawn* aired, Americans found themselves in a time of racial tension and violence not seen since the '60s, when between "1965 and 1968 three hundred race-related disturbances and race-related violent confrontations, usually referred to as 'riots,' gripped the nation, involving an estimated half million African Americans, a number equivalent to the number of US soldiers serving at the time in Vietnam. The battles resulted in over eight thousand causalities" (Greene 1998, 79). The days and months following the release of *Dawn* in July 2014 marked a flash point in what would become an epidemic of white police officers killing African Americans and being largely acquitted for their actions.[7]

A 2015 study revealed that young Black men die at the hands of police officers at five times the rate that white men do. "Despite making up only 2% of the population, African American males between the ages of 15 and 34 comprised more than 15% of all deaths logged this year [2015] by an ongoing investigation into the use of deadly force by police" (Swaine et al. 2015). On July 17, 2014, just six days after the release of *Dawn*, forty-three-year-old African

Apes ransack the city after Caesar frees them from ape jail. (*Rise of the Planet of the Apes*, 2011)

Unrest in Los Angeles, California, in 1992 after the acquittal of police officers in the beating of Rodney King. (Akili-Casundria Ramsess, Associated Press)

American Eric Garner was arrested in Staten Island, New York, for selling loose cigarettes. A white police officer, Daniel Pantaleo, applied a fatal chokehold on Garner, despite the prohibition of that form of restraint in the state of New York. Although the medical examiner declared Garner's death a homicide, a grand jury decided not to indict Pantaleo. Then, on August 9, 2014, just twenty-nine days after *Dawn*'s release, with racial tensions still high, Michael Brown, an eighteen-year-old unarmed Black man, was fatally shot on the street in Ferguson, Missouri, by police officer Darren Wilson, who believed Brown to be a robbery suspect. Eyewitnesses at the scene report Brown to have raised

Caesar and his escaped apes go on a rampage in the street. Scenes like these resonate visually with the violence of the King uprising. (*Rise of the Planet of the Apes*, 2011)

Caesar and his crew smash the glass windows of Gen-Sys, mirroring images of looters smashing store windows. (*Rise of the Planet of the Apes*, 2011)

his arms in surrender when he was shot six times by Wilson, though other witnesses claim Brown was running toward Wilson when shot.[8] Brown's body was left in the street uncovered for four hours, prompting a number of local residents to hold a vigil and erect makeshift memorials to Brown. The following day, protests erupted, provoking a heavily militarized police response involving riot gear, tear gas, and rubber bullets being sprayed into crowds of protestors. The Ferguson uprising lasted for two weeks, resulting in the Missouri governor calling for a state of emergency, the implementation of curfews, and ultimately, on August 18, the calling in of the National Guard. An armed police response of this scale had not been seen since Watts, which took place from August 11 to 16, 1965, almost exactly forty-nine years before.

As a result of an investigation into the nature of policing in Ferguson, Obama's Justice Department issued a report in March of 2015 detailing the unfair and unequal treatment of African Americans by Ferguson police, observing that the department's leadership fueled a culture of "explicit racial bias" (quoted in

Caesar and his apes overtake the Golden Gate Bridge, killing police and destroying property. (*Rise of the Planet of the Apes*, 2011)

Protestors take over Los Angeles, California, during the Watts riots of 1965. (Associated Press file)

Tesler 2016a, 231; see also Berman and Lowery 2015). To further inflame tensions, on November 22, 2014, just four months after *Dawn*'s release, a twelve-year-old African American boy, Tamir Rice, was killed by police for possession of a pellet gun that was assumed to be a pistol. In a December 2015 Gallup poll, 13 percent of Americans cited race relations and racism as the most significant problem facing the country, the greatest percentage to do so in a poll since the 1960s

Protestor returns a tear gas canister fired by police to disperse protestors in Ferguson, Missouri, 2014. (Robert Cohen/*St. Louis Post-Dispatch*, Associated Press)

(Tesler 2016a, 192). As Frank Wilderson makes clear, "Black people stand in a different relationship to the police, so even though the homicidal murderous violence of the police can be meted out to the white working class, white women, immigrants, Native Americans . . . the generative mechanism of the same *acts* of violence are not of the same *structure* . . . The police actually enforce the laws on all these other groups, but the police *make* the laws on Black bodies when they produce violence" (Wilderson et al. 2016, 15).

Freddie Gray, already visibly hurt, is put into police custody. Baltimore, Maryland, April 12, 2015.

Caesar is forcibly dragged into the primate facility. (Rise of the Planet of the Apes, 2011)

Protestor raises the Black Power fist in Baltimore, Maryland, in the aftermath of the death of Freddie Gray. (Patrick Semansky, Associated Press)

Caesar, having electrocuted Dodge, his evil guard, raises his fist in an echo of the Black Power symbol. (Rise of the Planet of the Apes, 2011)

MEDIA SPECTACLE AND TRAUMA: THE CASE OF TRAYVON MARTIN

In his examination of the role played by Hollywood in supporting and contesting the actions and policies of the Bush-Cheney administration and its "war on terror," Douglas Kellner argues that the media reporting of the attack on the World Trade Center on 9/11, which was repeatedly replayed in twenty-four-hour news cycles, not only had a material effect but also produced a psychic effect on the US populace, "traumatizing a nation with fear" (2010, 100). In their wall-to-wall coverage of traumatic events like 9/11, media outlets turn historical events into "powerful media spectacles" that "shape social memory" (Kellner 2010, 98).

The 2012 death of Trayvon Martin at the hands of Neighborhood Watch volunteer George Zimmerman and the aftermath of his acquittal in 2013 constitutes another historical event turned into a media spectacle. As scholars have noted, "the news coverage reflected an encompassing pro-white/antiblack master-frame that presented Black Americans as inadequate, lawless, criminal, threatening and at times biologically different" (Lane et al. 2020, 790; see also Banks 2018). In their examination of media reporting from 2012–2016 on the Martin case and the founding of the Black Lives Matter movement, Lane et al. found that even those news outlets considered more liberal, such as the *New York Times* and the *Washington Post*, relied on frames and sub-frames that emphasized Black criminality, white fear, and other racial stereotypes; characterized Martin as a "gangsta thug" with a truancy and drug problem; and depicted BLM as "scattered" and "ineffective" but also as a group of "terrorists" staging a "black militant uprising" (2020, 803, 801).

By contrast, Hispanic Zimmerman and the white police officers who decided initially not to charge him were described as "civilizers" and "protectors," attributes the media typically associates with whiteness (Lane et al. 2020, 801). While there is also evidence of counter-framing and attempts by some news outlets to reclaim Martin's humanity (Noble 2014), Trayvon's life became a mediated commodity. Consistent with colorblind media discourse, the coverage eschewed overt racial framing and instead utilized a new, though no less racist, frame that did not explicitly reference race but linked "racism indirectly to whites' policy preferences and white ideologies" (Lane et al. 2020, 804). In this way, the news reports "served to blame Trayvon Martin for his own death, as the image or 'figure in a hoodie' justified George Zimmerman fearing for his life" (Lane et al. 2020, 804). Martin became representative of a type of Black life that threatened the "cherished values" whites associate with American life, including gun control and family values (Lane et al. 2020, 805).

It wasn't only in the news media that white appropriation of the Martin narrative occurred. Internet culture was quick to adopt and adapt the Trayvon tragedy as a spectacle for white entertainment. Through a practice called "Trayvoning," popular on Facebook during the Zimmerman trial in 2013, white youth posted pictures of themselves in hoodies with Skittles and Arizona iced tea (items Martin was carrying when he was killed) in a pose suggesting they'd been shot in the chest. Since Martin's death, Skittles had become a symbol of Martin's innocence and protestors' resistance, as bags of the candy were like a "flag, waved, hung round necks, taped over mouths and even glued to placards" (Benedictus 2013). But as Gavan Titley notes, "once in circulation symbols are charged with memetic potential, in this instance appropriated as a mocking indicator of that life's historically sanctioned disposability" (2019, 24). And as Guerrero and Leonard argue, "the disregard for Black life, and the disparagement of Black death is nothing new" (2012). Whites deriving pleasure from Black pain has an extended and storied history in the lynching of Black men and rape of Black women; it also has a long-standing correlate in popular culture entertainment, where Black characters who perpetuate vile and violent acts are suitably and gratuitously punished by a white judicial system, exercising and enacting "the obligatory violence of whites toward the treachery of blacks" (Sexton 2017, 17). Importantly, though, this white pleasure goes beyond a mere denial of Black humanity and refusal of Black pain; rather, it is a conscious and deliberate manifestation of white power and privilege. And, like the news media coverage of Martin's death, it is one that occurs without naming or articulating the whiteness of that power. "White people don't take part in 'Trayvoning' to 'declare' white supremacy," Guerrero and Leonard note, "they take part in it because the declaration has been rendered unnecessary by various sociocultural, sociopolitical, and socioeconomic forces. In fact, the absence of the explicit claims to it emphasizes the power and privilege even more" (2012).

FERGUSON, BALTIMORE, AND BEYOND

The media spectacle of Black death became even more pronounced in the coverage of the unrest in Ferguson after the killing of Michael Brown, as well as those occurring in Baltimore following the death in police custody of Freddie Gray, and the subsequent other scenes of protest and violent clashes between police and BLM protestors and unorganized rioters erupting around the country. Analysts from outlets on both the conservative and progressive sides have weighed in on the role the media played in perpetuating specific accounts related to Ferguson. While they tend to disagree about the nature of that account—conservative sources suggest that a "false media narrative" perpetuated the "Hands up, Don't shoot" account (referring to initial reports that Brown was surrendering to Wilson when he was shot [Kurtz 2015; Christie 2015]), and more progressive analysts suggest that the media was quick to criminalize Michael Brown's past and thus provide justification for his death (Massie 2014; Khetpal 2014)—most pundits agree that the media's insatiable drive for ratings skewed the story and inflamed racial tensions.

In her analysis of the news coverage of protests surrounding the death of Freddie Gray and the visibility of an active BLM response, Chloe Banks argues that media outlets quickly shifted the rhetorical emphasis from peaceful protests with smaller violent elements to a framing of BLM as violent protestors looting and destroying property. Scenes of burning cars, crazed looters, aggressive militant police, and body after Black body shoved against police cars, hands behind backs or atop heads, saturated television screens and cemented the polarity of racial views already entrenched in America. As Banks notes, the *New York Times* frequently used images of protestors that "visualized deviance." In one prominent example, the *Times* printed a photo, shot from a low angle, of a Black man standing on top of a car and another of a Black man readying a chair to hurl into a shop window while a white woman cowers in fear and is ushered away by a white man (Banks 2018, 715). The comment sections of news stories and Twitter feeds revealed a wider sense among the white populace of Black people as dangerous and violent. The overrepresentation of "Black crime" and the depiction of "Black violence" in the media fueled bias and forestalled legitimate consideration of the cause of that violence, instead perpetuating stereotypes about African Americans (Gregory et al. 2014; Fitts 2014). Conservative radio talk show host Laura Ingraham's comments on Twitter exemplified such a view. Reacting to inflammatory images of rioters played on a never-ending loop on Fox News, she tweeted, "No fathers, no male role models, no discipline, no jobs, no values=no sense of right and wrong. #Family #Character" (quoted in Taibi 2015).

Kellner suggests that these "[s]pectacles of terror use dramatic images and narrative to catch attention and are intended thereby to catalyze unanticipated events that will spread further terror through domestic populations" (Kellner 2010, 99–100). Whereas the media spectacle of 9/11 traumatized and galvanized much of the populace,[9] inspiring Americans to support the "war on terror" through veiled appeals to patriotism and a ceding of their personal liberty to the government, the media spectacle around Ferguson and Baltimore had a divisive effect on Americans. Indeed, the nature of the "terror" produced in these media images differs according to the population watching/experiencing them. To a Black audience, continual reports of police shooting and killing of unarmed Black people further reinforce a reality already known to be true. However, the daily repetition of that story, in whatever city, in conjunction with the endless video of Black men shouting, "Don't shoot, don't shoot," right before being shot, and the ongoing fact of police acquittal can produce anger in addition to a very real fear that the agencies entrusted with guarding their civil liberties will no longer do so. If a citizen cannot seek redress for oppression from the government or the judiciary, our democracy is indeed in tatters. To a Black viewer, then, the media spectacle can produce a sense of disenfranchisement, despair, and racial isolation (Blake 2016). White audiences are also manipulated by these media spectacles, but rather than experiencing fear or isolation as Black people do, their terror is as old as racism itself. Because "popular media shape social memory and perceptions of the recent past and present that are still alive in the political discourse and struggles of the day" (Kellner 2010, 98), the media spectacle of race riots and lootings conjure up and redeploy narratives of the "scary Black man" burning with violence and revenge against whites for enslavement.

Regardless of the viewer's perspective, the perpetual reiteration of the racial spectacles of Ferguson and Baltimore produces a psychic effect similar to that experienced after 9/11. "These made-for-media events become global spectacles that create fearful populations more likely to be manipulated by reactionary forces who give simplistic answers to contemporary anxiety and problems" (Kellner 2010, 100). In this case, the media's continued sensationalized coverage of the violence in Ferguson and Baltimore worked to construct and reinforce the racial polarization of the nation, making us more susceptible to divisive political ideologies. Indeed, "existing research on the media framing of African Americans suggests that the crime frame can be an extraordinarily effective tool in shaping white views" (Abrajano and Hajnal 2015, 164). Interestingly, as violence against Black people became more pronounced in the US under Trump, this saturated media coverage has had the opposite effect than that seen in 2014. The televising of George Floyd's murder by Derek Chauvin, rather than reinforcing a belief in Black criminality, instead exposed police brutality and a pervasive police culture of anti-Black racism.

Hollywood, for its part, capitalizes on media spectacles by reproducing traumatic imagery and shaping audience response to them. Films, therefore, have the capacity to "construc[t] individuals' views of history and contemporary reality" (Kellner 2010, 98). The writers and producers of *Dawn of the Planet of the Apes* likely could not have predicted that their 2014 film would be released in an environment of extreme racial violence. But the social, political, and cultural context of a film always informs its reception. And the context surrounding this film was one of extreme racial division, an environment where legitimate calls for checks on police brutality against African Americans resulted in "Blue Lives" being pitted against "Black Lives." Because "cultural products work by accessing our cultural memories" (Greene 1998, 88) and because most viewers of the film were likely to see it concurrent with or after the racial uprisings of

Ferguson and in the framework of what neo-Nazi groups are labeling a twenty-first-century "race war" (Sheffield 2017; King 2016), *Dawn* elicits and indeed reinforces the same kind of white racial paranoia as the original films did. In the context of the film's release and its use of overt racial framing, the viewer is primed to interpret every scene of conflict between the apes and humans through the lens of contemporary racial strife

APE PARATEXTS AND MEMES

The racist association of Black people with apes took on a different connotation after the release of the original *Planet of the Apes* movies. As Eric Greene makes clear, the phrase "planet of the apes" signifies a specific kind of racial insult. "Using the phrase 'planet of the apes' is more than just an ethnic slur likening African Americans to apes. It is a statement expressing a sense of white powerlessness in a situation where the 'natural' order has been reversed and the despised racial 'other' now dominates" (Greene 1998, 176). Fictional narratives do not have the same political, social, or cultural resonance as real events, but they do perform the interpretive work of framing and rendering real meanings readable and relatable. Film and television representations are complex, and viewers enter texts from their own specific locations and with their own beliefs. Herman Gray contends that "commercial culture is increasingly the central place where various memories, myths, histories, traditions, and practices circulate. At the site of commercial culture, these practices and identifications are constantly assembled, torn apart, reassembled, and torn apart yet again by critics, viewers, and [film] makers such that they find discursive order resonance in everyday life" (Gray 1995, 4). While oppositional readings of *Rise* and *Dawn* are certainly possible, this new reboot is not easily separated from its paratexts. The original film franchise, the saturation in the news media of images of aggressive and lawless "Blackness," and popular memes which attempt to frame Obama and, by extension, other Black people within a racist discourse of bestialization reveals quite clearly the discursive resonance of everyday life in Obama's America.

In her analysis of the salience of memes in alt-right subcultures, Julia DeCook argues that, in a networked age, memes function as a significant form of political participation and are an important component of identity and community building (DeCook 2018, 486). The significance of these Obama/ape memes is not just their location in right-wing discourse; rather the linkage of the president of the United States with apes and the "Planet of the Apes" reveals the effortlessness of white privilege. As DeCook citing Bourdieu notes, "every interaction, no matter the context or the content, is both reifying and reproducing the power held in culture and society" (2018, 487). These forms

Two popular memes circulating on right-wing and mainstream social media platforms during the Barack Obama presidency.

of produsage make visible the politics that *Rise* and *Dawn* utilize but disguise in a postracial package. Despite the state-sanctioned power that Obama as president represents, these memes, because they "embody the social norms of the habitus," reveal his authority is incongruous with an Americanness that is implicitly and explicitly structured by whiteness. Just as the practice of "Trayvoning" exemplifies the disposability of Black life and the entertainment value of Black death, the casual association of a well-known, long-standing, profitable American film franchise with historically racist and eugenic views is a clear example of how popular culture utilizes and repackages racial ideologies of the past to define and reclaim white identity.

During the Obama presidency, alt-right and certain conservative media outlets frequently likened Obama's America to the "planet of the apes." In December 2008, just after Obama's election win, the white supremacist site stormfront.org published "Planet of the Apes: An Obama Years Survival Guide." Another neo-Nazi site, The Daily Stormer, routinely called Obama's presidency the "Planet of the Apes Occupation." In 2010, then *Fox News* host, Glenn Beck, discussing on air a critique of an Obama policy, asked his viewers, "What planet have I landed on? Did I slip through a wormhole in the middle of the night and this looks like America? It's like the damn Planet of the Apes!" (*HuffPost* 2010).

With the release of *Rise* in 2011, references to the Obamas and *Planet of the Apes* became more common. Images of the Obamas' faces superimposed over those of Zira and Cornelius from the original series proliferated, including one of them standing in the sand next to the iconic image from the original *Planet of the* battered, half-buried Statue of Liberty. In 2012, in the run-up to the election where Obama won a second term, one particularly virulent photoshopped image from *Escape from the Planet of the Apes* featured Hillary Clinton seated between Michelle and Barack Obama, depicted as Zira and Cornelius, with the caption, "It's a madhouse. A madhouse." Many of these pictures originate from neo-Nazi platforms like stormfront.org, which styles itself as "the voice of the new, embattled white minority" and is counted by the Southern Poverty Law Center as an active hate group. Michelle Obama, particularly, is a favorite target of internet trolls who compare her face to those of chimpanzees and gorillas, but the most common comparison made to her is Zira. This likening backfired for Univision network host Rodner Figueroa, who was forced to resign in 2015 after saying that Michelle Obama "looks like she's from the cast of Planet of the Apes" (McCormack 2015).

In documenting the legacy of the original series, including its adaptation for the small screen and in comic books, Greene remarks on the political value to the extreme right of appropriating a *Planet of the Apes* discourse. One reporter interviewed by Greene asserted that the phrase "planet of the apes" had surfaced as a racial insult at every KKK rally he had ever covered. Tellingly, Greene makes clear the ways in which the politics of the day inform and reinforce prevailing views about race. The "'*Apes*' movement from politically influenced fiction to fiction used to influence politics exemplifies the continual exchange in which politics flows into popular culture, which then flows back into politics" (Greene 1998, 179). The same claim can be made about the new franchise forty-three years later. As Jared Sexton makes clear in his analysis of the twenty-first-century resurgence of the *King Kong* films: the "resurfacing of the image of the simian black reveals the tenacity of the visual, narrative, and characterological paradigm established in Hollywood cinema by films like *Birth of a Nation* (1915) and *King Kong* (1933) and the versatility of ideological appropriation in the realm of culture work more broadly" (Sexton 2017, 28).

Greene makes clear that when the original *Planet of the Apes* franchise was produced and released, "the racial power dynamics of the United States were under sustained, often furious, attack" (Greene 1998, 12). Although *Dawn* was released days before the racial unrest in Ferguson, it was written and produced in a similar climate of racial division, in part fueled by the partisanship that developed during Obama's presidency. While polls taken on the eve of Obama's inauguration reflect optimism among Blacks and whites about the state of race relations in the country, polls taken later in his first term show that 37 percent of registered voters believed race relations had deteriorated under Obama. That number jumped to 43 percent in 2013 (Tesler 2016a, 208nn15, 16). While race relations did indeed worsen as a result of the violence in Ferguson and elsewhere, this pessimism about race can be attributed to the unique treatment Obama received as president. Where other presidents have certainly been pilloried in the press, they have not been diminished and personally disrespected. In a surreal echo of southern high-school traditions of crowning both a white homecoming king/queen and a Black one, Obama wasn't allowed to be "the President" because he was viewed by the electorate and the media first and foremost as "the Black President." Sexton argues that Obama's embodiment of "black masculinity as state-sanctioned authority ... should not be contrasted with the associations of illegitimacy, dispossession, and violence that seem to otherwise monopolize the signification of racial blackness. Rather the former should be understood as an extension of the latter" (Sexton 2017, xxiii). Every policy decision he made was refracted through a racial lens.

Shortly after Obama's inauguration in 2008, the Tea Party, an ultra-conservative branch of the Republican Party, formed. In 2010, members of the Tea Party won a number of congressional seats in the midterm elections, providing a vocal platform of opposition to Obama and his policies. A study published in 2013 measuring the relationship between racial prejudice, white identity, and the Tea Party found that "[i]dentification with the Tea Party was positively associated with anti-Black prejudice, libertarian ideology, social conservatism ... and national decline" (Knowles et al. 2013). To add to this, conservative news channels like Fox and alt-right sites like Breitbart and the National Review offered daily onslaughts of racially charged criticism of Obama and his administration. On numerous occasions, Bill O'Reilly used the bully pulpit of his Fox News cable show to critique Obama for his lack of leadership on America's race problem. The few times Obama did talk about race, such as when he addressed the killing of the unarmed Trayvon Martin, he was accused of being

Conservative politician and analyst Pat Buchanan being interviewed on CNN in 2016 before the presidential election.

a race-baiter because he suggested the outcome might have been different if Martin had been white (Hayward 2013; McCarthy 2013).

Surveys conducted from 2010–2012 measuring racial attitudes of self-identifying conservatives found that Americans were more comfortable talking explicitly about race than in previous decades, leading researchers to surmise that "when they heard public figures articulating feelings they shared perhaps some racially conservative Americans abandoned the old rules themselves" (Ehrenfreund 2016). A poll conducted by the Associated Press before the 2012 elections found that "79 percent of Republicans agreed with negative statements about racial minorities" (Ehrenfreund 2015). The racial divide saw Blacks and whites "unfriending" each other on Facebook and in real life as racist attitudes toward, and offensive caricatures of, Obama and his family circulated. For some African Americans, the presence of Obama on the political scene forced them to confront racism they thought "had been litigated and fought" in previous generations. At the base of it was the underlying feeling that "having a Black president didn't make any difference. If anything, it made things worse" (Blake 2016).

RACE AND MEDIA SPECTACLE

If this turbulent social and political environment contributed to the shootings and riots in Ferguson, Baltimore, Charlotte, and elsewhere, we might consider how the very same atmosphere provided the fodder for the plot and imagery of "racial" tension portrayed in *Dawn*. Here, as in the 1960–70s franchise, "the concerns and issues of the era may have been subconsciously incorporated into the films" (Greene 1998, 2). Although the filmmakers hadn't yet seen the media spectacle, they were surely able to predict what it might look like, especially with the history of LA and Watts in the rearview mirror. As Kellner makes clear, "Serious amounts of money are invested in the production of films and television, so they must resonate with audiences and often anticipate what people are thinking about, fantasizing, or yearning for" (Kellner 2010, 39). Furthermore, if we consider the racially charged political climate of *Dawn*'s production and take into account the racial allegory of the original *Planet of the Apes* franchise and the fact that it is released at the very moment that police killings and race riots are plastered on the news, it seems likely that many white viewers would associate the current state of race relations in America with the takeover of apes and the takedown of humans. By forming part of a media event, just like the first series, the films in the latest franchise do not "merely record and play back the society's ongoing discourses of racial difference and racial conflict, they ente[r] into it and are a part of those discourses" (Greene 1998, 19).

What is perhaps most striking, most disingenuous, or most politic about the confluence of events depicted in the films and those on the street is that in no interview (that I can find) do the writers, directors, or actors ever mention race. There seems to be collective amnesia or ignorance among them as to the historical and political legacy of the films they're rebooting. In one interview, when asked specifically about the political message of the films, director Matt Reeves sidelines the allegorical or metaphorical implications of the question, offering, instead, a diegesis of the film's universe and the importance of the "apes' perspective." Curiously, he ends by saying that *Dawn* helps us to see how "these problems" can exist and "how we find ourselves time and time again descending into violence." In the same clip, Gary Oldman and Keri Russell both struggle with the question, and then Oldman suggests the film "reflects what's currently happening in the Middle East," then uncomfortably adds, "you know, you could make the comparisons," as Russell looks down at her hands. Oldman quickly recovers and says, "I think it's timeless in that sense." Andy Serkis, for his part, praises Reeves for making a film "which is completely unbiased" (Ashurst 2014). So, while the destructive violence is acknowledged, no one associated with the film wants to tie it specifically to the tinderbox of US Black-white race relations. However awkwardly the stars tried to dismiss any political engagement with the films, some critics were quick to discern the legacy of the original franchise. Matt Seitz, writing at Roger Ebert.com, for example, suggests that *Dawn*, like *Rise*, "borrows situations and images from the 1960s and '70s" films in a "playfully political" way but "leaves an intriguingly bitter aftertaste" (Seitz 2014). Other critics call out the implied racial commentary in the films, beginning with the first: "The assertions made by *Rise* are not new; they've been present in cinema since *The Birth of a Nation* insisted that

Black savagery and inherent primitivism would presage the collapse of white civilization. In that sense, *Rise* is nothing more than an unoriginal but sparkly return to a 'rational' racism" (Goodkind 2011).

Politically, socially, and culturally, media events have larger implications for society as a whole. We cannot ignore the fact that the perception of African Americans as more prone to violence and criminality results in their higher rates of detention and incarceration. In fact, African Americans make up approximately 40 percent of the prison population, though they comprise only 13 percent of the overall population (Hagler 2015; Mauer and King 2007). In their study of the Black-ape connection, Goff et al. also found that "a Black-ape association influences the extent to which people condone and justify violence against Black suspects," and the association was linked "to the death-sentencing decision of jurors" (2008, 294). Indeed, "participants were more likely to believe that the beating the Black suspect received was justified when primed with apes than with big cats" (Goff et al. 2008, 302). As Michelle Alexander has shown in *The New Jim Crow*, the criminal justice system produces and enforces racial hierarchy in the United States. "In the era of colorblindness, it is no longer socially permissible to use race explicitly as a justification for discrimination, exclusion, and social contempt. So we don't. Rather than rely on race, we use our criminal justice system to label people of color 'criminals' and then engage in all the practices we supposedly left behind" (Alexander 2012, 2). Popular culture participates in and perpetuates social and political discourses of racial hierarchy. In depicting criminal "apes" in violent clashes first with police in *Rise* and as armed vigilantes in *Dawn*, the films cement an association of Blackness with animality and lawlessness and justify and naturalize the incarceration of African Americans. The implicit perception of African Americans as apes continues the legacy of Black people as not deserving of basic human rights and supports violent retaliation by a threatened hegemony.

Just like *Conquest of the Planet of the Apes* (1972), *Dawn* "establishes the terms of its conflict by playing on the audience's memory of extratextual historical references . . . of racial oppression" (Greene 1998, 89), and just like the earlier films, ends up contributing to racial divisions rather than racial unity. While *Dawn* tries to show both human and ape sides as weakened by a thirst for power and prone to violence, in the context of its reception, such a message is dangerously redirected. The cinematic mise-en-scène of Koba's fiery revenge bears an uncanny resemblance to the racially charged conflagrations in Ferguson and Baltimore. Just as in 1972, *Dawn* reinforces a dawning awareness among whites that Black America is ready to fight for justice and to stay "woke." Indeed, the main reason the ending of 1972's *Conquest* was changed from a violent ape revolt to a conciliatory message of peace was that "[e]ven liberal whites who wished—and wish—to see racial inequality eliminated would not—and do not—want to be punished, or even held accountable, for their profit from it" (Greene 1998, 110). Although Koba receives his comeuppance at the hands of Caesar, who breaks the one ape commandment "ape not kill ape" (Reeves 2014), the result does not appease the audience but instead forces viewers to set their sights and fears now on Caesar. As he makes clear at the end of *Dawn* when Malcolm urges him to leave the city to prevent war, "War has already begun." Yet, in a departure from *Rise*'s efforts to demonstrate the apes are retaliating against their unethical and inhumane treatment at the hands of humans, *Dawn* places the blame squarely at the feet of the apes: "Ape started war and human, human will not forgive" (Reeves 2014). Given the not-so-subtle substitution of ape for Black and human for white, in staging a "race" war that vilifies the apes and redeems the humans, *Dawn* adds oxygen to the incendiary race relations of its day. Functioning as a form of racial rearticulation, this franchise helps to vindicate white racism by containing and tempering legitimate calls for racial justice.

The use of dog whistles (code words), claims of "reverse racism," and a belief in "colorblindness" are all examples of the historic trajectory of the politics of rearticulation (Omi and Winant 2014). In a similar mode of racial rearticulation, *Dawn of the Planet of the Apes*, in its depiction of apes bent on revenge against humans and released in a cultural climate pitting Blacks against whites, delegitimizes African American claims for social justice and reinforces white beliefs that Blacks are inherently violent and pose a threat to white life. Because media spectacles manipulate our social memory and construct our reality, the racially divisive message of the film supports the climate of intense partisanship into which it was released and helped to fuel the claims of white extremists instrumental in Donald Trump's rise to power.

Chapter 5

"ANIMALS" WITH GUNS

In chapter 4, I argued that the conflation of apes and African Americans in the *Planet of the Apes* reboot contributes to the perception of Black Americans as animals, not merely capable of, but naturally inclined toward, violent retaliation. Real-life incidents of racial unrest, protests, and riots related to police brutality and Black death were interpreted through the representation of violent apes in the fictional *Apes* narratives, and these, in turn, shaped and ordered audience perceptions of ongoing racial conflict. In this chapter, I will examine how violence, and particularly gun violence, in *The Walking Dead* structures partisan views among the American populace about gun control and demonstrates how, in the age of Obama, the "gun itself is a conduit to the fantasy of white masculine redemption" (Kelly 2020, 107). I argue that the show associates gun violence with white hypermasculinity to give expression to both hard and soft forms of white identity politics. In *TWD*, overt white supremacist discourse supports and reifies white power narratives. However, consistent with colorblind racism, the show presents this noxious and over-the-top racist discourse in the context of a multiracial ensemble cast and alongside presentations of white male heroism and white female grit. By pitting hostile expressions of white identity against less antagonistic ones, *TWD* facilitates and cultivates latent racial ideologies—soft white identity politics. The voicing of white supremacist views allows white fans to revel in such outrageous, politically incorrect behavior and, at the same time, to separate it from their own investment in the uncontested superiority of whiteness.

Dawn Keetley has remarked of *TWD* that "[n]o one who has watched the show can fail to be aware of either the importance of fences (and securing them against the walkers and other, dangerous, humans) or the omnipresence of guns—the use of guns, training people in how to use guns, debates over who should have guns, giving guns to children, retrieving guns, lamenting the scarcity of guns" (Keetley 2014b, 10). Airing during a time of unprecedented mass shootings and efforts by Democrats to impose stricter gun laws, *TWD* utilizes a right-wing rhetoric that upholds a Second Amendment narrative justifying violence against the "Other," variously defined. In chapter 3, I examined how borders, walls, and fences in *TWD* reinforce a rhetoric of bioinsecurity as the threat that the zombie/immigrant represents is one of contagion to the nation-state. Here, I will examine how guns and their valorization and use in the series work to uphold white racial politics and underscore a prevailing narrative in white America, exploited by Trump, that white culture is vulnerable to attacks from non-white others and must be defended. Clearly, the zombies in *TWD* represent an obvious and imminent threat to the humans around them, as do, eventually, the humans from other communities who are vying for the scant remaining resources. However, I argue here that those overt and constant scenes of violence occlude the racial violence that takes place on an *intra*-group level between white and Black characters.

The first six seasons of *TWD* promote a survivalist, doomsday prepper culture that glorifies white masculinity at the same time as representing white men as victims that need to "take back" their country. Increasingly, African American characters, regardless of how complex or sympathetic their storyline, are either subject to or perpetrators of violence. *The Walking Dead* represents a clear example of what Casey Ryan Kelly calls the "apocalyptic turn" in white masculinity, where white men are "beseeched by an intoxicating fantasy of return to an imagined past before feminism, the Black freedom struggle, and queer activism fundamentally questioned cisgender heterosexual white men's primacy in all aspects of public and private life" (Kelly 2020, 2). Narratives of apocalypse appeal to these white men, for they offer them an opportunity to enjoy without censure the collapse of civil society and erosion of those liberal democratic protections afforded to all citizens but perceived as given, not earned, to "minority" groups, whether raced or gendered. Because guns are "prosthetic extensions of white male power" and because "[w]hite male bodies in particular are afforded credibility to act on behalf of the law and to exercise sovereignty over public space" (Kelly 2020, 26), I want to explore how *TWD* influenced and shaped the way Americans understood gun control, class issues, and racially motivated violence in the Obama-to-Trump era.

Certainly, there is considerable overlap in the blogosphere between fans of the show and hard-core gun enthusiasts. Numerous blogs devoted to the guns of *TWD* describe the kinds of weapons used in specific scenes and the skill or lack thereof of the characters using them. Some blogs, such as *Internet Movie Firearms Database*, merely catalog the weapons used in the show. Other bloggers provide more commentary, including Spike Bowman on a blog called *Tactical Shit News*, who writes, "I am a HUGE fan of AMC's 'the [sic] Walking Dead!' I am also an avid weapons enthusiast and Second Amendment advocate. It dawned on me as I was preparing for tonight's episode to put the two together" (Tactical Editor 2013). He then offers descriptions, statistics, and the average cost of the real versions of weapons used in the show. Ray, a blogger from *Armory.com*, notes that "[w]hat makes the weapon choices in *The Walking Dead* so interesting is that no one is using a tacticool [sic] assault rifle or is dual wielding pistols. They're not sporting anything too fancy" (Ray 2011). This blog also includes links to similar weapons for purchase on Amazon.

MILITIAS, INSURRECTIONS, AND WALLS OF MOMS

On June 1, 2020, in the midst of the ongoing public outcry over the death of George Floyd and in an effort to make Trump seem tough after weekend reports that he had fled to a bunker in the White House during protests, the Trump team staged a photo op in front of St. John's Episcopal Church, which had been damaged by fire in the protests of the night before. When Trump's attorney general, William Barr, realized that Trump would have to encounter protestors in Lafayette Square, across from the White House, he authorized the military to clear them out. Although the protestors were peacefully carrying placards and chanting Floyd's name, police and National Guard troops in full riot gear used tear gas and flash grenades to disperse the crowd. In what the *New York Times* suggests will be remembered as one of the Trump presidency's defining moments (Baker et al. 2020), the scene was captured by all major media outlets, prompting outrage among civilians and military leaders alike. The fallout from the event resulted in the country's top military official, General Mark Milley, who accompanied Trump on his walk, to issue a statement of regret: "I should not have been there," stating that it had created a "perception of the military involved in domestic politics" (*New York Times* 2020). Since the beginning of the protests, Trump had threatened to invoke the Insurrection Act of 1807, which would allow him to deploy the military to quell civil unrest. Gen. Milley and Secretary of Defense Mark Esper both rejected the idea, noting that the act should only be used as a last resort in the "most urgent and dire situations" (Kube and Schapiro 2020). Although Trump did have Constitutional authority to invoke the act, the politics and optics in doing so would likely have backfired, as even Republicans would likely have interpreted the move as threatening to their Constitutional rights.

Indeed, such a public outcry occurred in Portland, Oregon, in July 2020, when Trump sent federal troops to quell ongoing protests there. Amid reports that law enforcement officers dressed in camouflage were snatching peaceful demonstrators off the street and into unmarked cars (Ward 2020), a group of women, calling themselves the "Wall of Moms," gathered in downtown Portland, linking arms to protect protestors from police. A reporter for *The Guardian* noted that "[a]t the heart of it were hundreds of women dressed

A group of women, calling themselves the "Wall of Moms," gathered in downtown Portland, Oregon, linking arms to protect #BLM protestors from police, July 2020. (Noah Berger, Associated Press)

in yellow and singing 'Hands up, please don't shoot me'—evidence that not only has Trump's dispatch of federal agents failed to stop the protests, it has reinvigorated them" (McGreal 2020). When police fired tear gas at the women, a group of men dubbed "Dads with Leaf Blowers" joined the protests the following day using leaf blowers to disperse tear gas and send it back to the federal agents deploying it. Other protestors used hockey sticks to shoot back tear gas canisters as they approached the crowd (Walker 2020).

As Milley's comments warn and the actions of resisters in Portland reveal, military intervention in civil matters raises fears in the general populace about military occupation, revisits the specter of Waco, and is seen as a usurping of the freedom of individuals and states to exercise their Second Amendment rights, which, as framed by James Madison in the Federalist Papers, includes the implied right to form militias to combat a Federal Army.

"IN ZOMBIELAND, THERE ARE THREE KINDS OF PEOPLE: THOSE WHO KNOW HOW TO USE GUNS, THOSE WHO LEARN HOW TO USE GUNS, AND ZOMBIES"

Guns are a central component of *TWD*, but critics are not in agreement as to whether the series endorses or critiques gun violence. One commentator argues that the show "reflects moderate, popular US views on gun control," exhibiting a mix of American "conservative pragmatism and liberal concern about restraints and leadership" (Yuhas 2013). Others claim that it glorifies brutality and is "decidedly fascistic in nature" (Gencarella 2010, 2016). Certainly, in a program filled with violence of all sorts, the gun violence is frequently less violent than the boot-crushing, arrow-piercing kinds. As Gerry Canavan has argued, "Zombie narratives are ultimately about the motivation for and unleashing of total violence; what separates 'us' from 'them' in zombie narrative is always only the type of violence used. *They* attack *us* (like 'animals,' 'savages,' or 'cannibals') with their arms and mouths; we attack them back with horses, tanks, and guns" (2010, 442). But these "horses, tanks, and guns," while they may originate as instruments of the police or military, are found objects in *TWD*, which, taken out of context and repurposed by civilians for their own defense, support and reinforce the survivalist anti-establishment message of the show. Even though, as most critics note, Rick's pre-apocalyptic employment as a Sheriff's deputy, replete with badge and uniform, allows him to quickly assert control and reestablish law and order at least within his own group, *TWD* clearly demonstrates the incompatibility between the previous world's laws and the new world order instigated by the zombie apocalypse. Whatever law Rick is upholding, it's not the same as the one he was sworn to uphold. In fact, Rick's disillusionment with the law and its failure to inhere in these new circumstances becomes obvious in season 2, episode 4, "Cherokee Rose," when Rick gives his hat and badge to Carl, his young son, and retires his uniform (Darabont et al. 2011, 2:4). Losing the uniform doesn't change Rick's status as leader of the group, but it begins the period of Rick as a frontier lawman.

The show is careful to maintain a balance between the pragmatic operation of violence as self-defense and ruthless self-serving killing, but it is also quick to demonstrate the futility of non-violent confrontation. Fearing that he has gone too far in his quest for ultimate control and vengeance after his wife's death and worried that he has been a bad role model for Carl, season 4 opens with Rick relinquishing his role as leader and embracing a quiet, pastoral life raising pigs and planting crops in the prison complex they now call home. Critical of his father's pacifism and demanding the return of his own gun, Carl rebukes Rick for his inactivity and seeming lack of vigilance (Darabont et al. 2013, 4:1). Rick's bucolic retirement is short-lived, however, as a virus invades the prison, killing the inmates. Rick traces the infection to his pigs, burns them all, and renounces his call to the simpler life, resuming his place as armed leader (Darabont et al. 4:2). In this way, *TWD* deftly offers different narratives of survival and protection but ultimately endorses only one. Neither the individualist kill-or-be-killed ethos of Shane nor the totalitarian abuse of power exemplified by The Governor, Negan, or Alpha is valued; however, the humanitarian find-common-ground approach that his group first practices is shown to be lacking as well. Instead, *TWD* endorses a survivalist ethos that is intertwined with the embrace and performance of white masculinity, which, both physically and symbolically under attack, constantly needs defending. Rick is frequently understood by characters and critics alike as having a moral code, especially in relation to the extremely questionable ethics of his rivals, Shane, The Governor, and Negan. But this moral code is routinely compromised as he employs a utilitarian "ends justify the means" approach or a "sacrifice one for the good of the many" creed. Rick is as quick to kill humans whom he perceives as a threat as he is to dispatch a walker. As one critic astutely observes, "In zombieland, there are three kinds of people: those who know how to use guns, those who learn how to use guns, and zombies." By contrast, the few characters who, in the beginning, "stubbornly clung to their pre-apocalyptic fear and hatred of firearms.... are now dead" (French 2015). The moral code then that is validated and valorized by the series, at least in the early seasons, is an individualist, self-reliant, survivalist ethos, one typically associated with Second Amendment advocates and those on the far right.

While zombie stories and postapocalyptic narratives are increasingly popular forms of entertainment, the popularity of *TWD*, I would argue, stems from the fact that this postapocalypse locale isn't a generic midwestern zombie landscape; the show is set and filmed on location in the deep red South, in Georgia, and thus draws on the legacy of segregation and white supremacy, sexism, southern grit, and the right to "carry." As a writer for the conservative *National Review* notes, *TWD* draws its "dramatic energy from three principles every good Republican should understand: the government is incompetent and prone to collapse under pressure; the person who survives is the person who either knows how to shoot or learns quickly; and even when cities are overrun with undead, a living man is still the most dangerous animal of all" (French 2015).

"THE ONLY THING THAT STOPS A BAD GUY WITH A GUN IS A GOOD GUY WITH A GUN"

Republicans have long painted Democrats as anti-gun and eager to limit or repeal Second Amendment rights, but their concerns about Obama went beyond this. Part of their distrust arose from the statement Obama made on the campaign trail in 2008 before the Pennsylvania primary. Noting the tendency of white working-class voters to vote against their economic interests in favor of cultural politics, Obama opined: "[I]t's not surprising then that they get bitter, they cling to guns or religion or antipathy toward people who aren't like them or anti-immigrant sentiment or anti-trade sentiment as a way to explain their frustrations" (Pilkington 2008). This comment was exploited by Obama's primary opponent, Hillary Clinton, who jumped on it as an example of Obama's elitism. Many in the press and in the wider populace viewed the statement as evidence that Obama was not just tone-deaf to issues of class but as proof that he was out of touch with average Americans and had demonstrated a "profound misunderstanding of small-town values" (Seelye and Zeleny 2008). Here "small-town values" is code for "white values" and the remarks served as another example of how Obama's comments and policies would be refracted through his racial identity, "galvanizing supporters of extreme right-wing politics into heightened fear, organization, and activity" (Mills 2021, 340).

During Obama's presidency, numerous incidents of gun-related violence shook the nation and further inflamed gun control debates. There were two mass shootings in Fort Hood, Texas, one in 2009 and one in 2014; there were shootings on campuses and in movie theaters; in nightclubs; in temples and churches; and, in an elementary school. In December of 2012, just one month after Obama was elected to his second term, twenty-year-old Adam Lanza entered Sandy Hook Elementary School in Newtown, Connecticut, murdering twenty-six people, including twenty children between the ages of six and seven. Lanza had shot and killed his mother, a gun enthusiast and purported doomsday prepper, before entering the school. Stymied by a Republican-controlled Congress, Obama and the Democrats struggled to enact gun reform measures in the wake of Sandy Hook. They attempted to expand background checks (including closing the gun show loophole, where attendees of gun shows could purchase firearms without a background check), proposed a ban on high-capacity magazines, and sought to prevent people on terrorist watch lists from obtaining weapons. However, the NRA and its powerful lobby in Washington maintained their firm control over Republican members, spending more than $3 million on federal lobbying in 2013 and 2014 and more than $30 million in the 2016 elections (Shabad 2016; DiFazio 2018).

After the school shooting at Sandy Hook, when the national mood seemed more inclined toward reform, Wayne LaPierre, executive vice president of the NRA, delivered a speech where he claimed that "[t]he only thing that stops a bad guy with a gun is a good guy with a gun," and called for "armed police officers in every single school in this nation." Without the legal authority to propose or make laws of any kind, LaPierre nevertheless promised that the NRA would bring "all its knowledge, all its dedication and all its resources" to implement the proposed program. He then introduced a former Republican congressman and former administrator of the Federal Drug Enforcement Agency to present the "model security plan" in more detail (NRA 2012). Shortly after, a bipartisan bill requiring background checks on commercial gun purchases failed in the Senate, along with another proposal to reinstate the assault weapons ban, the 1994 Clinton era law which expired in 2004.

In January 2011, the year before the shooting at Sandy Hook, Congresswoman Gabby Giffords suffered a traumatic brain injury when she was shot in the head during a neighborhood political event with her constituents, of whom six were killed. Many in Washington saw the attack on Giffords as a result of an increase in inflammatory partisan rhetoric since Obama's election. The *New York Times* noted that not since the Oklahoma City bombing in 1995 "has an event generated as much attention as to whether extremism, antigovernment sentiment and even simple political passion at both ends of the ideological spectrum have created a climate promoting violence" (Hulse and Zernike 2011). News outlets at the time of the shooting made a connection between Gifford's assault and a map put out by Sarah Palin's political action committee. The map used crosshairs to target the districts of Democrats that Republicans sought to take in the midterms of 2010. Giffords's district was included on that map, prompting Giffords herself to note that "[w]e're on Sarah Palin's targeted list ... [with] the crosshairs of a gun sight over our district. When people do that, they've got to realize there's consequences to that" (Lee 2017a).[1]

In the aftermath of Giffords's shooting, although Congress was unable to pass substantive gun legislation, some states, including Connecticut, New York, and Maryland, did pass stricter gun measures; strikingly, ten states passed laws that weakened gun restrictions, and in 2013 "at least 36 states introduced legislation to nullify federal restrictions on gun rights." Clearly frustrated by the introduction of these measures, Obama accused "opponents of common-sense gun laws" of having "ginned up fears among responsible gun owners" that "feed into suspicions of government, that you need a gun to protect yourself from government" (Hartman 2013).

TWD'S IMPERILED WHITE MASCULINITY

It is in this contentiously partisan cultural moment of guns and gun violence that *TWD* premiered in 2010. Keetley argues that the "guns within the series refract the world beyond the show, as Americans have been constantly on the alert to the erosion of their right to protect themselves (and equally convinced that they need to protect themselves) since Barack Obama was elected in 2008" (Keetley 2014, 10). By utilizing prevailing anti-state fears about the government taking "our guns" and tying it to white survivalist culture, *TWD* validates a real-world narrative of imperiled white masculinity and "reflects the rise of a reactionary politics of white male resentment that seizes tropes of victimhood and marginalization even as it celebrates white male supremacy" (Kelly 2020, 2).

In a flashback that starts "TS-19," episode 6 of season 1, Shane (Jon Bernthal), in his deputy's uniform, enters the hospital where Rick (Andrew Lincoln) is being treated in an effort to wake him from his coma. While there, Shane observes the military enter the hospital and begin what can only be described as a kind of prophylactic killing, shooting people—doctors, nurses, patients, and children—before they become zombies. Horrified by this and unable to wake Rick, Shane retreats (Darabont et al. 2010, 1:6). Set against this clear representation of federal military overreach, *TWD* pits first the morals and values of the individual, local lawman, and then the backwoods code of the frontiersman. Yet, Rick's brand of law and order is also contrasted with the authoritarian violence and governance represented by The Governor (seasons 3–4), Negan (seasons 6–8), and in later seasons, Alpha (seasons 9–10). These dictators establish ultimate control by confiscating the weapons of group members and determining when and how they should be used. This kind of power is compared negatively to the kind of roving freedom that Rick and his group have.

One of Rick's first acts upon waking from his coma is to return to his sheriff's department to obtain weapons, giving one to his new Black friend, Morgan (Lennie James), so he can kill his undead wife. Overrun by zombies in Atlanta, Rick loses his bag of guns, but when he does retrieve them in "Vatos," he offers a Hispanic group part of the cache as a way to escape. In the early episodes, then, guns are represented as a necessary form of self-defense. Although they still largely reinforce white male power and the capacity of white male bodies to serve as a "metonymic substitute for the law" (Kelly 2020, 26), they're utilitarian, not glorified, and they are distributed among survivors in a recognition that humanity is worth protecting. But as the seasons progress and the threats to the survivors come as frequently from other humans as the zombies, the pro-gun message becomes sharper.

In season 2, episode 4, "Cherokee Rose," airing on November 6, 2011 (in the middle of the gun control debates following the attack on Giffords), Shane, as part of his shooting lesson, tells Andrea (Laurie Holden) that she has to "use her instinct." When Andrea asks how to do that, Shane tells her to "[t]urn off a switch. The Switch. The one that makes you scared or angry, sympathetic or whatever. You don't think. You just…you act. 'Cause odds are someone else is counting on you. That's your partner, that's your friend. There ain't nothing easy about taking a man's life. No matter how little value it may have. But when you get it done, you have to forget it" (Darabont et al. 2011, 2:4). Shane's justification is telling because it plays on the idea of a white brotherhood ("your partner, your friend") increasingly under attack from those with lives of "little value." This is a direct harbinger of LaPierre's creed that we need good guys with guns to stop bad guys with guns. In Shane's worldview, a view validated by the show, two things are clear: some lives have more value than others, and it's up to the guy with the gun, not the law, to determine that value.

FANS AND THE "RICKTATORSHIP"

Shane's Hobbesian survivalist ethos is often contrasted with the code of Rick, who is thought to exemplify a more balanced or ethical approach to life. In discussing Shane's sacrificing of Otis to the zombies to ensure his own getaway in "18 miles out" (Darabont et al. 2012, 2:10), Keetley notes that Shane is always motivated by survival. "For him, the law of survival pre-exists him. It is a kind of instinctive knowledge rooted not in the mind but in the body, in the organism's habit of living. Indeed, Shane never needs to think about the 'choices' he makes because for him, despite what Rick says, there are rules (not really choices at all), and he knows what they are. They are embodied rules, the rules of nature and of instinct" (Keetley 2014a, 164). Rick kills to protect the group, whereas Shane kills to protect himself. But eventually, Rick succumbs to baser survival instincts, which render considerations for larger group feelings or dynamics costly to the unit, or to those more valued individuals within the group. In fact, it is not until Rick abandons the pretense of democratic values and rules that he assumes full control and gains full respect from his followers.

Vulnerable after the attack on Hershel's farm and angered and upset that Rick has kept the truth about the virus from them, the remaining survivors question his leadership. Quickly and decisively, a harder Rick puts them in their place: "I didn't ask for this. I killed my best friend for you people, for Christ's sake! You saw what he was like. How he pushed me, how he compromised us, how he threatened us . . . He was my friend, but he came after me. My hands are clean." In killing Shane, Rick appears to have absorbed his values and is able to justify his actions because, in endangering them, in Rick's estimation, Shane became a life of "little value." Just as Shane had played dictator to the group before Rick's arrival, Rick asks them to make a choice, leave or follow his way: "You can do better? Let's see how far you get. No takers? Fine. But get one thing straight—you're staying. This isn't a democracy anymore" (Darabont et al. 2012, 2:13).

This episode, "Beside the Dying Fire," airing in March 2012, was the highest-rated episode in the series' history, with nine million viewers. Although popular among a cross-section of ages and groups, at the time of this episode's release, *TWD* ranked as the number one drama series in basic cable history among "adults and men" in all age groups, spanning eighteen to fifty-four (AMC 2012). Several critics and fans attribute the episode's strength to a return to the excitement and "momentum" of "zombie carnage" with fewer "annoying" or "inessential" moments of character development (Cinelinx 2012). In particular, Rick's more aggressive approach seems to have resonated with many viewers. Several fans express relief that Rick has become "the leader he should have been from the start," finally embracing "the no-nonsense leader that this group wants and needs him to be" (Hogan 2012). Another suggests that "[m]aybe we're meant to be troubled by Rick becoming more forceful and controlling (and a bit more Shane-like in his approach), but given the way some of these characters act, I'm all for it. Tell 'em, Rick!" (Goldman 2012).

COMPLEX TV

In his book *Complex TV*, Jason Mittell argues that changes to viewing, production, and distribution practices in American television "blu[r] the experiential borders between watching a program and engaging with its paratexts (Mittell 2015, 7). As I discussed in chapter 3, AMC was a forerunner in cultivating fan engagement for *The Walking Dead* through Story Sync, which allowed spectators to interact in real time with other viewers and producers of the show, and answer quiz questions and offer opinions about the characters' fates. Thanks to Story Sync and other of the serial's paratexts, including the aftershow, *The Talking Dead*—which features the show's stars commenting on the previously aired episode—as well as numerous blogs and wikis devoted to the program, *The Walking Dead* epitomizes Mittell's definition of "complex TV." As Mittell explains, complex television programs are "part of a lived cultural practice, not a static, bounded, and fixed creative work.... To understand television textually, we must look beyond what appears on a single screen to explore the range of sites where such texts are constituted, and serially reconstituted, through practices of cultural engagement" (Mittell 2015, 7). Mittell suggests that while only a minority of a show's fans typically participate in online forums and pursue other intertextual forms of engagement, the behaviors and views of active fans are "indicative of *broader tendencies* among many less participatory television viewers" (2015, 8, my emphasis). The blogs devoted to the guns of *TWD* and comments like those made by fans referenced above suggest that a big part of the show's appeal to viewers lies in its depiction of men who embody the values of hegemonic white masculinity or, in the case of Shane and the new Rick, a brand of toxic masculinity evident in, what the blogosphere aptly calls, the "Ricktatorship" (Hogan 2012). This, Gencarella suggests, represents "ideal masculinity as control of the body and suppression of emotions," resulting in a "fusion of fascism and patriarchy" (Gencarella 2016, 131).

    Rick's incorporation of Shane's hardline, take-no-prisoners approach indicates that there never really was an alternative to the Rick or Shane way. Although Daryl's brand of "hillbilly" grit might have offered a counterpoint to the men, at this early point in the series, he is still too much of a loner and identifies too strongly as an outsider to seek control or to be accepted as a leader. Rick and Shane's former roles as law enforcement officers suggest their fitness for leading the group, as does being "strong, male, heterosexual, and white." In contrast, "other strong leaders (Andrea, Dale, and Glenn) are rendered second-tier contenders because they are not hegemonic white men; they are female, older, and racialized" (Lavin and Lowe 2015, 118).

Mittell suggests that the pilot episode of any television serial is crucial to the direction the narrative will take and the meanings it wants to convey. Specifically, pilots play a pivotal role in "teaching viewers how to watch the ongoing narrative, and [in] inspiring them to commit to ongoing serialized consumption" (Mittell 2015, 13). As discussed in chapter 3, the pilot of *The Walking Dead*, "Days Gone Bye," lays out a discourse of "us" and "them" and sets the parameters for survival in the zombie apocalypse. At the same time, the pilot establishes a clear demarcation of gender roles, setting up the preapocalyptic white hypermasculine authority that Shane and Rick enjoy. Lamenting that this "chick . . . and every other pair of boobs" will "bitch about global warming" but can't turn off a light switch, Shane comes off as a stereotypical, white working-class southern man who, following the "guy gospel," is comfortable in his sexist essentialist views. Rick, though not as obviously caustic, laughs companionably with Shane and complains that his wife, Lori (the prize over whom the two men will ultimately spar in the postapocalypse), is frustrated with his lack of communication. Instead of assuming the blame for this, Rick views Lori to be at fault: "Lately, whenever I try, everything I say makes her impatient. Like she didn't want to hear it after all. It's like she's pissed at me all the time and I don't know why" (Darabont et al. 2010, 1:1).

Through their pilots, serials "establish intrinsic norms for ongoing narratives" (Mittell 2015, 13). Most of the action of *TWD*'s pilot occurs in the postapocalypse, and Lori's reliance on Shane in Rick's absence and Carol's abuse by her violent husband reinforce conservative gender roles of weak women and strong, aggressive men. As Dustin Dunaway makes clear, the gendered behaviors of characters in the early season imply that "the apocalypse *necessitates* a return to the 'natural order of things' where traits men already have are most valued" (Dunaway 2018, 12). That the sexist exchange between Shane and Rick occurs in a flashback prior to the zombie event indicates that what the pilot is "teaching" us is the durability of patriarchy in the world of *TWD*. In this way, the show wipes out "all the social progress that the authors see as 'superfluous' in favor of a 'hard reboot' of society" (Dunaway 2018, 12). And it is in this white hypermasculine, southern lawman setting that the series frames its representations of guns, gun violence, and race.

POSTAPOCALYPTIC PREPPERS

Casey Ryan Kelly has argued that "theatric performances of masculinity in popular culture have intensified the crisis motif to cultivate anticipation of an apocalyptic event that promises a final resolution to white male alienation." Troublingly, this kind of "apocalyptic paranoia has contributed to a surge in hypermasculine mass violence in American culture . . . where feelings of male alienation translate into militaristic preparations for an uncertain future" (Kelly 2016, 96). In other words, representations of white male alienation on TV not only mirror feelings of alienation and fear of "demographic replacement" by minority groups and emasculation by feminist women, but they actively produce that alienation and response to it in the culture. In the real world, those who hold survivalist views, so-called Doomsday Preppers, believe in self-sufficiency through the stockpiling of weapons and the hoarding of food and other supplies for a global catastrophe, whether nuclear, viral, or religious (holy war).

In his essay, "Obamageddon: Fear, the Far Right, and the Rise of 'Doomsday' Prepping in Obama's America," Michael F. Mills explains that preppers plan for catastrophes of medium- and long-term duration and for those that might result in "violent social breakdown." Preppers identify and organize around the maintenance of "six core needs: nutrition, hydration, shelter, security, hygiene, and medicine" (Mills 2019, 336). Although they were "non-existent leading up to 2008," in the period of 2009–2014 (during Obama's presidency), events and trade shows featuring preppers and prepper products drew visitors in the thousands. Central to the need for such preparation is the belief that the government cannot save us, and it will fall to individuals to protect themselves in the face of an apocalypse. The "strong links between prepping, religious fundamentalism and the far right" and the perception that Democratic leadership makes us more vulnerable to attack explain the rise in survivalist culture during Clinton's and then Obama's presidency (Wilson 2016).

Survivalism has long been linked to extremist culture and anti-government sentiment. The 1990s alone saw several high-profile stand-offs between the FBI or US Marshals involving firearms, including the shoot-out between the white supremacist Randy Weaver and the FBI at Ruby Ridge (1992), the Waco siege (1993), and the bombing of a federal building in Oklahoma City by anti-government terrorist Timothy McVeigh (1995). During Obama's tenure, conspiracy theories flourished that "explained mass shootings as pseudo-events manufactured by the Obama administration and the liberal media to justify disarming the public" (Kelly 2016, 110). In January 2017, just before Trump's inauguration, a survivalist website called concernedpatriot.com (with the tagline "Prepare Now, Survive Later") warned that Trump would not be able to undo the damage Obama had inflicted on the country. Such acts included his purported growing of the "surveillance state" and his intent to "destroy every prepper's hard work" by mobilizing "government agencies to seize American property in an emergency" (Campbell 2017).

In 2015, a military exercise called the Jade Helm 15 gave rise to suspicions in certain quarters that Obama was organizing a military takeover of Texas and other states. Conspiracy theories included the belief that the Federal Government intended to impose martial law in Texas and confiscate civilian firearms and that local Walmarts were going to be used for guerilla training centers and be subsequently set up as FEMA internment camps for political resisters. According to polls taken at the time, half of those identifying as Tea Party supporters believed that a military takeover of Texas was imminent. Texas Governor Abbot threw his support behind the alarmist fringe theory when he mobilized the Texas National Guard to oversee the federal operations, asserting that it was "important that Texans know their safety, constitutional rights, private property rights and civil liberties will not be infringed" (Goodwyn 2015; Fernandez 2015).

Experts say that the number of people identifying as preppers and the number of prepper businesses have diminished since Trump's election because "Trump relieves many of the worst fears of his voters, including conservative preppers" (Brueck 2019). What exactly those fears are and how they are thought to be relieved by Trump bears further investigation, but it becomes increasingly clear that the rhetoric supporting the protection of Second Amendment rights is frequently couched in terms of white identity politics; there is an obvious correlation between the belief that Democrats want to take away "our guns" and the perception that white identity needs to be defended in ways that it hadn't previously. Indeed, survivalism's late twentieth-century growth was tied to a broader expansion of American extremist movements. These included the "Posse Comitatus, the Ku Klux Klan, Christian Identity, and numerous militia groups, each organized around mixtures of overt white supremacism, hostility towards government, and theological views of America as a sacred Christian nation" (Mills 2019, 4).

Because "prepping is tied to time-honored American traditions of individualism and self-reliance" (Brueck 2019) and because it is largely a movement of the far right, it is instructive to examine how preppers and their culture are endorsed and made legible and sensible in the narrative of *The Walking Dead* and, further, how the show links survivalist instincts/behavior with an "us" and "them" narrative that is frequently racialized. The Second Amendment has historically represented the rights of white Americans over Black. It endowed white landowners with the power to form militias, and it facilitated and legitimated attacks on African Americans in the South by the KKK (Winkler 2011). As Chauncey DeVega makes clear, "Racism, guns, aggrieved masculinity, and a love of violence and militarism are not peripheral to movement conservatism, they are central to it" (DeVega 2015). Because "[z]ombification schematizes and renders livable . . . a particular sort of enemy, an unrecognizable, killable other," it is worthwhile to examine how *TWD* embeds its pro-gun white survivalist ethos within the zombie narrative. Scenes of violence between a clearly defined "us" and "them" reaffirm "disparate social realities" and offer a "convenient and durable symbol that stirs middle-class social anxieties" (Linneman 2014, 510, 508).

ZOMBIES, GUNS, AND WHITE SUPREMACY

Steven Pokornowski suggests that in zombie fictions, the "sleight of hand provided by monstrosity" utilizes the ubiquity and visibility of racialized violence while obscuring its racial dimension. In doing so, it "normalizes racial violence . . . in an effort to maintain or restore humanity, civilization, or some other grandiose analog for a white supremacist status quo" (Pokornowski 2016, 2). While violence against the zombie provides cover for racial violence, it is critical to note how frequently racism in *The Walking Dead* is not obscured but is instead given voice and validated. Postapocalyptic survival is represented in the context of white supremacy and Second Amendment freedoms in ways that link survival to a white working-class aesthetic, one where racial hatred is, if not explicitly endorsed, voiced and justified in the context of the survival event.

In the early seasons, the metaphorical substitution of the zombie for "racial Other" is repeatedly reversed so that *living* non-white humans, typically African Americans, occupy the structural place of the zombie. This reversal results in obvious and egregious expressions of racial hatred and violence, frequently sanctioned or given cover not by zombie aggression but by white redneck rhetoric or by a law-and-order script mandated by white hegemonic masculinity. Black lives are expendable to and work in the service of white masculine empowerment and advancement. Alexander Weheliye's concepts of "habeas viscus" and racializing assemblages provide a useful lens to examine how racial violence in the show is justified through the structural substitution of people of color for zombies. Weheliye is critical of the discourses of biopolitics and bare life because "neither sufficiently addresses how deeply anchored racialization is in the somatic field of the human" and assumes an a priori pre-racialized subjectivity unstructured by race or racism (Weheliye 2014, 4). In chapter 1, I argued that the zombies occupy the category of bare life in *TWD*; here, I consider how human lives in *The Walking Dead*, subject to the sociopolitical processes of racializing assemblages even in the postapocalypse, occupy the disciplinary subject positions of "full humans, not-quite-humans, and nonhumans" (Weheliye 2014, 4).

The possession and handling of guns serve a crucial function in setting the humans (white men) apart from the not-quite-humans and nonhumans (categories variously occupied by white women and people of color) in the show. In the hands of white men, "guns are virtually synonymous with power and authority, law and order, freedom and liberty" (Kelly 2020, 112), whereas Black men with guns are either overtly aggressive, mentally unstable, or just incompetent. While everyone uses guns in *TWD*, the series links a specific kind of responsible gun ownership to white male bodies and frequently represents gun use by African Americans as dangerous or inept. Guns are a natural extension of white male power and are necessary tools in restoring order from chaos, a chaos where white bodies are displaced and disenfranchised; armed Black bodies, by contrast, represent a threat to that restoration. Guns are the rightful expression of white power in the show, whereas swords, batons, and tigers provide a more anodyne, though in effect no less violent, means of defense for Black people.

"DADDY, I GOT THIS SUMBITCH! I'M GONNA SMACK HIM DEAD!"

How guns and gun violence and their relation to figurations of whiteness and Blackness will play out in the first several seasons of the show is apparent from the pilot episode, "Days Gone Bye," when a young Black boy, Duane, Morgan's son (Adrian Kali Turner), sneaks up behind our dazed white hero, Rick, and smacks him in the face with a shovel, yelling proudly to his father, "Daddy I got this sumbitch! I'm gonna smack him dead!" The reverse-shot reveals Morgan (Lennie James), an African American man, walking up to a zombie, shooting it in the head, and then pointing the same gun at a prone Rick, threatening to kill him if he doesn't tell him how he got his wounds. The scene cuts to Rick with his hands and feet tied to the posts of a bed with Duane standing guard close by with a baseball bat. Having tended to Rick's wounds, Morgan further interrogates Rick. Holding a hunting knife close to his face, Morgan tells Rick to "take a moment, look how sharp it is." Then pushing the knife close to Rick's eye, he says, "You try anything, I will kill you with it and don't you think I won't" (Darabont et al. 2010, 1:1). Narratively, Morgan and Duane's actions make perfect sense. Duane first assumes Rick is a zombie, and Morgan needs to verify that his wound is not a bite; however, the visual grammar of the scene reinforces a trenchant racial dynamic where, unprovoked, Black men and children attack innocent white people, thus encouraging sympathy for Rick, leveraging his

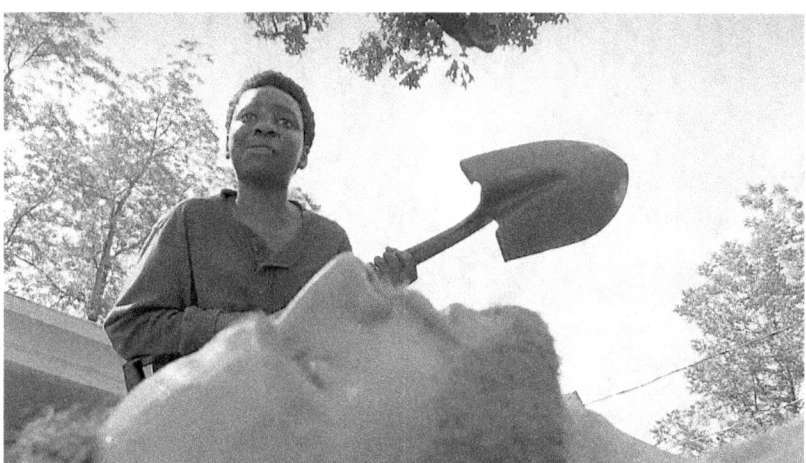

Assuming Rick is a zombie, Duane strikes him with a shovel. (*The Walking Dead*, "Days Gone Bye," season 1, episode 1, 2010)

safety over the safety of Duane and Morgan. Furthermore, when Rick gets up, he observes that he's in the house of "Fred and Cindy Drake," making it apparent that Morgan and Duane are squatting there and are offering no explanation for the Drakes' whereabouts.

In the first episode, then, guns are used by good white guys (cops), bad white guys (the "rednecks" that shot Rick and put him in the coma), and Morgan. Morgan's discharging of his firearm seems warranted, especially as the zombie was headed straight toward his son, but Morgan tells Rick later, "I never should have fired that gun today. Sounds draws them. Now they're all over the street. Stupid—using a gun." Not only is Morgan portrayed as inept, in Rick's eyes he's a killer: "[Y]ou shot that man today. You shot him in the street out front—a man." After Morgan explains how the virus is transmitted, he asks Rick how he got shot. "My boy says you're a bank robber." Rick replies, "Yeah. That's me. The deadliest Dillinger. Kapow." Morgan chuckles and then Rick admits he's a sheriff's deputy, to which Morgan guardedly responds, "Uh-uh" (Darabont et al. 2010, 1:1). Regardless of his circumstances and dress, Rick's authority and lawfulness are embodied by his whiteness, and Morgan's lack of judgment in relation to the gun and his distrust of Rick is tied to his Blackness.

At the sheriff station's armory, Rick retrieves his uniform and his guns and, with them, his formal authority. When Duane asks if he can learn to shoot, Rick tells him, "It's not a toy. You pull the trigger you have to mean it." Similarly, Rick hands Morgan what he considers to be a suitable weapon for his skill. "Take that one. It's nothing fancy. The scope's accurate," he says, then reminds him to conserve his ammo because "it goes faster than you think." Of his undead wife, Morgan acknowledges that he "should have put her down" but he "didn't

Rick reunited with his uniform and guns embodies white male authority and power. (*The Walking Dead*, "Days Gone Bye," season 1, episode 1, 2010)

have it in [him]." And even after he receives a rifle from Rick and goes home with the express purpose of shooting her, he cannot. Rick, by contrast, now reinforced with his uniform and sidearm, shows no hesitation in shooting a former colleague point blank in the forehead and returns to the encounter with the half-body zombie in the park, saying, "I'm sorry this happened to you" before swiftly shooting her in the head (Darabont et al. 2010, 1:1). Where Morgan vacillates and shows weakness, Rick is resolute.

By season 3, however, Morgan has become a hardened killer. Having lost his son to an attack by his undead wife, Morgan has booby-trapped the town square and is holed up, sniper-style, on the roof of a building. Unaware of the gunman's identity, Rick, Carl, and Michonne refuse to relinquish their weapons and engage in a shoot-out with Morgan, who, protected by body armor, is shot by Carl. When Rick realizes who Morgan is, he insists they get him off the street. They carry Morgan back to his house, now a house of horrors booby-trapped with bombs, bloody axes, and trip wire. On the walls are scrawled messages and other rantings of a deranged mind. Inside, they find an arsenal of weaponry, including shotguns, grenades, and various forms of artillery. Although Michonne wants to take the guns and leave, Rick insists on staying and ties Morgan to the bed, as he himself had been tied by Morgan. When Morgan wakes, he attacks Rick, who screams at him, "You know me," over and over. Morgan wrestles Rick to the ground, brandishing a knife, yelling, "I don't know anyone anymore!" and then stabs Rick in the shoulder. Rick, furious, throws Morgan off him and pulls his revolver, saying, "You crazy son of a bitch." When Morgan pulls the gun toward him, begging, "Please. Please kill me," Rick backs off (Darabont et al. 2013, 3:12).

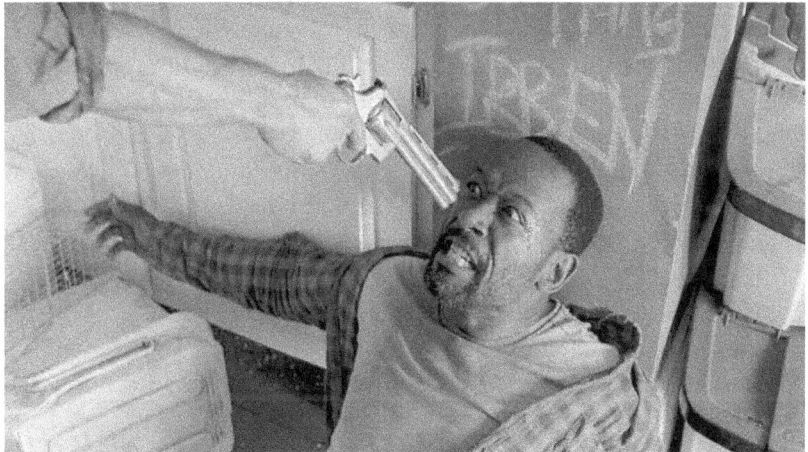

A deranged Morgan stockpiles weapons and begs Rick to kill him. (*The Walking Dead*, "Clear," season 3, episode 12, 2013)

Because guns are a metonym for white male authority and power, Morgan falls short. As Kelly makes clear, "The gun functions metonymically, and thus can be read as a stand-in for white identity without ever having to reference whiteness or maleness as the key identity categories that are actually at stake" (Kelly 2020, 111). Recounting his failure to kill his wife—"You tried to get me to do it 'cause I was supposed to do it. I was supposed to kill her, my Jenny. Knew I was supposed to, but I let it go. Let it go like there wasn't gonna be a reckoning . . . I was supposed to; I was selfish. I was weak. You gave me the gun" (Darabont et al. 2013, 3:12)—Morgan establishes Rick's authority, which doesn't stem from his background in law enforcement but seems to reside in a more existential dimension. As he tells Rick, "People like you, the good people, they always die. The bad people die, too. But the weak people, the people like me, we have inherited the earth." At first, Rick tries to rehabilitate Morgan by saying, "You can come back with us, you can heal," trying to see the humanity in Morgan, despite his mania. "We both started out in the same place. Things went bad for you, things went bad for me. But you're not seeing things right. . . . but you can come back from this, I know you can. You have to. This can't be it. It can't be. You've got to be able to come back from this." However, Morgan reverts back to his madness: "No! I have to clear. That's why I didn't die today. I have to man, I have to. I have to clear." Rick looks at Morgan as if he finally understands that he's lost, takes Morgan's guns, and walks away. When Michonne asks Rick if Morgan is okay, Rick says, "No, he's not" (Darabont et al. 2013, 3:12).

In relation to guns, Morgan is viewed as unhinged and mentally ill—as not being able to handle the trauma that the apocalypse brings. Although Morgan's kills are no less violent or gruesome than Rick's or Daryl's, theirs are represented as mostly dispassionate or utilitarian, whereas Morgan's are frantic and disturbed. Though by this point, Rick has lost his wife and Darryl has lost his brother, Morgan cannot recover from the death of his wife; where white men are strong enough to kill their undead loved ones (nine-year-old Carl killed his postpartum mother, after all), Morgan is too weak. Now he is forced to "clear"—trap the zombies and burn them so they can't kill again. In a culture of "kill or be killed," Morgan's need to kill and clear is seen as aberrant, further reinforcing his unsuitability for the real job undertaken by white men (and boys) of eliminating the actual threats to their survival.

"Clear" aired in March 2013, three months after the Sandy Hook shooting. In January 2013, Dianne Feinstein, Democratic Senator from California and author of the 1994 Assault Weapons Ban that expired in 2004, introduced into the US Senate a bill that would ban assault weapons of the kind that Lanza used in Sandy Hook. In addition, it banned the sale, transfer, importation, or manufacture of about 150 named firearms, large-capacity magazines, and high-capacity ammunition magazines (defined as those capable of holding more than ten rounds) (*USA Today* 2013). The Assault Weapons Ban was defeated in the Senate 40–60 in April 2013. In comparing Rick's responsible gun use with Morgan's, "Clear" underscores the popular mantra of gun enthusiasts everywhere: "Guns don't kill people; people kill people." Even though most mass shooters are white, the episode reinforces the sense that guns in the right (white) hands protect and save, and only in the wrong (Black) hands do they maim and kill.

WOMEN AND CHILDREN

While the white women on the show all shoot guns and participate in the greater defense of the group, their authority and standing, at least in the first several seasons, are always second to the male leadership, particularly that of Rick and Daryl. And in later seasons, white women serve to reinforce the inevitability of white masculine authority "by adopting the militarism and mannerism of the soldier male" (Gencarella 2016, 134). Even the all-woman community of Oceanside—which, after most of its members were brutally murdered, has survived by killing strangers on sight—has its guns stolen by Rick when the women won't help him fight Negan and the Saviors.

White masculine authority extends to the preteenage Carl (Chandler Riggs) as well. Not only does he defy his father's orders to stay away, but he also saves them by shooting Morgan. Earlier in the same episode, Carl questions Rick about why, on this scouting trip for weapons, he brought along Michonne, whom nobody trusts because she can defend herself and doesn't defer to anyone, especially the white men in the group. Rick makes clear that she's useful to them "just for right now" because of their "common interests" (Darabont et al. 2013, 3:12). As Rick's son, Carl seamlessly assumes the mantle that white male authority gives him. On their way out of town, he stops to apologize to Morgan for shooting him, to which Morgan says, "Don't ever be sorry," and when Rick asks Carl how it went with Michonne, Carl determines that "she might be one of us," effectively ensuring her place in the group (at least until the next episode, where she is bartered by Rick to save his people from The Governor). By the end of the season, however, Carl has killed a man who was surrendering and is critical of his father's perceived weakness: "You didn't kill Andrew and he came back and killed Mom. You were in a room with The Governor, and you let him go. And then he killed Merle. I did what I had to do. Now go, so he doesn't kill any more of us" (Darabont et al. 2013, 3:16).

WHITE RACISTS, COLORBLIND DISCOURSE, AND *TWD* FANDOM

Although there is considerable overlap between *The Walking Dead* comic book and the television series, there are notable differences, including the addition of the Dixon brothers: Daryl, the working-class loner and Merle, the southern racist. Comic creator Robert Kirkman and the TV series' developer and initial showrunner Frank Darabont created Merle Dixon, the bigoted misogynist "redneck," as a foil for the upstanding lawman Rick Grimes. Apparently, the character of Daryl, Merle's younger brother, was created after Norman Reedus impressed the show's producers when reading for the role of Merle. Although Merle only appeared in two episodes of the first season and received negative reviews from critics, he was popular with viewers. Appearing briefly in season 2, Merle reappeared as a regular in season 3 after fans clamored for his return. Michael Rooker, the actor who plays Merle, was himself surprised by his character's popularity: "*Nobody* expected this level of Merle worship. He's such an out-there, crazy, anything goes kind of guy" (Karlin 2011a). What Rooker doesn't say is that Merle's appeal is surprising because he is an overt racist who throws the N-word around with impunity. In other words, Merle isn't supposed to be likable, and yet he seems to have struck a chord with fans of *The Walking Dead*.

There is no question that the introduction of the Dixon brothers to the television series is the single most significant change from Kirkman's comic, and most *Walking Dead* fans consider their inclusion to be an improvement. The fans' unproblematic embracing of Merle is an example of how "fandom communities actively cite, circulate and produce discourses that sustain structural antagonisms," particularly "antiblack racial antagonisms" (Johnson 2015, 260). The Dixons appear in every ranked list of fan-favorite characters, with Daryl routinely earning the top spot. It's worth investigating what the addition of the Dixon duo to the story world of *TWD* reveals about the producers' perception of what would resonate with audiences in middle America and what the Dixons' popularity with fans, as well as the popularity of the show itself, tells us about the viewing tastes of the country in 2010. It's also interesting to note that while the show's creatives were eager to add the white "rednecks," they significantly altered and reduced the storylines and characterizations of many of the comic book's Black characters, including Michonne and T-Dog. Numerous fans of the comic were disappointed in the early portrayal of Michonne, for example, seeing in her onscreen representation a reduction of her complex character to a version of the recalcitrant, angry Black woman, who is "mysterious, violently angry, vengeful, silent to a fault, disloyal, and not to be trusted" (Johnson 2015, 271).

We are first introduced to Merle in the second episode of season 1, "Guts." Having left Morgan and Duane, Rick sets out to find Lori and Carl, his wife and son, but is overwhelmed by zombies in Atlanta. He is saved by Glenn, who is Korean American, and his group, comprising an African American man and woman (T-Dog and Jacquie), a Mexican American man (Morales), a white American woman (Andrea), and a white American man (Merle). Even though Rick admits he doesn't understand anything about the zombies, it doesn't take long for him to assert control over the group. In his sheriff's uniform and his white skin, Rick appears to be the logical choice to lead them. Upset that Merle, who is shooting zombies sniper-style from the roof of their hideout, is putting them at risk, the group attempts to stop him. Morales (Juan Pareja)

Merle displays hypermasculine strength and aggression towards the non-white members of his group, and is eventually subdued by another white man, Rick. (*The Walking Dead*, "Guts," season 1, episode 2, 2010)

and T-Dog (IronE Singleton) rush Merle, and T-Dog tells him to "chill" and to stop "wasting bullets we ain't even got." Incensed, Merle retorts, "Bad enough I've got this taco-bender on my ass all day. Now I'm going to take orders from you? I don't think so, bro. That'll be the day." When T-Dog pushes back at Merle, Morales tells him to "leave it. It ain't worth it." And Merle retorts: "You want to know the day? I'll tell you the day, Mr. 'Yo.' It's the day I take orders from a n----r" (Darabont et al. 2010, 1:2). When T-Dog attempts to strike him, Merle fights T-Dog and everyone else who tries to restrain him.

While Merle certainly acts like the foil to Rick that the producers intended, to viewers not used to this level of racist invective in prime time, Merle's vitriol is shocking. In his display of hypermasculine strength, initially overpowering

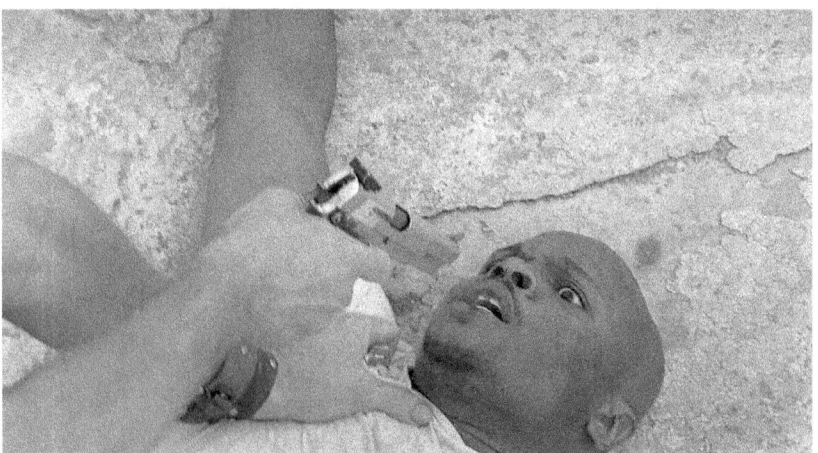

Merle verbally and physically attacks T-Dog and threatens to shoot him. (*The Walking Dead*, "Guts," season 1, episode 2, 2010)

everyone, including rule-follower Rick, Merle reestablishes a more traditional form of white masculinity and reifies dominant forms of patriarchal hegemony. It's clear from the way Rick intervenes and subdues Merle, even calling him "dumb-as-shit, inbred white-trash" that the show is cautious not to endorse Merle's views, but it's telling that in a world where humans are fighting for survival, where the salient binary is the living and the dead, the show chooses to foreground the divisive politics of its own age. As Johnson argues, "Instead of imagining worlds that are perhaps more inclusive of non-white subjects," *TWD* invites us "to desire, participate in the creation, and sustain the fantasy of white heterosexual normativity and cisgender male dominance as the optimal formation of humanity worth saving" (2015, 261).

This strategy of invoking and then renouncing white supremacist views enables *TWD* to align the plight of white working-class masculinity with an apocalyptic narrative of the end of days and to demonstrate the perceived irrelevance of identity claims in the new world order. As Michael Wayne has argued in another context, "the presence of prejudice alongside tolerance promotes the belief that race is no longer relevant while simultaneously turning racism into a transgressive pleasure" (Wayne 2014, 207). Merle epitomizes the doubleness of the racial message in the "Imperiled Whiteness" programming cycle. In his vocalization of overt, blatant prejudice, the show endorses colorblind discourse by attributing "real" racism to individuals and minimizing or ignoring the pervasiveness of structural racism. Expressions of racism in *TWD* (and, as C. Richard King argues, in other shows, including *Oz* and *Sons of Anarchy*) reassure viewers that "white racism where it exists is extreme, excessive, and marginal; white racists dwell elsewhere; white racists and, hence, white racism are bad" (King 2014, 219).

Because zombie narratives operate as expressions of cultural fear and anxiety, by showcasing "marginalized" whiteness in this context, *TWD* subtly points to and stokes extant fears about race and the dissolution of whiteness and tacitly legitimates hate speech and violence against people of color. Even though Morales, Glenn, Jacquie, and Andrea attempt to intervene in the struggle between Merle and T-Dog, they are rendered impotent in the face of Merle's powerful aggression. The close-up of T-Dog prone on the ground as Merle's white hands shove the pistol to his mouth foreshadows the many images that would populate our TV screens in the coming years of Black men victimized and murdered by white police officers. In representing a white hypermasculine subject overpowering and subduing a large, aggressive Black antagonist and then being schooled for his racism by a white cop, the show begins what will become a repeated formula—representing racial conflict not as a structural problem rooted in history but as an individual failing, a question of prejudice, not power. The racial slur Rick levels at Merle, "dumb as shit inbred white trash," is meant to carry the same weight as the racial slurs Merle directs to T-Dog and Morales. Later in the episode, Merle justifies his actions to T-Dog, saying, "It's just that your kind and my kind ain't meant to mix. That's all. It don't mean we can't work together" (Darabont et al. 2010, 1:2). As early as the second episode, then, *TWD* foregrounds race and pits the claims of disenfranchised ("hillbilly"/"redneck"/"white trash") whites against those of other minorities.

A number of critics have analyzed the race and gender politics in *The Walking Dead*. Many argue that it has developed from a hypermasculine fantasy where "white men kill off mostly white men in a sort of white male survivalist fantasy" (Turner and Perks 2019, 668) to a quasi-feminist portrayal of resilient female characters—Carol, Maggie, and Michonne, who occupy leadership roles and command respect. In its twelve-year run, the series has developed strong and compelling storylines for a number of Black characters: Morgan, Tyreese, Ezekiel, Sasha, and, of course, the katana-brandishing Michonne. But as a blogger at "Nerds of Color" points out, the show has, with the exception of Michonne, a "one Black character at a time" problem (Jenn 2013). Others have argued that T-Dog, Morgan, and Tyreese function as "Magical Negroes" supporting and extending the power of the white protagonists' quests (Jionde 2018). Following this line of argument, I would suggest the proliferation of characters of color provides a kind of "postracial cover," offering a visual display of difference without engaging in substantive ways with the lived experiences of people of color. King observes in his essay "Watching TV with White Supremacists," that "it is precisely the predominance of post-racial framings, typified by the ideology of colorblindness, that anchors resurgent formulations of white supremacy today, energizing their interpretations of television" (King 2014, 233). As the interests and objectives of the group are framed through the white lens of Rick and Shane and, later, Rick and Daryl, characters of color are either explicitly singled out in a negative way because of their race or entirely subsumed within and whitewashed by the show's colorblind discourse.

PERFORMING WHITENESS IN THE POSTMASCULINIST POSTAPOCALYPSE

Critics such as Michael Wayne and Geraldine Harris have argued that the cultural return to hegemonic masculinity previously perceived to be decentered and denaturalized by feminist and racial minorities is at the heart of shows like *The Sopranos, Deadwood, Sons of Anarchy,* and *The Shield* (Wayne 2014a, 2014b; Harris 2012). This kind of gender representation has been variously described by critics as hyperreal, postmasculinist, and anti-heroic. However, it's no longer just women that this new (old) male subject is set against, but rather alternate forms of masculinity embodied in non-white male bodies. According to the narrative, white men, particularly white working-class men, are left behind by diversity initiatives supporting minorities. This script was deployed effectively by Trump and his team in his 2016 campaign. "Trump's dark portraiture of contemporary American life signals to white men that the apocalypse is nigh: the country has been overrun by nonwhites and foreign enemies, violence and persecution define everyday life, the press and the 'deep state' have overthrown legitimate government, language, religion, and culture have become subject to the whims of tyrannical leftists" (Kelly 2020, 27). Accordingly, this reclamation of white masculinity sanctions a return to and expression of xenophobia and racism, now justified as an expression of white ethnic pride.

The reassertion of hegemonic white masculinity plays out in interesting ways in *The Walking Dead*. Many critics have examined Rick's role as "protector and progenitor" whose deputy sheriff's uniform legitimizes his leadership and the expectation that he is fair and impartial (Ho 2016). In fact, there are a number of white men who work to reassert hegemonic masculinity in the show as they do in the comics: Shane, The Governor, Negan etc., but the addition of the working-class Dixon brothers and their polarizing views sensationalize and capitalize on the divisions present in the political landscape. Specifically, the inclusion of white masculinity in the figure of the "hillbilly redneck" offers a deliberate counterpoint to the middle-class whiteness represented by Rick and offers a vocal platform to rural whites apparently longing for cultural validation in the age of Obama.

Part of Merle's appeal seems to reside in Michael Rooker himself. One article titled "How one *Walking Dead* Actor's Racist Maniac Makes for Must-See TV" connects Merle's appeal with fans to Rooker's own humble Alabama roots.

> Listen, I'm just a regular guy and I have a slightly different perspective than a lot of actors. I survived pretty poor circumstances. I grew up with eight siblings. Our house in Alabama had an outhouse and a dirt floor. When my folks divorced, our mom moved us to a rough Chicago neighborhood. To come from that, and make a life and a career, is pretty tough and takes a lot of fight. It's made me have to get the job done better than most. And I'm gonna enjoy it better than most. (Karlin 2011b)

When asked by another reporter how he felt about people's perception of Merle as a "racist redneck," Rooker defends his character:

> I never played Merle as a despicable racist guy. I've always played Merle as a straight forward guy living in a zombie f—ing apocalypse. There's no more political correct bulls— out there. It's survival of the fittest, and you better know how to survive in this world. If you don't, you're going to perish, plain and simple. (Abrams 2013)

Here Rooker implicitly ties Merle's behaviors and views to his own modest upbringing and subsequent professional success. In doing so, Rooker rationalizes and justifies Merle's racism as stemming from the exigency of group survival and highlights a key dimension of alt-right ideology—the disenfranchisement of white men by a PC culture that pits the claims of minorities over and above those of whites. Rooker makes clear that treating people as equals isn't central to an ethical moral code but rather is "political correct bullshit" that necessarily gets abandoned when survival is at stake. In the apocalypse, the codes of conduct governing social and race relations are expendable. Rooker's comments go beyond *TWD*, echoing and validating a particular brand of masculinity and white nationalism that was displayed so prominently in Charlottesville in 2017 and the Capitol riots on January 6, 2021. That Rooker is personally identified as an ambassador for this form of straight-talking masculinity is exemplified in his role as spokesman for NASCAR. A representative of NBC who hired Rooker for its promotional ads recognized in him the ability to speak to the "core values" of NASCAR fans. Although Rooker has played many popular roles, the persona of Merle has effectively become an extension of Rooker, enabling and empowering the form of performative whiteness that is central to the "core values" of white nationalist ideologies.

EXPENDABLE BLACK BODIES

The racial politics of the show are particularly apparent in season 3 with the introduction of Michonne (Danai Gurira), who, with her long, bandana-bound dreadlocks, leather vest, katana sword, and chained zombies, resembles an African militant or a Black female stereotype—the castrating woman (Berry 2013). Michonne will become a central member of the series, forming a romantic partnership with Rick and eventually raising his daughter and their son after his death. However, in the early seasons, Michonne is frequently depicted as an outsider, assumed to be untrustworthy and dangerous to the goals of the group. In her analysis of *TWD* fandom, Dominique Johnson remarks that "while a majority of fan content regarding the character recognizes her skill and abilities for survival with enthusiastic positivity, she is routinely regarded as an outsider, perpetually unfeeling or emotionally closed off, which results in a broad lack of empathy from a largely white, male audience" (2015, 261). In chapter 1, I explained how Michonne's distrust of The Governor puts her at odds with Andrea and reinforces the view of her as different and unadaptable. Even though Michonne's sense that the Governor is up to no good is proved right, Michonne is frequently punished for this knowledge, first by The Governor, then by Merle, then by Rick.

In *The Walking Dead* comics, The Governor rapes and tortures Michonne, who, along with other members of the group, has been captured. Kinitra Brooks has argued that Kirkman constructs Michonne through racial and gendered lenses that mark her as "rapeable." "Kirkman lazily relies on the creative myth of the strong black woman to show that Michonne is 'a machine' for whom sympathy and complexity need not exist" (Brooks 2014, 471). The TV series does not reproduce the rape but does include a violent fight between Michonne and The Governor when she finds his fish tank cache of zombie heads and his undead

Merle knocks Michonne out and drags her to the prison cellar. (*The Walking Dead*, "This Sorrowful Life," season 3, episode 15, 2013)

The visual representation of Merle binding Michonne's hands with wire and placing a sack over her head evokes lynching practices. (*The Walking Dead*, "This Sorrowful Life," season 3, episode 15, 2013)

daughter chained in a closet. So incensed is The Governor with Michonne's discovery and her ability to fight (she takes out his eye), he negotiates a truce with Rick on the condition that he relinquish Michonne, who, just the episode before, had been accepted into his group. Rick consults with Hershel and Daryl, and then, presumably because he needs the opinion of another white man, decides to run it by Merle, whose favorite epithet for Michonne is "that Black bitch." Merle tells Rick to restrain Michonne with wire, not rope: "[W]ire. Nothing she could chew through." Fearing that Rick is too weak to go through with the plan, Merle lures Michonne down to the cellar of the prison, knocks her out, ties her up, and hoods her (Darabont et al. 2013, 3:15).

There is a clear and obvious evocation of lynching here, which I would argue the show tries to pass off as "just Merle" and, in this way, justifies and excuses the action while visually engaging in the racial pornography that, just moments before, respectable everyman Rick had himself considered. When Daryl shows frustration at many of the evil deeds Merle performed while in the employ of the Governor, Merle upbraids him. "Your people look at me like I'm the devil . . . now y'all want to do the same damn thing I did. Snatch someone up and deliver them to The Governor. Just like me. People do what they got to do or they die" (Darabont et al. 2013, 3:15). The show tries to mitigate, justify, or excuse Merle's racism, just as Rooker does in the interview above, by suggesting that his motivations don't come from hate but from pragmatism, and that liberals (like Rick and Hershel) are hypocrites who are similarly motivated.

When Rick consults Merle on his plan to kidnap Michonne and deliver her to The Governor, Merle recognizes the true Rick, warning, "You go on give him that girl. He ain't gonna kill her, you know. He's just gonna do things to her, probably take out one of her eyes. Both of 'em most likely." When Merle asks Rick if he'd let that happen and Rick doesn't respond, Merle says, "You're as cold as ice, Officer Friendly" (Darabont et al. 2013, 3:15). Narratively, this is supposed to represent further evidence of Rick's decline after Lori's death. The real Rick, our morally judicious leader, would never consider such a thing. How could Rick be like Merle, we wonder. However, I would argue that Rick's request has the opposite effect. Because it is "reasonable Rick," who voices it, not "maniacal Merle," such a heinous act appears justified. After all, if the deal goes through, "no one else will die." When Rick decides he can't do it after all, it doesn't really matter; in voicing his desire to do it, in airing the possibility of him doing it, the show implicitly evokes the terms of the racial contract as defined by Charles Mills: "the moral and juridical rules normally regulating the behavior of whites in their dealings with one another either do not apply at all in dealings with nonwhites or apply only in a qualified form" (Mills 1997, 11). Black lives are fungible, disposable, ready at hand. It's only the moral restraint of white people that prevents them from being utilized in unethical ways. Even though Rick agrees that Michonne has "earned her place" with them, her life is still expendable, dependent on the whims of white men.

As Lorraine Berry reminds us, the deal between The Governor and Rick, two southern white men, is a historical echo of "white men using an African American woman's body as currency. We did that for 300 years. It was called slavery. Did the writers really want to remind us that, in this world, a Black woman's worth stems from her ability to be currency, something that can be bought or exchanged in order to stop a war?" (Berry 2013). However, as Johnson shows, fan commentary about Michonne disavows these obviously racialized elements. Fans' staunch denial of the racial and sexual politics that animate

Merle kidnaps Michonne to bring her to The Governor. (*The Walking Dead*, "This Sorrowful Life," season 3, episode 15, 2013)

TWD's story world reveals that Michonne's characterization in the TV series "neither disrupts nor challenges the confining archetypal images of black femininity that circulate in a white heteropatriarchal media economy" (Johnson 2015, 262). It is significant that Merle ultimately saves Michonne by letting her escape. By permitting Merle to do what Rick and Hershel (who explicitly states that his white daughters' lives are more important than Michonne's) cannot, *TWD* separates Merle's actions from his statements, thereby depicting his racist vitriol as harmless bluster and painting him as the emblem of a straight-talking, practical, white masculine ideal. This is a clear example of how "racial rhetorics reinvent themselves, taking on novel appearances to communicate seemingly antiquated ideologies" (King 2014, 232).

Season 3 also introduces two new Black characters, Tyreese (Chad Coleman) and his sister Sasha (Sonequa Martin-Green). The siblings, along with three white survivors, enter the prison where Rick's group has taken up residence and ask to join them. "Made to Suffer" opens with Tyreese, who is large and muscular, taking out a walker with an axe. Despite his strength, Tyreese is shown to be tenderhearted, allowing Donna, a white woman in their group, to come into the prison with them even though she has been bitten because her son, Ben, is "not ready" to let her go. It is Tyreese who will later save Rick's baby daughter, Judith, from The Governor's people during the attack on the prison and guard and protect her for weeks until they find Rick again. When Carl locks them in a prison cell to await Rick's return and his decision on the fate of the prisoners, Sasha, angered, begs Carl, "Come on, man. We're not animals." Tyreese, believing that reason will prevail, tells her to "[b]ack away from their door and let the man go." Tyreese tells Hershel that they were able to survive thanks to his neighbor Jerry, who was "one of those survivalist nuts." Although "everybody on the block thought he was crazy" because "he was always preparing for the end of the world . . . Jerry knew! He had a bunker under his shed in the backyard" (Darabont et al. 2012, 3:8).

Tyreese is nothing but calm, grateful, and cognizant of the break they're being given, but Hershel tells him not to "get too comfortable here." When Allen and Ben, Tyreese's white companions, calculate that it would be easy to take down "a little kid, a woman, a girl and a one-legged old man," Tyreese asks them if they are "going to smash the little baby's head with a rock," too, and insists that "this isn't what we do." When Rick returns, Tyreese tells him they will help to forage for food and fight alongside them, "anything to contribute." Rick refuses. Hershel disagrees and tells Rick that "he's got to start giving people a chance." But Rick, traumatized by the reappearance of Lori's ghost, unholsters his gun and starts screaming, "You don't belong here! Get out!" (Darabont et al. 2012, 3:8). Tyreese and his group find their way to Woodbury and are taken in by The Governor and his people. Tyreese and Allen provide The Governor with a layout of the prison, thus helping to precipitate his attack. Later, when Tyreese and Sasha learn the depths of The Governor's depravity, they rejoin the group at the prison and help to defend it against The Governor's assault.

In "Isolation," episode 3 of season 4, long after Tyreese has been accepted back in the fold and has proven himself on many occasions, he discovers that the body of his girlfriend, Karen, and another man, who had contracted a virus from Rick's pigs, have been burned and dragged into the courtyard of the prison so that they won't die undetected and reanimate. Visibly angered, Tyreese asks Rick to investigate. Rather than acknowledge that Tyreese is justified in his anger (when did they start burning the living?), Rick suggests that he is becoming deranged, just as Rick had been when Lori died: "I know what you're feeling. I've been there. You saw me there. It's dangerous." Daryl (Norman Reedus), apparently fearful for Rick's safety, pulls Tyreese away, causing him to lash out at Daryl. Holding Daryl by the neck and shoving him roughly against the gate, the reverse shot frames an angry, panting Tyrese in close-up through the prison bars. When Rick tells him to calm down because "we've all lost someone," Tyreese punches Rick twice. Rick, incensed, flattens the much larger Tyreese with one punch and then kicks him in the gut, pummeling him with his fist over and over as Daryl tries to stop him (Darabont et al. 2013, 4:3).

As Tyreese lies broken and sobbing on the ground, the camera pans to Rick's bloody fist. Because Rick later expresses remorse for what he's done and Tyreese accepts Rick's apology, saying, "It's on both of us," we could interpret this as one more episode in Rick's "post-Lori death" mania. Nevertheless, the scene provides a visually egregious example of the way Black bodies function in relation to white bodies in the show's political landscape. Although Rick's

Angered by the murder of his girlfriend, Tyreese shoves Daryl against the prison gate. (*The Walking Dead*, "Isolation," season 4, episode 3, 2013)

Tyreese is criminalized by the camera's framing of him behind prison bars. (*The Walking Dead*, "Isolation," season 4, episode 3, 2013)

actions are hyperaggressive, both Carol and Daryl's efforts to stop Tyreese from attacking Rick assume viewer alignment with the white characters and imply that Rick's response to Tyreese's actions is both understandable and inevitable. Further, Tyreese's framing through the prison bars and his rough handling of Daryl reinforces a white perspective of Black men as violent and criminal. Aggressive Black men, whether justified in that aggression or not, must be subdued unless they are working in the service of the "man."

Tyreese was not the first member of the in-group to challenge Rick's authority, but he was the first one to be savagely beaten for it. Even though Rick and Shane expressed substantive differences regarding the group's survival, they

Daryl holds Tyreese as Rick prepares to assault him. (*The Walking Dead*, "Isolation," season 4, episode 3, 2013)

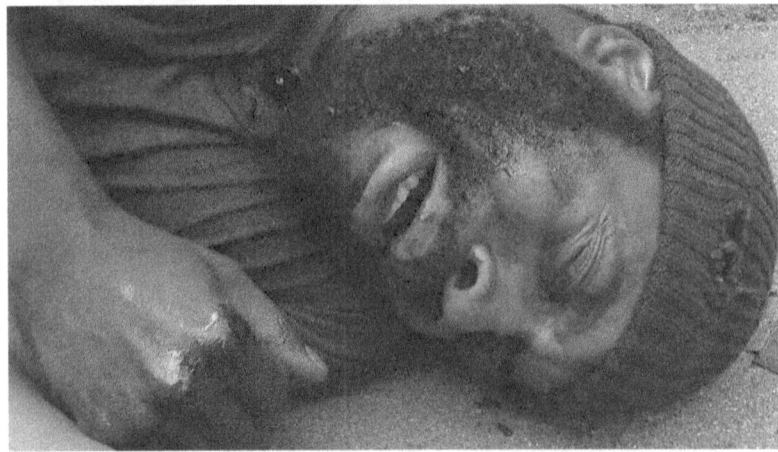

A close-up of Rick's bloody fist is juxtaposed with Tyreese's prone body. (*The Walking Dead*, "Isolation," season 4, episode 3, 2013)

didn't come to blows until the end, and that conflict was motivated by Shane's desire for Lori. Hypermasculine white men like Daryl and Abraham, the former US Army sergeant, both embody and reinforce Rick's authority, whereas Black men like T-Dog and Tyreese, by virtue of their racial outsider status, are viewed as potential threats to white male authority. Although Rick no longer wears his sheriff's uniform, Tyreese's explicit acknowledgment of it ("you're a cop") when he asks Rick to investigate the deaths seems a deliberate attempt on the part of the show to capitalize on, or even sound a dog-whistle to, those on the right for whom violence against people of color is not only justified but glorified. One might, perhaps, read this blatant display as a commentary on the excesses of police violence, but as Gencarella notes, "[T]he cascading glorification of soldier male mentality makes it difficult to accept the series as an admonitory tale against violence and a fractured republic, just as the murderous seriousness of its distinction between friends and enemies makes it difficult not to question its homage to fascism" (Gencarella 2016, 132).

"I'M NOT VERY GOOD WITH GUNS"

Season 5 of *TWD* aired from October 2014 to March 2015, after the August 2014 shooting of Michael Brown and during the ongoing protests over the failure of the grand jury to indict Darren Wilson, the officer who shot and killed Brown. Like season 3, season 5 engages in some problematic race-work, with narratives involving three African American men—Gabriel, Bob, and Morgan. On escaping Terminus, an outpost where the survivors eat the dead, Rick's group encounters Gabriel (Seth Gilliam), an African American preacher who, cowering on a rock, is being attacked by walkers. Rick asks his usual questions of Gabriel while roughly manhandling him: "How many walkers have you killed? How many people have you killed?" Gabriel, with his hands in the air in his preacher's garb, answers, "None, because the Lord abhors violence," making him seem like the antithesis of the image of the violent Black "predator" being mustered by the Wilson defense (Darabont et al. 2014, 5:2). However, rather than the pious man he claims to be, Gabriel is a coward and a liar. We subsequently learn that he barricaded himself inside the church and refused entry to his parishioners, who then faced their deaths outside his walls. Traumatized by this, Gabriel refuses to use a weapon, frequently putting the group in danger. Rick makes it clear that he doesn't trust Gabriel, and this suspicion is frequently borne out, culminating in Gabriel's attempt to betray them when they get to Alexandria. Neglecting to mention his own heinous acts, Gabriel tells Alexandria's leader, Deanna (Tovah Feldshuh), that Rick's group are full of monsters that have done unspeakable things.

In the same season, Bob (Lawrence Gilliard Jr.) gets overpowered by a walker in the food bank; although Sasha saves him, he is bitten on the shoulder. He is then captured by one of the cannibal men from Terminus, who amputates his leg to feed some of his men. Returning to the group, Bob admits that he has been bitten and subsequently dies from the bite. That Bob should suffer such an ignominious ending is hardly surprising. In season 4, his newly found friends learn that he is an alcoholic when he jeopardizes them all on a supply run for meds by knocking over a shelf of alcohol, resulting in one man's death. When set against the masculine stoicism of white Rick, Daryl, and Abraham, Black Gabriel and Bob are not only weak but a liability to the group, constantly threatening its safety by their lack of judgment or duplicity.

In season 5, Morgan returns a changed man, defending himself with only a staff but refusing to kill. In a flashback in season 6, we learn that after Rick left him, Morgan devolved further into madness. Having burned his house to the ground, he retreats to the woods and is rescued by a white man named Eastman (John Carroll Lynch), who inducts Morgan into the spiritual defensive art of Aikido, the goal of which, according to Eastman, is to "completely avoid killing even the most evil person" (Darabont et al. 2015, 6:4). Rehabilitated, Morgan eventually finds his way to Alexandria and becomes part of Rick's group. When the settlement is attacked by a rival group called the Wolves, Morgan refuses to kill them. When he recognizes one of the men as someone who had tried to kill him in a previous episode, he keeps him as a prisoner in an attempt to reason with him. Unlike Gabriel, Morgan is not shown to be weak or afraid. He certainly kills when he must, but unlike the white men of the group, he cannot handle guns and is clearly better suited to the noble warrior ("Magical Negro") duties. As Matthew Hughey argues, racial depictions of this sort "marginalize Black agency, empower normalized and hegemonic forms of whiteness, and glorify powerful Black characters in so long as they are placed in racially subservient positions" (Hughey 2009, 543). This is particularly obvious in Morgan's case. He scolds Carol (Melissa McBride) for slaying a "Wolf," who was trying to attack him: "You don't have to kill people!" "Of course we do," she says. When Morgan chooses to restrain, rather than kill, the Wolf that attacks Father Gabriel, Carol strides over and shoots him in the head. And when Carol, a white woman, gives these two Black men guns from the armory to defend themselves, Morgan hands Gabriel his gun. Gabriel looks at it, saying, "I'm not very good with guns." Morgan agrees, "Me neither" (Darabont et al. 2015, 6:2).

In season 7, the Magical Negro trope is in full force with the introduction of King Ezekiel (Khary Payton), who dresses in kingly robes, holds court in a theater, and is protected by a pet tiger, Shiva. Although Ezekiel has a sword, he seldom needs to use it, as he's surrounded by loyal subjects who not only support his charade but depend upon it. While Ezekiel is their leader, he doesn't display the kind of masculine qualities of hardness, resolve, and sacrifice consistent

"King" Ezekiel exemplifies the "Magical Negro" trope and asserts his authority through performance. (*The Walking Dead*, "The Well," season 7, episode 2, 2016)

in the representation of white hegemonic masculinity. Ezekiel's power is mere performance as Carol notes, "You're a joke. This place is.... You're selling these people a fairytale." Called out, Ezekiel drops his kingly speech and admits to Carol that when people "see a dude with a tiger, they start telling stories about finding it in the wild, wrestling it into submission, turning it into his pet. They make the guy larger than life, a hero. And who am I to burst their bubble? Next thing you know, they treat me like royalty. They wanted.... They *needed* someone to follow, s-so I-I acted the part. And I faked it till I made it" (Darabont et al. 2016, 7:2).

By installing Ezekiel in a leadership role, *TWD* attempts to mitigate the white masculine hegemony it has erected in the previous seven seasons. However, in depicting his leadership as a performance, one that does not follow naturally from innate qualities of strength and good judgment and is bolstered only by its association with the savagery of the jungle, the show promotes the idea that leadership comes naturally to white men, while Black men must act the part. These kinds of representations "subversively reaffirm the racial status quo and relations of domination by echoing the changing and mystified forms of contemporary racism rather than serving as evidence of racial progress or a decline in the significance of race" (Hughey 2009, 543). Where the Black men in the show are shown as crazed, weak, inept, or fake, the primary Black women, Michonne and Sasha, are competent and effective with their weapons. Sasha even makes fun of Tyreese's inability to shoot straight, telling him he needs more practice. When she scoffs that his last shot "wasn't even close," he asks her if she wants to take the shot. She quickly retorts, "I have been" (Darabont et al. 2013, 3:14).

POSTRACIAL POSTURING AND HONORABLE HILLBILLIES

Overall, I would argue that the show is inconsistent in its representation of minority characters. For example, Glenn Rhee, who is Korean American, though initially depicted as an infantilized pizza delivery boy in a costume that made him resemble Indiana Jones's sidekick Short Round, develops into an integral member of the group. He was a loyal husband to Maggie, and his brutal death by baseball bat in the premiere of season 7 shocked and infuriated his many devoted fans. Michonne, when introduced in season 3, appears as an aggressive, distrustful loner but eventually earns the respect of the group. She has a romantic relationship with Rick, becomes a mother to Judith, and, on Rick's death in season 9, becomes the leader of Alexandria. In fact, from seasons 5–9, the show seems to want to have it both ways, appealing to both conservative and liberal viewers alike. However, these seemingly progressive representations of race don't undermine the narrative of disenfranchised whiteness as much as they support it. "Ideologically, the juxtaposition of an anti-hero with postrace signifiers including interracial relationships with the racially marked, marginalized form of white masculinity associated with the label 'white trash' promotes the myth that 'it is only "those people" who are racist' while still allowing for the depiction of unacceptable racist attitudes and behaviour" (Wayne 2014a, 212). Disenfranchised whiteness orders the racial politics of the show and undermines whatever progressive statements on race that the series, in later seasons, might attempt.

Merle's racist, misogynistic neo-Nazi views represent a far-right perspective easily dismissed by critics and some fans as "over the top"; however, Daryl, with his strong "hillbilly" reserve and clearly defined boundaries of right and wrong, "us" and "them," enables Merle's values to be packaged in a more palatable heroic figure, what critics Kom Kunyosying and Carter Soles have called the "Hyperreal Hillbilly." Applying Baudrillard's concept of the hyperreal, they argue that Daryl "function[s] as a manifestation of the sign 'hillbilly' stripped of its vicissitudes, racism, and homophobia" and that the muting of racial tension in Daryl's character "make[s] him a more powerful point of identification within the show" (Kunyosying and Soles 2018, 34). In his discussion of postmasculinist television, Michael Wayne shows how an ambivalent antihero is frequently juxtaposed with a racist redneck. Whereas the ambivalent antihero tacitly reinforces postracial ideology, the racist redneck gives voice to racist views and allows "white audiences to take 'ironic' pleasure in expressions of overt racism" (Wayne 2014a, 205). As Merle's brother, Daryl shares Merle's working-class grit and social marginalization as a result of their poor upbringing; where Merle is loquacious, Daryl is laconic, so we never really know where Daryl's politics lie, but by tying them together through a narrative of childhood abuse at the hands of their alcoholic father, the series links economic class to specific social views. Even though Daryl sometimes calls Merle out for his actions, he does it in private and just as frequently defends Merle to the group.

The show does set up explicit distinctions between Merle and Daryl. An example of this is when the brothers save a Hispanic family from walkers and Daryl threatens to shoot Merle when he tries to rob them, but only after watching Merle rummage through their car. Daryl then turns on the family, yelling at them to leave, as if he blames them for putting him in that position with Merle in the first place. However, there are also numerous occasions when Daryl is implicitly tied to Merle and his racist views. When Merle disappears from the rooftop where Rick has handcuffed him in season 1, Daryl takes Merle's motorcycle. Although no overt comment is made of it in the show, the chopper has the SS Nazi insignia painted on its gas tank. Like his crossbow, the chopper becomes a staple of Daryl's identity—so much so that there is a Funko Pop! of Daryl on his bike, allowing Merle's white nationalist neo-Nazi identity to be absorbed by Daryl, the good brother. In this way, Daryl's character perpetuates and justifies the views of "disenfranchised whites" without explicitly stating them. This strategy, as Wayne makes clear, "provides white audiences with the opportunity to both take pleasure in overt expressions of racial superiority and generally disavow the existence of structural racism" (Wayne 2014a, 207). After all, Daryl's not the racist, Merle is.

Daryl inherits Merle's Chopper with the SS insignia. (*The Walking Dead*)

Daryl's association with his bike is reflected in the Funko Pop! figure of him.

Merle appears to Daryl in a hallucination. (*The Walking Dead*, "Chupacabra," season 2, episode 5, 2011)

In season 2, episode 5, Daryl has distinguished himself from the others in his group by refusing to give up looking for Carol's lost daughter, Sophia. Having fallen down a ravine and been struck by his own arrow, Darryl moves in and out of consciousness. Merle appears to him in a hallucination. "All those years I spent trying to make a man of you. This is what I get? Look at you. Lying in the dirt like a used rubber." Merle accuses Daryl of abandoning him and of being Rick's "bitch." "You're a joke is what you are, playing errand boy to a bunch of pansy-asses, n----rs and Democrats" (Darabont et al. 2011, 2:5). As noted above, Merle's guest appearance in season 2 and his return as a series regular in seasons 3–4 were motivated by fan demand. Obviously, the writers aligned Merle's popularity with his outspoken prejudice and wanted to give the fans more of the same. While Merle still expresses overt racism in this scene, he notably now includes the other whites in Daryl's group, the "pansy asses" and "Democrats." "You're nothing but a freak to them," he sneers. To them, Daryl is "redneck trash," someone to laugh at and make their "bitch."

Dawn Keetley argues that "[t]he Merle whom Daryl conjures up in his fevered state has a deep sense of identity rooted in white, working-class heteronormativity that is most likely supposed to code as Republican and that is expressly *not* Democrat" (Keetley 2014a, 157). Yet, as it is Daryl's hallucination, these sentiments don't belong to Merle; they are Daryl's. Subconsciously, Daryl believes that he'll always be the outsider, that his social status renders him a perpetual freak to the respectable middle-class whiteness embodied by the others in his group. And because audiences are primed to like and respect Daryl, we're more inclined to accept these fears as valid, which further reinforces Daryl's social position—his rugged working-class authenticity over the

Daryl pierces the skull of a recently undead Black zombie. The iconography of the skull pierced by an arrow and suspended in medium close-up evokes colonial imagery of cannibals and savagery and aligns Daryl's battle with the history of white men killing or being killed. (*The Walking Dead*, "Chupacabra," season 2, episode 5, 2011)

others in his group. Considering the stark racial landscape evoked by Merle of "us" and "them," white and Black, Republicans and Democrats, hard men and "pansy-asses," it's no surprise that Daryl musters superhuman strength to extricate the arrow from his side and load his crossbow to kill the Black zombie lumbering toward him. In fact, this zombie is remarkably alive looking, only recently undead. Moreover, the iconography of the skull pierced by an arrow and suspended in medium close-up evokes the colonial imagery of cannibals and savagery and aligns Daryl's battle with the history of white men killing or being killed, thus helping to justify and reinforce Merle's warning to Daryl.

Effectively, then, I would argue that Daryl performs the same function as Merle, first articulating and then redeeming the narrative of working-class whiteness. However, by separating the claims to white masculine identity from the expression of racism and misogyny, the show encourages either an identification with or sympathy for Daryl, and by extension Merle, and suggests that overt racism of the kind expressed by Merle is personal, not structural, and, perhaps more pointedly, that the Dixon brothers' trauma is on par with or exceeds that experienced by minority groups in the US.

"PANSY-ASS" DEMOCRATS

In season 5, Rick's group is invited into the Alexandria Safe-Zone, a walled-off community led by a former Democratic congresswoman, Deanna Monroe

(Tovah Feldshuh). Alexandria, built to be an eco-friendly, sustainable community, is the Democrats' version of Woodbury, or at least a stereotypical representation of how the right-wing media frames Democrats' liberal elitism. Defense and security are not the first priority; rather, community building and quality of life are the group's main goals. As Deanna subjects Rick's group members to an interview, assessing their suitability for the new community, an overt class narrative is introduced. In "Remember" (2015, 5:12), Deanna is shown living the life of privilege she had before the apocalypse and we learn that she and her architecture professor husband were brought to Alexandria for protection by the military. In her opulent surroundings and disdain for guns, Deanna represents the stereotypical privilege of the Washington (left) elite. She has never left her gated community, considers armed watch patrols unnecessary, and refuses to allow members of her group to use their guns inside the walls. However, she recognizes Rick's authority immediately: "I want you to help us survive. I know you can help us do that." When Michonne asks Rick to consider staying, she mentions that Deanna "seems smart." Rick quips, "smart for then or smart for now?" (Darabont et al. 2015, 5:13).

In his hypermasculine presentation, Rick appears to be a better bet than refined Deanna or gay Aaron (Ross Marquand). As relieved as they are to have shelter and food, the group worries that the comfort of Alexandria will make them go soft. As soon as they arrive, there is tension among them about whether staying will make them lose their edge and become weak. They hide weapons outside the community, and Rick and Carl frequently go beyond the walls of Alexandria to maintain their skill in killing walkers. Rick gradually adjusts successfully to Alexandria, installing himself as the community's constable, effectively reestablishing his old life. Daryl, by contrast, is like a caged animal. He refuses to shower or sleep indoors and roves the grounds ever alert to danger. Although food is plentiful, he still hunts and eats whatever animals he can find, skinning and disemboweling them on the porch instead of in the kitchen. Daryl is clearly uncomfortable and out of place in these opulent surroundings, suggesting not that he *won't* adapt but that he *can't*.

The group was recruited to Alexandria by Aaron, a gay man who lives with his partner, Eric (Jordan Woods-Robinson). In "Forget," Aaron befriends Daryl and compares their relative outsiderness, sharing that he and Eric have heard their "fair share of well-meaning but hilariously offensive things from otherwise really nice men and women." Aaron suggests to Daryl that the community is "scared of you and me for different reasons. They're less scared of me because they know me.... So, let them get to know you." Daryl responds, "I got nothing to prove." That Daryl's difference, his class standing, is not at all like Aaron's difference and cannot be overcome in this privileged community is apparent when Aaron asks Daryl to join him and Eric for dinner. Unclean and unkempt,

Daryl slurps his spaghetti and wipes his mouth with his sleeve. Aaron and Eric exchange amused glances, and, as if to demonstrate how far apart the men are, Eric asks Daryl to pick up a pasta maker "if you happen to be in a store or something" on his next scavenging run (Darabont et al. 2015, 5:13).

While Daryl is coarse and completely lacking in social skills, it is Aaron and Eric who come across poorly. In their smug condescension of Daryl, their behavior reifies the belief that (effete) liberals are laughing at white working-class people. Far from the discrimination that minority groups claim to experience, this episode suggests that they are living the good life at the expense of the "rest of us." At the same time, the scene affirms the elevation of the hard, straight masculinity that Daryl and Rick embody, disparaging men like Eric and, by extension, Aaron, who, even in the postapocalypse, are concerned about trivial (stereotypical) things like pasta makers. When Aaron accompanies Daryl to hunt rabbits, they come across a wild stallion. Attempting to tether the horse, Daryl notes, "The longer they're out there, the more they become what they really are." When he gets close to it, he whispers, "You used to be somebody's, huh? Now you're just yours" (Darabont et al. 2015, 5:13). Like the horse, Daryl doesn't want to relinquish the freedom and authority that he enjoys in the wild. He fears being relegated, in Deanna's world, to the limitations of his pre-apocalypse class position. That the horse runs off before Daryl can harness it foreshadows how Daryl will not be tamed or made weak by the soft liberal values of Alexandria. However, the horse is later devoured by walkers and has to be shot by Aaron, reinforcing the dangers of compromising your true self for the false comforts of the elite class.

Airing in March 2015, just three months before Trump announced his presidential campaign, this episode reads like a litmus test of American class politics. Merle was the extreme version of this kind of masculinity, and though he appealed to fans, he was too toxic, too much. Darryl's outsiderness, by contrast, has come to signify insiderness, real American heroism— the kind of working class "real" American that Trump championed and that whites, supposedly left behind by globalization, low-wage immigrant labor, and free trade, responded to. As a journalist noted in 2016:

> These Americans know that they're being left behind, by the economy and by the culture. They sense the indifference or disdain of the winners on the prosperous coasts and in the innovative cities, and it is reciprocated. Trump has seized the Republican nomination by finding scapegoats for the economic hardships and disintegrating lives of working-class whites, while giving these voters a reassuring but false promise of their restoration to the center of American life. (Packer 2016)

Tapping into this resentment and indeed helping to foster it, serials like *TWD* contribute to the narrative of white alienation and Black criminality, pedaled by the Trump campaign, and suggest that real (white) men will rise up and protect "us" whether we want them to or not.

Keetley argues that in seasons 4–8, *TWD* "offers a utopian alternative to a United States that in the late 2010s, is increasingly fractured along the lines of identity politics" (Keetley 2018, 157). Certainly, in season 9, all the families are blended and interracial families become the norm, as previous partners die and orphaned children are absorbed into existing family units. However, I would argue that *TWD* depicts postapocalyptic America as postracial and postfeminist in order to reassert the claims of white masculinity. Portrayals of masculinity in *TWD* engage with and attempt to resolve the disaffection felt by white men in the age of Obama, but the racial politics of the show are clearly bound to its class politics. White working-class masculinity, synonymous as it is with grit, determination, and survival, is the commodity valorized time and again in the series. Of course, representations are always open to contestation, and audiences can respond in diverse ways. Indeed, as Saha argues, "[T]he unpredictability of audience behavior means that cultural production is fundamentally a negotiation with risk and uncertainty, which cultural industries respond to with vertical and horizontal integration, and rationalizing strategies and other forms of 'tight control'" (2018, 75). While the overtly racist statements made by *TWD*'s Merle produce different reactions from liberals and conservatives, his speech clears a space of recognition (Hall) that puts whites in a position to define themselves in relation to Merle, or, as Dominique Johnson demonstrates, in relation to the racial debris circulating around Michonne.

Herman Gray has argued that "[i]n order for television to achieve its work—that is, to make meaning and produce pleasure—it has to draw upon and operate on the basis of a kind of generalized societal common sense about the terms of the society and people's social location in it. The social ground and the cultural terms on which it works depend on assumptions about experience, knowledge, familiarity, and the accessibility of viewers to these assumptions" (Gray 1995, 9). *TWD* effectively utilizes this formula by tapping into social currents of disaffected whiteness and depicting a world where white men regain their so-called lost ground. That the show organizes these hierarchies in the context of a zombie apocalypse is ironic but consistent with postracial posturing. Richard King observes that "characters emblematic of white power not only allow some audience members to indulge in the pleasures of representations that openly speak the language of white supremacy and overtly ties whiteness to (antiquated) vestiges of superiority, but also, for many more viewers, render white racism outdated, antisocial, and disturbing, affirming their enlightenment and taste" (King 2014, 221). The show's social landscape requires a brutal and violent killing of the undead. That this violence sometimes extends to the killing of those who don't conform to or who threaten the hierarchy of dominant white masculinity is revealed as expedient and necessary in the postapocalypse.

Part III
MONSTROSITY

Chapter 6

BIOENGINEERED MONSTERS

In 2016, the year of Trump's election, discrimination and diversity were the buzzwords in Hollywood. For the second year in a row, The Academy of Motion Picture Arts and Sciences had failed to honor actors of color. Of the twenty Oscar nominations for acting, including Best Actor and Actresses in Lead and Supporting Roles, not one person of color was included. This had occurred in previous years when there weren't any viable contenders, but that was not the case in 2016, where there were several potential nominees, including Idris Elba for *Beasts of No Nation*, Benicio del Toro for *Sicario*, Samuel L. Jackson for *The Hateful Eight*, Michael B. Jordan for *Creed*, and Will Smith for *Concussion*. Similarly, the nominees for Best Picture included white leads and predominantly white casts. Neither *Creed*, *Concussion*, nor *Straight Out of Compton* received recognition in the Best Picture category. While *Straight Out of Compton* did receive a nomination for Best Original Screenplay, the writers of the screenplay were all white. The hashtag #OscarsSoWhite (which first appeared in 2015 when the director and star of *Selma*, Ava DuVernay and David Oyelowo, were overlooked by the Academy even though the film itself was nominated for Best Picture) trended on Twitter and drew attention to the lack of diversity in Hollywood and in the Academy. Just a few days later, with rumors of a threatened boycott abounding, Cheryl Boone Isaacs, the Academy's first African American president, announced that it would double the membership of women and minorities in the academy by 2020 (Jagernauth 2016).

A few weeks later, J. J. Abrams announced that his production company, Bad Robot, would institute a diversity policy with the aim of increasing the number of women and people of color involved in his productions. Citing the Oscars controversy as a "wake-up call," Abrams declared that Bad Robot would work with its agency partner CAA, as well as Warner and Paramount, "to ensure women and minorities are submitted for writing, directing and acting jobs for the company in direct proportion to their representation among the US population" (Ford and Kits 2016; Ryzik 2016). It's tempting to view Abrams's policy as his response to the "whitewashing" (a disparaging term used when white actors are cast for non-white roles in film) controversy surrounding his 2013 reboot, *Star Trek Into Darkness*, which cast white British actor Benedict Cumberbatch as Khan Noonien Singh, a South Asian, brown-skinned Sikh played by Ricardo Montalbán in both *The Original Series* episode "Space Seed" (1967) and *Star Trek II: The Wrath of Khan* (1982). But it's also interesting in light of the progressive casting of John Boyega and Daisy Ridley as the leads in Abrams's *Star Wars: Episode VII—The Force Awakens*, the long-anticipated sequel to the *Star Wars* franchise. *The Force Awakens* (2015) might even be viewed as a corrective to the Khan debacle, generating its own racial backlash and hashtag, #BoycottStarWarsVII. Released at the height of Trump's campaign fever, rather than being too white, *The Force Awakens* was considered by some diehard *Star Wars* fans as anti-white, some going so far as to say it promoted "white genocide" (Griggs 2015).

In 2016, Abrams produced the third installment of the *Star Trek* reboot, directed by Asian American director Justin Lin and featuring Black British actor Idris Elba in the lead role as the evil Krall. On the surface, this film appears to be consistent with Abrams's stated commitment to diversity. *Star Trek Beyond* includes the most diverse cast of all the reboots, and actors of color are given extended story arcs. Idris Elba's character Krall, who plays the lead antagonist, is central to the film's exploration of identity and belonging. Far from the progressive film it seems to be, *Beyond* traffics in racial stereotypes and reveals white anxieties about the superiority of African Americans. Indeed, rather than standing as a corrective to *Into Darkness*, *Beyond* can be viewed as its natural successor, extending the troubling racial politics of that film.

The whitewashing controversy wasn't the only one that beset *Into Darkness*; it also received criticism for its irresponsible celebration of urban terrorism, which included an aircraft destroying a building. Instead of departing from these themes, *Beyond* continues them with a Black character in the role of terrorist. While the rhetoric of fear has associated brown skin and terrorism in the popular imaginary since 9/11, there is a different emphasis in these films. Brown or Black people are not simply waging terrorist acts; their bodies are themselves weapons—not suicide bombs, but biological agents with the potential to destroy the purity and uncontested superiority of whiteness. *Into Darkness* and *Beyond* raise troubling yet timely questions about bioengineering and biological warfare. This chapter will examine these issues through a reading of the two *Star Trek* films, demonstrating how fears about biology and developments in genetic science are tied to white fears about race.

The representations of both Khan and Krall go far beyond the well-traveled sketch of the terrorist frequently populating our big and small screens; rather, like the apes in the new *Planet of the Apes* films, *Into Darkness* and *Beyond* betray a palpable ambivalence about whiteness and Blackness, and "us" and "them," which mirrors shared anxieties about race in so-called postracial America. Released in 2013 and 2016 respectively, these science fiction films, just like *The Walking Dead* and *Rise* and *Dawn*, offer a roadmap for understanding the rise of white identity politics in the Obama-to-Trump era. Operating as a form of popular fantasy, science fiction both imagines and projects our current social and political realities into a future time. Most obviously, science fiction attempts to articulate the anxieties people feel in relation to scientific experimentation and weighs both the benefits and costs to our current world and life as we know it. Science fiction can offer a productive space to express cultural concerns about science and technology. Frequently, these concerns are tied to racial anxieties. As Sean Redmond has argued, science fiction often connects the innovative, salvific, and technological power of science to whiteness, which is threatened by an evil "alien" Other who is frequently racialized. The "finely drawn symbiotic relationship between salvation and whiteness works to confirm and reaffirm white people's racial superiority and therefore their primary, essentialized position on a racially-inscribed evolutionary ladder" (Redmond 2006, 10). In the twenty-first century, anxieties about emergent technologies can be seen to be linked to fears about race and the effects that advances in bioengineering might have on the prevailing racial hierarchy.

STAR TREK'S RACIAL SPACESCAPE

In his important work on *Star Trek* and race, Daniel Bernardi notes the well-documented efforts by the original series' writers and production team to engage with the racial politics of the 1960s. Despite Roddenberry's stated objectives to imagine a progressive and liberal universe where difference was valued, Bernardi notes, "[T]his project was inconsistent and contradictory—often participating in and facilitating racist practice" (Bernardi 1999, 30). Frequently constrained by NBC censors, *Star Trek: The Original Series* (*TOS*) attempted to mitigate potentially explosive racial elements, like the kiss between Kirk and Uhuru in "Plato's Stepchildren" (1968) by cutting away before their lips touched, and by downplaying Sulu's Japanese ancestry characterizing him as "confused and mystified by Asians." As Bernardi notes, "Sulu's intended integration into the space of the starship comes at the expense of a recognizable identity with Japanese "culture" (1999, 40). Like many science fiction productions, *TOS* and other *Star Trek* vehicles since then have attempted to work through the racial politics of their time by depicting racial conflict through alien conflict. Adilifu Nama and Isiah Lavender have argued that science fiction has a history of using alien difference to comment upon issues of racial difference. "Science fiction often talks about race by not talking about race.... Even though it is a literature that talks a lot about underclasses or oppressed classes, it does so from a privileged if somewhat generic white space" (Lavender 2011, 7). In Abrams's and Lin's productions, however, racial difference is not transposed onto alien otherness; rather, racial difference is clearly marked as human difference, even in the case of Cumberbatch's lily-white Khan.

The whitewashing of Khan has implications for the cultural moment of the early twenty-first century that go far beyond the Hollywood tendency to cast white actors in roles written for people of color. It betrays a significant unease about the power people of color possess in a time when the US population is expected to be majority minority by 2050 and feeds into the Great Replacement theory popular among white supremacists.[1] As a journalist covering the early days of the Trump presidency revealed in a 2017 interview: "[T]here's a kind of deeper cultural discomfort with the growing population of people who are not white in this country, coming from a kind of traditional white sense of propriety of what America is about . . . and it's part of what's driving the more extreme elements of this presidency" (Bazelon 2017).

#OSCARSSOWHITE AND #BLACKLIVESMATTER

It seems evident that #OSW was attempting to reckon with more than the problem of racial diversity in the Academy. Its use and popularity sprang from fertile ground tilled by explosive racial relations between members of the Black community, police, and the justice system and should be viewed in the context of the activism of the Black Lives Matter movement. The hashtag #BlackLivesMatter first appeared in 2013 after the acquittal of George Zimmerman for the murder of unarmed Black teenager Trayvon Martin. Black Lives Matter became increasingly visible and assumed a greater political and public role as violence against African Americans escalated in subsequent years. In 2014, communities of color were reeling from the fatal shooting of unarmed Michael Brown and the riots that followed the acquittal of Brown's killer, police officer Darren Wilson. In 2015, racial tensions between African Americans and police escalated further. In April 2015, Freddie Gray, subject to unnecessary force upon arrest and subsequently unrestrained in a police van, suffered extreme injuries to his spinal cord and died while being transported to a police station. Days of protest in Baltimore followed Gray's death and turned violent, prompting the Governor of Maryland to declare a state of emergency and deploy the state's National Guard. A grand jury indicted the police officers on charges ranging from second-degree murder to illegal arrest. The trial of one officer ended in a mistrial, and the others were acquitted of all charges. These events reflected heightened tensions among the populace about issues of racism and race relations. In May of 2015, the *New York Times* reported that "sixty-one percent of Americans now say race relations in this country are generally bad. ... The negative sentiment is echoed by broad majorities of blacks and whites alike, a stark change from earlier this year, when 58 percent of blacks thought race relations were bad, but just 35 percent of whites agreed. In August, 48 percent of blacks and 41 percent of whites said they felt that way" (Sussman 2015).

That race itself was the story at the 2016 Oscars reveals a number of things about the cultural politics of the second decade of the twenty-first century, specifically, that "postracial" or "colorblind" ideologies, so prevalent after the election of Barack Obama in 2008, are not only myths but covert exercises of white privilege. The attempt to sweep race under the rug by liberals and conservatives alike, demonstrated in the subtly aggressive #AllLivesMatter, speaks to a greater fear among whites about racial presence. Racial difference, it seems, is too visible, too threatening, and needs to be contained. As respected sociologists and theorists Michael Omi and Howard Winant make clear, "colorblindness" is not race-neutral at all; rather, it is a tactic utilized by the dominant racial hegemony for the purposes of containment and redirection. "As hegemonic racial ideology, colorblindness has to be enforced, not only in state policies and court decisions, but in popular culture and everyday life as well" (Omi and Winant 2014, 263). Conservative anxiety about whiteness and its ability to stay dominant was heightened by Obama's presence in the White House and his popularity among diverse segments of the population.

Hollywood is adept at exercising covert racism. In fact, Hollywood is a reliable barometer of race relations and prejudices within the larger populace (Downing and Husband 2005; Courtney 2005). #OscarsSoWhite was effective in that it drew attention to the fact that Hollywood, in its hydra-like involvement in business, politics, foreign markets, etc., is not quite the liberal mouthpiece the right so often accuses it of being:

> Of the 100 most popular movies released in 2014, only 12.5 percent of the movies' characters were Black, according to a study done by the University of Southern California—and that statistic correlates to every year since 2007. It isn't just that the Academy—which was hugely revamped in June 2015 to become more diverse (a self-imposed change, by the way)—is largely uninterested in stories they consider "other." ... The Academy picked a largely white slate of nominees this year (and last year), because that's mostly all they had to pick *from*. Yes, #OscarsSo White, but #HollywoodSoWhite is closer to the truth. (Gruttadaro 2016)

Hollywood's disinterest toward, or active rejection of, representations of race on the big screen provides a context for the 2014 Sony Pictures email scandal. In

December of that year, exactly one month before the first appearance of #OSW, Sony made news when the emails of two of its key executives, Scott Rudin and Amy Pascal, were leaked to the press. The emails revealed a number of racist comments the two had made about President Obama, Denzel Washington, and Kevin Hart. They also speculated on Denzel Washington's lack of box office bankability in overseas markets (Steadman 2014).

Far from liberal, these racially reactionary products coming out of Hollywood reflect a perception among white executives that racial diversity onscreen is not marketable to predominantly white audiences. Such attitudes stem from a growing backlash among whites against issues of race or, at least, reflect a degree of what some have called "racial fatigue."[2] But importantly, these films don't just reflect; they also construct and fashion those views about race at home and abroad. As Bernardi makes clear, "[S]tate and cultural power brokers like Hollywood's rely on a hegemonic strategy of coercion and consent to support a center of white power and a periphery of colored exclusion and degradation" (1999, 22). Moreover, overtly racist representations often appear in movies without specific racial storylines. Science fiction texts frequently obfuscate race, as Edward James notes in his seminal essay, "Yellow, Black, Metal, and Tentacled: The Race Question in American Science Fiction" (1990). It's in the overt allegorization of otherness in fantasy and science fiction that racial tension is evident. As Nama has argued, "For the most part, Black characters are absent from SF cinema, yet their omission does not eliminate Blackness as a source of anxiety. Churning just below the narrative surface of many SF films, Blackness is symbolically present" (2008, 11).

As the #BoycottStarWarsVII "white genocide" claims reveal, when Hollywood remediates this absence, the white backlash is swift and decisive. Donald Trump's upset victory in the 2016 presidential election demonstrates that expressions of racist views are as popular as ever. Trump, who ran on a racially divisive populist-nationalist platform, appealed, in part, to conservative working-class whites who felt invisible in the political landscape of Washington and ridiculed by what they perceived as a discourse of liberal elitism emanating from the East and West coasts. As #OscarsSoWhite and my reading of *Into Darkness* and *Beyond* demonstrate, the assumption of the right that Hollywood is part of an out-of-touch liberal elite needs further scrutiny. Social scientists have long recognized that various forms of media reflect and reproduce social inequalities. Indeed, "[T]he production, content, and consumption of media may be used to justify and encourage racist, sexist, classist, and heterosexist understandings of the way the world is or should be" (Sumerau and Jirek 2015, 72).

I suggest that, like *The Walking Dead* and the new *Planet of the Apes* franchise, these recent *Star Trek* reboots reflect but also work to *construct* America's changing views on race. These forms of entertainment media are exemplars of the social discourse of the Obama-to-Trump era and play a key role in responding to and shaping our racial landscape. Interpreting and analyzing films like these make visible the work that allegories of race in film perform and the ideologies that they veil. These ideologies seem particularly crucial to investigate in the new *Star Trek* franchise because of Gene Roddenberry's desire for *Star Trek* to reflect his own liberal views. As he said of his series, "*Star Trek* is my statement to the world . . . [it] is more than just my political philosophy. It is my social philosophy, my racial philosophy, my overview on life and the human condition" (quoted in O'Connor 2012, 185). *Star Trek* of the 1960s expressed the "utopian passions of countercultural relativism." "Refus[ing] to impose its values on alien races," it spent its time "spreading the gospel of liberal understanding" (Rothstein 2009). Despite this, scholars have suggested that the politics of Roddenberry's *Trek*, which relied on a "liberal-humanistic discourse particular to the 1960s," was "fundamentally and pervasively contradictory" in its representation of race and racial difference (Bernardi 1999, 23). However contradictory, Roddenberry reflected the politics of his age. In a similar way, Abrams's reboots reflect our age, utilizing the discourse of colorblindness to reinforce a neoconservative world order where whiteness "trumps" all.

INTO WHITENESS

Many Trekkers were outraged when it was revealed that Benedict Cumberbatch was to reprise the role of Khan Noonien Singh in the second *Star Trek* reboot. Fans immediately reacted with claims of whitewashing. Whitewashing was a common device in the early days of Hollywood film, where white actors would don blackface or yellowface or adopt ethnically stereotyped accents or gestures. Some of the more egregious examples include Laurence Olivier as Othello in the 1965 film version of Shakespeare's play, John Wayne as Genghis Khan in the 1956 movie *The Conqueror*, and Mickey Rooney's hideous caricature of the Japanese I. Y. Yunioshi in 1965's *Breakfast at Tiffany's*. Whitewashing is related to "racebending," where the ethnicity of the character is changed in a remake or alternative media version (video game, etc.) of the original production. The website racebending.com was swift to condemn the whitewashing of Khan in *Into Darkness*:

> Racebending.com has always pointed out that villains are generally played by people with darker skin, and that's true . . . unless the villain is one with intelligence, depth, complexity. One who garners sympathy from the audience, or if not sympathy, then—as from Kirk—grudging

Ricardo Montalbán as Khan. (*Star Trek: The Original Series*, "Space Seed," season 1, episode 22, 1967)

Benedict Cumberbatch as Khan. (*Star Trek Into Darkness*, 2013)

admiration. What this new *Trek* movie tells us, what JJ Abrams is telling us, is that no brown-skinned man can accomplish all that. That only by having Khan played by a white actor can the audience engage with and feel for him, believe that he's smart and capable and a match for our Enterprise crew. (Sammy 2013)

Into Darkness manages to perform whitewashing and racebending at the same time. Benedict Cumberbatch is a white actor playing both a white character, John Harrison, and an Indian character, Khan Noonien Singh. *Into Darkness* doesn't attempt to explain the illogic of this, but as I argue below, the film's two narrative strands of terrorism and superhumanness explain why Cumberbatch has to inhabit two entirely different ethnic identities simultaneously.

Whitewashed Khan embodies what Sean Redmond calls the "white Alien Messiah," which is "fetishized as the supreme rationalist and archetype techno-scientist, brought to Earth through superior technology, furnished with advanced weaponry and scientific knowledge, and motivated by scientific reasoning and logic alone" (Redmond 2006). In "Space Seed" (Rodenberry 1967), we learn that Ricardo Montalbán's Khan is a genetically bred superman from twentieth-century India who was part of the Eugenics Wars on Earth. He and his crew were cryogenically frozen and drifted through space until the year 2267, when they were discovered by the Enterprise. Khan is literally the greatest man alive. (Although Khan's crew is similarly engineered, he still assumes a position of power over them.) When Cumberbatch's Khan explains his unique abilities to Kirk (Chris Pine) in *Into Darkness*, the facts of his "breeding" carry a different resonance: the threateningly superior Brown man is completely erased by the white British man. When Khan explains to Kirk that his intellect and savagery were exploited by Admiral Marcus (Peter Weller), Kirk asks, "Why would a Starfleet admiral ask a 300-year-old frozen man for help?" Khan responds, "Because I am better." Kirk: "At what?" Khan responds, "Everything" (Abrams 2013). From the mouth of the crisply British Cumberbatch, who offers an emotionally wrenching performance worthy of the Royal Shakespeare Company, superhumanness gets tied yet again to Imperial British Whiteness. In this way, "the finely drawn symbiotic relationship between salvation science and whiteness works to confirm and reaffirm white people's racial superiority and therefore their primary, essentialized position on a racially-inscribed evolutionary ladder" (Redmond 2006).

ONE-DROP RULE

The sanctity and entitlement of whiteness saturates the film from the depiction in the opening scene of indigenous white "primitives," and Kirk's hubris in breaking the prime directive of non-interference, to futuristic London of 2259, where a Black man (Noel Clarke) devastated by the debilitating disease of his dying daughter performs a terrorist act for the white mastermind. In the Faustian pact, the child survives thanks to the restorative properties of Khan's white blood, while the father must pay the price with his life. In this film, as in others of the genre, "[W]hite blood [is] presented as a means to cure and repopulate a diseased and dying world . . . [and] draws on the dual racial eugenic propositions that not only is Black blood a contaminant to white bloodlines but white blood is also considered a neutralizing agent for biologically dictated mental deficiencies in Blacks" (Nama 2008, 49). Khan's recasting from Brown to white enhances this meaning; however, it's also instructive to note that the blood of Montalbán's Brown Khan, in both "Space Seed" and *The Wrath of Khan*, has no such lifesaving properties. Moreover, in the *Wrath of Khan* it is Spock (Leonard Nimoy), the perennial Other, who heroically saves the ship, sacrificially locking himself into a radiation chamber. In *Into Darkness*, the heroics are left to Kirk, who does the same thing as Spock in the previous film, but rather than dying, he is brought back to life by Khan's blood. Here the symbolism of the transfusion takes on a different quality as Khan passes on symbolic superman properties to Kirk, reinforcing Kirk's natural "fitness" to lead the *Enterprise*. Furthermore, white Khan's transfusion of blood to white Kirk prevents any suggestion of miscegenation. The "racial convention" of the one-drop rule "is an integral part of the cultural politics of race in American society in which 'Black blood' is viewed as not only a potent pollutant but also a fundamental element in assembling an essentialized racial identity for both whites and Blacks" (Nama 2008, 43). Although Khan is not Black, Brown blood has historically carried the same stigma.

BROWN ÜBERMENSCH?

While it is not directly addressed, the question of the ethical use of eugenics or genetic engineering undergirds the premise of *Into Darkness*. In 1967 and 1982, when it is revealed that Khan was a product of the Eugenic Wars, the kind of eugenics that could produce a superhuman "species" like Khan seemed far off. Not so today, where we are capable of genetically modifying food, have the capacity to screen for and correct genetic deficiencies through somatic gene therapy, can transplant embryonic stem cells to repair any diseased or injured organ, and, thanks to the completion of the Human Genome Project, can identify which genes control intelligence and how they can be manipulated. The possibility that a man like Khan could exist seems inevitable, if not now, in the near future.

Part of the ethical conversation around genetic engineering involves equity and access to new technologies, but these concerns usually refer to the disproportionate benefits that the wealthy would obtain from human improvements, such as designer babies with exceptional IQs. Here, however, in replacing the Brown man with the white one as the perfect specimen of humanness, *Into Darkness* exposes and eradicates a latent fear expressed by some conservative commentators about bioengineering. Could genetic engineering level the racial playing field, or worse, make whites inferior? Far from the state-sponsored sterilization and lobotomization of years past, the "new eugenics" threaten to enhance those whom society deems weaker or less intelligent. As conservative commentator Francis Fukuyama, a member of George Bush's Council on Bioethics from 2001 to 2004, has noted, "Under this scenario it is entirely plausible that an advanced, democratic welfare state would reenter the eugenics game, intervening this time not to prevent low-IQ people from breeding, but to help genetically disadvantaged people raise their IQs and the IQs of their offspring" (Fukuyama 2003, 81). Lest there is any doubt that Fukuyama is making a connection between race and low IQ, elsewhere in his book, he endorses Murray and Herrnstein's controversial findings in *The Bell Curve* that up to 70 percent (Fukuyama says the rate is closer to 40–50 percent) of IQ is heritable and that African Americans are genetically predisposed to have lower IQs. Further, he sees these new technologies as posing a danger to the political world order of the twenty-first century and cautions that such technologies "will change our understanding of human personality and identity; they will upend existing social hierarchies and affect the rate of intellectual, material, and political progress; and they will affect the nature of global politics" (Fukuyama 2003, 174, 82). In other words, they have the potential to push the white West off its perch.

By transforming superhuman Indian Khan Noonien Singh into the genetically gifted, white, British John Harrison, whose blood self-replicates and rejuvenates life, *Into Darkness* removes any suggestion that non-whites could be stronger, smarter, and better than whites. This representation is consistent with other post-war science fiction texts, which construct "an imaginary timeline that has white people as navigators of all human history, and also imagines a human teleology that has been singularly driven by the ingenuity, by the brilliance, of white people. It is as if they were and are, finally, the origin and the future of the species" (Redmond 2006). This rewriting is a form of "racial rearticulation" (Omi and Winant 2014), utilized by a dominant hegemony that "cannot explicitly name, utilize, or exploit the race concept; instead, it is forced to exercise racial rule covertly.... This is a contradictory and conflictual situation, in which the racial regime simultaneously *disavows* its raciality and *deploys* it as broadly and as deeply as ever" (Omi and Winant 2014, 263). Understood in these terms, the whitewashing of Khan not only reinforces the association between whiteness and superiority that the casting of Ricardo Montalbán as Khan disrupted, it offers tacit support to expressions of hard and soft white identity politics traversing the cultural landscape in the Obama-to-Trump era. When Khan reveals that he will undertake mass genocide of any species he finds inferior, the cautionary tale is complete. In a eugenic race war, whites will prevail.

COLORBLIND FANDOM

The link between whiteness and superiority is reflected in some fans' commentary on Cumberbatch's casting in the role of Khan. Although many fans objected to the whitewashing of Khan, others noted that his whiteness was consistent with his superior enhancements. In a Quora forum dedicated to the question, "Am I the only person really bothered by the whitewashing?" one fan writes, "I'm not bothered as [Cumberbatch] did a great acting job, no mention of or care was placed upon his heritage, and in the canon he was 'genetically' altered so could have been modified to be taller, stronger, and why not have his appearance modified toward whomever his genes came from . . . ." (Metcalfe 2013). Consistent with this sentiment, another fan urges viewers to "[i]gnore the cries of whitewashing[.] . . . [A]nyone versed in the mythos of the character knows that his name is the only ethnic thing about him. Khan is a superman bred to be above the pitfalls of typical humanity" (Maidy 2016). One of those pitfalls, apparently, is non-white skin. Another fan on the Quora string suggests that the casting of Cumberbatch is consistent with *Trek* history: "The original Khan was just as whitewashed. Ricardo was a Spaniard, which means European, white, non-Latino" (Leech-Steffens 2013). Montalbán was, in fact, Mexican, and while the fan is right in her observation that the racial substitution of a Mexican man for an Indian one is problematic, the change doesn't carry the same symbolic resonance because Brownness is valued differently than whiteness in the racial hierarchy. In fact, casting a Mexican man to play a gifted superhuman was consistent with the ideological project of Roddenberry's text. Not only did Montalbán's Khan provide visual diversity (an important objective for Roddenberry), but his casting also disassociated the concept of übermensch from its connection with whiteness.

As a genre, SF fosters and cultivates fan engagement, and *Star Trek* fans are arguably the most engaged fans of all, in part because of the extensive *ST* franchise, which includes the original television series, nine spin-off television series, thirteen feature movies, and an animated television series, as well as numerous fan paratexts, including comics, novels, shorts, and conventions. Bernardi notes that *ST* fans are extremely conscious of Roddenberry's stated aims regarding the franchise's representation of difference and diversity and "are consistently and consciously reading race into and out of the mega-text" (1999, 143). Reading the debate over whitewashing in *Into Darkness* in the larger context of *ST* fan engagement is instructive. In his book *Textual Poachers: Television Fans & Participatory Culture*, Henry Jenkins explains the process by which fans utilize elements of a storyworld, adapting and shaping them to fit their own experiences and desires. However, Jenkins notes that fan readings of texts typically reside within the ideological frame of their storyworlds and usually reflect the politics and ideologies of their creators: "[F]andom originates in response to specific historical conditions (not only specific configurations of television programming, but also the development of feminism, the development of new technologies, the atomization and alienation of contemporary

American culture, etc.) and remains constantly in flux" (Jenkins [1992] 2013, 3). It is the ideology of colorblindness inherent to neoliberalism in the Obama-to-Trump era that is front and center in Abrams's film. *Into Darkness* reinscribes colonialist racial hierarchies and its elevation of whiteness not by demonizing people of color but through an erasure of Brown agency altogether. Similarly, the sentiments of the fans cited above reflect the cultural zeitgeist of their era. In ways consistent with the language of diversity and difference, the fans utilize colorblind rhetoric to justify the casting of a white actor in a role originally written for and made famous by a person of color. As Bernardi notes of *ST* fans generally, "whether racist or not, reactionary or progressive, historicity is not weakened by the fans; rather, it is realized and politicized" (1999, 156).

WHITE TERROR

The casting of a white Khan has considerably different implications, however, when we examine the film's terrorist plot. Damon Lindelof, one of the film's screenwriters, has said of the emphasis on terror in the film, "All that stuff was in the air and I think we weren't trying to make a sociopolitical statement when we wrote the story, but we just started gravitating towards those ideas because that's what was on the news" (Sacks 2013). Lindelof makes clear how different aspects of media work together to form media events. A Brown actor, it seems, would be the perfect vehicle to feed Western hysteria about terrorism and to demonstrate the interconnectedness of race and violence. However, according to Robert Orci, the filmmakers were conscious of that association, and he, personally, was "uncomfortable demonizing anyone" on the basis of their race. Instead, "by choosing a white actor, the film-makers decoupled Khan's villainy from his brownness—which was significant, especially in the light of Khan's terrorist attack on a skyscraper in the film" (Yo 2016).

It's certainly the case that a white Anglo terrorist is less of a political hot potato than a Brown one. But why, if the filmmakers wanted to "decouple" Brownness and villainy, did they borrow so carefully and obviously from terror events perpetrated by Al Qaeda and its affiliates, and subsequent attacks by ISIS? Precisely because the film depicts scenes of urban terrorism like 9/11 as well as attacks in London and Paris, these representations are always already racialized. We don't need a narrative about John Harrison's radicalization by Islam to understand the film is pulling from the cultural zeitgeist of terrorism waged by Islamic militants, especially when the terrorist is a man named Khan. Within the first twenty minutes of the film, a bomb has destroyed a top-secret Starfleet research center in London. This, it turns out, is a mere prelude to his larger attack on Starfleet, where Khan uses a jumpship (a helicopter-like vehicle) to target a skyscraper and kill a majority of the Starship senior command. He then escapes to Kronos, the homeworld of the Federation's greatest enemy—the Klingon—where he is in hiding. Kirk and his crew are given orders to launch missiles on Kronos and destroy Khan. In pursuing this line of action, the film is clearly drawing from and commenting upon US policy regarding Osama bin Laden, the architect of the attacks of 9/11. Before Admiral Marcus knows that Khan has escaped off-world to Kronos, he makes a speech reminiscent of Bush's avowal to capture Bin Laden "dead or alive." Marcus says, "In the name of those we lost, you will run this bastard down. This is a manhunt, pure and simple, so let's get to work" (Abrams 2013). However, when he finds out that Khan is hiding on the remote Klingon homeworld, he orders Kirk to deploy missiles to kill, not capture, Khan.

Into Darkness both highlights and remarks on US policy, and the ethics of kill or capture become evident when Spock (Zachary Quinto) finds out the true nature of their mission. Spock "strongly object[s] to [the] mission parameters" because "there is no Starfleet regulation that condemns a man to die without a trial." And then, if the case wasn't clear enough, he argues that "[r]egulations aside, this action is morally wrong." "Captain, our mission could start a war with the Klingons and it is by its very definition immoral" (Abrams 2013). Because Spock is logical and can always intuit the correct path, even when not successful, the moral high ground is his, at least temporarily. Reluctantly, Kirk agrees to Spock's demands, but as the plot unfolds, Kirk's capitulation to Spock's ethical path is shown to be wrong. Sparing Khan's life results in significantly more lives lost. While Roddenberry's vision "both championed, and dissented from, [the counterculture's] peaceful, anti-militaristic vision" (Rothstein 2009), Abrams's vision is jingoism at its finest. Ethical concerns about the taking of enemy life, whether Khan's or Bin Laden's, are shown to be soft and foolish, while the view of the military hardliners is shown as correct.[3] This overt support, whether legal or ethical, of military ops is consonant with the politics of the right and the "war on terror." Although it was Obama's administration that found and killed Bin Laden, his military operations were often criticized as not going far enough, as being "soft on terror," or, in the words of Donald Trump, being "sympathetic to Islamic Terrorism" (Blatter 2016; Stein 2016).

BEYOND RACISM?

Anxieties about bioengineering and racial difference are also on display in the third reboot in the new franchise: *Star Trek Beyond*. However, the terrorist narrative shifts in *Beyond*. Whereas *Into Darkness* uses whiteness to try to avoid making a political point about race and terrorism (even though,

Krall sustains his life by sucking the life force from humans of Starfleet. (*Star Trek Beyond*, 2016)

as I've explained above, it does so covertly), *Beyond* goes one step further by transposing fears of Islamic otherness to African American otherness. This is homegrown terrorism, but the cause of radicalization is different. Far from being created by an evil Other, Krall/Edison (Idris Elba) is a product of the Federation. A former soldier turned captain, Balthazar Edison and his crew were abandoned by the Federation. As the defeated, resigned captain states in the last entry of his captain's log, "All distress calls unanswered. Of the crew, only three remain.... I will do whatever it takes for me and my crew. The Federation do [sic] not care about us" (Lin 2016). This backstory of a soldier discarded and forgotten by the military finds an analog to contemporary stories about soldiers returning home from war with PTSD and a broken Veteran's Administration that cannot adequately cater to them. Following this reading, Edison's anger at the Federation is justified. But instead of pursuing this storyline and allowing a sympathetic interpretation of Krall/Edison, the film demonizes and "others" him, and his race is central to that demonization.

Beyond's narrative builds and develops a theme of unity and disunity, of "us" and "them," which resonates quite differently when we learn that Krall/Edison is not an alien "them" but a human "us." When questioning Uhura (Zoë Saldaña) as to why she sacrificed herself to save Kirk, he taunts her: "You think you know what sacrifice really means. Federation has taught you that conflict should not exist. Ha! But without struggle, you would never know who you really are." When Sulu (John Cho) tells him that he has "no idea who we are," Krall reveals his plan to attack Yorktown: "Millions of souls from every Federation world holding hands. It's a perfect target." Uhura challenges him: "You're wrong, there is strength in unity," to which Krall counters, "The strength of others, Lieutenant, is what has kept me alive" (Lin 2016). And to demonstrate this, he transfers the life out of two Enterprise crewmembers—one white, one Black—to himself through a biotechnological machine. When voiced by someone/something which appears so completely other to the humanity that Uhura and Sulu represent, these words support the idea of Krall's monstrosity. Here, he is othered not just in his species difference but by his philosophical view of the world, and this incapacity to recognize their ethical code can be explained by his difference, his otherness. Why would this murderous alien subscribe to the same theory of liberal humanism, of unity, as they do? Obviously, he has no idea who they really are! But this easy philosophical binary is troubled by the fact that he does know who they are. He *is* who they are. Or is he?

NO ONE LEFT BEHIND

It is significant, of course, that we don't know that Krall is Edison until near the end of the film. Our first impression of him is as a reptilian humanoid alien creature who attacks the Enterprise and literally sucks the life out of his prisoners. When Krall's true identity is revealed and we learn of Edison's plight, the film offers a more sympathetic view of the abandoned captain. In Krall/Edison, we get an unflattering reflection of the Federation. It's Edison's story, the solider left behind who did what he was supposed to do—protect his crew and wait for his rescue that never came, that forces us to question the shibboleths on which the Federation depends. Indeed, the mantra of not leaving anyone behind is reiterated several times in the film. Scotty (Simon Pegg), in trying to encourage Jaylah (Sofia Boutella) to join them on their rescue mission, pleads, "Look, that's our friends out there, lassie. We cannae just leave them behind." Bones (Karl Urban) refuses to beam back to the ship with the majority of the crew until Spock (Zachary Quinto), Uhura, and Kirk (Chris Pine) are present, exclaiming, "Damn it man, we're not leaving without them!" Scotty comments to Jaylah that "[y]ou're part of something bigger now . . . we'll sure as hell never give up on you. That is what being part of a crew is all about" (Lin 2016). And he's right. They don't give up on her; in fact, Kirk, who consistently goes out of his way to save his crew, risks his own safe passage to the ship in order to secure Jaylah's return and her ultimate admission to Starfleet. This stands in stark contrast to the experience of Edison, who, though remembered as "one of the first heroes of Starfleet," is never rescued.

Watching the captain's slow unraveling on the ship's logs, Kirk, Scotty, and Uhura are appalled at his fate. Kirk notes, "[H]e was a solider," and Scotty affirms that he "was a pretty good one." But because military operations came to an end with the establishment of the Federation, Edison could no longer fight and was made a captain and given a ship. Stranded on a planet abandoned by an "indigenous race" that left behind "sophisticated mining equipment" with the capacity to prolong life, Edison tries to save his crew. The Starfleet officers' sympathies shift, however, when they see the last log; Edison comes across as

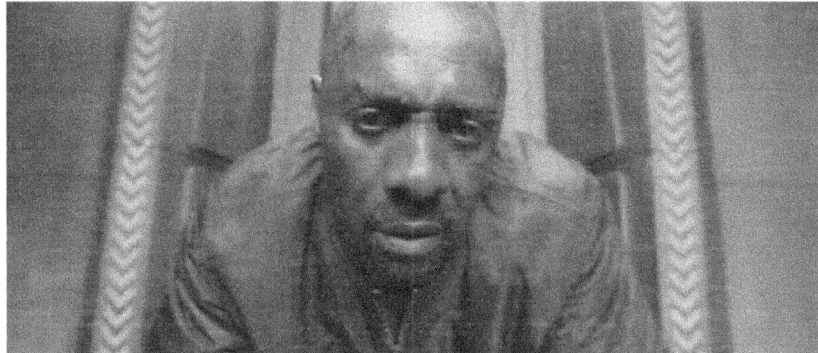

Edison's video captain's log shows his mental decline. (*Star Trek Beyond*, 2016)

a desperate and unhinged captain who tells them that though he'll probably never see them again, they should "be ready" (Lin 2016).

Bathed in a saturated green light, Edison's devolution seems already to have begun, even without the alien technology that will eventually transform him. Through this visual depiction, the film quickly pivots away from feelings of sympathy toward Edison and instead aligns him with an alien biotechnological life force that is anathema to humans.

The possibility of reading Krall/Edison's story as a critique of the Federation is withheld by the film as Uhura and Sulu are proved right. They will all work together to secure their rescue, Yorktown will be saved, and Krall's evil counterphilosophy will be destroyed. However, what this simple resolution obscures is that it's not the monstrous Krall that gets destroyed; it's the Black Edison. For by the end of the film, the monster has returned to his human form and, dressed in his Starfleet uniform, faces Kirk man to man, captain to captain. Though his body is now human in appearance, Edison's face is not the same; it is marked by Krall or traces of Krall. Narratively, this suggests that the evil is still within Edison, it helps explain his desire to destroy Yorktown, and it provides justification for Kirk's destruction of him. However, as the film's

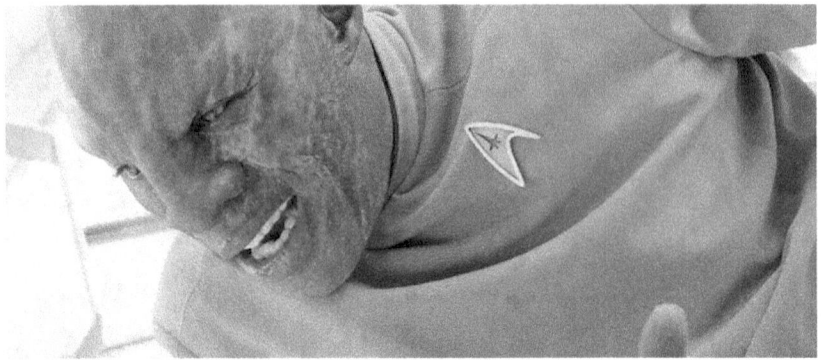

Edison's human face is marked by the traces of Krall's monstrosity. (*Star Trek Beyond*, 2016)

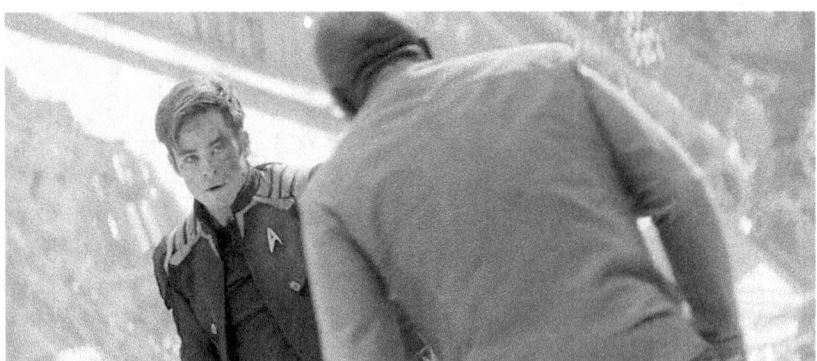

Kirk and Krall engage in a Manichean struggle over the fate of humanity. (*Star Trek Beyond*, 2016)

disclosure of Krall-as-Edison demonstrates, Krall never occupied the place of Other. Krall was a product of the Federation. And the scarred, distorted face that he wears in the final battle with Kirk is the outward manifestation of his betrayal by his own.

Beyond holds fast to the unassimilable evil and otherness of Krall. The reason why Krall remains effectively othered in the film and why the sympathetic abandoned soldier narrative and the pointed critique of Starfleet don't prevail is because Krall is doubly othered. He is monstrous *and* Black—what monstrosity is to Krall, Blackness is to Edison. Idris Elba's black skin, (mostly) disguised for the majority of the movie, contributes in definitive ways to the film's representation of Krall as evil and treacherous and, when exposed, takes on a narrative emphasis similar to Cumberbatch's white skin in *Into Darkness*. Nama has astutely noted that in science fiction, "[t]he Black body is a representational canvas coated with signifiers of alien unsightliness, danger, fear, social inferiority, and even transgressive sexuality that evoke a wide range of racial anxieties and cultural politics circulating in American society" (2008, 72). Just as Edison bears the mark of alien Krall at the end, retroactively, Krall, too, is marked by black Edison; and when read in the context of his race, Edison's struggles as an abandoned and forgotten outsider allow for an alternate reading.

FIGHT THE POWER

It is telling that Krall speaks only to Uhura, the ship's Black communication specialist, about strength and unity. When Syl (Melissa Roxburgh) gives up the Abronath to save Sulu, Krall turns to Uhura and says, "Lieutenant, unity is not your strength, it is your weakness." Uhura is insistent that there is strength in unity, and he is insistent that there is not. Where Uhura speaks of unity, Krall champions sacrifice and struggle. In their first encounter, he practically spits at her: "You think you know what sacrifice really means. Federation has taught you that conflict should not exist. Ha! But without struggle, you would never know who you really are." And in a later scene, he reinforces this idea: "The world I was born into was very different from yours, Lieutenant. We knew pain. We knew terror. Struggle made us strong. Not peace. Not unity. These are myths the Federation would have you believe" (Lin 2016). From Krall's mouth, these words highlight his difference and secure him squarely in the box of Other. But when Krall is revealed to be Edison, a Black man born a century prior, the words take on a different resonance. If we understand that the goal of the Federation is to uphold the liberal democratic ideals of Western nation-states, Krall/Edison's words serve as a critique of Uhura's racial politics, of her naïve belief in inclusion and colorblindness. Krall repeatedly ties his actions against the Federation to an act of resistance, even using the language of colonized oppressed peoples to justify his position. As he makes clear to Uhura, "The Federation has pushed the frontier for centuries. But no longer. This is where it begins, Lieutenant. This is where the Frontier pushes back" (Lin 2016).

Uhura tries to convince Krall that "unity is our strength." (*Star Trek Beyond*, 2016)

This interpretation is further affirmed in the music that Jaylah finds on Edison's ship. Both Public Enemy's "Fight the Power" and Beastie Boys' "Sabotage" figure in prominent ways in the narrative action of the film. Both songs are protest hip-hop anthems that challenge establishment views and positions. "Fight the Power" was written for Spike Lee's 1989 film *Do the Right Thing*, which explores racial and ethnic divisions in Brooklyn in the 1980s, specifically how the interests of minority groups are pitted against each other—in Lee's film, those of Italians and African Americans. "Fight the Power" functions as the film's refrain and reinforces the sense of the simultaneous racial disenfranchisement of Black people and their strong history of resistance. *Do the Right Thing* culminates in the murder by police of a Black character, Radio Raheem, who broadcast the song "Fight the Power" from his boom box wherever he went. In the racial climate of *Beyond*'s release in 2016, when Black lives were routinely terrorized and taken by police, the choice of "Fight the Power" as one of the key songs in the film is significant.[4]

First, the song works to "fill in" Edison, to give more weight to his backstory, to tell us something about his politics, not just his music. Public Enemy was known as a "hard-core" rap group that used its music to comment on the treatment of African Americans in US culture and media. That Edison, as the captain of the ship, brought this music with him "colors" his statements about struggle and resistance and situates those statements firmly within a narrative of Black power, which is anathema to Uhura's assimilationist philosophy of unity. Second, the song works to further "other" Edison from the crew of the Enterprise, for the only person who appreciates the song and perhaps the sentiment, "Fight the Power," is the unconventional Jaylah (she likes the "beats and shouting"), who has the audacity to ruffle Kirk by sitting in the USS *Franklin*'s captain's seat.[5] By tying Krall to Edison's Black roots, the narrative provides a tacit justification for his betrayal of the Federation and conveniently explains the need for Kirk, the white savior, to vanquish him. As Edison makes clear in his final captain's log, "You'll probably never see me again. But if you do, be ready," and then he punches the monitor. Beastie Boys' "Sabotage," also a protest song, lends further support to Edison's political views. However, in the film, Kirk and his crew use the song against Krall to disrupt the swarm pattern of his drones. Sabotage here, far from being an instrument of resistance, is appropriated by the power to quell the resistance. And because the song is already linked to Kirk and his stealing of his stepfather's car in the first reboot, *Star Trek* (2009), Kirk's use of the song and the recoding of the nature of sabotage is endorsed by the film.

SUPERHUMAN BLACKNESS

Beyond, like *Into Darkness*, links anxieties about biotechnology to race. As I've argued above, in its rewriting of the genetically enhanced, brown-skinned Sikh, Khan Noonien Singh, as white, British John Harrison, *Into Darkness* does not simply eradicate the threat the posthuman/superhuman represents to the human, it links that threat to people of color and the fear that they, too, will take over the white race. Teeming hordes of Black, Brown, and "Yellow" skins are revealed to be as existential a threat as the "skin jobs" of science fiction. The representation of this fear is particularly interesting in *Beyond* where Krall devolves from a techno monster capable of drawing energy from humans to feed his power into a Black human male. The Black man, it seems, is even more monstrous than the monster, scarred as he is by his difference and his hatred of the Federation that abandoned him. Krall's biotechnological cannibalism, which draws energy from sacrificed life forms and enables him to extend his lifespan, is the epitome of white fear—a racial vampirism that strengthens the Black man by weakening the rest.

As noted above, science fiction plots routinely employ a Manichean struggle of good and evil, human and alien, which frequently gets worked out in racial terms. In Bernardi's view, Montalbán's Khan is "an overdetermined bearer of meaning in this regard" because of his ethnic identity and because "his postapocalyptic clothes reveal a super-sized chest" (1999, 85). However, I would argue that Montalbán's role as nemesis to heroic whiteness is significantly different than other racialized characters (both human and alien) in *ST*. Certainly, the casting of an African American woman, Nichelle Nichols, as Uhura, and a Japanese American man, George Takei, as Sulu, was an important step in changing an all-white television landscape. However, as Bernardi notes, the two characters were frequently relegated to the "spatial and narrative background" providing "color" to the majority white cast but offering little else in the way of diverse experiences or views (1999, 40). Khan, by contrast, is a complex villain, a role Montalbán could perform with depth and range. Although evil, Brown Khan is represented as superior; Krall, on the other hand, is pure evil, made heinous by his bloody revenge toward the Federation. Unlike Cumberbatch's white Khan, whose life-prolonging power renders him beautiful and virile and recognizably human until the end, the analogous power of Elba's Black Krall/Edison makes him monstrous and repulsive, a deformed, freakish human at the end. Far from offering racially progressive narratives, these *Star Trek* films, like others in the SF genre, reveal once again that "[j]ust beneath the special effects, monster makeup, and futuristic narratives churn and bubble repressed racial conflicts, mythologies, desires, sexual impulses, wishes, and fears" (Nama 2008, 72).

These historic fears of the Black body take on a new urgency in the age of bioengineering and provoke a galvanized white response. Rather than dying a forgotten death, Edison chooses to fight back by harnessing the technology of the indigenous peoples of his adopted planet. In doing so, he demonstrates the threat that advanced biotechnology represents to whiteness when placed in the hands of people of color. As one bioethicist observes, "'Genetic engineering' is now a slogan used to rally conservative and neoconservative forces against a godless and soulless science. . . . [C]onservatives, pro-lifers, neoconservatives, and even an odd crew of neogreen thinkers . . . see the genetic revolution as holding the seeds of the degradation and destruction of humanity" (Caplan 2002, 58). In science fiction, biotechnology, whether in the form of AI, cloning, or genetic engineering, increasingly stands in for and justifies what was formerly understood as scientific racism. Moreover, both *Beyond* and *Into Darkness* link fears of biotechnology to raced bodies and terrorism. As Spock realizes, "Armed with this bioweapon [Krall] could rid [Yorktown] of all life and use the base's advanced technology to attack an untold number of Federation planets" (Lin 2016). Whereas *Into Darkness* consciously avoided associating terrorism with people of color, *Beyond* reaffirms the connection. Krall/Edison attacks Yorktown because he wants to destroy the Federation's way of life. The name "Yorktown" carries double significance here: *strength*, by evoking the battle of the successful repulsion of the British by the Americans during the Revolutionary War, and *terror*, by evoking the assault on "American values" represented by the terrorist attack in New York on 9/11 (particularly as Krall's aircraft crashes into the city). Krall/Edison's attack on Yorktown secures his position as un-American; or, more accurately, it demonstrates that his kind of Americanness, the experience of the disenfranchised minority, is dangerous and must be defeated at all costs.

In the final battle scene between Krall/Edison and Kirk, the competing philosophies of the two men are fully exposed. Kirk, obviously shocked by the morphing of Krall into Edison, asks Edison what happened to him. On hearing his name again, Edison admits that he's "missed being me" but has found his purpose: "the means to bring the galaxy back to the struggle that made humanity strong." When Kirk suggests that he "underestimates humanity," Edison angrily reminds him that he "fought for humanity. Lost millions to the Xindi and Romulan wars. And for what? For the Federation to sit me in a captain's chair and break bread with the enemy." Like Uhura, Kirk embraces a politics of assimilation: "We change, we have to, or we spend the rest of our lives fighting the same battles" (Lin 2016). From Edison's perspective, such politics fail to acknowledge the specificity of his struggle and the fact that the same battles need to be fought. Here, as before, the film pulls back from a sympathetic view of Edison and instead connects his struggle for justice to violence. Kirk and Edison engage in a battle of good vs. evil, represented as white vs. Black. When Kirk tells Edison to "give up," Edison makes a pointed comparison between the two men: "What, like you did?" he says to Kirk. "I read your ship's log. Captain James T. Kirk. At least I know what I am. I am a soldier." Kirk, employing reason to Edison's passion, says, "You won the war, Edison. You gave us peace." Edison responds, "Peace is not what I was born into" (Lin 2016). And with that final statement, he resumes his efforts to vaporize Yorktown. Rather than explain Edison's defection as a result of his abandonment by the Federation, the film situates it in his preference for fighting over peace—and by implication, in his inherent unfitness to captain a ship. As the Admiral regretfully makes clear to Kirk, "For decades, the Federation taught that he was a hero" (Lin 2016). As Krall transitions from the reptilian alien form to a Black human body in a Starfleet uniform, and the good and noble white man fights the hateful demonic Black man and wins, white superiority is affirmed. Kirk, of course, gets the last word: "Better to die saving lives than live with taking them. That is what I was born into" (Lin 2016). The struggle and defeat of Edison have strengthened Kirk's wavering purpose, demonstrating his ability to save not only his crew but all of humanity.

While there are moments in *Beyond* where alternatives to hegemonic whiteness can be seen, the film entertains such possibilities only to rearticulate them in the service of the dominant power structure. Although such blatant racial coding would seem anathema to the long-standing philosophy of the *Star Trek* franchise, we get a better understanding of the racism expressed in the film when viewed in the context of the racial politics of the Obama-to-Trump era. By tying racial fears to advances in biotechnology and genetic engineering, *Into Darkness* and *Beyond* engage in a new form of social Darwinism or scientific racism. These films reflect the fact that current concerns about biotechnology intersect with anxieties about race and help explain the new brand of populist conservatism underwritten by race hatred that is the "Trump phenomenon." If bioengineering attempts to "solve biological problems through the application of technology, including engineering at the molecular and cellular level,"[6] these reboots appear to suggest that racial difference is the biological "problem" that bioengineering sets out to solve and, in exploring the ramifications of this, arrive at some frightening conclusions. Both *Into Darkness* and *Beyond* expose a conservative fear that if biotechnology is not controlled, white people will be dominated by racial "others."

Chapter 7

OF CHIMERAS AND MEN

The concerns about bioengineering and the "superhuman" potential of Black or Brown bodies raised by *Into Darkness* and *Beyond* mirror those explored in the *Planet of the Apes* franchise in the metaphor of the ape itself. In chapter 2, I examined how the biologically engineered intelligence of the apes in the new franchise represents white fears about Black advancement. I want to return to the scientific questions raised in the *Apes* films, specifically those related to chimeras and germline manipulation, as these targeted concerns reflect anxieties similar to those expressed in the *Star Trek* reboots and signal larger concerns among the white populace. *Rise of the Planet of the Apes* explores issues relating to the ethics of bioengineering and big pharma and the extent to which we should utilize animals as test subjects in human drug trials. To that end, the film also questions species boundaries and what constitutes the difference between the human and the animal. On the one hand, *Rise* elicits sympathy for animals but then suggests that these non-human animals represent an existential threat to humans. On the surface, the film warns that advances in bioengineering challenge the "us" vs. "them" of the human/animal divide. Both *Rise* and its 2014 sequel *Dawn of the Planet of the Apes* expose these anxieties overtly—apes are empowered and refuse to stay subjugated to humans; however, because the films are successors to the original franchise, which utilized apes as stand-ins for African Americans and employ many of the same storylines and characters, fears about the dissolution of species boundaries can be seen to be entwined with fears about the dissolution of racial boundaries and the social and cultural hierarchies that keep those boundaries in place.

In the tumult of the civil rights movements of the '60s and '70s, "*Planet* . . . identifie[d] fear of the 'others' difference as a central cause of racism and racial violence. *Conquest* and *Battle* later provided the further insight, present just below the surface in *Planet*, that racism stems not only from a fear of the 'other's' difference, but also from the fear that the 'other' may in fact—and in very significant ways—be the same" (Greene 1998, 36). These questions still motivate racist ideology today, but they are also increasingly being applied to animals, forcing us to reexamine the human/animal divide. Whereas in the original franchise racial conflict is reinscribed as species conflict (Greene 1998, 21), the new films deal with fears associated with both race *and* species conflict, and specifically the capacity of science to eradicate the boundaries that maintain differences between humans and animals and whites and Blacks. Anxieties arising from developments in bioengineering and genomic science due to the mapping of the human genome are expressed in terms of race in the new franchise because these technologies have the capacity to challenge fundamental conceptions of the human and its place in the social hierarchy in the same way that legal and political changes in the twentieth century challenged the privileged place of whiteness. In this twenty-first-century iteration, these concerns are married together, revealing fears that biotechnology will not only eradicate human dominance over animals but will potentially eradicate white dominance over non-whites. To understand these issues more fully, I turn now to a brief examination of some of the recent debates in bioengineering specifically related to stem cell technology and the implications of that technology for humanity in the twenty-first century.

STEM CELLS AND CLONES

Opposing views on bioengineering and genomic technology, particularly in relation to stem cells, tend to line up along partisan political lines: Republican pro-life advocates see the use of embryonic stem cells in research as ethically and morally wrong insofar as they consider experimentation with and destruction or reproduction of these stem cells to be an affront to the sanctity of life and to potentially result in the manufacture of embryos for research (fetal farming). Those in favor of stem cell research argue that there is no cause for ethical or moral concern because stem cells come from donor eggs left over from assisted reproductive treatments like IVF, which would be destroyed anyway. They advocate instead for the lives of people suffering from Parkinson's, ALS, heart disease, and spinal cord injuries, which could be saved by the advances brought about by stem cell research. The conservative view on stem cells is certainly consistent with the pro-life/right-to-life platform of the Republicans insofar as they view the embryos from which the stem cells are taken as fetuses themselves because they have the *capacity* for potential life. Stem cell advocates, by contrast, point out that the stem cells aren't taken from embryos but from blastocysts, a mass of cells too small to be seen by the human eye, which, without successful transplantation, could never grow into human life.

However there is more to conservative opposition to bioengineering than simply pro-life concerns over the destruction or misuse of embryonic stem cells. Since 1996, when Scottish embryologists Ian Wilmut and Keith Campbell successfully cloned Dolly the sheep from an adult somatic cell, fears about the possibility of using stem cells to clone humans have dominated ethical debates in the field of bioengineering. At that time, concerns over human cloning were expressed by both Republicans and Democrats. In 1997, Democratic President Bill Clinton issued an executive order banning federal funding for human cloning research and a US Senate Subcommittee on Public Health and Safety held hearings addressing the need for regulation of scientific research utilizing stem cells for human cloning. In 1998, Republican Senators Bill Frist and Kit Bond proposed a bill to ban human cloning, which included felony charges with sentences of up to ten years for scientists conducting research in "somatic nuclear transfer" in humans. The vote on the bill was shelved due to a lack of agreement among senators as to whether a human life merits legal protection at conception or at birth. In the mid to late '90s, concern over cloning related primarily to humans. At that time, the ethics of animal cloning and stem cell transfer involving animals were not being debated by ethicists or politicians, and there were no attempts to regulate it.

All of that changed, however, in 2003, when the mapping of the human genome was completed. For the first time, scientists were able to identify and isolate specific gene sequences, prompting renewed fears about human cloning and designer babies. Once again, the moral, ethical, financial, and scientific impact of "genetic medicine" was of concern to politicians and world leaders alike. During their terms in office, both US President Bill Clinton and UK Prime Minister Tony Blair had invested money in the international Human Genome Project, hoping to "secure an economic advantage for their nations by making them the world leaders in biotechnology" (Caplan 2002, 57). President George W. Bush, by contrast, was hesitant to embrace advances in genetic science. Although aware of the potential for biotechnology to cure diseases in humans, Bush cautioned Americans, in a speech in the White House Rose Garden in 2002, not to "travel without an ethical compass into a world we could live to regret" (quoted in Caplan 2002, 57). Consistent with the politics of his Republican Party platform, Bush had earlier, in 2001, signaled his opposition to stem cell research. As the science improved during the Bush presidency, Republican pushback to advances in genetic medicine continued to grow.

In his State of the Union address in 2006, President Bush asked Congress "to pass legislation to prohibit the most egregious abuses of medical research: human cloning in all its forms; [and] creating or implanting embryos for experiments." He added a new cautionary note this time, calling for a ban on "creating human-animal hybrids" (Bush 2006). Bush briefly became a target of late-night talk-show hosts, as critics puzzled over his claim that researchers were creating "human-animal hybrids." Did he really imagine scientists were mating animals and humans? Were we living on the island of Dr. Moreau? Undoubtedly, Bush meant to say human-animal *chimeras*, which are routinely produced in laboratories to facilitate the testing of drugs on human tissue without harm to humans. Human-mouse chimeras, to offer just one example, are bred to study neurodegenerative disorders, autoimmune diseases, and various forms of cancer in humans; and transgenic pigs are created for use as donors of organs for human transplantation. Animal *hybrids*, by contrast, are created when an egg from one species is fertilized with sperm from another species, creating a third species, such as a mule, which is the offspring of a male donkey and a female horse. Chimeras, however, occur through the transplanting of genetically different cells (from a separate fertilization event) from one organism into another organism. Thus, a patient who receives a heart transplant from a human donor and a patient who undergoes porcine heart valve replacement are both chimeras—intraspecies and interspecies, respectively—because the cells introduced are from genetically different organisms. A human-animal embryonic chimera, specifically, is produced by introducing human stem cells into an animal embryo so that the chimera is composed of cells containing the complete human genome and the complete genome of the animal species.

Whether in the form of a chimera or hybrid, it is the idea of mixing human DNA with animal DNA that seems to cause the most concern to bioethicists and legislators who seek to regulate the practice. To some bioethicists, human "dignity" would be eroded by the presence of a human-animal chimera that could possess functional and cognitive human-like capacities. "Human dignity is based on the recognition that human beings possess, will possess, or have possessed functional and emergent psychological capacities that indicate they are worthy of respect" (Karpowics et al. 2004, quoted in Palacios-González 2015b, 489). According to this view, the respect accorded to humans is a result of their advanced cognitive and psychological abilities; if this capacity for higher-order thinking was expressed in chimeric forms, the concept of human dignity, which for these critics defines, in part, what it means to be human, would be eroded. Other critics fear the moral, and by extension legal, confusion that could result from crossing species boundaries, forcing us "to confront the possibility that humanness is neither necessary nor sufficient for personhood (the term typically used to denote a being with full moral standing)" (Robert and Baylis 2003, 10).

ECCE HOMO/ECCE MONO

In 2005, two years after the final mapping of the human genome was released, a draft sequence of the common chimpanzee genome was published, confirming what evolutionists had long claimed, that humans share common ancestry with African great apes (Coors et al. 2010, 658), and, further, that humans differ genomically from chimps by no more than 1.2–1.6 percent (Robert and Baylis 2003, 4). The result fueled the conversation about the efficacy of using non-human primates to study "human lineage specific (HLS) sequences." As researchers have noted, "[T]he high level of similarity between their genetic background and that of humans makes [apes] an attractive host species for transgenic studies of the function of HLS sequences"; however, the scientific insights "are outweighed by ethical concerns regarding the generation of such 'humanized' apes" (Coors et al. 2010, 658).

At the center of these fears and reservations about stem cells and the uses to which they might be put, whether through cloning or in the creation of chimeras, is the effect such organisms would have on the definition and status of the human. Conservative critics of bioengineering William Kristol and Eric Cohen have likened stem cell research and human cloning to "genetic terrorism," which threatens the "meaning of human mortality," and they argue that the very essence of human life is being held ransom by "hubristic scientists" and "squishy liberals" (Kristol and Cohen 2002, 299). But it's not just the science of bioengineering that is forcing us to examine the claim of human exceptionalism. Philosophers, scientists, and ethicists working in the field of animal studies recognize the human/animal binary as a false one and remind us that humans are animals, too. Preferring the terms "human animals" and "non-human animals," animal studies scholars view our culture's pervasive anthropocentrism as "speciesism," a form of discrimination toward animals that is analogous to racism and sexism. Speciesism "relies upon the tacit agreement that the transcendence of that fantasy figure called the 'human' requires the sacrifice of the 'animal' and the animalistic, which in turn makes possible a symbolic economy in which we can engage in a 'non-criminal putting to death' (as Derrida puts it) of other humans as well by marking them as animal" (Wolfe 1999, 116). Whether you support human exceptionalism or not, there is no question that the bioengineering of humans and animals requires a reexamination of species boundaries and the rights and benefits accorded to those within a species. "Interspecies hybrids and chimeras made with human materials 'straddle the line between *us* and *them*.' As such, these beings threaten our social identity, our unambiguous status as human beings" (Robert and Baylis 2003, 8).

Concerns about chimeras among scholars and ethicists stem primarily from the ethics of crossing species boundaries and the effect of such a practice on both humans and the chimeric animal. But Henry Greely demonstrates that the main issues having to do with the opposition to human/non-human chimeras stem from fears about "brains, gametes, and looks" (Greely 2013, 681). These concerns are most marked in relation to the implanting of human stem cells into non-human primates and anxiety about the potential capacity for them to develop human brain function and reproduce offspring with human DNA. Because apes "have the greatest potential to produce human-like phenotypes ... [they] carry a unique potential for harm" (Coors et al. 2010, 658). To that end, "The Human Chimera Prohibition Act" of 2005, sponsored by former senator and governor of Kansas, Sam Brownback, would "classify as federal felonies a variety of activities that would mix genes, cells, or tissues from human and non-human animals" Greely 2013, 672). But as Greely notes, the bill's definition of chimera makes clear that the impetus for the regulation stems from fears about the impact human DNA would have on the cognition and reproduction of non-human species, specifically primates. Mouse DNA also bears a striking similarity to human DNA, sharing 85 percent of the same genes as humans, and 90 percent of genes linked to disease are the same in mice as in humans. No one is particularly concerned about the cognitive capacity of mice, however, because the small size of their brains prevents any possibility that they could mimic human consciousness; a non-human primate, particularly a great ape, on the other hand, represents a real threat to human dominance. As one study concluded, "[I]t is not absurd to think that a gorilla with a brain derived from human embryonic stem cells or human brain stem cells would have a substantially 'humanlike' brain and possibly humanlike behaviors" (Greely 2013, 683). And if human stem cells were introduced at the embryonic stage, they could permanently alter the germline of the ape species.

The current fascination on both sides with the impact the genome has on race and identity marks a return to the racialist thinking of the past, where biology was used as proof to justify inequality and shore up white power. Historically, "[T]he extremity of beliefs in essential racial distinctiveness has been correlated with the severity of racial discrimination" (Phelan et al. 2014, 297). Today, the mapping of the human genome gives rise to concurrent fears about species boundaries and racial boundaries. Or, to put it another way, anxiety over species boundaries gets articulated in the same way as anxiety about racial boundaries. In fact, bioethicists often utilize the example of miscegenation to discuss the ethics of crossing species boundaries (Palacios-González 2015a). Two leading voices in the case against species crossing, Jason Robert and Françoise Baylis, suggest that we might classify human-animal hybrids according to "the relatively recent practice in the United States of classifying octoroons (persons with one-eight Negro blood; the offspring of a quadroon and a white person) as Black. By analogy, perhaps 1% animal DNA (i.e., mitochondrial DNA) makes for an animal" (2003, 8). The arguments advanced by bioethicists concerned with violations of human dignity and species crossing in chimera debates sound alarmingly like arguments mounted by eugenicists in the nineteenth and twentieth century to safeguard the purity of the white race against race mixing. Recall that the opposition to human/animal chimeras is grounded in concerns about cognition and reproduction. Just as antebellum southern whites refused literacy to Black slaves for fear that they would organize and revolt and created laws against miscegenation to uphold the fiction of racial inviolability, humans fear a loss of control over animals who are intelligent and could reproduce that intelligence in subsequent generations through alterations in the species germline. This link between species and races is not mere analogy; it betrays the associative connection in some white minds between Black people and apes.

Produced and released when social and ethical concerns about bioengineering were gathering steam in the media and in political and scientific communities, the films in the new *Planet of the Apes* franchise express anxiety and ambivalence about enhancing animals through biotechnology, and these fears can be seen to intersect with white anxieties about racial difference and its permanence. Bioethicists' primary concern about non-human primates possessing human intelligence and the trepidation about the reproduction of such creatures are clearly on display in the newest *Planet of the Apes* movies. In these films, just as in the previous franchise, the fear of enhanced apes, or advanced apes who can no longer be kept in their place, mirrors white fear about the empowerment of Blacks. Further, the portrayal of human hubris resulting in science running amok and producing human victims serves as a cautionary tale about how genetic engineering might overturn the "natural" order of things.

Captured in the wild by African traffickers, apes are sent to the labs of Gen-Sys, a pharmaceutical corporation, as test subjects for a potential treatment for Alzheimer's disease. The lead researcher in the trial, Will Rodman (James Franco), explains that the drug, ALZ-112, is a "gene therapy that allows the brain to create its own cells in order to repair itself," thus enabling "neurogenesis" (Wyatt 2011). Right away, Will and his team notice an improvement in the apes. Performing a task called the Lucas Tower, which consists of moving different-sized disks from one rod to another in the fewest number of moves without placing a larger disk on a smaller one, an ape called Bright Eyes (in the first of many references to the 1968 *Planet of the Apes*) exhibits improved cognitive capacity. Before the drug, Bright Eyes (Terry Notary) is unable to perform the puzzle; after the treatment, she can complete the task in twenty moves, just five shy of the optimal result. Her transformation encourages Will to obtain permission from the board to test the drug on humans. As the technicians attempt to bring Bright Eyes to the board room for observation, she becomes aggressive and attacks the technician who is trying to remove her. She then runs rampant in the building, destroying everything in her path, until she is shot dead by a security guard. Considering the apes to be "contaminated," Steven

Jacobs (David Oyelowo), the profit-driven African American CEO, orders all of them to be put down in the most "cost-effective way." Bright Eyes's aggression is later understood to be attributed to the fact that she had given birth and was trying to protect her infant. As neither Franklin, the lab's ape handler, nor Will can bring themselves to kill the baby, Will takes it home to his father, who is suffering from Alzheimer's.

It is with this development that the film begins to explore the implications of enhanced cognition and the effects of an altered germline in non-human primates. In doing so, Rise thematizes the prevailing anxiety in chimera debates about species confusion—that is, the cost of blurring the boundaries between humans and animals and the resulting consequences for humans. In showing that a genetic transference from mother to child results in hyperintelligence that far exceeds that of the mother and the human counterpart, the film sets the stage to explore the ramifications of bioengineering animals and targets those anxieties expressed by bioethicists about the blurring of species boundaries and, by extension, racial ones.

OUT OF AFRICA

From the opening scene, *Rise of the Planet of the Apes* foregrounds the fundamental binaries that the film will explore: human vs. animal and nature vs. science against the larger racial division of white vs. Black. A clear analogy is established right from the beginning between the plight of the apes and the plight of African slaves captured and brought to North America. The film opens with a panning aerial shot over a canopy of lush greenery. This "Africa" of the opening scene is a bucolic Eden where a caravan of chimpanzees travels through the forest, unaware of the predators that stalk them. Their peace is quickly disrupted by human traffickers snaking through the trees who capture the apes and transport them to the labs of big pharma in America. Wielding machetes and pursuing the apes with nets, the African men are shown as predators, creating a parallel between human savagery and animality. Further, by juxtaposing shots of Black faces with ape faces in medium close-up and situating human ululating "war" cries with the agitated screeching of chimps, the film performs a visually racist substitution, associating Black bodies with ape bodies. The "ape-trade" is a neo-slave trade. In this iteration, the apes are sold into a form of scientific slavery that will callously exploit and maim their bodies for profit. Consistent with this representation, Black men in the film are either evil opportunists, such as the pharmaceutical company's CEO and the African ape traffickers, or hapless victims who kill or get killed by the apes. In this, the film follows a strategy utilized in *Conquest of the Planet of the Apes*

(1972), where African American actors were cast as ape slavers and as high-ranking officials. Greene suggests that this form of casting helps to expose the racial subtext of the film:

> The association of ape slave and black handler is crucial for establishing and disclaiming the film's concern. The film strives to tell the audience that its concern is not about black Americans, primarily through the roles they play in the society envisioned by the film. . . . Having African-Americans run the slavery apparatus is another signal that, on the surface, the condition of blacks and black-white relationships are sufficiently non-problematic that the blacks involved see no problem with being part of the master class in relation to the apes and have no difficulty with participating in the subjugation of another race. Establishing that textually nonproblematic relationship, while keeping it subtextually ironic, was one of the strategies employed both to hold off and engage the issue of the oppression of black Americans. (Greene 1998, 101)

The demonization of Black humans in *Rise* occurs principally through the main character Steven Jacobs. Where Will is motivated by the desire to do good by helping people with a "wide range of brain disorders," Jacobs is only interested in the profits. He shows no consideration for the apes or the humans that would be helped by the treatment, just the bottom line. Jacobs occupies an important function in the film; thematically, his role as the evil agent behind the testing displaces white culpability and seemingly removes the allegorical racial implications of the human/ape opposition, but at the same time, the film works to associate him both with Africa and with the apes.

A far cry from the sterile steel and glass of the rest of the building, his office is saturated in warm light with African-inspired art and native plants. In one particularly revealing scene, Jacobs is juxtaposed with the most dangerous ape in the series, Koba. The first ape in the lab to receive the new and improved serum, ALZ-113, Koba responds quickly to the treatment. Jacobs, fascinated with the potential of the drug, watches Koba from the hallway and then enters the lab space. Initially, the mise-en-scène establishes a distance between the man and the ape; framed by the door of the lab, Jacobs is on the threshold between the outside and the inside, whereas Koba's slightly out-of-focus body occupies the foreground of the shot. Eventually, Jacobs enters Koba's space as the camera moves to a medium shot, bringing the two closer together and obscuring the glass partition that separates them. Koba, without turning toward Jacobs, grunts and begins writing Jacobs's name with his finger on a touch screen monitor. Now shot in a tight close-up, Jacobs is observing Koba's writing on the monitor. Only when he's finished does Koba turn to Jacobs, prompting Jacobs to turn and

Jacobs and Koba confront each other. (*Rise of the Planet of the Apes*, 2011)

The juxtaposition of Koba and the name "Jacobs" creates an association between the ape and the Black man. (*Rise of the Planet of the Apes*, 2011)

Jacobs recognizes Koba's intelligence. (*Rise of the Planet of the Apes*, 2011)

acknowledge Koba head-on. In the shot/reverse shot sequence, Jacobs remains framed within the center of his close-up, but Koba is positioned to the right with the monitor bearing "Jacobs" included in his tight frame. Narratively, the writing of the name signifies Koba's now advanced intelligence, but the choice of the name and the composition of the shot all work to create an association between Koba and Jacobs, between the ape and the Black man.

Furthermore, as Koba seeks bloody revenge in the second film, *Dawn of the Planet of the Apes*, the connection established between them suggests that Jacobs is always already an advanced ape whose ambition and greed will be the downfall of civilization. As Susana Loza observes, "The emphasis on black complicity and the erasure of white responsibility allows for the reverence of past white heroes and denial of any accountability for the cumulative effects of centuries of white supremacy" (2017, 116). When Will wants to proceed cautiously with the ALZ-113 trials until they know all of the effects, Jacobs overrules him, revealing once again his purely venal interests. As he says to Will, "You make history, I make money. Wasn't that our arrangement?" (Wyatt 2011).

"I LOVE CHIMPANZEES. I'M ALSO AFRAID OF THEM. IT'S APPROPRIATE TO BE AFRAID OF THEM."

There are several early scenes in the film which consciously frame an association between Caesar's experiences and those of Black people subject to racism, which is to say there are numerous occasions in the film where Caesar is coded as Black. The first is when young Caesar, spying an open door, leaves the house to play with the neighbor's kids. He is treated like a violent intruder, beaten off with a baseball bat and told to "get out." When the neighbor threatens, "If I see that animal anywhere near my house or my kids again. . . ." Will's father, Charles, replies that "he's not dangerous." Caesar is like a racial interloper who, by entering the white domain of the neighbor's house, has violated not just the physical boundaries of the yard but the racial boundaries of the family. Later, Caroline, Will's veterinarian girlfriend, echoing racist fears about Black masculinity, warns that Caesar "won't stay this way for long. He's gonna soon grow into a large and powerful animal." As a "child," Caesar believes the world is open to him, but that gets taken away from him as people begin to fear him. As Caroline makes clear, "I love chimpanzees. I'm also afraid of them. It's appropriate to be afraid of them" (Wyatt 2011).

We might argue that the problem with Caesar is that he doesn't know his place; he thinks he's human and realizes the hard way that he's not. He is like the colonized person described by Fanon, who, in his home colony of Martinique, identifies with Tarzan but, in the colonial metropole of Paris, is forced to identify with the "savages."[1] Indeed, a clear parallel is drawn between Caesar's coming into awareness of the humans' perception of him as an animal and a Black person's experience of white people's perception of him or her as incommensurably "Other." On one of adult Caesar's outings in the park, he encounters an animal, a dog on a leash, who barks and growls at him. Caesar looks puzzled and then silences the dog with a loud hiss. When Will pulls him away, Caesar becomes aware of his leash and how he is positioned in relation to the animal and not to the human. When Will tries to put him in the back of the station wagon, Caesar refuses and walks around to sit in the seat. Caesar's refusal to be treated like an animal sent to the back echoes Rosa Parks's refusal to sit in the back of the bus. And by mapping his refusal onto hers, the film both racializes Caesar and animalizes Blackness. Clearly upset, Caesar asks Will, by signing, if he is a pet. In a shot/reverse shot sequence where each is framed in medium close-up, the camera gives equal footing to the two characters. But when Will tells Caesar that he is his father and Caesar asks, "What is Caesar?" we know the jig is up. The origin story that Will gives Caesar is an unnatural one: he was born in a laboratory. The ultimate message here is that Caesar's existential crisis would have been avoided if Will had not tampered with nature. However, because of the prior coding of Caesar's animalness as Blackness, we get an additional reading: Caesar isn't human because Caesar isn't white.

The film is at its most overt in racing Caesar when he is incarcerated after attacking the neighbor who was attacking Charles. Narratively, the events of this plot point in *Rise* closely follow both the first film in the original series, *Planet of the Apes* (1968), and the fourth film, *Conquest of the Planet of the Apes* (1972). In the first film, George Taylor (Charlton Heston) and his crew crash-land on the ape "planet" and encounter a group of mute, "primitive" humans. The new arrivals are soon rounded up by gorillas on horseback and taken into captivity. Taylor is the only one of the original crew that makes it; Dodge, an African American astronaut, is shot and killed (and later stuffed and displayed in a museum), and Landon, a white astronaut, is lobotomized. Taylor is shot in the throat, temporarily impairing his speech and preventing him from distinguishing himself from the mute humans that are imprisoned and studied by the apes.

Taylor, named "Bright Eyes" by Zira (Kim Hunter), the chimpanzee scientist, is subject to a variety of dehumanizing treatments in captivity; he is stripped, beaten, tied up, gagged, and, in an obvious echo of the tensions of the film's 1960s political moment, hosed. On one level, he resembles a hunted animal, but in the context of the civil rights movement and the reversal of racial station that the original film wanted to depict, his situation and the mistreatment he endures mirror those experienced by African Americans during that period. The effect of this racial role reversal is two-fold, however, as Taylor's subjugation forces a white audience to see the unfairness and cruelty of the treatment endured by Black people, but at the same time, because the apes (coded as Black [Greene 1998]) are the ones who mete out the punishment and behave in malicious and illogical ways, it reinforces a white perception of Black people as aggressive and bestial.

Taylor strung up by the apes. (*Planet of the Apes*, 1968)

Dehumanizing treatment of humans by apes. (*Planet of the Apes*, 1968)

Zira views the humans as beasts and curiosities. (*Planet of the Apes*, 1968)

In effect, the film functions as an object lesson for whites about the consequences of relinquishing white power and spurs anger and incredulity among them that a white man (Charlton Heston!) could be subject to such treatment. Curiously, then, Taylor embodies the disenfranchised position of the African American at the same time as he reflects the seemingly unquestionable superiority of the white man. Moreover, because Taylor's degradation occurs through a process of overt animalization, an interpellation that we recognize as false, his animality gets transferred to the apes, who become stripped of the veneer of civilization and returned to their rightful place as "savage beasts." The ape ascendency is thus revealed to be temporary and inevitably doomed.

DAMN DIRTY APES

Consistent with its explicit message about the bioethical treatment of animals, *Rise* extends the animalization of Taylor by the apes to the experience of modern-day lab animals. In *Rise*, "Bright Eyes" is the ultimate victim: captured, trafficked, experimented upon, and killed. But just as Taylor was both a lab animal and a prisoner, *Rise* broadens the analogy beyond the lab to include Caesar, who, locked up in the "primate shelter" like Taylor, is considered a dumb beast by his cruel human jailors and is harassed and hosed by one particularly vindictive "prison" guard.

From this point in the narrative, the plot closely follows the plot of *Conquest of the Planet of the Apes* (1972), where apes are enslaved by humans. The effect of this is to duplicate the problematic doubling of sympathy and fear, victim and oppressor, seen in the original film. Both Caesars, endowed with intelligence and speech, infiltrate the subordinated ape population, emancipate them, and lead them in revolution against their human oppressors. There are obvious parallels between Taylor and Caesar. Like Taylor, who was rendered temporarily mute, Caesar does not speak at first. Both captives utter their first words under extreme duress and, in doing so, mark the beginning of their separation from their "kind." What's different is the framing of these two parallel themes and the distinctive resonance of each when race and racial context is taken into account.

In *Planet*, Taylor attempts to escape his captors but is ruthlessly pursued, pelted, whipped, roped, dragged by a horse, and ultimately hung up by the apes. When they go to cut him down, he speaks to the apes for the first time, delivering the famous line, "Get your stinking paws off me, you damn dirty ape!" (Wilson 1968). Arguably one of the most famous movie lines of all time, the rebuke strikes a chord with members of a white audience because it seems to affirm what has been obscured all along: the blatant (stinking, dirty) bestialization of the apes and their incredible overreach in attempting to usurp

Taylor is hosed by ape prison guards. (*Planet of the Apes*, 1968)

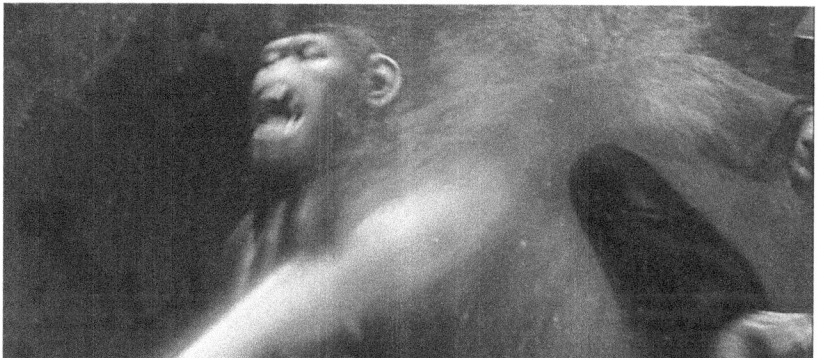
Caesar is hosed by human prison guards. (*Rise of the Planet of the Apes*, 2011)

human power. Though Taylor remains captive, undergoes a rigged trial, and eventually escapes again, he has the moral high ground. While the film sets out to analogize the humans' experience under ape rule with African American experiences under white rule, it only reinforces the purported superiority of whiteness, thus providing tacit justification for racial oppression.

This position is echoed in *Rise*, where it's the evil Dodge Landon (in a curious amalgamation of the names of Taylor's fellow astronauts) who utters the iconic "dirty ape" line to Caesar, who angrily rages out his first word, "No!"[2] While I think it's probably the case that most (non-white supremacist) viewers sympathize with Caesar at this moment, the riot that ensues when the apes are freed, culminating in Caesar's electrocution of Landon and their violent confrontation with the police on the San Francisco bridge, leverages fear over sympathy. It is also Dodge Landon (Tom Felton) who utters Taylor's other famous line, "It's a madhouse!" when the apes first reject the newly incarcerated Caesar. By giving Taylor's lines to the vindictive antagonist, *Rise* betrays the ambivalent racial message of *Planet*, evoking white sympathy along with white fear.

The racial reversal works for the most part in *Planet* because there is something obviously incongruous about humans being jailed by apes. Heston's Taylor always seems out of place and ready to right the wrong that deprives him of his liberty. This incongruity is supposed to force the viewer to see the treatment of African Americans as equally arbitrary and dehumanizing because it "imputes to white humans, through the use of one of Hollywood's favorite symbols of *specifically* white humanity [Heston], the very animalistic qualities usually ascribed to non-whites" Greene 1998, 45–46). The same cannot be said of the imprisoned apes in *Rise*. There is something disturbingly familiar and unsettling in the way these jailed apes are represented. When Caesar is apprehended after committing his "crime," he is transported to the shelter in a paddy wagon and dragged by the neck into the facility. Caesar's difference from the other apes is obvious. He is dressed in jeans and a sweater, making him appear more man than beast, and is able to communicate with Will by signing. Will and Caroline are reluctant to leave him, but John Landon (Brian Cox), the manager of the shelter, assures Will that they'll "integrate him." Dazzled at first by the mural of the fake outdoors on the wall and the extensive tree-like jungle gym, Caesar, having heeded Will's command to "trust me," asks permission to explore his new surroundings. Too late, Caesar realizes the illusion, and so begins his institutionalization. Slowly and painfully, Caesar is forced to recognize his true place in the world. And like a slave who must feign ignorance so as not to provoke his master, Maurice reminds him to be "[c]areful. Human no like smart ape." Harassed and taunted by inmates and jailors alike, Caesar throws off his "white mask" and embraces his "Black skin," eventually becoming the alpha of the other apes.

Though technically an animal shelter, the mise-en-scène is carefully crafted to resemble a prison, with rows of cages and faces pressed to the bars. The fact that the inmates, except for Maurice the Orangutan, are darkened by their fur and the jailors are white and employ classic prison control techniques all work to cement the association of apes and Blacks and to naturalize the incarceration of African American men. Shot with low lighting and in medium close-up, the apes are vicious and menacing to Caesar; in a frenzy, they pound their cages and screech at him. The jailors call the apes "stupid monkeys" and "lazy baboons," epithets that are technically appropriate in this instance but read as racial slurs when put in the context of the themes of the film and its history.

Michelle Alexander has argued that the mass incarceration of Black people since the second half of the twentieth century has operated culturally as a form of racial control. Although committing as many crimes as whites in the United States, Black men are imprisoned at rates twenty to fifty times greater (Alexander 2012, 7). "[M]ass incarceration defines the meaning of Blackness in America: Black people, especially Black men, are criminals. That is what it means to

Caesar imprisoned for his crimes. (*Rise of the Planet of the Apes*, 2011)

The "primate shelter" functions as a symbolic analog of a contemporary prison and reflects the disproportionate numbers of African Americans in custody. (*Rise of the Planet of the Apes*, 2011)

be Black" (Alexander 2012, 197). When Will finally arrives to release Caesar, recognizing the captivity of his fellow inmates, Caesar refuses to accompany him. Seeing this, the "warden" Landon muses: "I guess he likes it better here with his own kind." The species difference that Landon observes is layered over by the other formal and diegetic elements that racialize the prison and Caesar's experience there, seemingly pointing to the inevitability of the incarceration of Caesar and his "kind." In this way, *Rise* endorses and indeed participates on a cultural level in the "tightly networked system of laws, policies, customs, and institutions that operate collectively to ensure the subordinate status of a group defined largely by race" (Alexander 2012, 13).

"THESE APES ARE SMARTER THAN YOU THINK! WE'VE GOT TO KILL THE LEADER."

The original apocalyptic ending of racial uprising and revolt in 1972's *Conquest of the Planet of the Apes* was changed, according to Greene, due to fears that it would incite real racial violence. "Following the pessimistic pattern of the first three films, *Conquest* was intended to end with MacDonald's call for mercy going unheeded and the apes planning to reverse the system of domination, envisioning, indeed plotting, humanity's destruction in a fanatical vision of racial nationalism" (Greene 1998, 109). Thus, the film originally ended with Caesar's inflammatory speech: "[F]rom this day forward, my people will crouch and conspire and plot and plan for the inevitable day of man's downfall . . . And we shall build our own cities, in which there will be no place for humans except to serve our ends . . . that day is upon you now!" In the released version, Caesar takes a more accommodationist position, advocating compassion and understanding.

Where *Conquest* pulls away from racial apocalypse, *Rise* and *Dawn* engage it directly. Freed from prison and enhanced by ALZ-113, the apes invade the city, attacking police, overturning cars, and destroying property. If the revolts and violence in *Conquest* called to mind the Watts rebellion of 1965 Los Angeles, as I argued in chapter 4, the ape revolution in *Rise* evokes images of the 1992 LA uprising and foreshadows those that would take place in Ferguson after the killing of Michael Brown and in Baltimore after the murder of Freddie Gray. In fact, just as the white audience of the original series was primed to associate the ape uprising with Black nationalism, a contemporary audience recognizes the metaphor of persecuted apes being attacked by police. The difference, however, is that in *Rise* the persecuted prevail and successfully push back against the police. Outmatched in size and strength, the police have no chance against the apes. While the almost complete destruction of humanity is not directly attributed to the apes but rather to the ALZ-113, which is toxic to humans, the disease will come to be known as "simian flu." And as the narrative of *Dawn* reveals, though the apes have created a peaceful society for themselves, the humans want to eliminate them and take back the "power."

Where Caesar is assimilationist and conciliatory, Koba, by contrast, will neither forgive nor forget. His scarred body betrays the truth that he's "seen inside of a whole lot of labs" and wants revenge. Pointing to his body when Caesar advocates peace, Koba makes clear that each of his scars recalls "[t]his human work. . . . This human work. . . ." (Reeves 2014). As the narrative arc of the original movies reveals, white anxiety about Blackness stems from the fear that the evils visited on the slave will be returned on the master. *Rise* exploits this fear, depicting intellectually advanced apes escaping "prison," destroying

Apes take over the Golden Gate Bridge. (*Rise of the Planet of the Apes*, 2011)

property, killing police, and overtaking the city. Interestingly, Jacobs is the one who voices the driving motivation here, echoing a racist strategy employed against black leaders during the civil rights era (and more recently during Obama's presidency): "These apes are smarter than you think! We've got to kill the leader" (Wyatt 2011). Curiously, the acquired intelligence has no bearing on the apes' behavior; they are depicted as angry beasts out for revenge, instinctively reverting to their "savage" nature. Once again, sympathy turns to fear as the apes, by virtue of their numbers and their unmatched strength, completely take over.

Of all the humans on the bridge, Jacobs is the only one whose fate is meted out deliberately by the apes as the gorilla, "Buck," (yes, Buck) launches himself off the bridge and takes down the helicopter with Jacobs and the pilot in it. Filmed first in an aerial long shot from Jacobs's perspective and then in a reverse shot behind the advancing Buck, the camera pulls in for a tight close-up, for the second time in the sequence, on Buck's angry face and wide gaping mouth; this enraged "Black" face filling the entire screen is the iconic historic catalyst of white fear. As the scared white pilot attempts to shoot him with his pistol, Buck keeps coming, flying through the air, straight into the spray of bullets.

Jacobs somehow survives, so it's Koba who is left to finish the kill after Buck goes down. When Jacobs sees Koba rising up out of the fog toward him, he knows his fate is sealed and begs, "Not you!" When Koba pushes the crashed helicopter off its precarious perch on the bridge, Jacobs's last words are "stupid monkey!" The association between Koba and Jacobs is reasserted here as neither one is redeemed. Dismayed by the deaths of innocent police, the audience is happy for Jacobs to meet his end; however, Koba's deadly act marks the beginning of his "turn" and reveals a vindictive side which will ultimately lead to Caesar's downfall in *Dawn*.

"Buck" the gorilla sacrifices his life to kill Jacobs. (*Rise of the Planet of the Apes*, 2011)

Close-up of Buck's angry face as he encounters Jacobs. (*Rise of the Planet of the Apes*, 2011)

Jacobs begs for mercy. (*Rise of the Planet of the Apes*, 2011)

Koba pushes Jacobs to his death. (*Rise of the Planet of the Apes*, 2011)

ALL IN OUR GENES?

Those involved in the Human Genome Project assert that their findings demonstrate once and for all that there is no genetic basis for race. "Recent biology has confirmed the conviction of those who have long insisted that racial kinds were social kinds, and it has undermined any possible argument for placing these kinds in the realm of the biological. In its broadest and most common understanding, the concept of race remains little more than the reified residue of racism" (Dupre 2008, 53). And yet those invested in maintaining the fiction of racial difference see in the findings definitive proof not just of separate races but of Caucasian superiority. Released in Obama's second term, a recent instance of this line of thinking is the book, *A Troublesome Inheritance* (2014), written by former *New York Times* science writer Nicholas Wade. Wade, who is not a geneticist or a scientist of any kind, uses data selectively from the human genome to rehash Johann Blumenbach's eighteenth-century theory that human evolution has produced several discrete races and that those races have evolved differentially as a result of environmental pressures. Moreover, Wade argues that those differences—including behaviors like violence, work ethic, and group organization—are social traits that, over time, produce change at the genetic level. A highly speculative book, Wade's main argument is that genes, not environment, resources, or geography, determine the success of one race over another. Caucasians, he claims, have developed a genetic propensity to delay gratification and save money. This, coupled with Europeans'"instinct for fairness and reciprocity," has ensured the rise of the West. Africans, by contrast, he asserts, remain rooted in *genetic* tribalism (Wade 2014, 124). According to his argument, in order to progress, Africans and African-descended peoples need to evolve from their capacity for "violent, short-term, impulsive behavior" and develop the "more disciplined, future-oriented behavior" of East Asians and Europeans (Wade 2014, 178). Ultimately, however, according to Wade, it is the West's superior adaptation that will ensure its continued dominance over other geographic groups, for "East Asian societies seem too authoritarian and conformist, despite the high abilities of their citizens, to challenge the innovation of the West" (2014, 248). Wade revives the debate that IQ is largely heritable and not environmental, asserting that "[i]ntelligence is almost certainly under genetic influence" but is forced to acknowledge that "none of the responsible alleles has yet been identified with any certainty" (2014, 190).

Although a bestseller, Wade's book has been roundly denounced by biologists and geneticists. Over one hundred of them signed a letter published in the *New York Times Book Review* stating that Wade "misappropriated" their research and confirmed that "there is no support from the field of population genetics for Wade's conjectures" (Coop et al. 2014). Population geneticists Sarah Tishkoff of the University of Pennsylvania and David Reich of Harvard University, both of whom have published extensively on patterns of human variation, were particularly aggrieved with the misuse of their data. Tishkoff, whose work was used to ground Wade's claim of the existence of three to five races, said she signed the letter to the *Times* because her work does not support the claim that Wade asserts. As Reich makes clear, "[o]ur findings do not even provide a hint of support in favor of Wade's guesswork" (quoted in Balter 2014).

FINDING YOUR ROOTS

The current popularity of services that claim to provide a personal genetic history for consumers also contributes to a reification of genetic concepts of race. While there are no racial genes, genomicists have identified alleles (gene variations) that occur in greater frequency among populations in certain geographical areas. Genetic drift occurred as groups of humans variously migrated out of Africa and populated other parts of the globe, adapting over time to those geographical environs. As a result of migration and in-group reproduction, discrete units of people share a cluster of alleles in greater frequency than individuals from other population groups (Bolnick 2008). This is not to say that specific alleles are unique to racial types or groups; rather, they occur more frequently in certain geographical populations and help to explain patterns of phenotypical variation or disease resistance/susceptibility among humans. It is this clustering specific to a geographical region that informs the commercial proliferation of companies devoted to exploring individuals' "ancestry." As critics note, the marketplace demand for such services provides a "tremendous financial incentive to package 'race' as a genetically underwritten commodity" (Koenig et al. 2008, 4). The ease and relative affordability of the tests make them appealing to the average person curious about their heritage. However, because these tests "suggest genetic differentiation among what are essentially races based on continental ancestry" (Bolnick 2008, 73), they reify a popular belief in discrete genetic races.

A not surprising result of the ready availability of these services is the widespread use of the tests by alt-right groups seeking to demonstrate an unequivocal whiteness: "[I]f you believe in the superiority of European culture and white people, then it follows that one of the most important facts you should establish is that you are white yourself" (Reeve 2016). At the same time, African Americans are also avid consumers of the tests, seeking records of ethnic kinships eradicated by diasporic dispersal, forced displacements, and the violent uprooting of the Middle Passage. Alondra Nelson argues that purveyors of these tests believe that they are getting a complete picture of their ancestral forebears. However, "at present, matching a consumer's DNA against proprietary genetic databases comprised of samples from contemporary populations, as African Ancestry and other genetic ancestry tracing companies do, cannot establish kinship with any certainty; *ethnic lineage analysis does not associate a root-seeker with specific persons at precise spatial-temporal locations*" (Nelson 2008, 260). A number of recent genomic studies have found that genetic clusters correspond to major geographic regions, typically Africa, Eurasia, East Asia, Oceania, and America, and have therefore "been interpreted as showing that racial divisions based on continental ancestry are biologically significant" (Bolnick 2008, 73–4). However, the data generated by computer programs used to estimate the number of genetic clusters present in a data set to determine ancestry based on population group are flawed. As Bolnick makes clear, the number of population groups the program finds in a sample is determined *in advance* by the programmer (2008, 74). In the same way that Morton nearly two centuries ago interpreted racial cranial capacity in terms of his belief in

Caucasian superiority, genomic researchers already subscribe to the belief in racially defined population groups and set the parameters of the program to provide data to support evidence of discrete genetic clusters. "These particular results have been emphasized simply because they fit the general notion in our society that continental groupings are biologically significant. This notion is a legacy of traditional racial thought and seems to persist even when not clearly supported by biological data" (Bolnick 2008, 77). By contrast, if the users set the program to find genetic variation beyond the five to six geographical "races," gradients of genetic change are seen between geographical regions, thus disrupting a correlation between race and geographic or continental area.

The problem with Wade's analysis and attempts by others to determine racial meanings from the genome is that racial meanings change depending on how well they "conform to existing social, political cultural loci" (Williams 2015, 1499). In other words, "'Race's' variability gives it the ability to conceptually reconfigure itself to sustain white supremacy's basic structures in response to unforeseen legitimacy challenges" (Williams 2015, 1497). In a historical echo, science is again pitted against science so that data from the human genome is used both to refute and support genetic racial difference. Wade and others of his ilk are remarkably similar in their rush to dispel any concern that their inquiries are racist. In fact, in books arguing for biological genetic differences between races, this accusation is typically the first to be addressed. Yet, as Johnny Williams argues in his examination of the way societal perceptions of race affect scientific findings, "By assigning responsibility for scientific racism to a bygone era, genomicists frame contemporary genomics as an exceptional site of scientific 'race' neutrality. However, genomicists' continuous concern with racial genetic differences suggests they remain 'race-centric' in thinking and practice" (Williams 2015, 1498). Incredibly, Wade justifies his work by suggesting that "opposition to racism is now well entrenched, at least in the Western world. It is hard to conceive of any circumstance that would reverse or weaken this judgment, particularly scientific evidence" (Wade 2014, 7). One is tempted to reach out and welcome Wade to Trump's America and remind him that his own book, in its revivification of scientific racism and its embrace by neo-Nazis, does exactly that.[3]

In 2016, the ascendancy of neo-Nazi groups and more than 900 separate incidents of hate crimes in the ten days after Trump's election, in the aftermath of the first "Black Presidency," revealed that the myth of white exceptionalism had been exposed. As a result, in the early twenty-first century, as in the nineteenth century, scientific racism and biological determinism are being deployed to shore up a fragile belief in white superiority. Now, as before, science serves as the handmaid to politics. As Omi and Winant make clear, these "[e]fforts to 're-biologize' race . . . are principally framed on the terrain of politics . . . race is now a preeminently political phenomenon" (2014, 120). In its twenty-first-century incarnation, findings from the genome are being used to reify race and bolster beliefs in essential racial differences. However, if we consider the legacy of scientific racism, which from its earliest articulations interpreted racial difference as species difference, we might consider whether these two fears about difference are essentially articulations of the same thing. Where the race question had seemingly been settled at the end of the twentieth century, the twenty-first century sees a return to outmoded views on race which are linked, temporally, to the bioengineering of animals and fears about the dissolution of species' boundaries. Science media, news media, and entertainment media work in a continuous feedback loop to perpetuate these views and affect the way audiences interpret and understand race relations in real time and in real life.

Part IV

POSTRACIAL RESISTANCE

INTERLUDE

On July 3, 2020, with the coronavirus pandemic resurging in the southern and western United States and on the heels of nationwide demonstrations protesting racism and racially motivated police violence, Donald Trump gave a divisive speech at the foot of the Mt. Rushmore monument in South Dakota. Resorting to the same kind of culturally inflammatory rhetoric that he employed on the 2016 campaign trail, in this Independence Day speech, Trump warned of a purported "far-left fascism that demands absolute allegiance." Early in June, Virginia announced the removal of several Confederate statues, including those of General Robert E. Lee and Andrew Jackson, in the city of Richmond, and just a few days prior to Trump's speech, Mississippi announced the retiring of its state flag, the last flag in the nation to incorporate the Confederate emblem. Following Trump's vehement rejection of the Pentagon's plan to rebrand bases named after military leaders of the Confederacy, the Republican-led Senate Armed Services Committee approved an amendment that would require the Pentagon to rename those bases within three years. Responding to these events, Trump introduced an executive order that would prosecute and imprison those found damaging or defacing federal monuments.

In the context of this cultural flashpoint, Trump used his Mt. Rushmore speech to vilify the left, accusing them of engineering a cultural revolution to "wipe out our history, defame our heroes, erase our values, and indoctrinate our children," whom, he claimed, are "taught in school to hate their own country." Calling out "radical" ideologues who are turning our "free and inclusive society into a place of a repression, domination, and exclusion" and accusing those who labor "under the banner of social justice" of "want[ing] to silence us," he affirmed that "we will not be silenced," again utilizing the rhetoric of "us" and "them" to further inflame national divisions that lie along racial lines. Trump gave lip service to the rights of "citizens of every race, background, religion and creed" in reinforcing his support for the police and the Second Amendment, but his suggestion that "we only kneel to Almighty God" was a clear reference to NFL player Colin Kaepernick and others who kneeled during the playing of the American anthem in protest of police brutality. At the same time, Trump implicitly invoked the racially explicit language he used just days earlier when he called the Black Lives Matter movement a "symbol of hate" (Livak and Holmes 2020) and connected protests against the police to the defacing of monuments by suggesting both were attacks on "our great country" (Trump 2020). Obviously, the "us" here refers to those on the right who share Trump's inflammatory views. However, at the time of this speech, that group was diminishing. Polls taken in the last week of June 2020 showed Trump trailing Joe Biden by as many as nine points in some states and only marginally beating or tying with him in many reliably conservative states. In addition to Trump's bungling of the country's coronavirus response, many Americans felt that Trump badly mishandled race relations in the aftermath of George Floyd's death and was out of step with rapidly evolving views on race and racially motivated police brutality. These issues, in addition to a flagging economy, would eventually secure Biden's victory in the 2020 election.

Several cultural and political crises in the spring of 2020 had an impact on Trump's falling popularity, but his misreading of the country's views on and feelings about racism and the ongoing discrimination faced by African Americans contributed to his loss of standing among voters and his ultimate loss of the presidency. In polls taken in July 2020, only 31 percent of voters surveyed had faith in Trump's ability to bring the country closer together, with only about 35 percent expressing confidence in his ability to handle race relations (Pew Research Center 2020). A CBS poll taken in June 2020 found that eight in ten Americans believed that African Americans faced discrimination compared to polls taken in 2015, which saw only 39 percent of Americans believing that whites fared better than Blacks; the 2020 poll showed 50 percent of Americans viewed white people as having a better chance of getting ahead (DePinto et al. 2020). Attitudes of white liberals on race also changed during Trump's presidency. Seventy percent of those polled in 2019 believed that "racial discrimination is the main reason why many Black people can't get ahead these days" versus 40 percent of those polled in 2010, the year that support for the Tea Party resulted in a Republican sweep of the Democratic-led House (Herndon 2019). As I've argued, film and television productions released during the Obama administration cultivated racial resentment against Black and Hispanic people and targeted white fears of demographic replacement by associating them with contamination and criminal behavior. At the same time, many Black filmmakers in the age of President Trump utilized entertainment media to combat those racially inflamed images and offer alternative versions of race and racial identity.

RACE AND THE BURDEN OF REPRESENTATION

Two years after the racial maelstrom unleashed by Trump's election, several films like Spike Lee's *BlacKkKlansman*, Carlos Lopez Estrada's *Blindspotting*, Ryan Coogler's *Creed II*, Boots Riley's *Sorry to Bother You*, and Barry Jenkins's *If Beale Street Could Talk* directly or indirectly explored structural racism and white privilege. With the exception of the satirical *Sorry to Bother You*, these films are realist narratives and illustrate contemporary racism using the lens of the past in the case of *BlacKkKlansman* and *If Beale Street Could Talk*. A key premise of my argument in *Imperiled Whiteness* is that speculative fiction film and television, including science fiction and horror, perform cultural and political race-work. Historically, science fiction texts have engaged issues of class, gender, and race differences in future worlds by using Marxist, feminist, or postcolonial perspectives as a means of commenting upon and critiquing contemporary power structures and systems of domination and inequality. However, popular science fiction texts of the twentieth century commonly use "the indirection of metaphor or allegory to consider issues of race and prejudice" and frequently render Black life in naïve opposition to or untouched by technological progress (Bould 2007, 179).

In discussing the underrepresentation of Black directors and other Black culture producers in the lucrative, blockbuster, franchise-heavy field of SF cinema, Maryann Erigha observes the impact of this exclusion on the careers of Black filmmakers as well as on the kinds of stories that get told. "Few self-consciously Black characters exist in sci-fi films," she notes. Unlike independent films, "sci-fi and fantasy blockbuster franchise films, by and large, propagate fantasies of White patriarchy and conservatively depict a nostalgic White masculinity that is unchallenged by race, class, or gender hierarchies" (Erigha 2016, 554). The sidelining of Black directors, actors, and fans in the horror genre is noted by Jordan Peele as a key motivation behind his 2017 horror film *Get Out*:

> The reason Chris in the film is falling into this place, being forced to watch this screen, that no matter how hard he screams at the screen he can't get agency across. He's not represented. And that, to me, was this metaphor for the Black horror audience, a very loyal fan base who comes to these movies, and we're the ones that are going to die first. So, the movie for me became almost about representation within the genre, within itself, in a weird way. (Quoted in Sharf 2017)

The marginalization of Black lives and Black stories in speculative fiction genres of science fiction and horror means that Black filmmakers typically tell Black stories in realist films and, as a result, as critics like Kobena Mercer, Nicole Fleetwood, and Michael Boyce Gillespie have noted, are "burdened with the rope chain of 'reality' in ways that white people simply aren't" (Allen 1995, quoted in Gillespie 2016).

Fleetwood observes that Black cultural producers are tasked with the enormous and impossible job of producing corrective interpretations to the visual field of Blackness and "to do something to alter a history and system of racial inequality that is in part constituted through visual discourse." And "[t]hat something," she contends, "is the desire to have the cultural product solve the very problem that it represents" (2011, 3). Along the same lines, Michael Boyce Gillespie has argued for the importance of separating Black art from Black life, for the "belief in black film's indexical ties to the black lifeworld foregoes a focus on nuance and occults the complexity of black film to interpret, render, incite, and speculate" (2016, 2). The expectation of racial veracity in realist film limits the artistic range of the filmmakers' vision and produces normative discourses about Black life and appears to make Black lived experience and subjects knowable to non-Black audiences.

In this final part of the book, I pivot away from cinematic and televisual texts that foreground whiteness and turn to the ways Black directors Jordan Peele and Ryan Coogler "trouble" prevailing representations of Blackness in the realm of cinema. Specifically, I will explore how they utilize the genre of speculative fiction to disrupt the visual field in which Black life has been presented as knowable and consumable. SF enables Black filmmakers to forego the responsibility and weight of having to represent the "truth" of Black life. In doing so, Black SF alleviates the problem of representational "correctness" and highlights the constitutive and cultural fictions of race (Fleetwood 2011, 13; Gillespie 2016, 6). In part, SF does this by effectively redeploying through parody or fantasy the colonial/imperial tropes of Blackness as contagion, animality, and monstrosity, which sustain white racial imaginaries. Gillespie notes that Black film should offer "a critical range of potentialities for understanding blackness as multiaccentual and multidisciplinary" (Gillespie 2016, 6). In my readings of the horror and fantasy films of Peele and Coogler, I show how Black SF foregrounds the discursivity of Blackness, thus enabling new figurations that refashion the sign of Blackness in the white gaze. Because, as Fleetwood notes, "[B]lack subjectivity is constituted through visual discourse and performed through visual technologies" (2011, 12), Blackness is rendered, made, in the visual field of whiteness.

The horror genre offers a unique space for Peele to disrupt the visual representation of Blackness and to "trouble" the racial field in a way that allows for alternative possibilities for Black representation and a way to make apparent the white investment in Black bodies. In both *Get Out* and *Us*, Peele draws attention to a white rendering of Black bodies by parodying the rendering itself and exposing the meaning of Blackness in a white field of vision. I argue that while Black horror, like realist film, depicts Black suffering, its capacity to elicit an *affective* response from the white viewer produces a form of viewer engagement not witnessed in realist films or other kinds of horror films. In this way, Peele highlights what Fleetwood argues is the "affective power of Black cultural production" and "call[s] upon the spectator to do certain work, to perform a function as arbiter, or decoder, of visual signs that become aligned with blackness" (Fleetwood 2011, 7).

In a similar way, Coogler uses Afrofuturist concepts and conceits to reimagine Black power in ways that trouble and enhance the canonical white Marvel Cinematic Universe. Excluded in substantive, transformative ways from science fiction's white worlds, people of color inspire and ground Afrofuturist texts. And while Afrofuturism certainly participates in and furthers political critiques related to Black people's forced enmeshment in Euro-Western histories of empire and capital, the future orientation of the genre also seeks alternate possibilities, or counter-histories, as forms of positive projections of possibility for African-descended peoples. In his analysis of the rise and role of Black superheroes in American popular culture, Adilifu Nama argues that in the 1960s and '70s, "the bright line between the popular and political was obliterated as American pop culture began to shed its escapist impulses and boldly engage the racial tensions that America was experiencing" (2011, 11). In the similarly turbulent racial landscape of the Trump era, where the violent vitriol and actions of white supremacists are sanctioned by the president and calls for Black equality are characterized as attacks on American values, it is worth revisiting the power of speculative fiction to intervene and revise dominant hegemonic narratives.

Chapter 8

BLACK HORROR

> It seems like every film—if it is in any way going to communicate some type of empathy that the audience can walk away with—has to have Black death as its precondition.
> —WILDERSON, "POSITION OF THE UNTHOUGHT"

> Black history **is** Black horror.
> —TANANARIVE DUE

According to Brigid Cherry, the horror genre is hard to define, as it is marked by a "sheer diversity of conventions, plots and styles." She argues that a "more crucial defining trait of the horror genre" is its capacity to "scare, shock, revolt or otherwise horrify the viewer" (2009, 2, 4). On its face, this seems a reasonable enough assumption, but it raises the question of how and where the viewer is located socially and culturally in relation to the depiction of the horror unfolding. Do viewers identify and root for victims unlike themselves? If a hallmark of the horror genre is its capacity to evoke an emotional and physiological response in the viewer (Cherry 2009, 46), it seems likely that a film proficient in its craft will produce the desired physical effect. But can it produce an empathetic response—an emotional identification at the social and cultural level with a member of an out-group, even when the viewer shares in-group identification with the monstrous antagonist? Peele seems to think so:

> What I've been really pleasantly surprised with was that, you know, the very people who are villains in this movie get it and support it and appreciate the fact that when they're watching the movie they are taken on a journey to see the world through Chris's eyes. And that to me is the power of story.... The best tool we have to promote empathy is ... through the film which is, I believe, the most perfect collaborative art form. We can deliver people into a different perspective for two hours at

a time and that missing piece of the conversation, I think, you know not to get too bold with it, but is connected to why we're here in this climate we're in today. (GoldDerby 2017)

Appealing to white empathy is a time-honored tactic in the discourse of race relations. Abolitionists in the nineteenth century and civil rights leaders in the twentieth century used moral suasion in an attempt to influence whites of the evils of slavery on ethical and religious grounds. Saidiya Hartman explains the problem with these kinds of appeals in her analysis of *Letters on American Slavery* by noted abolitionist John Rankin, who sought to "rouse the sensibility of those indifferent to slavery by exhibiting the suffering of the enslaved and facilitating an identification between those free and those enslaved." However, as Hartman argues, "By slipping into the black body and figuratively occupying the position of the enslaved, Rankin plays the role of captive and attester and in so doing articulates the crisis of witnessing determined by the legal incapacity of slaves or free blacks to act as witnesses against whites" (Hartman 1997, 22).

As most critics have noted, *Get Out*'s politics are quite straightforward. The film functions as a critique of our so-called postracial moment, exposing white fragility and the various economies of racism. One critic calls it "the best damn movie I've ever seen about American slavery" (Thrasher 2017). Another says, "[I]t probes the systematic devaluation of black life that killed people like Trayvon Martin, Walter Scott, Tamir Rice, and Eric Garner" (Staples 2017). In this regard, the film belongs to the recent, post-Trump, growing corpus of "Black resistance films," in company with dramas such as *Straight Outta Compton, Fruitvale Station, BlacKkKlansman, If Beale Street Could Talk*, and others that offer powerful critiques of white racism. However, by taking as their central concern the violation and disposability of Black life, dramas like these operate and indeed depend upon the spectacle of Black suffering and, in doing so, risk "reproduc[ing] the hyperembodiness of the powerless" (Hartman 1997, 19). As a critic for *The Ringer* notes, in realist dramatic films:

> The nuances of Black life get cut down to a few familiar rites of passage—police encounters, for example. By the time we get to a movie like the N.W.A biopic *Straight Outta Compton*, in which interactions with the LAPD are meant to establish formative moments that would become the substance of the young artists' work, director F. Gary Gray barely has to work to dramatize these incidents. We know what the cops will do, how the Black heroes will feel; we know the routine. The director has to do only so much. We can rely on our cinematic memories, and our own lives, for the moment to have power—hence the moment gradually being emptied, over time, of its immediacy. Now, it's a meme. (Collins 2016)

While there is obviously a difference in the subject position of a Black filmmaker and a white abolitionist, the aim is often the same—to elicit empathy/outrage/action in their audience. Importantly, Hartman asks us to consider the "precariousness of empathy and the thin line between witness and spectator":

> The effort to counteract the commonplace callousness to black suffering requires that the white body be positioned in the place of the black body in order to make this suffering visible and intelligible. Yet if this violence can become palpable and indignation can be fully aroused only through masochistic fantasy, then it becomes clear that empathy is double-edged, for in making the other's suffering one's own, this suffering is occluded by the other's obliteration. (Hartman 1997, 19)

I'm interested in the possibilities that the genre of horror can offer for acts of racial witnessing that narratives employing forms of moral suasion cannot. Horror films often serve as barometers of our time as they "tap into the cultural moment by encoding the anxieties of the moment into their depictions of monstrosity" (Cherry 2009, 11). What does horror allow? What can horror do that realist films cannot or do not?

Get Out has a 98 percent "fresh" rating on Rotten Tomatoes, and several critics have opined about the film's social message, its "wokeness." That *Get Out* appeals to liberals and progressives—one critic called the film "the first great film of the Trump Era," is hardly surprising, but the wide arc of its popularity across demographics is of interest to me precisely because of its release in the Age of Trump.[1] Its original premise—the kidnapping of Black people for the purpose of transplanting in them the brains of aging white people—draws on traditional horror tropes of murder, entrapment, repressed fears, and the uncanny and successfully elicits the emotional and psychological responses of tension, anxiety, fear, and paranoia germane to the horror film. The fact that *Get Out* couches these effects within a racial narrative makes its broad popularity with white audiences even more extraordinary. The film at first appears to be a modern take on *Guess Who's Coming to Dinner* but turns into an extended engagement with the history of the commodification and trafficking of Black bodies, the libidinal economy of white desire, and ends with the triumphant escape of the Black protagonist, with no white savior in sight. Similarly, Peele's second film, *Us*, boasts a 93 percent "fresh" rating on *Rotten Tomatoes* and has won numerous awards. Acknowledging the double entendre in his title *Us*/US and Red's claim that she and her "tethered" family are "American," Peele states that a guiding theme in *Us* is "our" tendency to make an enemy of "them." Maybe, he ponders, "'we' are our own worst enemy" (Chang 2019).

What accounts for the broad appeal of these films that call white Americans to task for their racism and privilege and comment upon and critique the kind of commodity fetishism that blinds them to the social underclass? What can "racial horror" do that traditional horror cannot? George Lipsitz has argued that "small changes in generic forms serve as a register of broader alterations in society at large. In moments of crisis, old stories may seem inadequate or at least incomplete. Pressing problems of the present may intrude into seemingly fixed genres" (Lipsitz 1998, 208). If Black people (and women) have historically been the horror genre's grisly victims, what does it mean for a Black protagonist to defy victimhood and slay the white monster, as Chris does in *Get Out*? And more importantly, what does it mean when a white viewer identifies with the Black victim-hero and effectively roots for and participates in their own annihilation? After all, "[c]onfronting race in a horror film would mean confronting, and troubling, the idea of a white protagonist. Who, but a white person, would be the villain of a Black horror movie?" (Collins 2016). What are the political and ethical stakes when the spectator identifies both with the aggressor and the victim?

Certainly, much feminist work in horror has explored the gendered potential in the mutual embodiment of both positions (Clover 1992; Williams 1991), but there has been little to no discussion of how this dual identification functions at the racial level. Because "identification with the filmic body [is] at the heart of the horror experience" (Reyes 2012, 247), what I'm calling "cross-racial identification" in horror involves more than a white person empathizing with the Black victim; rather, the formal affective conventions of horror thrust the spectator in the place of the victim into a position where they not only identify but also experience the victimization experienced by the Black characters in the film. Peele is very clear about wanting to produce this kind of cross-racial identification in *Get Out*: "I wanted to make this an experience where everybody's Chris (Daniel Kaluuya) when you're in the movie. So, everybody is Black. If you're a white person in the audience, you're experiencing a piece of the Black experience through this character" (*PBS NewsHour* 2017). In *Us*, although the plot is different, the same kind of identification is apparent in Peele's choice to make the victims and perpetrators both Black and white.

In this chapter, I will offer a reading of both *Get Out* and *Us*, which, while recognizing the political and cultural importance of the films' narratives, extends our understanding of their significance by attending more closely to the generic elements of the films and the underexamined role that form can play in an analysis of the politics of Black film. If, as George Lipsitz notes, genre films are satisfying and familiar to audiences in part because generic codes typically reinforce established gender, class, and racial hierarchies (Lipsitz

1998, 209), how might viewer satisfaction and comfort change when a genre film, in the hands of a Black filmmaker like Peele, consciously manipulates those generic codes?

AFFECTIVE HORROR

In her work on fear and affect, Sara Ahmed has argued that the emotion of fear is primarily affective because it "works through and on the bodies of those who are transformed into its subjects, as well as its objects" (Ahmed [2004] 2014, 62). In her reading of Fanon's discussion of his encounter with a white child who expresses fear of him, the "Negro," Ahmed suggests that racial fear "does not have its origins in the psyche" but is circumscribed and "shaped by multiple histories." She contends that "[f]ear does something; it re-establishes distance between bodies whose difference is read off the surface, as a reading which produces the surface (shivering, recolouring). Fear involves relationships of proximity, which are crucial to establishing the 'apartness' of white bodies" (Ahmed [2004] 2014, 63). As I've shown in previous chapters, myths of Black aggression and animality certainly frame white fear; while I agree with Ahmed's reading of Fanon, I would suggest that racial horror films present alternative possibilities for interpreting affective fear and produce a different relationship between Black and white bodies that collapses the idea of racial "apartness." As Xavier Aldana Reyes notes, horror's "identifying trait is its capacity to emote, to instill affect" (2012, 247). I argue that while Black horror, like realist film, depicts Black suffering, its capacity to elicit an *affective* response from the white viewer produces a form of viewer engagement not witnessed in realist films or other kinds of horror films. The doubling that takes place between viewer and victim in the traditional horror encounter is complicated in the Black horror film. In conventional horror films, spectators are largely victim-identified (Carroll 1990; Clover 1992; Reyes 2012; Reyes 2016); in racial horror, however, white viewer identification oscillates between the monster and the victim. In traditional horror, spectators are not invited to inhabit the place of or identify with the slasher/killer/monster as whites are asked to do in *Get Out*. In the figures of the progressive white Armitage family, Peele depicts whiteness as both comforting, because it's familiar, *and* horrific.[2] At the same time, because "horror normally aligns the viewer with the predicament and ordeal of the victim" (Reyes 2016, 164), the white viewer of the Black horror film also identifies with the Black subject position, a position in *Get Out* which is structurally antagonistic to white identity.

In *Us*, this oscillation between positions is further complicated not simply because the spectator identifies with both the victim and the monster but because they are the *same person*. Peele performs a bait and switch by changing the white spectator's orientation halfway through the film. What begins as a story seemingly about *Black* American lives, the underclass that structural racism produces, and Black people's tenuous hold on capitalism's promised riches turns swiftly into an interrogation of *all* American lives. Whether we characterize the Trump political landscape as populist, neo-liberalist, or fascist, Peele suggests that regardless of our standpoint, we are all implicated in the horrors now. Arguing that both films offer new opportunities for racial witnessing, this chapter will explore the mechanics and politics of cross-racial identification and examine the potential for Black horror to disrupt the visible field of Blackness—the way Black images are circulated and consumed on screen.[3]

HORROR NOIRE

> I think one of the most important milestones in that process was just realizing that every true horror, human horror, American horror has a horror movie that deals with it and allows us to face that fear, except [that] race in a modern sense, hadn't been touched. It really hadn't been touched in my opinion since *Night of the Living Dead* 50 years ago. Maybe with the film *Candyman*. That to me, I just saw a void there. So it really started with this notion of like, *this has to be possible, let's figure it out.*
> —JORDAN PEELE

The second and third decades of the twenty-first century have seen a renaissance of Black horror. Certainly, the success of Peele's films has contributed to the resurgence of interest in the genre and has paved the way for others. The year 2018 alone saw the release of three mainstream horror films featuring Black actors and written or directed by Black filmmakers: *Cloverfield Paradox* (2018), *The First Purge* (2018), and *Tales from the Hood 2* (2018). Black horror as a genre is not new. But how do we define the genre? Robin Means Coleman, in her book *Horror Noire: Blacks in American Horror Films from the 1890s to Present*, distinguishes between Blacks *in* horror films and *Black* horror films. Blacks in horror films "present Blacks and Blackness in the context of horror, even if the horror film is not wholly or substantially focused on either one." These films have "historically, and typically, been produced by non-Black filmmakers for mainstream consumption." In this category, Coleman also includes films that encode Blackness in monstrous otherness, regardless of whether Black actors are featured in the film and regardless of whether the film would typically be considered horror. Accordingly, films like *The Birth of a Nation* (1915) are included in this category (2011, 6). Black horror films, by contrast, "have an added narrative focus that calls attention to racial identity, in this case Blackness—Black culture, history, ideologies, experiences, politics, language, humor, aesthetics, style, music, and the like" (Coleman 2011, 7). Taken together, Coleman's main objective, in her analysis of both types of films, is to demonstrate "when and how they variously position Blacks as the thing that horrifies, or as the victim or that which is horrified" (2011, 8). The website *BlackHorrorMovies.com* doesn't distinguish between kinds of Black horror films but instead provides an extensive list of horror films featuring Black actors and includes a variety of articles and posts on the evolution of Blacks in horror. As "Blacula" (Mark Harris), the site's creator, explains, Black character types in horror "tend to include disposable characters like criminals, high school jocks, voodoo practitioners, one-dimensional authority figures and sidekicks willing to sacrifice themselves for the hero." Blacks, he argues, have largely been confined to the subgenre of "urban horror" and "frequently revel in 'hood' stereotypes, sacrificing plot for hip-hop swagger" (Blacula 2018). But as Tananarive Due, who teaches a course at UCLA called "The Sunken Place: Racism, Survival and the Black Horror Aesthetic," argues, "When Black creators like Peele write Black Horror, those tropes disappear—and something new, exciting and often revolutionary, emerges" (Due 2019).

Xavier Burgin's 2019 documentary *Horror Noire: A History of Black Horror* explores the representation of Blacks in horror films from the nineteenth century to the present. Based on Coleman's book, *Horror Noire* features Black actors such as Tony Todd (*Candyman*), Keith David (*The Thing*), Loretta Devine (*Urban Legend*), and Ken Foree (*Dawn of the Dead*) along with directors including William Crane (*Blacula*), Rusty Cundieff (*Tales from the Hood*), and Ernest Dickerson (*Bones*), as well as Peele. In conversational style and interspersed with commentary by Coleman, Ashlee Smith, and Tananarive Due, these artists discuss Blacks in horror and in Hollywood more broadly as well as their own films and the racial context surrounding their production. Just as in Coleman's book, most of the films discussed in *Horror Noire* focus on the quality or lack of the representation of Blackness, the significance of the authorial stamp that a Black writer/director brings to a film, and the importance for Black viewers to see Black actors onscreen, even when they are victims.

Without doubt a driving impetus for the documentary and the revival of Black horror was the critical and commercial success of *Get Out*. As "Blacula" makes clear:

> *Get Out*'s success . . . not only legitimizes black horror to studios (whose modest $5 million investment in its budget illustrates how little Hollywood is willing to risk on African-American films in general, but especially in unproven genre fare), but it also legitimizes black horror to

audiences whose expectations for this sub-genre were understandably low. Finally, it legitimizes black horror for filmmakers interested in the genre and sets a high bar of excellence, while reawakening the possibilities in the genre for allegory, satire and social commentary. (Blacula 2018)

Horror writer and executive producer of *Horror Noire*, Tananarive Due, expresses a similar view about the film's significance. Expressing her delight on seeing *Get Out*'s theatrical trailer for the first time, she remarks, "This is a story through a Black lens by a Black artist and it's horror. I thought I was in heaven" (Burgin 2019). However, the generic classification of *Get Out* has itself provoked much commentary. When the film was nominated in the Best Musical or Comedy category at the Golden Globes, Peele tweeted in response that the film was a documentary:

> I think the issue here is that the movie subverts the idea of all genres ... Call it what you want, but the movie is an expression of my truth, my experience, the experiences of a lot of Black people, and minorities. Anyone who feels like the other. Any conversation that limits what it can be is putting it in a box. (Kohn 2017)

Peele ultimately seems to have decided that "social thriller," defined as "thriller/horror movies where the ultimate villain is society" (Phillips 2017), is the most apt categorization for the film. Regardless of Peele's preference, *Get Out* has all of the elements of horror and is generally viewed as a horror movie by critics and fans.

Although I will be dealing predominately with Black horror in this chapter, I am defining it as a subset of a genre I'm calling "racial horror." Racial horror is horror that features a non-white protagonist(s) and is written or directed by a filmmaker of color and directly or indirectly offers a critique of racial norms. While *Candyman, People Under the Stairs*, and to some extent *Night of the Living Dead* are considered Black horror films because of their Black stars and implicit racial commentary, they are all products of a white creative team. *Blacula* (1972), directed by William Crane and starring William Marshall, aligns more closely with my concept of the genre, but as part of the Blaxploitation subgenre, its commercial aims and audience reception set it apart from the kind of political racial horror that Peele is producing. While my definition aligns with Coleman's definition of the Black horror film, of particular interest to me is the way contemporary racial horror films utilize horror conventions to provoke the identification of a white viewer with a non-white victim *in the context of* a narrative exposing white fragility and/or critiquing white power. Rusty Cundieff's *Tales from the Hood* (1995), *Tales from the Hood 2* (2018),

Ernest Dickerson's *Bones* (2011), and Gerard McMurray's *The First Purge* (2018) are exemplary of this kind of politically inflected racial critique.

AFROPESSIMISM AND THE FUNGIBILITY OF BLACK BODIES

In my argument, cross-racial identification in horror has the capacity to produce a structural and psychic alignment between a white spectator and a Black victim. But how do we distinguish between an appropriative voyeuristic consumption of Black pain—the kind of libidinal investment in Black bodies that is foundational to structural racism in the US and which *Get Out* parodies—and the type of cross-racial spectatorship that Black horror might produce? In defining the field of Afropessimism, Frank Wilderson, following Fanon, argues that Blacks exist in a state of ontological death. "The Black" is always already positioned as Slave and, as such, experiences a perpetual, gratuitous violence, not as a response to a transgression, but one permitted and indeed enabled by the ontological status of the Slave (the Black) as nothing—as existing in a relation of non-relation to the white (Wilderson 2010). Wilderson defines this relation as an antagonism rather than a conflict, for, unlike conflict, the aim of which is resolution, antagonism is irreconcilable. Blackness in this antagonistic relation occupies the space of ontological nothingness. Afropessimism understands "racism as a relation grounded in anti-blackness rather than white supremacy." As Jared Sexton elaborates, "Afro-Pessimism is, among other things, an attempt to formulate an account of such suffering, to establish the rules of its grammar" (Sexton 2016). Both Wilderson and Sexton ground their critique in Saidiya Hartman's analysis of the slave as a fungible object, "an abstract and empty vessel vulnerable to the projection of others' feelings, ideas, desires, and values ... a surrogate for master's body since it guarantees his disembodied universality and acts as the sign of his power and dominion" (Hartman 1997, 21).

In *Red, White & Black: Cinema and the Structure of U.S. Antagonisms*, Wilderson argues that "cinematic and political discourse since the 1980s tends to hide rather than make explicit the grammar of suffering which underwrites the United States and its foundational antagonisms" (2010, 6). In an attempt to analyze the racial subtext of Hollywood film and the cultural and political effects it engenders, Wilderson argues that white "Master" cinema (white director/white cast) operates hegemonically toward Blacks, offering them a false interpellation to the human categories/human relations from which the Black is excluded by virtue of their ontology as "non-human." Such a cinema, he argues, enacts and perpetuates the Black's exclusion from relational positionality. However, Wilderson is also critical of Black "Slave" films (Black director/ Black cast), which "labor imaginatively in ways which accompany the discursive labor of Slave ethics, ethics manifest in the ontology of captivity and death or accumulation and fungibility" (2010, 26).

The fungibility of Blackness, "its abstractness and immateriality, [that which] enables the Black body or Blackface mask to serve as the vehicle of white self-exploration, renunciation, and enjoyment" (Hartman 1997, 26) is a central motif in *Get Out*. Opening with the abduction of a young Black man, Andre Logan King (LaKeith Stanfield), the film quickly depicts the state of affairs for the Black body. There is nothing unusual or out of place about Andre—he is on the phone, minding his own business, looking for an address. But in a specific, suburban (coded white) space, he is *made* out of place. The very geography of the neighborhood estranges him and makes Andre uneasy: "What kind of sick individual names a street Edgewood Way and then put it half a mile away from Edgewood Lane?" Expressing his apprehension in "this creepy, confusing-ass suburb," he is acutely aware of his displacement. "I feel like a sore thumb out here" in this "fucking hedge maze." We don't know what he's doing there or whose house he's looking for, but when a car slowly pulls next to him and the refrain "Run rabbit, run rabbit, run! Run! Run!" is heard emanating from the car's stereo, every audience member, regardless of race, knows that something bad is about to happen to this Black man. Although the music, creepy in its campy jauntiness, situates the scene squarely in the horror genre, there is nothing surprising or unusual about this scene. The horror is experienced not in the mise en scène but in our quotidian knowledge of race relations. "Just keep on walking, bruh," he tells himself. "Don't do nothin' stupid." But Andre knows as well as we do that his actions cannot change the outcome. "Fuck this," he says, and decides to turn back the way he came. "Not today. Not me. You know how they like to do motherfuckers out here, man. I'm gone." But it's too late; the guy in the car gets the jump on him and chokes him, dragging him to the vehicle. At the same time, the music moves from playing in the intradiegetic space of the car to the extradiegetic world of the film and we finally hear the full refrain: "Run rabbit, run rabbit, run! Run! Run! Don't give the farmer his fun, fun, fun." We don't need a horror movie to tell us that Black men are hunted (Peele 2017).

In *Us*, the fungibility of Blackness is represented by Adelaide's (Lupita Nyong'o) shadow-family, which occupies a life under the surface. Tethered to their doppelgängers above, the shadows are forced to mime the actions of their counterparts in empty and unfulfilling ways. Explaining her motivation for seeking their untethering, Red recounts the repetitive, soulless existence wholly dependent on the actions of those above them: "[W]hen the girl ate, her food was given to her warm and tasty. But when the shadow was hungry, she had to eat rabbit, raw and bloody." Where the girl received "wonderful toys, soft and cushy," the shadow's toys were "so sharp and cold they'd slice through her fingers." Deprived of free will or agency, Red's life is an empty simulation of Adelaide's. She is forced to couple with Abraham, whether she "loved him or not." When Adelaide gives birth to a "beautiful baby girl," Red produces "a little monster," and for their second birth, where Adelaide has a doctor-performed cesarean, Red has to cut the boy out of her belly herself. "So, you see," Red explains, "the shadow hated the girl so much for so long" (Peele 2019). Fungible, disposable, invisible, Red represents "the returned revenge of the dispossessed, the purposely forgotten, those who have been used and sloughed off so that America's project of civilization can succeed" (Brooks 2019).

In an interview with Wilderson, Hartman speaks of the "limits of most available narratives to explain the position of the enslaved" (Hartman and Wilderson 2003, 184). Even though the "slave is the foundation of the national order," she argues that "the slave occupies the position of the unthought." And she wonders how it is possible to "bring that position into view without making it a locus of positive value, or without trying to fill the void" (2003, 185). *Get Out* and *Us* make visible the ontological status of Black life, the libidinal economy of anti-Black racism, and, through the formal elements of horror, offer a way of thinking the unthought. Perhaps the unthought can only be represented in filmic forms that eschew realist representation. Horror and fantasy (as discussed in the next chapter), because they are not bound by the strictures of realism which demand either participation in or accommodation to the master narrative—even in their seeming resistance—provide an opening for both a parodic, satirical exploration of anti-Blackness and, in the case of horror, the possibility of cross-racial identification through shared somatic suffering. Wilderson sees an impossibility in Black films that try to apply the three-point progression of classical narrative—equilibrium, disequilibrium, equilibrium—because "the three-point progression of a drama for the living cannot be applied to a being that is socially dead (natally alienated, open to gratuitous violence, and generally dishonored)" (Wilderson 2010, 27):

> [F]or Blackness, there is no narrative moment prior to slavery. Furthermore, a hypothetical moment after slavery would entail the emergence of new ontological relations (the end of both Blackness and Humanness) and a new episteme. It is impossible for narrative to enunciate from beyond the episteme in which it stands, not knowingly, at least. At the heart of my deliberations on Slave cinema is the question *How does a film tell the story of a being that has no story?* (Wilderson 2010, 28)

Both *Get Out* and *Us* thematize, in an overwrought, satirical, horrific manner, the story of a being that has no story, whose very fungibility is the fact driving the plot. But it is through its form, in its hyperbolic, carnivalesque, grotesque plot, that the "lived experience of the Black [person]" is revealed.[4] Wilderson argues that "Black cinema deploys a host of narrative strategies to slip the noose of a life shaped and compromised by the existence of slavery" and, ultimately, does not consider it to be successful. His concern is with the impossibility of depicting a void without filling it, and he argues that cinema frequently offers the viewer the "pleasure of seeing Blacks maimed as well as the pleasure of Blacks taking pleasure in the process" (Wilderson 2010, 96, 97, 115).

Horror films, of course, rely upon physical maiming and mutilation of bodies, and often those bodies are Black and/or female. But the horror film can offer something else in the depiction of that violence. Rather than reproducing the voyeuristic, gratuitous pleasures attendant in the victim's abasement, *Get Out* and *Us* belong to the genre of "post-millennial horror" films whose challenge, according to Reyes, is to "make the viewer experience fear" through an experience of "full-bodied affect" (Reyes 2012, 244, 256). In *Get Out*, that fear is not fear of the Black Other but fear of the white self. Because the mechanics of the horror genre solicit viewer empathy with the victim and fear of the perpetrator, the white viewer identifies with the Black experience of fungibility, which triggers an active fear of the mechanics of white power. Far more effective than anger, shame, and/or revulsion toward the behavior of the white characters, this white fear of whiteness produces a displacement, a break in the "possessive investment in whiteness" (Lipsitz 1998). If the pleasure experienced by the appropriability of the Black body is central to white self-fashioning (Hartman 1997, 26), in replacing pleasure with horror, Peele disrupts the fantastic investment in Black bodies. In this sense, both whiteness and Blackness are the sites of pleasure and horror for the white viewer.

AFFECT AND CROSS-RACIAL IDENTIFICATION

The role of affect in horror is central to the theory of cross-racial identification I'm proposing. Following Christian Metz, critics observe two modes of identification in cinema: primary identification with the camera and secondary identification with the "character of empathic choice." While it is the case that competing figures resonate with competing parts of the viewer's psyche (masochistic victim and sadistic monster, for example), "audience sympathy in horror is primarily oriented to the position of the victim" (Clover 1992, 8). Following Carol Clover, subsequent critics, specifically Noel Carroll and Xavier Aldana Reyes, consider the role of affect in viewer identification, particularly in relation to the horror film. Horror, through affect, allows for a specific kind of empathic identification. "Affect, at its most anthropomorphic, is the name we give to those forces—visceral forces beneath, alongside, or generally *other than* conscious knowing, vital forces insisting beyond emotion—that can serve to drive us toward movement, toward thought and extension" (Seigworth and Gregg 2010, 1). Horror is saturated in spectacle and hyper-embodiedness; entrapment, mutilation, and death are the stock-in-trade of the horror film. What better vehicle to explore the condition of anti-Blackness and the precarity of Black life than the genre of horror? "Race is a horror story. The bodycam footage of Black death tells me that; old images of lynchings tell me that. The fabricated fears of suburbanites, the stuff horror is made of, afflict Blacks in real time" (Collins 2017).

Reyes argues that "horror uses bodies in order to affect ours" (Ryes 2016, 3) and that its primary function is to represent a fictional body-in-suffering that can be consumed by the spectator. "Alignment with the on-screen body is therefore crucial for affect to occur" (Reyes 2012, 253). But the question is whether empathic identification is possible at the racial level. Is racial witnessing possible in horror's space of exaggerated spectacularity? Recognizing horror's disruptive power, one critic avers that "horror will be our most powerful form of screen activism in this period of raw and rampant social unrest" (Cruchiola 2017). Can the formal conventions of horror, because they anticipate victimization, provide opportunities for political engagement with racial oppression in ways that don't reproduce that oppression through its consumption? After all, the horror movie is "the space of exception, where paranoia is always founded, though its object may be misrecognized; there *is* something dangerous under the bed, in the dark, in the thoughts and bodies of those around you" (Jarvis 2018, 102). My goal here is to examine how racial horror functions, how it complicates what many critics see as the purely affective relation between spectator and victim. Does it prompt and then utilize a specific reaction in the white viewer that's different from other kinds of viewer identification in horror? And what might such a reaction signify for race relations?

SLASHER FILMS AND FINAL GIRLS

In her classic text *Men, Women, and Chainsaws*, Carol Clover examines the kind of cross-identification that takes place in horror films whereby a "majority viewer"—in her account, a younger male—identifies with a "minority" female victim-hero (Clover 1992). Clover suggests that rather than rejoice gratuitously in the female's victimization, male viewers actually root for her and experience a climactic moment of female power when the "Final Girl" overpowers and outsmarts her male aggressor, resulting in an "active power with bi-sexual components" (Williams 1991, 7). If a horrific encounter between a male killer and a female victim can produce an experience of cross-sexual identification in the male viewer, might an encounter between a white killer and a Black victim produce an experience of cross-racial identification in the white viewer? And what would this look like?

Both *Get Out* and *Us* could be classified as slasher films. In the traditional slasher film, the "killer is the psychotic product of a sick family but still recognizably human; the victim is a beautiful, sexually active woman; the location is not-home, at a Terrible Place; the weapon is something other than a gun; the attack is registered from the victim's point of view and comes with a shocking suddenness" (Clover 1992, 23–24). The killer is "an insider, a man who functions normally in the action until, at the end, his other self is revealed." The persecution of the victim occurs in a "Terrible Place" (Sunken Place), "most often a house or tunnel" occupied by "terrible families—murderous, incestuous, cannibalistic." The preferred weapons are pre-technological—"knives and needles, like teeth, beaks, fangs, and claws, are personal extensions of the body that bring attacker and attacked into primitive, animalistic embrace." The slasher film "evinces a fascination with flesh or meat itself as that which is hidden from view" and an interest in the "opened" body. Clover argues that the killer usually exhibits signs of gender confusion and victims are sexual transgressors: "killing those who seek or engage in unauthorized sex amounts to a generic imperative of the slasher film . . . men and boys who go after 'wrong' sex also die" (Clover 1992, 30, 32).

It is interesting to see how Peele reverses the traditional sex roles in slasher films and further subverts their meanings by adding race to the mix. While the "killer" in *Get Out* is a collective one—a "terrible family" (Jeremy, Missy, and Dean all play pivotal roles in securing the victims)—the white woman (Rose) occupies the traditional place of sadistic aggressor, the supposedly normal insider, while the Black man (Chris) is the seemingly passive victim. Chris's "sexual transgression" is his interracial relationship with Rose, and the killers' "gender confusion" is here replaced by racial confusion as the Armitages and their white community engage in an elaborate kind of miscegenation in the grisly "Coagula Procedure," where the brains of aging white people are transplanted into the bodies of young black people. *Us* also follows the slasher formula. The scissor-wielding monsters come from tunnels into the home, where the attacks take place. The trope of the killer "insider" is taken to its furthest extreme here, for whether white or black, the killer *is* us.

Clover observes that post-1970s slasher films invariably feature a "final girl" who survives the horrific scene and escapes. She is "chased, cornered, wounded. . . . She is abject terror personified. . . . She alone looks death in the face, but she alone also finds the strength either to stay the killer long enough to be rescued (ending A) or to kill him herself (ending B)." However, Clover argues that there is always something boyish about the final girl, from a gender-ambiguous name to a competence in "mechanical and other practical matters" (Clover 1992, 35), and this female masculinity is crucial to the male viewer's capacity to identify with her. The "Final Girl is (apparently) female not despite the maleness of the audience, but precisely because of it. The discourse is wholly masculine, and females figure in it only insofar as they 'read' some aspect of male experience" (1992, 53).

The implications of this are particularly salient in *Get Out*. Chris (a gender-ambiguous name) is a final "girl"[5] who kills the white male killer (Armitage) and attacks but does not kill the white female sadistic aggressor (Rose). She is instead killed by a different one of her Black victims (Walter), while Chris is rescued by another Black man (Rod). Adelaide is the final girl in *Us*, exhibiting a confidence and competence in defense of her family and the pursuit of her would-be killer Red. If we consider the reversals of gendered and raced subject positions in *Get Out*, we are forced to inquire as to the nature of viewer/victim identification in the film. If the white female functions as "congenial double" for the adolescent male viewer in the conventional slasher film, what is the nature of identification in this Black horror film? Clover suggests that, ultimately, the heroic final girl in the slasher film serves as a vehicle for the "sadomasochistic fantasies" of the male viewer. Does Chris function in the same way for the white viewer? And does this explain the film's appeal to white audiences? And how does *Us*'s Red/Adelaide, who occupies the position of "victim and villain, threat and threatened, protagonist and antagonist" (Brooks 2019), complicate the racial politics of the final girl trope?

Ahmed argues that "fear is felt differently by different bodies, in the sense that there is a relationship to space and mobility at stake in the differential organisation of fear itself" (Ahmed [2004] 2014, 68). In the horror film, however, the spatial logic of fear is altered through corporeal identification. In his analysis of horror affect, Reyes distinguishes between character identification and corporeal identification. Identification, he argues, is more than the process of merging with the personality or identity of the character; rather, it is a state where the "situations and, most importantly, the bodies of the characters and their vulnerability can be apprehended" (Reyes 2016, 164). This has significant implications for cross-racial identification because it suggests that the white viewer is capable of *inhabiting* the corporeal experience of the Black victim. Realist dramatic films generate their empathic appeals on the basis that whites have a *cognitive* understanding of the predicament of Black lives. The reality depicted onscreen is, of course, already known to whites in that it is a shared history of possession/dispossession and enslaving/enslavement, passed down through history books and reinforced daily in news media, music, and in the experiences of family and friends. But white viewers of those genre films have typically not felt the *corporeal* experience of Blackness. "Horror, by virtue of its intention to scare, puts the viewer in a situation of threat that either mirrors (in dread) or, in most places, relies on the extrapolability of, that of an intradiegetic victim" (Reyes 2016, 166).

In *Get Out*, the white spectator not only witnesses but, according to horror affect theory, is forced to vicariously experience the immobility and paralysis, the silencing and physical dispossession of being a Black body, not as a singular traumatic event—a rape, a murder, a mutilation common to classic horror victims—but as an ongoing trauma that extends beyond the life of the film, backward and forward, repeatedly, systemically. Through somatic identification with Chris, the white viewer experiences what it is like to be sold at auction; to have to smile through the ignorant, self-satisfied assumptions about your exaggerated physical capabilities and mental incapacities; to be thrust into the Sunken Place with the knowledge that this horror, though constructed narratively in this instance, is not a fiction at all—and that you, as a white person, are complicit in the victimization. As Peele explains, "It was very important to me to just get the entire audience in touch in some way with the fears inherent [in] being Black in this country" (*NPR* 2017).

If such identification is possible, what does it mean to inhabit this place? What does it mean for a white person not merely to witness the "spectacular character of Black suffering" (Hartman 1997, 3) but to dwell there, to embody it? In *Us*, a similar dynamic is at work when Red details the raw life of the tethered, empty of signification, and stripped of material comfort. With the exception of Rod (Lil Rel Howery), most of the Black characters in *Get Out*—Chris (Daniel Kaluuya), Walter (Marcus Henderson), Georgina (Betty Gabriel), and Andre—occupy the position of the Black victim in the film; however, *Us* offers two versions of Black life—Red's family and Adelaide's family. Whereas Red's family members inhabit the sunken place and are victims of a purported government cloning plot, they are also the monsters attacking the other Black family. Furthermore, because fake Adelaide swapped places with the real Adelaide (Red) when they were children, she is effectively the catalyst for the whole gruesome murderous event, complicating viewer identification with the victim. Indeed, as I will argue below, the doubling of the Black subject position and the addition of the doubled white family in *Us* offers a variant to the mechanics of affect in racial horror.

In *Get Out*, Andre reappears halfway through the movie, only so altered that he is almost unrecognizable. He is introduced as Logan King and is apparently married to an older white woman. He is dressed in the garb of an earlier era—a straw hat and plain, tan slacks and jacket. He looks out of step even with the older white people, who are wearing modern outfits. The clothes on this young Black man, coupled with his old-fashioned speech and generic midwestern accent, render him strange, out of place. Just like Walter, the groundskeeper, and Georgina, the maid, Logan is conspicuous in this older white crowd, but it's not his Blackness that makes him stand out; it's that his Blackness is *uncanny*, "signalled by the chasm between the appearance of the black body and the elderly, white mannerisms of its comportment" (Jarvis 2018, 106). Victims of the Coagula Procedure, Walter, Georgina, and Logan have had the brains of three older white people transplanted into their bodies. As Jim Hudson (Stephen Root), who has bought Chris's body at auction for the same purpose, explains to him:

> The piece of your brain connected to your nervous system needs to stay put, keeping those intricate connections intact. So, you won't be gone, not completely. A sliver of you will still be in there, somewhere, limited consciousness. You'll be able to see and hear what your body is doing, but your existence will be as a passenger. An audience. You'll live in The Sunken Place. . . . Now, I'll control the motor functions, so I'll be. . . .

Chris interrupts: "Me. You'll be me." "Why us, huh? Why Black people?" Jim laughs awkwardly. "Who knows?" he says. "People want a change. Some people wanna be stronger, faster, cooler. . . . But please don't lump me in with that. I could give a shit what color you are. No. What I want is deeper. I want your eye, man. I want those things you see through" (Peele 2017).

Hartman makes clear that the pleasures of life in the exercise of white power (aka white life) "is virtually unimaginable without recourse to the Black body and the subjection of the captive, the diversions engendered by the dispossession of the enslaved, or the fantasies launched by the myriad uses of the Black body" (Hartman 1997, 26). If we consider the relationship between spectator and victim in the horror film, then the intradiegetic depiction, in the Coagula Procedure, of a white person occupying the body of a Black person is mirrored extradiegetically in the corporeal identification of the white spectator and Black victim. As Reyes notes, "[t]he spectatorial body is deeply affected by the image and feeling of what is virtually not there: a second body or bodies that have a direct impact on it" (Reyes 2012, 252). But is this extradiegetic cross-racial identification as much a violation as the intradiegetic one? In other words, what is at stake in this white possession of Blackness? And how does the inclusion of uncanny doubling in *Us* complicate this potentially appropriative relation?

Uncanniness is "concerned with the phenomenon of the 'double,' which appears in every shape and in every degree of development." Thus, according to Freud, characters "are to be considered identical because they look alike." "On the one hand," the uncanny refers to "what is familiar and agreeable, and on the other, what is concealed and kept out of sight" (Freud [1919] 2010, 827). When the previously concealed tethered people come into sight, they function as a return of the repressed, and in *Us*, white and Black characters alike are rendered uncanny by the presence of their doppelgängers. In the first half of the film, the white spectator has an affective connection to the Black victims (Adelaide, Gabe [Winston Duke], Zora [Shahadi Wright Joseph], and Jason [Evan Alex]),[6] but with the introduction of the white Tyler family's doubles, the white spectator's affective identification transfers to the white victims, who occupy the same structural position heretofore occupied by the Black victims. As Freud makes clear, this uncanny "relation is accentuated by mental processes leaping from one of these characters to another . . . so that the one possesses knowledge, feelings and experience in common with the other." The white tethers produce this uncanny effect in the white spectator because they come after the introduction of the Black tethers and the very personal revenge plot instigated by Red; however, because the relationship is uncanny, the white spectator's affective response to the fear experienced by the Black victim is transferred to the white one, and throws the spectator "in doubt as to which [their] self is, or substitutes the extraneous self for [their] own. In other words, there is a doubling, dividing and interchanging of the self" (Freud [1919] 2010, 940) occurring between the place of the Black and the white victim.

Reyes argues that the affective response engendered by horror's use of violence exposes our organic body, the Deleuzian "body without organs (BwO)," which allows us to approach a form of pre Symbolic materiality that "makes sensations accessible" (Reyes 2012, 256). In producing doppelgängers of the Black family *and* the white family, Peele connects white viewers to the visceral experience of being flesh and ties them to an othering within the self that produces the position of the white body as fungible object, meat. In this substitution, "[w]hat is evacuated is not the body or the self, understood at its most organic level, but rather everything else: the socially constructed or immaterial" (Reyes 2012, 255), the workings of white privilege.

AFFECT VS. COGNITION

To examine this further, it's useful to understand the relationship between cognitive affect and physical affect and whether they produce different responses in the white spectator. In *The Philosophy of Horror*, Noel Carroll asks why audiences derive pleasure from being frightened and why they subject themselves to a repulsive and fearful experience repeatedly. He argues that it's not the fear that produces pleasure but rather the narrative vehicle, the story, which is pleasurable insofar as it enables an encounter with the impossible and the unknown. Disgust and fear are emotional effects, byproducts, of the cognitive, evaluative experience that literary or filmic horror provides; Carroll calls this emotion "art-horror" (as distinct from real-life horror). In the horror genre, it's the *idea* of the monster, not the monster itself, which is truly frightening. The experience is more cognitive than corporeal. The pleasure in the horror experience, he argues, doesn't arise from the involuntary response produced in the viewer (sudden fright, the goosebumps, the nausea) but rather the belief and thoughts viewers possess about certain situations and events (terrifying scenarios) based on their cognitive evaluation of their own position in relation to those known objects (*How would I escape? What would I do?*)—not to mention the corollary pleasure and satisfaction in knowing that it's not happening to them—as well as the moral and ethical dilemmas that horrific and bloody acts onscreen trigger in the viewer (Carroll 1990).

Similarly, Reyes suggests that cognition plays a significant role in the way that corporeal affect manifests itself on the viewer, arguing that the viewer's corporeal affect can be "undermined, overwritten or emphasized by moral implications connected to viewer interpellation" (Reyes 2016, 85). At the same time, Reyes and other critics[7] consider Carroll's emphasis on the cognitive to ignore the role and importance of the corporeal response produced by horror: "[W]hen somatic reactions are triggered in Horror, this can be either a result of a sensory attack or of an emotional connection at a corporeal level." Reyes argues that not all physical responses are triggered by emotional states and "the fact that some reactions are not cognitively processed sets them apart from others that require rational evaluation or complex thinking" (2016, 86). In short, Reyes insists on the separation of "two sides of the horror emotion: the physical one, which is connected to the somatic and informs feeling, and the cognitive process, which involves emotive states and reflection" (2016, 94). According to Reyes, the experience between viewer and victim relies on both an "emotional-cognitive" and "affective-reflective" identification (2016, 167). While I agree that both of these are operative in the cinemagoing experience, I suggest that in racial horror, they are not two components of one interaction (the viewer/victim encounter) but rather describe two different kinds of viewer identification: viewer/victim and viewer/monster, and that the viewer effectively oscillates between them. Identification with the monster occurs as a result of an emotional-cognitive connection and identification with the victim is an affective-reflective one.

Reyes argues that in horror, the body of the actor is "virtually interchangeable" with the body of the viewer and is "empathically approximated so that its specificities (gender, age, race) become irrelevant to the moment of horror" (2016, 167). Because horror is a "form of compulsion" that provides gratification as a result of being immersed in a "vulnerable and unpleasant state" (2016, 165), Reyes considers race/gender/class differences as immaterial to the experience. Viewers do not necessarily feel sympathy for the victim, then; they just identify with the vulnerability of the onscreen body "as sentient flesh (devoid of a specific subject and their personalities)" (2016, 169). However, this form of somatic empathy has problematic implications if we consider the colonial and racist practice of viewing non-white bodies as flesh. As Amber Musser makes clear, "Historically, flesh is the province of marginalized subjects" and the "disembering of bodies into flesh is part of the equation of Blackness with depersonalization and nonsubjectivity" (Musser 2014, 19).

At issue for many critics in Carroll's analysis is his insistence that for horror to be classified as horror, it requires a monster or other non-human, supernatural antagonist.[8] Carroll argues that monsters are central to horror because they "breach the norms of ontological propriety," which elicits horror in the victim and, subsequently, the audience. A truly horrifying monster provokes feelings of fear and disgust in the viewer (Carroll 1990, 16, 22). "The audience thinking of a monster is prompted in this response by the responses of fictional human characters whose actions they are attending to, and that audience, like said characters, may also wish to avoid physical contact with such types of things as monsters" (Carroll 1990, 35). Critics rightly point out that human monsters in slasher films like *Halloween* and *Saw*, which, according to Carroll's schema, don't qualify as horror but rather action/suspense or "tales of terror," are just as monstrous as supernatural villains and are certainly capable of provoking fear and disgust in viewers. In conventional horror, whether we understand the audience's reaction to the horror as primarily cognitive (Carroll) or corporeal (Reyes), the viewer is aligned with the victim and, specifically, the victim's assessment of the threat that the monster represents. While for Carroll, "The audience's psychological state, therefore, diverges from the psychological state of characters with respect to belief," it "converges on that of characters with respect to the way in which the properties of said monsters are emotively assessed" (Carroll 1990, 53).

In my view, what these accounts don't address is the possibility of audience identification *with* the monster. In racial horror, the cognitive affect of the white viewer produces identification with the white *killer*, and somatic affect produces identification with the Black *victim*. That the Armitages initially appear to be "good" whites (liberals) is key to the identification process. It is the purpose of the "monster" to evoke disgust, but in the case of the white spectator of *Get Out*, that disgust is self-directed. While Reyes continues to emphasize the interchangeability of the bodies of spectator and victim, he does note that this association can be disrupted if the "narrative manipulates one's feelings otherwise" (2016, 167). The Armitages and the doppelgängers of the white Tyler family in *Us* provide this alternate manipulation of viewer feelings. It's not just a case of a viewer having empathy with a character of another race; obviously, viewers can empathize with characters who share different traits, outlooks, and experiences, as is the case in narratives involving animals, robots, and animated characters. But in racial horror, the character is involved in a narrative *about* race/racism in which the viewer, by virtue of their race, is also implicated. In this case, the identification is more than somatic; it involves a cognitive dimension, an oscillation between insider and outsider because history itself, the history of race relations in this country, intrudes upon or at least interferes with the kind of simple somatic exchange that Reyes describes. And in the case of *Us*, we are quite literally forced to identify with the killer within ourselves.

WHITE LIBERAL MONSTERS?

There is an important difference between viewer allegiance and viewer alignment, however. While the viewer may align with one character, typically the POV character, their allegiances may lie elsewhere. Carl Plantinga considers this to be particularly likely in the case of gender difference. While many scholars, after Mulvey, suggest the apparatus of Hollywood film assumes a male viewer and caters to heterosexual male desires—thereby *aligning* both male and female viewers with that perspective—viewers, particularly female viewers, are also likely to share an *allegiance* with the female victim. In other words, "[A]udiences tend to sympathize most strongly with those who are familiar to them and whom they like" (Plantinga 2009, 98). The Armitage family represents a specific kind of East Coast liberal privilege often depicted in Hollywood film; these are lake house-owning, groundskeeper-hiring, lacrosse-playing elites. Similarly, the self-absorbed nouveau riche West Coast Tylers embody another well-traveled white stereotype. Most white spectators are unlikely to share the wealth or background of these white families, but they recognize it; it may be grating, but it's familiar. While a majority of viewers, regardless of standpoint, share an *alignment* with Chris and Adelaide and her family—we want them to escape—white viewers share an *allegiance* with the Armitages and the Tylers. This is what Wayne Booth calls "'the sustained inside view,' or what we might call sustained attachment, [which] may lead to a kind of 'insider sympathy' with the character and her or his allies and antipathy toward other characters portrayed as 'out' group members" (Plantinga 2009, 107).

Having opened with Andre's kidnapping, *Get Out* cuts to a title sequence evoking slavery's past with panning shots of the Alabama countryside and a haunting Swahili song ("Sikiliza Kwa Wahenga," ["Listen to the Ancestors"]). The next cut transports the viewer to a new present where the smooth sounds of Childish Gambino's "Redbone" offer a warning to "Stay Woke." This present is one where Black men are free to own nice things and to date beautiful white women if they so choose. When we first see Rose (Allison Williams), she is shopping for pastries, which she eventually brings home to Chris. As he prepares his bag for the weekend away to meet her parents, she lolls comfortably on his couch, playing with the dog and implicitly teasing him about his discomfort. "Do they know I'm Black?" he asks. "No. Should they?" Both white and Black viewers know the answer to this question: of course they should know he's Black, but the fact that Rose doesn't consider it important suggests her politics, while problematically colorblind, are squarely left of center. It's not important to her; she doesn't think it matters. After all, as she tells Chris: "My dad would have voted for Obama a third time if he could have. Like the love is so real" (Peele 2017). Rose warns Chris that her dad will bring this up and that "it will definitely fucking suck," suggesting that she recognizes the awkwardness of her dad's liberal posturing and doesn't herself buy into it. This contrast between Rose's stance and her family's telegraphs to the audience that, while Rose is certainly curiously oblivious to Chris's concerns, at least from the perspective of a liberal-leaning white audience, she is the real deal, and it's okay to like her. Trying to reassure Chris that her parents aren't racist, she emphasizes, "I would have told you. I wouldn't be bringing you home to them; think about that for like two seconds" (Peele 2017). The next "test" of Rose's character comes en route to her parent's house when, driving, she hits a deer and stands up to the cop who wants to see Chris's ID. Although Chris is ready to oblige, she won't let him. "No. Fuck that. You don't have to give him your ID because you haven't done anything wrong." What's interesting about this scene is that Rose isn't outraged or incredulous. One doesn't get the impression that she's shocked by the double standard. When the cop justifies his actions by saying, "Anytime there's an incident, we have every right to ask . . . ." she cuts him off with a half-smile and a cocked head. "That's bullshit." And with that, the cop backs down. In both of these scenes, Rose displays staggering levels of white privilege (and not a small amount of paternalism), but because she uses that privilege to stand up for/protect her Black boyfriend, it looks like the system has the problem, not Rose. When Chris tells her he finds her actions "hot," she tells him that she's "not going to let anyone fuck with her man" (Peele 2017). Whatever doubt might have crept into the viewer's mind as a result of Rose's reckless behavior, Chris's sanctioning of her actions works to reinforce the liberal white viewer's perception that she's all right.

Similarly, when Chris meets the parents, Dean (Bradley Whitford) embraces Chris, saying, "You call me Dean. And you hug me, my man. . . . We're huggers." There's no doubt that Dean is awkward with Chris, asking the couple how long this "thang" has been going on and delivering the anticipated Obama line; however, because both Missy (Catherine Keener) and Rose dismiss him with eye rolls and embarrassment ("Does he have an off button? This is exhausting!") and because Rose has already warned us that Dean is a "lame dad more than anything else," the white viewer might feel annoyed or frustrated by Dean's missteps rather than concerned or fearful (Peele 2017). The awkwardness of the ingratiating progressive is, in any case, better than the vitriol of the racist. When the camera pulls back in a wide-angle long shot, we see Walter (Marcus Henderson), the Black groundskeeper, from behind, watching the house. Walter's presence and the fact of his employment, silently noted by Chris as they arrive, is the first inkling that something doesn't quite jibe. The concern is heightened by the behavior of Georgina (Betty Gabriel), the Black maid, whose Stepford-wife antics—overfilling the tea glass and repeating phrases robotically—immediately raise Chris's suspicions.

In *Us*, spectatorial alignment and allegiance are disrupted initially because the Black victims are attacked by Black perpetrators inhibiting the kind of oscillation that the Black victim/white monster produces in the white spectator. This disruption will play a key role in the white spectators' cross-racial identification with the Black victims when the Tylers' tethers attack them. The caustic, snarky, competitive Tylers seem extraneous to the victim/monster model until they become victims themselves. And when that occurs, the white spectator, who has already aligned with the Black victim, occupies three positions at once: identification with the Black victim, identification with the white victim, and identification with the white monster. In this way, the horror film provides the white spectator with the affective sensation of "being stripped down to meat," an embodiment "constructed out of the experience of vicarious suffering and its concomitant affect" (Reyes 2012, 257). But does this spectatorial location merely return us to the realm of "masochistic fantasy" that Hartman cautions against? What role does masochism play in the identificatory relationship between viewer and victim?

RACE AND MASOCHISM

Reyes argues that critiques of the sadistic nature of horror, which suggest that there is a pleasurable component for the spectator in watching the suffering or vicariously imposing suffering on the victim, fail to account for the pleasures spectators might derive from identification with the suffering or trauma of the victim. Steven Shaviro defines the kind of somatic affect produced in cinema as one that is not fended off but passionately sought out by the spectator, for "[a]nxiety over the disruption of identity is concomitant with, and perhaps necessary to, the very intensity of sensual gratification. Fearfulness is itself a thrill and a powerful turn-on" (Shaviro 1993). However, we cannot overlook the implications of sexual and racial power when the cinematic body is Black, and the spectator is white. Indeed, from Deleuze to Silverman, Creed to Shaviro, critics interpreting the history of masochistic identification in film and particularly in horror, while ostensibly concerned with power and lack, pleasure and perversion, curiously flatten relations of power even in their very articulation of them. Reyes, too, argues that "there is a certain scopophilic and masochistic pleasure in rediscovering the materiality of our bodies through images or descriptions of mutilation, [and] these must be understood as potentialities" (Reyes 2012, 257). If this is the case, perhaps cross-racial identification is less an ethical encounter than a repackaging of a fungible Black body for white self-actualization?

In her book *Sensational Flesh: Race, Power, and Masochism*, Amber Musser suggests that masochism should be understood as "the desire to abdicate control in exchange for sensation—pleasure, pain, or a combination thereof." However, Musser cautions against reading masochism as an "exceptional practice linked to subversive politics," for questions of difference are often "elided in that collapse" (Musser 2014, 1, 3). White film theory's failure to discuss race or, in the main, to even acknowledge Fanon's work on masochism with regard to the colonial relation, signals a critical lacuna at the very site at which these scholars seek to reverse traditional hierarchies of power. This oversight presumes that corporeal sensations and reactions are shared atemporally and ahistorically across bodies, and that all bodies experience affective responses in the same way, or, more precisely, that the stimulus for the affective responses are the same, are shared. Even when we acknowledge the capacities of bodies to respond affectively to cinematic horror, we might ask as to the nature of that affect. Whatever fear the spectator feels is only a simulation, though no less real, of the imagined or felt fear experienced by the victim. Reyes recognizes that it is impossible for the spectator to feel exactly the same experience as the victim and that our emotions will always be different; however, he argues that successful horror can "short-circuit reality, or appear to bring us as experientially as close as possible to the bodies of the onscreen characters" (Reyes 2016, 170). On the other hand, as Julian Hanich argues, the degree to which the body responds empathically depends on how closely the viewer's experience aligns with the victim's: "Since the viewer is dependent on the personal *carnal knowledge* of the object and the pain it inflicts, *familiar* weapons and affected body parts tend to cause stronger somatic empathy . . . [and] enhance the likelihood of a collective response" (Hanich 2010, 106). In the case of racial victimization, the white spectator can certainly feel the fear of persecution, but only insofar as they have already felt terrors of a similar order. Peele notes that he wanted *Get Out* to be inclusive, but he also recognized that Black viewers and white viewers would have different responses to the film. "This was an exercise in . . . making a movie that is meant to be inclusive. . . . In any good story, whoever you are, you should be able to relate to the protagonist. At the same time, I had to recognize that Black people would be watching this movie and having a different experience ... than white people would ...." (*NPR* 2017).

Consequently, even when we recognize that viewers can share fearful experiences, those experiences vary qualitatively depending on the proximity of the threat to one's own experience. The cognitive always informs the somatic. This is not to say that the physical affect is simulated, that the horripilation is not real, but rather that the somatic response arises from and is preconditioned by the viewer's previously lived cache of experiences, even when the fear is anticipatory—when the action hasn't yet occurred. I can quite easily identify with the character's fear of being pursued and her fear of death, but unless I've been attacked and pursued by a knife-wielding killer, my fear will always be constituted in the space of how I imagine such a fear to feel in conjunction with the memory of real fears I've experienced in other threatening scenarios. Therefore, the supposed liberatory potential of masochistic affect, which Shaviro views as a "necessary condition for any political intervention" (Shaviro 1993, 57), must necessarily acknowledge the role of analogy and simulation in the experience. And in the case of cross-racial identification, the masochistic viewer relation needs even further analysis. As Musser makes clear, "In contrast to Blackness, which is overdetermined from without, masochism is a stance that one has to adopt. Though the Negro's passivity looks similar, he has none of the masochist's powers of transformation.... While he plays at objecthood and passivity, the Negro cannot escape it" (Musser 2014, 105–6).

Reyes explains that in horror the *trauma* of the victim cannot be compared to the *pleasure in trauma* experienced by the masochist viewer, for the "masochist in the masochistic contract wishes the torturer to fulfill a form of violent fantasy, whilst the victim of the sadist does not wish pain to be inflicted upon them" (Reyes 2016, 165). So, even though there is a corporeal identification or an affective relationship between the viewer and victim, in the case of the masochist, the somatic identification is of a different order. Rather than experience the fear and terror that the victim exhibits, the viewer derives supplemental pleasure in and from the victim's fear and terror. This is an important distinction, for it recognizes a somatic connection to exist between the two but acknowledges that the feeling is not shared or even vicarious; it is instead a parallel corporeal experience. In other words, both viewer and victim feel *some*thing as a result of the sadist's actions, it's just not the *same* thing. Masochism, then, is an impediment to the kind of racial recognition that cross-racial identification would seek to produce. As Musser makes clear:

> Masochism cloaks the fact that one *could* act in the face of another's suffering and produces a discourse of innocence. This innocence is complicated; it is constructed through a focus on the suffering that guilt

produces, which, in turn, manifests itself as empathy and analogizes the white body's current guilt to the Black body's past (and present) trauma. (Musser 2014, 102)

WHITE PROGRESSIVE LIBERAL GUILT

The connection between Black trauma and its potential to trigger masochistic white guilt offers a clue as to the popularity of *Get Out* among white viewers and the significance of Peele's choice to write the Armitages as progressives. In the original ending of the film, Chris, bloodied from his own brush with death and standing next to Rose's corpse, is apprehended by the police and sent to prison, presumably for life. Peele explains that this ending was supposed to signal the fallacy of a postracial America and point to the illusory and dangerous nature of the narrative. "That's what the movie was meant to address. Like look, you recognize this interaction. These are all clues, if you don't already know, that racism isn't over. . . . So the ending in that era was meant to say, look, 'You think race isn't an issue? Well at the end, we all know this is how this movie would end right here'" (Verhoeven 2017). But between the writing of the movie and its release in 2017, the myth was unraveling, the lie exposed daily on our streets and in our neighborhoods in the murders of Trayvon Martin, Michael Brown, Eric Garner, Sandra Bland, and the many others whose lives were stolen by visible and invisible systems undergirding white power and extending its reach. Peele decided he couldn't release the film with its original ending. "It was very clear that the ending needed to transform into something that gives us a hero, that gives us an escape, gives us a positive feeling when we leave this movie. . . . There's nothing more satisfying than seeing the audience go crazy when Rod [Lil Rel Howery] shows up" (Verhoeven 2017). And he's right; audience members, regardless of race, do cheer when it's Rod, not the cops, who gets out of the police car, lights blazing. We cheer because we're relieved, but that relief plays differently for whites and for Blacks. When Peele suggests we need a hero, he means that Black viewers need a hero. Being Black in America in 2017 (and 2018, 2019, 2020, 2021, and 2022) is not just depressing, it's deadly; and those who believed that Obama's presidency would change the racial landscape in this country for the better, by this point, understood that it had changed for the worse. Black relief, then, is release, an escape from the trauma produced by the relentless slaughter of Black people and a needed break from bearing witness to Black death. But whites are relieved, too, because their guilt is alleviated. As Musser makes clear, "[U]ltimately liberal guilt is born from spectatorship: 'When those who suffer gaze back at those who do not, guilt is the consequence'. . . . Through empathy, the substitution of the white body for the Black body, current guilt or suffering distracts from the choice of inaction and produces color blindness" (Musser 2014, 102). Imagine the horror for the white viewer in being forced to watch the original ending, the one where the white liberal Obama voter, secure in his "wokeness," reveals the indispensability of anti-Blackness to white life—which is to say, reveals not only his complicity in but his dependence on Black death—and gets away with it! As one critic elaborates:

> Peele doesn't allow white liberals to view the theft of Black bodies in a faraway frame of an Antebellum Southern plantation, nor to blame crude Trump supporters. Instead, *Get Out* blames the theft on contemporary, Northern white Obamaniacs. American liberalism, not just Trumpism, continues to make race by way of bodily theft. (Thrasher 2017)

Considering the masochistic structure of viewer/victim identification, we might also examine whether those white cheers at the end are not just relief but pleasure, pleasure in witnessing the grisly deaths of the Armitages, pleasure in the restoration of a moral order where fake white liberals are punished. After all, "Masochism cloaks the fact that one *could* act in the face of another's suffering and produces a discourse of innocence." Because, in the masochistic structure, the viewer derives a supplemental pleasure in and from the victim's fear and terror, there is pleasure for the white viewer in witnessing the persecution of Chris, not just his ability to overcome it. The ending provides a catharsis for them. Plantinga argues that catharsis is not simply the purgation of negative moments; rather, catharsis in film requires a "cognitive reframing" of the emotions elicited by the film "in such a way that their overall impact is both cognitively and emotionally satisfying, comforting, and pleasurable" (Plantinga 2009, 179). The catharsis for the white viewer in the film's ending is relief that this time, in this film, they're not responsible for Black death. They get a pass. The original ending would have withheld catharsis—no cognitive reframing, no emotional satisfaction, no jubilant cheering.

Clover suggests that in the slasher film, the final girl often functions as a "congenial double" for the adolescent male viewer. "She is feminine enough to act out in a gratifying way, a way unapproved for adult males, the terrors and masochistic pleasures of the underlying fantasy, but not so feminine as to disturb the structures of male competence and sexuality" (Clover 1992, 51). Ultimately, then, the heroic final girl in the slasher film serves as a vehicle for the "sadomasochistic fantasies" of the male viewer. If the female masculinity of the final girl is key to the male spectator's identification with her, then Chris might function in a similarly analogous way for the white viewer. As I have argued, white viewer identification oscillates between the killer and the victim in *Get Out*, but both identifications are rooted in masochistic fantasy. There is pain/embarrassment/shame for the white viewer in watching the Armitages defend their liberalism, while seemingly oblivious to their string of offensive microaggressions, because the white viewer identifies *as* the Armitages, which is to say they identify with the whiteness of the Armitages, even while, as discussed above, they identify with Chris as a persecuted victim and experience pleasure in his fear. But when Chris escapes his murderous captors by killing them, chokes Rose, and finally GETS OUT, the white viewer identifies with Chris not as victim but as victor. In the moment of his escape, to the white viewer, Chris "acts white" (acts like the white viewer imagines they would act)[9] in the same way that the final girl, who successfully escapes her victimization, appeals to the male viewer because she acts like a man imagines he would act.

Reyes assumes that the work of affective mimicry and somatic empathy collapses the distance and difference between spectator and victim. However, even when we consider the role of the somatic in this kind of cross-identification, as Hanich has argued, the identification works most effectively when the viewer is familiar with the threat imposed on the victim; that is, when they can conjure the sensation itself. Therefore, the cognitive component of horror affect can be seen to be central in cross-racial identification because white empathy is informed by cognitive/emotional knowledge and understanding of the Black predicament (whites are troubled at an ethical/moral level by the threat against Chris); however, in *Get Out*, the liberal progressive Armitages confuse the cognitive empathic association with Chris because the viewer cognitively identifies with them at the same time as they identify with Chris's victimization. This combination of affect produces a masochistic structure, whereby the white viewer seeks to identify with the victim's pain as a means of self-flagellation for their own role in the structural displacement of Black bodies.

It is significant to note that white identification with the Armitages doesn't cease when their murderous plot is known; it remains with the white viewer even while they experience empathic and somatic affect with Chris. Even though the "reveal" in the film makes clear that the Armitages are using Chris in unforeseen ways, their characters, with the arguable exception of Rose, don't change at all. There is never a sense that they were just pretending to like Chris or to be liberals or that Dean Armitage's love of Obama and all things Black was an act, no sense that they are really motivated by hatred or a desire to hurt Black people. On the contrary, Peele effectively demonstrates that their actions—their murderous, body-snatching, mind-numbing actions—are consistent with white progressivism. In other words, the Armitages aren't really racists pretending to be liberals; effectively, there's no difference between them because both groups are animated and sustained by the fungibility of Blackness. After all, racism is not an action committed by individuals but rather a system into which everyone is socialized.[10] The cognitive and somatic affect produced within the white spectator in Black horror unveils the racial grammar of American whiteness. Here the lie of the postracial is exposed—whiteness still presumes to arrogate to itself the functionality of the Black body but refuses to acknowledge its act as racist. As Peele acknowledges, "Part of being Black in this country, and I presume being any minority, is constantly being told that . . . we're seeing racism where there just isn't racism" (NPR 2017).

In demonstrating and reinforcing the position of the slave as ontological nothingness existing in the Sunken Place, *Get Out* exposes and parodies the non-subjecthood of the Black (Wilderson) and the emptiness of whiteness. Peele highlights this history but distorts this relationship by having the white characters occupy Black bodies to demonstrate how white survival depends on the vitality of Blackness. At a narrative level, then, Peele demonstrates how the historical condition of Black fungibility is tied to the racial libidinal economy of white desire: "the fantasies of murderous hatred and unlimited destruction, of sexual consumption and social availability that animate the realization of such [anti-Black] violence" and, most importantly, how "anti-Black fantasies attain objective value in the political and economic life of society and in the psychic life of culture as well" (Sexton 2016).

In *Us*, however, Peele revisits the question of cross-racial identification. By creating in the tethered shadow bodies, "Bodies without Organs," bodies that are doubles of us, he avoids the masochistic appropriation involved in cross-racial identification and is able to make a larger point: what if we were *all* terrorized and hunted on the basis of our embodiment, on the way we look? Where the white spectator's identification with Chris in *Get Out* risks a masochistic identification, the introduction in *Us* of the white victim who is victimized in the same way as the Black victim allows empathic connection through somatic affect. Cross-racial identification is achieved in *Us* because every person, whether Black or white, has a tethered Other who is victimized by the politics of the prevailing hegemony. The masochistic fantasy of the white spectator, evident in the possession of Chris's body, is disrupted in the abjection of the white body, which comes to occupy the same structural location, the place of fungibility that was perceived to be historically unique to Blackness. In this reordering, the white spectator first has an affective encounter with Adelaide and her family, recognizing and fearing the power of whiteness to order and hierarchize Black life according to its utility and its plasticity, and then is forced to experience it via the proxy of the white bodies of the Tylers.

Reyes and Shaviro claim that horror is the perfect vehicle for the exposure of the Body without Organs, that body which in its corporeal immediacy creates an "alignment between . . . bodies [that] brings about a moment of organic recognition" (Reyes 2012, 257). Racial horror has the potential to offer an alignment between Black and white bodies, which can trigger not simply the *cognitive* awareness of "the potentiality of the 'body as meat'" also put the white spectator into the *corporeal* location of that experience. In other words, white spectators must understand themselves as "meat" before they can recognize the humanity of the Black Other who has been viewed as meat all along. In this way, Us completes the racial critique of *Get Out*—not just at the thematic narrative level, but importantly, at the formal affective level. "If only for a moment, the immanence of the body-as-meat is capable of bringing [Whites] back to a perception of [their] own bodies as organic, sentient and intensive" (Reyes 2012, 258). In *Get Out*, the Black victim instantiates an affective connection to the white spectator, but the oscillation between white monster and Black victim precludes a transcorporeal substitution that would enable true identification. Witnessing is possible in this model, but not corporeal identification. However, through the doubling, doppelgänger motif, cross-racial identification *is* made possible in *Us*, not because the white spectator inhabits the Black victim's body, but because they inhabit the white victim's body, which occupies the same structural position—has been made meat—by the ordering regime of white power.

Chapter 9

ANIMALS WITH TECHNOLOGY

As I've argued throughout this book, the genre of speculative fiction provides cover for racist themes and representations in *Planet of the Apes*, *The Walking Dead*, and *Star Trek*. At the same time, speculative fiction offers Black filmmakers an opportunity to explore racism in ways that redeem Black life rather than trafficking in its subjection. Black superheroes offer a "powerful source of racial meaning, narrative, and imagination in American society." They function as "ripe metaphors for race relations in America, and are often reflective of escalating and declining racial unrest" (Nama 2008, 4). In an age where politics, news, social networking, and entertainment media representations don't merely reflect race relations but construct, inflame, and litigate them, I'm interested in the particular kind of political resistance that speculative fiction and fantasy, specifically in the case of *Black Panther*, animate or give voice to in Trump's America. As Jamil Smith notes, "In the midst of a regressive cultural and political moment fueled in part by the white-nativist movement, the very existence of *Black Panther* feels like resistance" (Smith n.d.).

It is the nature and scope of that resistance that concerns me here and how and why the genre of Afrofuturist fantasy offers an effective vehicle to voice it. I argue that *Black Panther* engages in a form of world-making "where dissenting voices can reshape the production and circulation of culture and, in turn, publicize counternarratives to dominant ideologies" (Fawaz 2016, 14). *Black Panther* asks us to consider how the kind of world-making central to the fantastic offers new possibilities for Black identity at both a political and ontological level and what cultural difference it might make. This chapter will explore these questions, arguing that Coogler's Wakanda forces viewers to wrangle with the promise of American democracy and offers possibilities for interrogating and undermining colonial logic, which has excluded people of African descent from the category "human" since the transatlantic slave trade and produced an ontological crisis for the Black subject. *Black Panther*, I argue, redefines Black life in an anti-Black world in both political and philosophical ways.

An intersectional, interdisciplinary movement, Afrofuturism, whether through music, art, literature, or film, imagines alternative pasts, futures, and, inevitably, presents through technological innovation, space travel, tradition, culture, and cosmic time. Through mysticism, mythology, or metaphysics, Afrofuturists imagine an Africa free of colonization, violence, and death. By producing what Kodwo Eshun calls "countermemories that contest the colonial archive," Afrofuturists "bring Africa and its subjects into history denied by Hegel et al." (Eshun 2003, 288). In this way, Afrofuturist texts offer an antidote to The Void, and (what Afropessimists call) the violence of the nothingness of Black being, through an exploration and celebration of Black presence—a writing in of all that has been written out. As Isiah Lavender makes clear, "Afrofuturism presents an age-old yearning to exceed racial limitations and to produce the necessary social changes that go with it; such desire is what makes black worlds possible" (Lavender 2019).

In their introduction to *Afrofuturism 2.0*, Reynaldo Anderson and Charles E. Jones suggest that twenty-first-century Afrofuturism—Afrofuturism 2.0—is the "early twenty-first-century technogenesis of Black Identity" and encompasses a "Diasporic techno-cultural 'Pan-African' movement." Anderson and Jones identify five main dimensions of Afrofuturism 2.0: "metaphysics; aesthetics; theoretical and applied science; social sciences; and programmatic spaces" (Anderson and Jones 2016, x). Metaphysics and aesthetics work together in Coogler's production in ways that extend and develop Afrofuturist readings of the film. *Black Panther* explores questions related to Black being, interrogating ontological possibilities in the context of cosmology and pan-African spiritualism, and utilizes that revision to articulate a new inclusive American democracy.

Black Panther earned $1.3 billion in worldwide sales, was nominated for 232 nominations overall, including an Oscar nomination for Best Picture, and won eighty-one awards, including Movie of the Year at the AFI Awards, as well as three Oscars for Costume Design, Original Score, and Production Design. As of December 2022, *Black Panther* has a 96 percent "fresh" rating on *Rotten Tomatoes* and is in first place in its Top 100 list. With its advanced technology powered by the super metal vibranium and engineered by Black Panther's sister Shuri (Letitia Wright), there is no question that *Black Panther* is an Afrofuturist text, but it is also a meditation on colonialism, slavery, patriarchy, and revolution. Critics have described the film as "revolutionary," a "love letter to people of African descent all over the world," and have seen it as offering a "redemptive counter-mythology" (T. Johnson 2018; Serwer 2018; Cobb 2018). But there is also a palpable divide among filmgoers and critics that mirrors the struggle between T'Challa (Chadwick Boseman) and Erik (Michael B. Jordan). T'Challa, like his father T'Chaka (John Kani) before him, has hidden

Wakanda's wealth from other nations to avoid the kind of colonization the rest of Africa endured. They refuse aid and provide none. In the eyes of the world, Wakanda is a poor Third World nation of farmers, and Wakanda intends to keep it that way. Erik, abandoned in Oakland after his father, N'Jobu (Sterling K. Brown), was killed at the hands of his brother King T'Chaka, has suffered the consequences of Wakandan isolation. Without choice or agency, Erik and his people, African Americans, have borne the burden Wakanda refused. Given the moniker "Killmonger" and bearing the self-inflicted scars of every kill the American military trained him to deploy, including those of his kin on the African continent, Erik wants a reckoning. Demanding an audience from the Royal Court, Erik notes, "Y'all sitting up here comfortable. Must feel good. It's about two billion people all over the world that looks like us. But their lives are a lot harder. Wakanda has the tool to liberate 'em all" (Coogler 2018). In pitting the ideal of resistance against that of revolution, isolationism against globalism, the film "recreates the most significant and contentious debate in anti-colonial movements and post-colonial development: black sovereignty versus black solidarity" (Faramelli 2019).

Raised on the streets of Oakland, where the Black Panther Party originated, and consumed by "The Void, the psychic and cultural wound caused by the Trans-Atlantic slave trade, the loss of life, culture, language, and history," Erik wants to take what Wakanda won't give and liberate Black people of the diaspora. The movie appears to set Erik up as T'Challa's adversary, but to many, it is Erik who has the more compelling case. After all, "[I]f an African superpower like Wakanda existed, with all its power, its monopoly on the invaluable sci-fi metal vibranium, and its advanced technology, how could it have remained silent, remained still, as millions of Africans were devoured by The Void?" (Serwer 2018). Even Chadwick Boseman, the actor who plays Black Panther, has noted, T'Challa was "born with a vibranium spoon in [his] mouth. . . . I actually am the enemy. . . . It's the enemy I've always known. It's power. It's having privilege" (Sims 2018). The very things that make Wakanda appealing, its technological advancement, its wealth, its sovereignty, are the very things that motivate Erik and, for many viewers, justify his attempt at violent revolution.

FROM LIBERALISM TO DEMOCRACY: THE PATH OF BLACK PANTHER

In his examination of comics produced in the Cold War era, Ramzi Fawaz argues that fantasy can operate as a "political resource for recognizing and taking pleasure in social identities and collective ways of life commonly denigrated as deviant or subversive," and he demonstrates how fantasy utilizes superhero figures to give expression to "a variety of left-wing projects for political freedom" (Fawaz 2016, 4). Readers consumed comic books in the Cold War era not as an escape but rather to see represented alternative concepts of America and its possible futures. Fawaz argues that the twentieth-century superhero succeeds mythic heroes of previous centuries, particularly the "frontier adventurers and cowboy vigilantes of nineteenth-century westerns," but is distinguished from them through its relationship to scientific and technological innovations of the twentieth century. As exemplars of liberalist ideology, the cowboy or frontiersman represents "a belief in the unfettered autonomy of the individual," whereas the superhero values democracy over liberalism, works in the service of a collective good, and champions those people, especially who, by virtue of their difference from the "universal citizen," have been excluded from the democratic ideal. Fawaz argues that "in its commitment to protecting the political interests of the alienated social groups, the superhero had the potential to redefine the meaning of political freedom in America by recognizing the rights of those excluded from the national community" (2016, 7).

In depicting a superpowered hero and a nation unwilling to help people in Africa or abroad, *Black Panther* deviates from this model; at the beginning of the film, the character Black Panther embraces the values of liberalism and only later embraces democracy. Although set in Africa and in dialogue with a future past that Wakanda represents, *Black Panther* is at its base a discourse on America and the mythical values of equality and liberty it purportedly embodies. In Coogler's representation, Black Panther does not initially exemplify the values and attributes of traditional superhero figures as outlined by Fawaz. Like his father, T'Challa actively resists contributing to the greater good. But it's in his journey from one to the other that *Black Panther* explores this tension between liberalism and democracy, between the needs of the local over the demands of the global, and in doing so, offers a critique of the kind of individualism particular to the founding narrative of the United States. Although some critics find it compromised by urban stereotypes (LeBron 2018; Gates and Warner 2018; Serwer 2018), Erik's rhetorical entreaty is the voice of democracy, reminding the American viewer of America's failed promise to the collective good. The violence of Erik's appeal is central to its power.

As I have argued in Parts 1–3, the cultural zeitgeist of Obama's America, as expressed in film and television, tilted toward the mythos of earlier folk heroes, ones that resonated with and were constructed for white audiences. When we strip away the postapocalyptic framing, the white men of *The Walking Dead* are reminiscent of the nineteenth-century folk heroes who functioned as agents of national(ist) fortification, defending America from those foreign/racial others who would endanger America's white sovereignty. A different meditation on race and nation is produced in Trump's America in the hands of Black filmmakers. Where *TWD* demonstrates that science and technology will prove irrelevant to white survival, privileging instead grit and individualism, *Black Panther* situates Black resistance to white nation-building firmly in the realm of scientific advancement, refusing to be defined by and resisting the return to those myths that fueled colonial conquests in the nineteenth century and empower white nationalists/neo-Nazis today.

Although some critics chafe against what they view as an elevation of the "African noble over the black American man," thus upholding "every crass principle of modern black respectability politics" (LeBron 2018), it is T'Challa's journey from liberalism to democracy, his awakening to a responsibility to the diasporic peoples of Africa whose claims he had previously eschewed, that offers a paradigm for political resistance. But most importantly, it is Erik who is the catalyst for that transformation and who, despite his violent methods, or perhaps because of them, represents a different kind of superhero. As Boseman notes, "T'Challa and Killmonger are mirror images, separated only by the accident of where they were born. . . . What they don't realize is that the greatest conflict you will ever face will be the conflict with yourself" (quoted in Smith n.d.). Unlike Nakia, whose pleas to T'Challa for refugee relief in Africa fall on deaf ears, Erik's strident demands provoke action in T'Challa. In this way, Coogler's film, like comic books before it, offers "a space for modeling new modes of radical critique that offer alternatives to direct-action politics and the discourse of civil liberties" (Fawaz 2011, 357). Indeed, in T'Challa and Erik, both of whom have earned the title "Black Panther," Coogler develops a Black superhero who offers a "generative site for imagining democracy in its most radical form, as a universally expansive ethical responsibility for the well-being of the world rather than an institutional structure upholding national citizenship" (Fawaz 2016, 7).

"I CHOSE WAKANDA"

Encountering his father on the ancestral plane for the second time, after he learns of T'Chaka's murder of N'Jobu and his abandonment of Erik, T'Challa asks, "Why didn't you bring the boy home?" In an uncharacteristic rebuke, T'Challa calls his father out: "You were wrong to abandon him!" When T'Chaka repeats the Wakandan dictum, "I chose my people. I chose Wakanda," T'Challa angrily denounces him: "You were wrong!" Gesturing to the ancestors surrounding his father, he expresses his own frustration and dawning awareness of the consequences of Wakanda's geopolitical policies: "You were all wrong to turn your backs on the rest of the world!" (Coogler 2018). T'Challa will go on to defeat Erik, ultimately killing him, and reclaim his throne. On one level, one can certainly read this, as several critics have done, as a rebuke of Black

America and its call for global accountability. Christopher LeBron argues that Coogler makes us choose between T'Challa, "a man of African nobility," and Erik, a "black thug from Oakland, hell[-]bent on killing for killing's sake . . . a receptacle for tropes of inner-city gangsterism" (LeBron 2018). However, I would argue that even despite his brutal methods (he kills his girlfriend rather than relinquish the vibranium to Klaue and burns the field of purple heart-shaped herbs that give Black Panthers their strength), Erik is not the sympathetic villain of the piece; Wakanda is. I don't mean to suggest only that the film raises questions about diaspora and the responsibility that Black people bear "to help one another escape oppression" (Serwer 2018). Rather, Wakanda's wealth and privilege and its disinterest in the suffering of Black people are a metaphor for American neoliberalism.

T'Challa notes that Erik "is a monster of our own making," but America created "Killmonger" in the void that Wakanda left. Abandoned by his paternal family, Erik was "raised" by the military-industrial complex of Annapolis, the

T'Challa returns to the ancestral plains of Africa after imbibing the purple heart-shaped herb that transforms him into the Black Panther. By contrast, robbed of his history and heritage, Erik returns to Oakland, where he relives the last moments of his father's life. (*Black Panther*, 2018)

Navy Seals, and JSOC. He was taught how to "commit assassinations and take down governments." But even before that, as a young Black boy in Oakland, he knew that "everybody dies. It's just life around here" (Coogler 2018). When T'Challa imbibes the purple heart-shaped herb, he returns to the ancestral planes of Africa; when Erik consumes it, he ends up back in Oakland. By substituting the grown Erik for his younger self, we don't see a "killmonger." Instead, we are presented with a boy robbed of a history and a heritage and resigned to the knowledge that his life doesn't matter, a boy excluded by and from the democratic promise of the United States.

Fawaz argues that:

[M]any readers and cultural critics of comics understood that *differences* (whether of race, class, sex, or gender, geographical location, ability, or religious orientation) were not only sites of political oppression but potent cultural resources for articulating new forms of social and political affiliation, questioning the limits of democratic inclusion, and developing new knowledge about the world from the position of the outcast and the marginalized. (Fawaz 2016, 21)

Erik occupies this function in *Black Panther*. It is his radicalism, his political truth which forces T'Challa to change. The benevolence and diplomacy that Wakanda displays at the end of the film is only possible because of Erik's radical philosophy and the violence he uses to implement it.

By suggesting that Wakanda is an analog of America, I don't mean to undermine the important and soul-affirming space that it occupies for many African Americans, but merely to argue that Afrofuturism as a form of aesthetic resistance allows and invites both critique and celebration. Critics note the joy and freedom, the power, that representations of independent, intelligent, technologically savvy, and wealthy Black people engender in a Black audience. Wakanda liberates the viewer: "We're not dealing with black pain, and black suffering, and black poverty—the usual topics of acclaimed movies about the black experience" (Wallace 2018). Valerie Babb argues that Wakanda "embodies what Africa as an invention has meant in much of the black American imagination: a utopian memory, a site for creating traditions and narratives filling the lacunae of slavery, a means of establishing continuity between the black African past and the black American present" (Babb 2020, 96). Coogler has stated that he wanted to explore "what it means to be African . . . this concept of us as a people being marooned in this place that we're not from" (Eels 2020). In doing so, he offers "a vivid re-imagination of something black Americans have cherished for centuries—Africa as a dream of our wholeness, greatness and self-realization. . . . There exists, somewhere within us, an image in which we are whole, in which we are home. Afrofuturism is, if nothing else, an attempt to imagine what that home would be" (Wallace 2018).

But at the same time, *Black Panther* asks the Black viewer to measure the value and potential cost in dreaming, positing, and creating a fantasy of Africa as home, even when that fantasy is by and for African Americans. What is the role of Africa in imagining African American freedom? And specifically, what is the function of an imagined Africa untouched by the West? Wakanda offers the dream of what might have been had colonization and the transatlantic slave trade not violently altered or ended the lives of so many African people. In the fertile imagining of a place like Wakanda, we can glimpse the possibilities for freedoms denied in the current socio-political imaginary of the United States. A place like Wakanda forces us to ask more of America, as Ricardo Guthrie does: "[H]ow can Black speculative fiction re-fashion a de-colonial space beyond Wakanda, in the current nation-states and community places within which Afro-diasporic people struggle daily for sustenance, power, and joy?" (Guthrie 2019, 15).

AFRICA AND THE WAKE

Frank Wilderson is critical of those who would see in Africa a prelapsarian past. For Wilderson, Africa is not a diasporic homeland to which African Americans might return. Africa only represents "dispersal, which is to say that it does not rest upon some plenitude in the past":

> But what is even more problematic about the word diaspora, when applied to Blacks, is its grammatical coupling with a possessive pronoun "their"—"their homeland," or "their original homeland." The viability of such phrases falters in the face of Africa because the word "Africa" is a shorthand for technologies of force that rob possessive pronouns and place names of their integrity.... Blacks, in other words, cannot claim their bodies, cannot claim their families, cannot claim their cities, cannot claim their countries, they cannot lay claim to a personal pronoun. It is (or was, sticking with diaspora) no more "their continent" than the slave cabin was "their home".... Africa is a slave dwelling as well; it's just that it is a slave dwelling at a higher level of abstraction than the cabin. (Wilderson et al. 2016, 8)

Wilderson's critique raises relevant points about the efficacy of grounding political movements in a retro-positing of African wholeness and a belief in its capacity to heal significant wounds in its historical wake. But as Christina

Sharpe makes clear, "while the wake produces Black death and trauma . . . we, Black people everywhere and anywhere we are, still produce in, into, and through the wake an insistence on existing: we insist Black being into the wake" (Sharpe 2016, 11). For Sharpe, this means attending to the ways that "literature, performance, and visual culture observe and mediate this un/survival . . . representing the paradoxes of blackness within and after the legacies of slavery's denial of Black humanity" (2016, 14). If, as Wilderson suggests, it's not only foolish but dangerous to base political work in a mythical African past, we might consider how aesthetic productions, and particularly Afrofuturist texts, take up those questions and are able to explore and imagine ontological resistance and sovereign integrity of real Black bodies, not imaginary ones.

Nama explains that in 1960s America, the comic hero Black Panther offered not only a representation of Black self-determination and economic independence to Black Americans fighting for their civil rights, but it also spoke to the anticolonialist movements of 1950s Africa where leaders like Jomo Kenyatta, Patrice Lumumba, and Kwame Nkrumah "embodied the hopes of their people and captured the imagination of the anticolonialist movement with their charisma and promise to be free." In this way, the figure of Black Panther "not only symbolized a politically provocative and wildly imaginative convergence of African tradition with advanced technology, but he also stood as a progressive racial symbol and anticolonialist critique of the economic exploitation of Africa" (Nama 2011, 43). Coogler's desire to adapt the story of Black Panther speaks to a yearning to offer an equally compelling critique of today's racial context. At a narrative level, the film engages with the legacy of the transatlantic slave trade and the social and economic consequences of dispossession for Black people in America. And it is Erik, the other superhero, whose radical democratic ideals catalyze T'Challa, who must begin the work of constructing an equitable and empowering future for Black Americans and others around the globe.

In addition to this political critique of racism in America, I argue that the film offers a significant philosophical meditation on Blackness and a revision of the divisions that have shaped colonial logic and excluded Black life from categories of human. More than a projection of aspirational what-ifs, *Black Panther* posits an Africa and Wakanda so clearly fantastical that it illustrates through its cosmological and ontological beliefs and practices an alternative conception of Black "being" in America. The film unsettles prevailing conceptions of the human, particularly reductive conceptions of Black humanity, and engages in a form of what Zakiyyah Jackson calls "imaginative practices of worlding from the perspective of a history of blackness's bestialization and thingification" (Jackson 2020, 1).

ANIMALS REDUX

The presidency of Barack Obama animated and revived in political and popular cultural discourse nineteenth-century tropes that associated Black bodies with animal bodies. On the one hand, as I argued in chapter 2, this rendering animal of Black bodies has enabled and justified violence against African Americans while at the same time stirring fears among disenfranchised white voters that Blacks, as evidenced by Obama himself, might not belong to a different category of being after all. That realization, it seems, promotes anxiety among whites about maintaining their lead or, in the case of Obama and the advantages he was perceived to bestow on "his people," catching up. I've argued throughout this book that popular culture in the age of Obama deployed animal/African tropes, cultivating and shaping specific views about African Americans both as inferior and a threat to white supremacy and that the production of this sentiment among whites primed the way for Trump's racist nativism. Here, through further analysis of *Black Panther*, I extend my examination of the "animal," exploring the possibilities that the fantasy genre, and Afrofuturism specifically, holds for disrupting, subverting, and rewriting the association of Blacks as animals.

Zakiyyah Jackson has argued that the bestialization of Black bodies does not exclude Black people from the category of human but rather positions them along a scale of humanity, rendering Blackness plastic, "produced as sub/super/human at once, a form where form shall not hold: potentially everything and nothing at the register of ontology." In this reading, the "animal" is just one ontological manifestation of Black flesh and functions, conventionally, to delimit white humanity but also to define Black humanity. Rather than seeking inclusion into a humanity from which Blacks are purportedly excluded, Jackson suggests instead that we examine "alternative conceptions of being and the nonhuman that have been produced by blackened people." She exhorts us to move beyond prevailing Western conceptions of the human and instead explore Africanist texts that require us to rethink the ontology of Blackness and "displace the very terms of black(ened) animality as abjection" (2020, 3, 1). In doing so, she calls those scholars to account whose work, in Jared Sexton's words, exhibits the "tendency to depart from the faulty premise of black pathology and thereby carry along the discourse being criticized within the assumptions of the critique" (Sexton 2011, 12).

In expanding the definition of Black life beyond "denied humanity," Jackson engages with a view espoused by Afropessimists such as Frank Wilderson, Jared Sexton, Saidiya Hartman, Calvin Warren, and others, who consider Blackness always to be in an antagonistic, irreconcilable relation to the concept "Human."

For Afropessimists, the anti-Black foundations of Euro-Western philosophy, politics, history, and art depend upon and produce the "nothing" of Black being or, more accurately, Black being(s) as nothing. According to Calvin Warren, "Black being incarnates metaphysical nothing, the terror of metaphysics, in an antiblack world. Blacks, then, have function but not Being" (Warren 2018, 5). Social justice movements and socio-critical-political attempts to reclaim or restore Black identity, they argue, fundamentally misconstrue the conditions by which Blackness is instantiated in the first place. According to the Afropessimist view, the violence involved in the rhetorical and literal substitution of "slave" for "Black" provides the foundation of (white) humanity and ensures that Blackness is perpetually offset against the ideals of liberty and reason that ground the bourgeois subject. As Wilderson explains, "By *describing* the ways in which Blacks are barred, ab initio, from Human recognition and incorporation, Afro-pessimism argues that the Human would lose all coherence were it to jettison the violence and libidinal investments of anti-Blackness against which it is able to define its constituent elements" (Wilderson et al. 2016, 7). Accordingly, the "Black," lacking the conferral of subjectivity or selfhood, is perpetually exiled from the human condition because such a being is robbed of the reciprocal recognition that subjectivity requires.

Jackson argues that instead of assuming that Black aesthetic texts, literature, and visual art labor strenuously to humanize Blackness, as though vying for a place in the category of human (or, alternatively, reproduce, for purposes of exposure and critique, the fungibility and disposability of Black life), we might recognize instead how diasporic texts alter the "meaning and significance of being (human) and engag[e] in imaginative practices of worlding from the perspective of a history of blackness's bestialization and thingification" (2020, 1). For Jackson, then, though Blackness is frequently represented or depicted by the Euro-West as an inversion of the humanity of the white Enlightenment subject, Black writers, thinkers, and artists have frequently disputed such characterizations not by laying claim to an identity that invalidates them, but by offering divergent definitions of humanity itself. Such representations refigure the racialization of the human-animal distinction and allow us to see how the abjection of animals "has historically been essential to producing classes of abject humans" (Jackson 2020, 2).

In the place of violence, which Afropessimists view as central to explorations of Black identity because "violence not only makes thought possible, but it makes black metaphysical being and black relationality impossible" (Douglass and Wilderson 2013, 117), Afrofuturism offers a fantasy of Blackness free of violence and untrammeled by colonial domination and the transatlantic slave trade. Where Blackness in the Afropessimist view is mere void, Afrofuturists, by contrast, see in Blackness infinite possibilities. "Blackness invites speculation. The

The visual transformation of both T'Challa and Erik/N'Jadaka into Black Panther depicts a coextensive belonging of human and animal bodies capable of dismantling and revising the concept of Blackness as bestialization. (*Black Panther*, 2018)

very idea of a global African diaspora creates the most fertile of grounds for a field of *what-ifs*" (Newkirk 2018). Wilderson is critical of Black films that attempt to produce an "illusive symbolic resistance" to the nothingness of Black life. In his view, Blackness is forever underwritten by The Void produced by slavery. As he makes clear, "Africans went into the ships and came out as Blacks.... This violence which turns a body into flesh, ripped apart literally and imaginatively, destroys the possibility of ontology because it positions the Black in an infinite and indeterminately horrifying and open vulnerability, an object made available (which is to say fungible) for any subject" (2010, 38). Wilderson's critique is applicable to realistic films that depict and even traffic in the "social life of social death" (Sexton 2011), films that attempt, falsely in Wilderson's view, "to aspire to the very ontological capacity which modernity foreclosed to them" by assuming that all lives exist on the same ontological ground, in spite of historically racist laws and practices that suggest otherwise (2010, 42). In other words, realist films that revisit our racist past and potentially evoke in the white spectator feelings of pity, shame, and/or guilt reinforce rather than challenge the nothingness of Black life. By contrast, speculative fiction and Afrofuturist fantasy like *Black Panther* can offer an alternative metaphysical model because they originate in an Africa untouched by the colonial and imperial rhetorics that produce Black nothingness in the diaspora. In Ava DuVernay's view, Wakanda prompts us to consider questions such as, "What if they didn't come? And what if they didn't take us? What would that have been?" (Quoted in Wallace 2018). In doing so, Afrofuturism posits an alternative imagining of Black life.

In *becoming human*, Jackson argues that instead of accepting the Euro-Western model in which Black people are "representative of the abject animalistic dimensions of humanity or the beast," we should look to texts that "generate conceptions of being that defy the disparagement of the nonhuman and 'the animal'" (2020, 3). The salient task for metaphysics, then, is not to reject the logic of animalization but rather to embrace it. Because there is no outside to the rhetorical positioning of Black flesh as Other and because discursive and visual grammars of Blackness rob Black people of "ontological resistance," we should look to creative texts for alternative ontological models of Blackness. In *Black Panther*, this fantasy of Black presence is achieved through its depiction of a coextensive belonging of human and animal bodies, which dismantles and revises the concept of Blackness as bestialization. *Black Panther* presents nonbinary models of animal-human relations in the characters of Black Panther and M'Baku (Winston Duke). Just as comic book creators in the Cold War period "used the biologically unstable body of the superhero to explore, and potentially bring into being, the states of bodily and psychic liberation espoused by a variety of countercultural movements" (Fawaz 2011, 357), *Black Panther* uses animals to render the category of humanity unstable.

TRANSMATERIAL/TRANSSPECIES BECOMING

Although it is vibranium that fuels Wakanda and accounts for its wealth and stealth, it is the power of the Black Panther that guides and defends Wakanda. In a voiceover at the film's start, Erik asks his father for a story of home, and N'Jobu recounts the history of Wakanda, which millions of years ago was struck by a meteorite containing vibranium. As competing tribes warred over its riches, the Panther Goddess Bast led a "warrior shaman" to the heart-shaped herb that granted him "superhuman strength, speed and instincts" (Coogler 2018). The power of the first Black Panther is transmaterial and transspecies in nature, a combination of human, animal, and mineral substances. This cross-species relationality does not render T'Challa abject or beast-like; instead, it is the source of his power.

In the *Black Panther* comics, M'Baku, a supervillain, appears as a racist caricature. Known as Man-Ape, he gained his power by killing a white gorilla, bathing in its blood, and eating its flesh (Rovin 1987, 203). Although many supervillains are violent, M'Baku's violence was imbued with a primitivism grounded in a belief in African otherness. His goal was to strip Wakanda of its vibranium and revert the country to a primitive state. In imbibing the blood of the white gorilla, M'Baku is infused with its strength and speed, allowing him powers that rival Black Panther's. Coogler and Cole retain elements of M'Baku's backstory—the gorilla is still the totem of his tribe, and the Jabari worship Hanuman, the monkey god—but rather than reinforcing a bestial connection between Black people and apes as the *Planet of the Apes* reboot does, Coogler and Cole endow M'Baku with a nobility and a legitimate counter-philosophy.

In contrast to the racist caricature of M'Baku in the comics, M'Baku wears a gorilla mask representing the totem of the Jabari during his contest with T'Challa for the throne of Wakanda. (*Black Panther*, 2018)

When M'Baku challenges T'Challa's claim to the throne, his tribe enters the arena chanting, adorned with white ceremonial paint. M'Baku, as their leader, wears a tribal mask of the gorilla totem rather than a realistic gorilla headdress. This distinction is important because the comic book M'Baku was frequently depicted in a "full gorilla mask" that "often made him literally look like that creature," erasing his humanity entirely (Breznican 2017).

The gorilla is sacred to the Jabari, an object of religious reverence and a vehicle for enhancing their humanity, not replacing it. M'Baku is critical of T'Challa's ability to defend Wakanda, especially as he was unable to save T'Chaka, and is concerned that Wakanda's technological advancements "have been overseen by a child who scoffs at tradition" (Coogler 2018). As is his right, he challenges T'Challa for his place on the throne and, when outmatched, yields to his authority. Surrounded by rhythmic drumming and Wakandans dressed in their traditional tribal clothes, the challenge begins with the two men donning their ceremonial masks. It is easy to imagine how this scene, with men in masks fighting with spears and shields, could have utilized primitive stereotypes central to Hollywood's conception of Africa, but Coogler and his creative team instead depict a dignified ceremonial event with significant consequences. According to M'Baku, without his "claws" and "special suit," T'Challa is "just a boy not fit to lead." Badly beaten and almost defeated, T'Challa demonstrates that it's not the suit that gives him strength but the power of the panther itself. When his mother, Ramonda (Angela Bassett), tells T'Challa to "show him who you are!" he rebounds and defeats M'Baku and is immediately crowned "King T'Challa, the Black Panther" (Coogler 2018). Just as the panther confers nobility on T'Challa and T'Chaka before him, the gorilla becomes an extension of M'Baku, guiding him first in his attempted defeat of T'Challa and then in his rescue and defense of him.

Whereas prevailing metaphysical conceptions of the human figure Black bodies as beasts, Wakandans are free to embrace and find power in the human/animal connection because animals offer agency and strength. The film doesn't simply repurpose or repackage material histories; it reinvents *epistemologies* of racialized humanity and bestialization both in its animal and human form, ultimately producing alterior *ontologies*. *Black Panther* thematizes and, importantly, visualizes the possibility of a human/animal co-dependence that, unburdened by colonial rhetoric and philosophy, realizes, reclaims, and refigures the potential in the animal. The white rhinoceroses that protect the border and become part of the Border Tribe's army in the battle against T'Challa are perfect examples of this. The rhinoceroses are not just tools or weapons to be utilized; they are an extension of W'Kabi's (Daniel Kaluuya) powers when he is on the brink of defeat. Although the Wakandans have the capacity to utilize the most advanced weaponry, they settle their tribal disputes in traditional

Black Panther demonstrates how indigenous forms of knowledge flourish beyond the colonial episteme and have the capacity to challenge it. (*Black Panther*, 2018)

ways, employing spears and charging rhinos. In these representations, *Black Panther* not only dismantles the binary of human/animal, but it also provides an alternative grammatology to humanism, one not dependent on Enlightenment discourses of hierarchy and division. *Black Panther* demonstrates how indigenous forms of knowledge flourish beyond the colonial episteme and then challenge it.

Wilderson suggests that "[p]olitical ontology is thought through two ensembles of questions: a descriptive ensemble asks 'What does it mean to suffer?' and a prescriptive ensemble asks 'How does one become free of suffering?'" For Wilderson, the descriptive ensemble demonstrates how "gratuitous violence structures and positions the Black," whereas the prescriptive ensemble represents the turning of that structuring violence against "civil society writ large" (2010, 126). Erik and T'Challa represent these two poles. *Black Panther* establishes that to "become free of suffering," Black people can refuse the pejorative association of African/animal and instead imagine ontologies beyond the trauma of the bestialized Black body. Erik embodies the position "what does it mean to suffer?" and reminds us of the political urgency of these ontological becomings. As a representative of American Blackness, it seems that Erik is granted "no reprieve from ontologizing dominance and violence" (Jackson 2020, 20). Deployed by the US military as a killing machine, he is a clear example of how Black flesh is made animal by the ordering logic of Western humanism.

In the two men, the film offers two versions of Black life; one possessing an expansive transcorporeal, transspecies potential, and one that is "appropriated, inverted, and ultimately plasticized" by a Western humanism that elevates its own humanity in contrast to a bestialized humanity (Jackson 2020, 23). Having inflicted the fatal blow to Erik, T'Challa's loaded suggestion "maybe we can still heal you" is rejected by Erik: "Why? So you can just lock me up?" (Coogler

W'Kabi calls rhinos to battle. (*Black Panther*, 2018)

2018). In refusing, Erik recognizes his difference from T'Challa and his place in The Void. Jared Sexton suggests that "captivity is always an unsettled condition, open to an outside about which it will not know anything and about which it cannot stop thinking, a nervous system always in pursuit of the fugitive movement it cannot afford to lose and cannot live without, if it is to go on existing in and as a mode of capturing" (Sexton 2011, 10). Erik "Killmonger" Stevens represents the abjected bestialized inhumanity that the cosmological ontology of *Black Panther* questions. However, when he is transformed in and through the power of the Black Panther, Erik becomes N'Jadaka again. In demanding to be buried in the ocean with his ancestors "that jumped from the ships 'cause they knew death was better than bondage," Erik refuses captivity and the violence of diaspora (Coogler 2018). *Black Panther*'s achievement is ultimately political and philosophical; not only does it offer a fantasy of pre-diasporic belonging and a neoliberal critique of American democracy, but it also challenges the very apparatus on which such claims to universalist humanitarianism rest.

The white rhinoceroses that protect the border and become part of the Border Tribe's army in the battle against T'Challa are not just tools or weapons to be utilized; they are an extension of W'Kabi's powers when he is on the brink of defeat. (*Black Panther*, 2018)

In Afrofuturist fashion, *Black Panther* offers an exploration of science and technological wonders in and through a celebration of the Africa of huts, tribes, totems, and animals. Indeed, as Edward Ademolu notes, "[I]t is the 'futurism' aspect that makes Black Panther stand head and shoulders above the rest. Showcasing an iteration of Africa that is more imaginatively radical than merely culturally palatable for audiences who are used to being spoon-fed—better yet, force-fed—microwavable doses of an Africa that is melancholic, benighted and savage, to satisfy their visually myopic cravings" (Ademolu 2018). Nevertheless, the film's resistant textuality resides not only in its depiction of Black excellence, advanced technology, and spirit untrammeled by centuries of white oppression—though, of course, these are important and inspiring things; rather, resistance is explored in demonstrating the fungibility of American Blackness and a voicing through Erik of the uses to which it has been put.

In this way, the film uses concepts of Afropessimism to articulate its Afrofuturist vision. As Wilderson claims, "If one tilts the analytic lens of Afropessimism properly one will be engaged not in a project which pathologizes Black people for being inhuman, but a project which pathologizes Humanity for its violent consumption of Blackness" (Wilderson et al. 2016, 7). Erik doesn't represent one face of Black life and Wakanda another; instead, the fantasy of Wakanda, however marvelous, is a fantasy that cannot hold while Black people are expendable, fungible, socially dead. For "all black(ened) people must contend with the burden of the antiblack animalization of the global paradigm of Blackness, which will infringe on all articulations and political maneuverings that seek redress for present and historical violence" (Jackson 2020, 19). In *Black Panther*, we are offered an alterior cosmology where animal being informs and empowers rather than minimizes Black life. In this rendering, the animal is as potent as the vibranium that powers Wakanda, and together they challenge the animalizing discourse that secures the abjection of both Black people and animals and extend the possibilities for imagining Black life beyond the Euro-Western model.

Conclusion

MEDIA MATTERS

In its broadest conception, *Imperiled Whiteness* is an examination of how media make race and how those racial makings shape and construct white Americans' sense of their racial identity in a "postracial" era. My analysis of representations of Black, Brown, and white bodies in news, entertainment, and social media in the Obama-to-Trump era demonstrates how media narratives converge to produce racial "truths" that animate and bolster white identity politics. Herman Gray observes that a proliferation of media technologies, rather than ameliorating deficiencies in racial representation, instead represents a shift in cultural politics from race to difference. These "crowded social and cultural spaces like [i]nternet-based social network sites (Twitter, Facebook) and user-generated content sites and distribution platforms (Instagram and YouTube)" obscure the power relations that structure racist discourses and representations and signal a "shift from antiracist struggle to antiracial ones" so that "visibility is an end in itself" (Gray 2013, 771). Sarah Banet-Weiser calls the curation of identity that is central to user participation in social media a form of "self-branding" that serves a neoliberal marketplace invested in commodifying diversity and visibility (Banet-Weiser 2012). Both Gray and Banet-Weiser note that the magnification of identity differences on social media platforms stems from and caters to a desire among users for recognition, what Gray calls an "*incitement* to visibility" (2013, 777). I've argued that in the Obama-to-Trump era, the "proliferation and marketing of difference and diversity" (Gray 2013, 772) in media outlets is extended to whiteness as white identity is made recognizable and visible in a purportedly postracial landscape. Heretofore untapped by the politics of diversity, white identity and whiteness become salient commodities in a mediascape sustained by and dependent on the production of racial meanings for consumer consumption. Media framing of cultural, frequently racialized, flashpoints of immigration, racial protest, and gun control—along with developments in molecular and genetic science and in conjunction with consumer-generated produsage—foster and produce an *affective politics* of whiteness and facilitate the organization and mobilization of white "resistance" to a perceived displacement/replacement. Speculative fiction provides a particularly effective and versatile platform for the exchange and circulation of racial visibilities through the recuperation of historically racist tropes that utilize colorblind discourses to mask and obscure its race-work, enabling a discourse of "imperiled whiteness." In the most recent iteration of their franchises, *Planet of the Apes*, *The Walking Dead*, and *Star Trek* cultivate and curate this discourse, helping to animate fears about white precarity and "demographic replacement." I've argued that their location in the science fiction genre facilitated and enabled a re-racing of white identity and the expression of racist discourse through fantastic obfuscation in ways that other genres could not achieve.

In targeting the idea of Americanness and defining it through the rhetoric of whiteness, these shows operate as "discursive relay stations," drawing on increasingly strident political discourse emanating from the Right and repackaging it in fantastic, futuristic, apocalyptic ways. These seemingly anodyne speculative fictions were avidly consumed by a wide and varied demographic of viewers and effectively fostered and developed new forms of white identity politics that were simultaneously finding expression in the news and social media spheres. As Fiske makes clear, "television," as well as film and other forms of entertainment media, "acts like a relay station: it rarely originates topics of public interest (though it may repress them); rather, what it does is give them high visibility, energize them, and direct or redirect their general orientation before relaying them out again into public circulation" ([1996] 2016, 25). Popular entertainment media *interpret* political discourse—those relations of power and conflict that animate and provide ceaseless fodder for the news media—and *translate* it into social discourse, which becomes the means by which those political conditions "are made to make sense within the social relations that structure them" (Fiske [1996] 2016, 3). As I've argued throughout, speculative fiction is particularly adept at this because social relations in the intradiegetic world of the text frequently obscure, through science or technology, or in the case of *TWD* in the exigencies of the postapocalypse, the real-world extradiegetic social relations informing those fantastic scenarios. Nevertheless, as I've argued in my analysis of *Get Out*, *Us*, and *Black Panther*, the same generic codes that speculative fiction employs to cloak its political race-work can be used to expose it, redeploying the fetishism of race and racism to progressive and productive ends.

In an effort to conclude this examination of how film and television, far from being isolated entertainment vehicles, are coextensive with media events, which together make and manipulate the cultural and political views of their audience, I want now to return to two of the franchises discussed in this book, *The Walking Dead* and *Planet of the Apes*. In my argument, these shows, developed and screened during the Obama years, provide instructive examples of how entertainment media make race by creating, shaping, and reinforcing prevailing fears of "us" and "them." I want to conclude with these productions because both franchises continued into the Trump era, yet the latest installments differ in significant ways from the earlier iterations produced in the Obama years. Because, as I've demonstrated throughout this book, there is a relationship between political discourse and media representation, we shouldn't overlook how *TWD* and *Planet of the Apes* respond to the racial backlash they helped to produce, offering an alternative to the fears stoked by media vehicles in the Obama era. In the persons of Negan and The Colonel, both *TWD* and *Planet of the Apes* respectively develop authoritarian, fascist characters that represent the kind of right-wing extremism voiced by Trump and embodied in the not-so-veiled neo-Nazi politics pervading his administration. Instead of glorifying the violent, oppressive tactics both men deploy, I argue that seasons 7–10 of *TWD* and the third film in the *Planet of the Apes* franchise, *War for the Planet of the Apes*, offer The Colonel and Negan as portents of what awaits an America supportive of and manipulated by the oppressive tyranny of leaders like Trump.

"YOU THOUGHT YOU WERE SAFE. I GET IT. BUT THE WORD IS OUT. YOU ARE NOT SAFE. NOT EVEN CLOSE."

Negan (Jeffrey Dean Morgan) makes his first appearance in *TWD* in the last episode of season 6, "Last Day on Earth." Many fans of the comic books had long awaited Negan's arrival, as his role as the dictatorial, violent leader of the Saviors was well established in Kirkman's graphic universe. The episode, which featured an unsatisfying cliffhanger, was not particularly popular with viewers, but Morgan's performance as Negan was praised by critics and fans as "terrific" and "deliciously evil." One critic said Negan added a "nerve-racking electricity to the show [and] his smirk and swagger were a wonderful sight to behold" (Rotten Tomatoes 2016; Fowler 2017). Warning Rick and his group that "he's going to beat the holy hell" out of one of them with "Lucille," his barbed wire-wrapped baseball bat, Negan asserts his authority through humiliation: "[W]hatever you do, no matter what, you don't mess with the New World Order. . . . You ruled the roost. You built something. You thought you were safe. I get it. But the word is out. You are not safe. Not even close" (Darabont et al. 2016; 6:16). With totalitarian bombast, Negan rules by targeting and exploiting the fears of his audience. The episode aired on April 3, 2016, at the height of Trump's jingoistic politicking, which included a memorable campaign event in Florida in January of 2016. In front of a live audience, three little girls, dubbed by the campaign "The Freedom Girls," arrayed in sparkly dresses of red, white, and blue, performed a bizarre "anthem" to Trump, which included the lyrics "President Donald Trump knows how to make America great. Deal from strength or get crushed every time" (Hafner 2016).

Negan shares the same philosophy of crush or be crushed and takes pleasure in taunting and bullying his adversaries. The similarity between Negan and Trump, noted by many critics, forced Scott Gimple, *TWD*'s showrunner, to deny any association, citing Kirkman's comic as his source material: "I'm really trying to hold onto Negan from the book, and tell human stories that reflect reality. If people draw conclusions about current events, it's just coincidence" (Huver 2017). Gimple does, of course, have a point. Negan's character is very similar to that represented in the comics, but in a show that routinely deviates from the comic's timeline and introduces new characters (Daryl and Merle) or conflates two or more existing characters (Andrea and Carol), the timing of Negan's introduction in the series in 2016 is worthy of examination. From the perspective of media event analysis, the precedent of comic book Negan is, critically, beside the point. Popular entertainment echoes an epoch's political discourse and its media-framed narratives and has the capacity to perpetuate or contest those narratives. Jeffrey Dean Morgan's representation of Negan on screen at a time when contentious partisan messaging was circulating broadly on other media platforms highlights the connection between political discourse and audience attitudes. Negan's character and fans' reaction to him serve as a barometer, for better or worse, of the country's prevailing mood. Perhaps the popularity of, and the media's cringing delight in, Trump's outrageous rhetoric signaled to the show's creative team that the run-up to the election of 2016 might be a good time to introduce the authoritarian, shockingly profane Negan.

What the *TWD* creative team probably didn't anticipate was the swift backlash to Negan's gratuitous violence and extreme posturing. Headlines such as "Why People Stopped Watching *The Walking Dead*" and "*The Walking Dead* Quitter's Club: Goodbye for Real" suggest that critics and most fans were sickened by the vicious and oppressive bullying depicted onscreen, with many claiming it was "torture-porn masquerading as storytelling" (Bishop and Statt 2016):

> [A]fter Negan and his not-so-merry band of Saviors came to town, *The Walking Dead* experienced a dramatic shift in tone. No longer did it feel like a cautionary tale, a series exploring the intricacies of existence and the darkness of human nature; it became something that takes pleasure in causing pain, transforming into physical and emotional "torture porn." (Caulfield 2021)

Airing just days before the 2016 election, the premiere of season 7, "The Day Will Come When You Won't Be"—which resolves the season 6 cliffhanger

Negan threatens Rick and his posse with his barbed-wire bat "Lucille." (*The Walking Dead*, "Last Day on Earth," season 6, episode 16, 2016)

with Negan's brutal and gory slaying by "Lucille" of Abraham and fan-favorite Glenn—sparked intense criticism among fans and critics and a precipitous drop in ratings. Reviewers slammed the episode's "sadistic acts of gut-wrenching violence," and another called it "to put it mildly, uncomfortable viewing: 45-plus minutes of torture porn mingled with something even more unpalatable—bitter feelings about the systematic humiliation of the characters we've taken for so many years of this drama to be the good guys" (Jeffries 2016). Watching the assault on the group, it becomes very clear to the audience that Rick's usual heroics don't work in this new world; not only will he not save the day, he can't. Rick is beaten, bloodied, and humiliated by Negan, who, demanding Rick's obeisance, has ordered him to cut off Carl's arm.

Negan bashes Abraham's skull with "Lucille." (*The Walking Dead*, "The Day Will Come When You Won't Be," season 7, episode 1, 2016)

Rick eventually capitulates to the demand, only to be given a last-minute reprieve by Negan, who makes the stakes clear to Rick: "You answer to me. You provide for me. You belong to me" (Darabont et al. 2016; 7:1). If the producers had hoped that Negan would provide fans the opportunity to root for another seemingly impossible challenge for Rick and his people to overcome, they were wrong:

> [T]o watch the murders of humans unfold was not just painful, but called into question what we think we're doing when we watch this stuff for entertainment. "You bunch of pussies," snarled Negan at one point, silhouetted apocalyptically by headlights. "I'm just getting started!" He was addressing the remaining members of Rick's gang, but he could have been talking to us as we hid behind our hands. How much more of this could we take? Personally, not much more. "This," Negan rightly observed, "is some screwed-up shit." (Jeffries 2016)

When fans complained about the excessive violence in the episode, Executive Producer Gale Anne Hurd said they had lessened the gore and violence in later episodes in response to criticism (Lieberman 2017). Interestingly, a week later, Scott Gimple said that the violence in the premiere was intentional: "The awfulness of what happened to the characters was very specific to that episode and the beginning of this whole new story . . . there was a purpose of traumatizing these characters to a point where maybe they would have been docile for the rest of their lives, which was Negan's point. But I will say again, the violence in the premiere was for a specific narrative purpose" (quoted in Ross 2017).

Negan prepares to bludgeon Glenn. (*The Walking Dead*, "The Day Will Come When You Won't Be," season 7, episode 1, 2016)

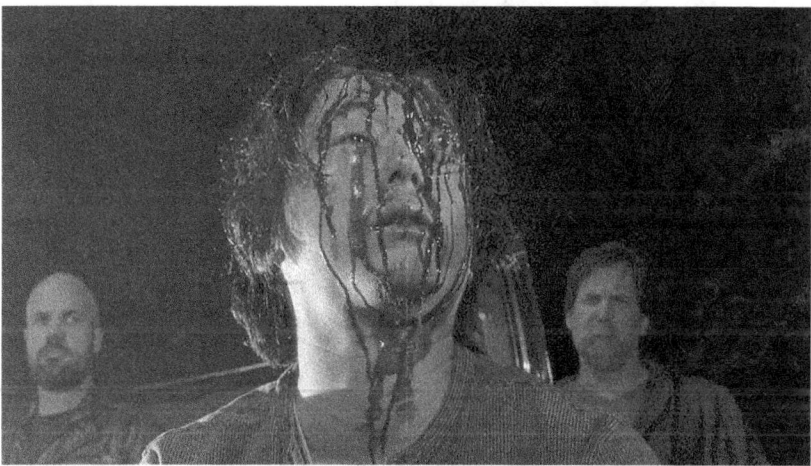

Negan's swift, brutal, and unexpected beating, and then murder of Glenn. (*The Walking Dead*, "The Day Will Come When You Won't Be," season 7, episode 1, 2016)

Gimple's language is noteworthy here if we consider the parallels between Negan and Trump. As the critical response reveals, while fans are concerned about the characters, they are more concerned with their own experience of trauma brought on by the episode. If the purpose of this shocking narrative is to warn us against docility in the face of tyranny, the gratuitous violence serves an extradiegetic purpose, cautioning us against our own complicity in prevailing systems of domination as we begin the "whole new story" of America under Trump. In season 10, a (mostly) changed Negan reflects on his former power and offers a justification for his ruthlessness: "I did what I had to do back then.

Negan pressures Rick into cutting off Carl's arm. (*The Walking Dead*, "The Day Will Come When You Won't Be," season 7, episode 1, 2016)

... One simple fact. One truth kept my people going. If you don't protect what belongs to you, then sooner or later, it belongs to someone else. That goes for your land, your wallet, your home, your country. Everything. It is your job as a man to protect it. That's the story of America, the story of the whole goddamn world. And ain't nothing changing it" (Darabont et al. 2019; 10:3).

In demanding the capitulation of all to his rule, in mocking and demeaning those whom he deems weak, in his egregious misogyny and sexism, and, above all, in suggesting that ruthless tactics are necessary to protect "us" from those who would take what's ours, Negan's philosophy is a consistent reflection of Trump's. The fact that fans, critics, and even actors on the show note the parallels between the two men demonstrates how fictional discourse is easily translated and interpreted in the context of real social relations (St. John 2016; Roe 2017). Ross Marquand, who plays Aaron, notes that "there's no right or wrong way to look at the show, but it is interesting that a lot of people are seeing parallels to world leaders; those who seem a bit dictatorial, like Negan" (Huver 2017). In 2016, Michael Cudlitz, who plays Abraham, compared the matchup of Negan and Rick to Trump and Hillary, noting, "Negan's a little bit of a loose cannon, and Trump is a little bit of a loose cannon," he continued. "And that's not me being political. That's by his own description, so yeah, I think we actually have our Negan and our Rick. And neither one is perfect" (Bradley 2016). Jeffrey Dean Morgan, for his part, has made clear that despite the similarities, he is not a fan of Trump. In fact, as though to separate himself further, in October 2016, just days before the season 7 premiere, Morgan called Trump's presidential campaign "a joke that has gone on way too long," saying, "He's an embarrassment to the world, not just America. He's a thug and an idiot" (Adams 2016).

Although The Governor of season 4 was a twisted and tortured nemesis to Rick's group, he operated through duplicity and misdirection; he was a liar and a lunatic, but the people of Woodbury felt safe and bought into the social contract that The Governor offered them. By contrast, Negan is a "straight talker" who tells it like it is. The "Saviors" are represented as ruthless sociopaths who suffer totalitarian abuse at Negan's hands. No individualism is allowed; everyone must identify themselves as "Negan" and abide by the hierarchical structure of his "government" or endure grotesque physical punishment, such as facial branding by a hot iron. Not unlike the Senate Republicans or contestants on *The Apprentice*, who answer to Trump, Negan's chain of command includes lieutenants who report directly to him and soldiers who provide the muscle and enforce the rules. The rest of the vast group is undesignated and they perform essential labor for the community for which they receive "points" that can be exchanged for desirable commodities (down-ballot votes?). One critic writing for *Forbes* notes:

> Negan . . . is basically a Donald Trump of the post-apocalypse. As we see him giving Dwight and the rest of his minions a pep talk of sorts, it becomes clear that Negan's just a demagogue. . . . Negan seems to select his inner circle through a series of contests that look a bit like some twisted version of *The Apprentice*. The nerds and weaklings love him because he makes them feel safe and strong. All he asks for in return is, well, *everything*. (St. John 2016)

"YOU GOTTA BECOME THEM, FEEL WHAT THEY FEEL"

The Walking Dead's dark turn, even for a particularly dark show, occurs in episode 3 of season 7, "The Cell." Airing just two days before the November 2016 election, this episode goes beyond the violence and gore of the previous episodes, representing psychological deprivation and torture along the lines of that inflicted on prisoners at Abu Ghraib by US soldiers. Daryl, who was taken as Negan's hostage in the first episode of the season, is brought to the Sanctuary, the Saviors' home. In an effort to recruit Daryl to their cause, they attempt to break him psychologically through sensory deprivation. Holding him naked in a dark cell, Dwight, the lieutenant, who is charged by Negan to break Daryl, subjects him to the annoyingly repetitive song "Easy Street" on a playback loop and gives him only dog food sandwiches to eat. At the time of its release, the episode received the second-lowest rating in the series' history (Porter 2016).

It is horrific and degrading viewing. Watching these "heroes" brought so low is not suspenseful, it's depressing; it's also instructive, forcing those of us still watching to ask: How did we get here? How did this narcissistic power-hungry sociopath establish himself as the one who gets to call the shots? By demonstrating how it reduces and diminishes the other characters, the people that we root for, *TWD* questions and condemns the tactics of Negan and his followers.

It is the character of Alpha (Samantha Morton) who epitomizes most clearly the dangers of fanaticism and fealty prevalent among supporters of Trump. Alpha and her group don't just fight the zombies, they choose to become them, wearing the skins of the dead so they can walk among them undetected. In a flashback, in season 10, episode 2, "We are the End of the World," Alpha tells Beta that "it's not just about moving with them. You gotta become them, feel what they feel." When Beta asks, "And what do they feel?" Alpha responds, "Nothing," adding that there are "only two kinds of people left in this world, the ones brave enough to walk with the dead and everybody else" (Darabont et al. 2019; 10:2).

Airing from October 2019 to February 2020 in the run-up to the 2020 election that would determine whether Trump would serve a second term, the nihilism of Alpha resonates in disturbing and pointed ways with the prevailing political environment. In episode 11, "Morning Star," Alpha leads her followers to an attack on Hilltop. Walking with the herd of zombies, as is their practice, the Whisperers shamble along, chanting, "We are the end of the world." In her paranoid isolationism, Alpha's chant resembles the hate-filled vitriol of neo-Nazi messaging. "I'm no longer weak. I'm stronger than ever. Our horde

Daryl is held naked in a cell by the saviors and forced to eat dog food. (*The Walking Dead*, "The Cell," season 7, episode 3, 2016)

will butcher and consume them. Screams will be song to me. . . . We bathe in blood. We are free. We love no one. We are free. We fear nothing. We are free. This is the end of the world. Now is the end of the world. We are the end of the world" (Darabont et al. 2020; 10:11). The repetitive incantation and marching function like a parodic echo of the 2017 "Unite the Right" march in Charlottesville, where neo-Nazis chanted in unison, "You/Jews will not replace us." Whereas Negan runs a fascist dictatorship, which in exaggerated form, mirrors Trump's, the Whisperers resemble Trump's followers. These normal people, though gaslighted and brainwashed into following Alpha, have become true believers, blindly following the commands of a leader with no conscience and no values.

Alpha and her crew wear the skins of the dead to walk safely among them. (*The Walking Dead*, "We Are the End of the World," season 10, episode 2, 2019)

WAR. WHAT IS IT GOOD FOR?

In a similar fashion, the last installment of the *Planet of the Apes* reboot, *War for the Planet of the Apes*, features a maniacal, deranged, power-hungry figure named The Colonel who stands as a warning to the audience of fascist tyranny. Where *Rise of the Planet of the Apes* and *Dawn of the Planet of the Apes* reflect white fear of a racial takeover, which can be tied to the hysteria around Obama's presidency and the visibility of Blackness and perceived diminishing of whiteness, *War* insinuates the pendulum has swung too far back. Released six months after Trump took office, the warning in *War* is not fear of the Other, but, rather, fear of what has become of us. Kellner argues that "when there is dissatisfaction in a society with a political regime, Hollywood is quick to exploit it with films transcoding the dissatisfaction or anger with the ruling group, whatever its politics" (2010, 34). While the humans are still fighting the apes, humanness no longer stands for a generic whiteness; it represents white *Americanness*, as *War* skewers the privilege that Americans have assumed for themselves. Whiteness is anything but redemptive; instead, it is represented by a jack-booted thug, Colonel McCullough (Woody Harrelson), who lacks the humanity that the apes exhibit in spades, and a weak, scared traitor in the figure of an albino gorilla named Winter (Aleks Paunovic).

War moves away from a critique of Black/white relations and instead utilizes the prevailing Trumpian rhetoric of immigration: of building a wall and securing the border, as well as the discourse of terrorism: of an unnatural enemy and "holy war." Where *Dawn* finds itself in the midst of, or reluctantly endorsing(?), the divisive racial politics that followed its release, *War* seems determined not to be on the wrong side of history. Matt Reeves casts a wide net in his aggressive takedown of an America whose insularity and divisive nationalism brought us Donald Trump and the craven Republican officials who slavishly follow him. The heightened militarization of Americanness since 9/11, involving the capture and killings of "high-profile targets" and culminating in the most notorious of all, Osama bin Laden, in 2011 have not made us safer or less prone to terrorist attacks. Rather, the film suggests, such actions have diminished us. As film critic Justin Chang observes, "This is hardly the first 'Planet of the Apes' movie to function as an allegory of oppression, hysteria and xenophobia, but it is almost certainly the most trenchant and serious-minded of the lot. It's impossible not to root for these brave and beautiful apes or to feel a sense of alienation from our own comparatively stupid, prideful, and empathy-deficient species" (Chang 2017).

War opens with a military contingent stealing through the pre-dawn California forest. The apes have been hiding out in a fortified tree camp awaiting the arrival of these soldiers, who were summoned by Dreyfus (Gary Oldman) and his team at the end of *Dawn*. On first glance, the mise-en-scène of the first few frames echoes the racialized divisions of human and ape evident in *Dawn*. The soldiers wear helmets with slogans such as "Monkey Killer," "Bedtime for Bonzo," and "Endangered Species." The soldiers are apprehensive as they look up at the apes on horseback patrolling their forest, unaware they are being hunted. When the African American captain, looking through his rifle scope, is stopped by a big, black gorilla hand on his shoulder, we assume the jig is up. However, as the shot widens to include the gorilla, it's clear they are in collusion. In the intervening period, several apes have turned and are working as "donkeys" for the humans. These apes, we learn, are what's left of Koba's followers and, fearing Caesar, have joined forces with the humans. While we have seen how African American characters die quickly or are demonized in the original *Planet* series and in *Rise*, here, the quick dispatching of the Black captain (Roger Cross) makes way for his Hispanic successor, Preacher (Gabriel Chavarria), whose watchful presence in the film serves as a constant reminder of the complex racial landscape the film will traverse. *War* positions Preacher as a kind of racial intermediary, expressing allegiance to The Colonel but showing admiration and empathy for Caesar.

Although there are rumors that he is holed away in a "hidden command base," when the soldiers come upon Caesar, Preacher, whose face shot in side light suggests his duality, expresses surprise that he's alive. "You're him," he says. "We've been searching for you for so long.... Some of us were beginning to think you might be dead." It's hard not to draw a parallel here between the search for Caesar, in his protective fortified seclusion, and the US military's hunt for Osama bin Laden. However, the comparison functions not to equate Caesar's actions or intentions with the mastermind of 9/11 but instead to condemn America and its jingoistic excess. Caesar shows mercy to the humans by letting the captured soldiers go, but he also wants to send a message to The Colonel: "He'll see we are not savages." Predictably, The Colonel seeks nothing less than the annihilation of the apes, and, in a dramatic nighttime incursion reminiscent of the Navy Seal mission to get bin Laden, the soldiers rappel into the compound on ropes with laser beam flashlights. Believing that he has killed Caesar and unaware that he has, in fact, killed Caesar's wife and son, The Colonel, in camo blackface, radios to his men, "Target acquired. King Kong is Dead" (Reeves 2017).[1]

Consumed by revenge, Caesar sets out to find The Colonel. When Caesar, with the help of Bad Ape (Steve Zahn), a similarly enhanced primate raised in a zoo, comes upon the prison where The Colonel and his army are based, he finds his apes have been captured and forced into labor. In this former California Border Quarantine Facility, the apes are enslaved and are forced to build a

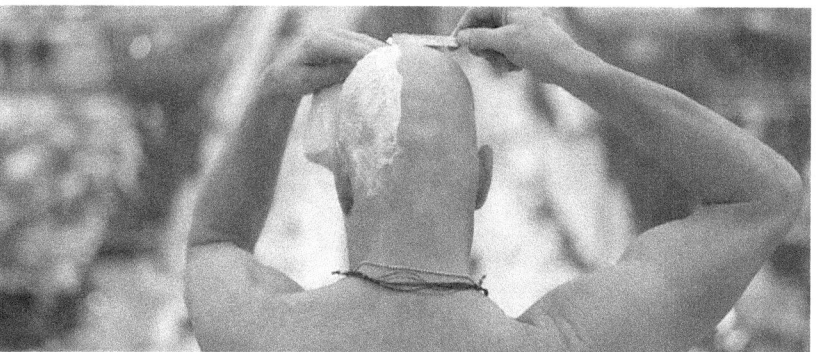

The Colonel is fashioned after a neo-Nazi skinhead. (*War for the Planet of the Apes*, 2017)

border wall. When Caesar asks, "Why do they need a wall?" the film critiques the insanity of Donald Trump's plan to bar illegal immigrants from Mexico. However, this wall is not for keeping out the apes, even though as virus carriers they are an existential threat to humans; the purpose of the wall is to keep out the other humans who seek to eliminate The Colonel. The virus, we learn, has mutated, robbing humans of the power of speech. Having killed his own son, who developed the mutation, The Colonel has ordered his men to kill anyone who exhibits its symptoms. The Colonel fears that if the remaining humans contract the mutated strain, it would "ro[b] us of those things that make us human. Our speech, our higher thinking. It will turn us into beasts" (Reeves 2017). But as the film painfully delineates in The Colonel's crude fanaticism and violent treatment of outsiders and his own people, the humans are already beasts. Where *Rise* and *Dawn* imply that science will destroy humans, *War* makes clear that our own hubris and hatred for the Other will be our downfall. The Colonel's "holy war" finishes us all in the end.

There is an obvious and palpable critique of America in this film. As I've argued, the ape shelter in *Rise* evokes the US prison complex and makes a connection between imprisoned apes and disproportionally incarcerated African Americans. The military facility where the apes are imprisoned in *War*, by contrast, recalls Guantanamo Bay and the illegal detention of presumed terrorists. Just like Guantanamo, an American flag bears witness to the atrocities within it, but this flag is defaced and ultimately burns. Like a tagged neo-Nazi flag, the symbols of alpha and omega are scrawled across the flag in the compound. In a scathing parody of American patriotism, the soldiers assemble in formation and salute it as they chant, "We are the beginning and the end." When the American anthem begins to play, on cue, they rush to the apes' cells to observe the "donkeys" beat their fellow apes, readying them for work on the wall. Watching all of this from on high is The Colonel, who, shaving his head and sipping from his flask, epitomizes an evil "skinhead," dispassionately

American soldiers chant, "We are the beginning and the end." (*War for the Planet of the Apes*, 2017)

overseeing the apes' torture. The Colonel frequently dismisses the anger and grief of the now-captured Caesar by calling him "emotional." Accusing him of being "confused in [his] purpose" and of "taking this all much too personally," The Colonel crafts his own version of "special snowflake," the epithet appropriated by the alt-right and used broadly by conservatives to attack liberals outraged at Trump and his policies.

While *War* is clearly invested in critiquing American policies on immigration, illegal detention, and terrorism, like its predecessors, it continues to utilize racial imagery associated with African Americans and slavery. The apes are routinely lashed and strung up on trees as punishment. However, unlike the other films, here the discourse of racial protest is used to critique America. Caesar stands up to the inhumane treatment the apes receive. When Caesar yells, "Leave him!" to the "donkey" whipping an orangutan, we get a dark reminder of America's past and the courage required to challenge it. Punished for his outburst, Caesar is lashed and tied to a tree in a crucifixion pose. Caesar, in a state of delirium, imagines Koba is talking to him. "Slave," he says to Caesar, "you cannot save them. Apes all die here" (Reeves 2017). But Koba is wrong, for

The "Alpha-Omega" American flag burns in the final battle between humans and apes. (*War for the Planet of the Apes*, 2017)

Apes are forced to build a border wall under guard supervision. (*War for the Planet of the Apes*, 2017)

ultimately, they all work together to save themselves. In raising their hands in the "ape together strong" sign, the film evokes the Black Power fist and offers a cautionary message to whites about repeating history's crimes.

In its exploration of the darker side of human nature, *War* evokes Conrad's *Heart of Darkness*, and Harrelson's aggressive, troubled Colonel resembles Marlon Brando's Kurtz in Coppola's adaptation of the book *Apocalypse Now*. The lesson of Conrad's novel is that humans' capacity for evil and darkness does not come from an exterior mythical "dark continent" but rather from within us. The sinister threat we project onto others, whether they be Congolese, Vietnamese, or ape, is really a distorted reflection of ourselves. *War* does interesting things with this trope. Rather than pursuing The Colonel into the "heart of darkness," Caesar is instead forced into an empty whiteness. The cinematography provides as vivid a visual contrast between the warm, lush darkness of the forest and the bleak, stark, snowy landscape beyond it as does the Manichean narrative itself. While it is The Colonel who epitomizes the rottenness at the core of white nationalism, Caesar, too, is sullied and darkened by his proximity to it. When

"Apes Together Strong" symbol mirrors the Black Power fist. (*War for the Planet of the Apes*, 2017)

Caesar first comes face-to-face with The Colonel at the prison, they are both shot in medium close-up in hard, high-contrast lighting. The deep shadows on their faces emphasize their conflicted, divided natures. It is only in seeing his own vindictive anger reflected back at him in The Colonel's radicalism that Caesar can regain his own humanity.

Caesar's journey to the heart of darkness/whiteness involves an encounter with three versions of whiteness—one, the sadistic, power-hungry Colonel; two, the frightened traitorous albino gorilla, Winter; and three, the mute, guileless girl, Nova. When The Colonel kills Caesar's wife and oldest son, he stokes the embers of rage and hatred dormant in Caesar since he killed Koba. Consumed by thoughts of revenge, Caesar abandons his baby son, Cornelius, and the rest of the apes and sets off to find and kill The Colonel. However, aware that Caesar is as much a danger to himself as The Colonel, Maurice (Karin Konoval), Rocket (Terry Notary), and Luca (Michael Adamthwaite) accompany him. The group comes across a seemingly abandoned homestead where a man tries to shoot them but is swiftly gunned down by Caesar. Upon entering the house, Maurice finds a mute white girl (Amiah Miller) hiding in her bed. Deliberately lowering the gun in Caesar's hand, Maurice approaches the girl and offers her the white doll he spies on the ground. (It is this white doll, and not Caesar's rage, that will be the catalyst for The Colonel's death as it is contaminated with the virus that causes the mutation.) In a tight close-up, Maurice's kind eyes and brown face peer gently at the girl, and then the camera cuts to the darkness of the bed where the girl lies. When the camera zooms in, the girl's pale face emerges from the darkness as she looks cautiously but not fearfully at Maurice. Caesar wants to abandon the girl who "can't speak," but Maurice says he "cannot leave her." Caesar's initial coldness and watchful wariness of the girl are an indication of how he retains no vestige of respect or faith in humanity. Indeed, not long after they find her, Caesar breaks the ape commandment again, killing Winter, who, having betrayed Caesar, is now working as a "donkey" for the

Nova's big fur hood resembles Maurice's facial flange. (*War for the Planet of the Apes*, 2017)

humans. It is this girl, known as Nova (in a nod to the original series), however, who represents a different kind of human.

As her name indicates, Nova is "new" and seems to have no allegiance to her own people, who have been corrupted by the bitter and divisive war. If Caesar is a Moses figure, Nova is Christ-like.[2] Not only does she help to liberate him from his physical enslavement in the jail, but her innocence and trust lift Caesar out of his mental and emotional prison. Although Nova is clearly human in appearance, the big fur hood of the warm, oversized coat that frames her face resembles Maurice's facial flange. Indeed, Nova identifies more with the nurturing apes than with the callous humans. When she asks Maurice, who is both a parent and teacher to the young girl, if she is an ape, he pauses and tells her she is "brave." Like Christ, who was prophesied to come from among the Israelites and redeem mankind, this white-skinned, blue-eyed, blonde-haired girl who vocalizes like an ape and dresses like an ape, the film implies, is the prophet that will redeem white humanity. In *War*, the equation of whiteness with desolation and a desperate hatred, in addition to its embodiment by a neo-Nazi-type figure, requires us to reflect on the myth of "imperiled whiteness." Building a wall and securing a border cannot protect us from the real threat—ourselves and the parody of humanity America has come to represent. Rather than sympathize with the plight of the humans, *War* puts us into Caesar's shoes, and we watch, as he does, with "horror, the horror" at the zero-sum game the humans engage in to destroy themselves. In Nova, by contrast, *War* offers us the possibility of redemption, a way out of the darkness of whiteness toward a new future of inclusiveness.

"MAY MY MERCY PREVAIL OVER MY WRATH"

The Walking Dead, too, depicts a similar Christ-like figure of hope in the character of Rick's son, Carl. Airing from October 2017 to April 2018, just four months after the neo-Nazi rally in Charlottesville, season 8 offers Carl as a counterpoint to the brutally senseless regime embodied by Negan. Carl, who, as a preteen, was hardened by a life of killing enemies alive and dead, has softened. In the season premiere, "Mercy," Carl comes across a man who, hidden by cars at a hollowed-out gas station, calls out to him. Making a compassionate appeal for Carl's help, the man shares a sentiment his mother taught him: "'Whatever you have of good, spend on the traveler'. . . . My mom said that helping the traveler, the person without a home—that's everything." The man then quotes a verse from the Quran, "May my mercy prevail over my wrath," but quickly realizes that he "probably shouldn't have said that." Having overheard the man speaking to Carl, Rick enters the area and shoots above his head to warn him away. Where Rick retains his healthy distrust of outsiders ("he could have been one of them"), Carl is clearly disgusted with his father's rush to judgment (Darabont et al. 2017; 8:1).

Carl encounters the man again in episode 6, "The King, the Widow, and Rick." Apparently looking for him all this time, Carl learns that the man's name is Siddiq, and he offers him food and water, explaining that he's helping him because his mom also told him that "you've got to do what's right. It's hard to know what that is sometimes, but sometimes it's not." When Siddiq clarifies that he doesn't want to make trouble (after all, "your dad didn't want anything to do with me"), Carl suggests that "sometimes kids have to find their own way to show their parents the way" (Darabont et al. 2017; 8:6). This plot development is remarkable in a number of ways. For the first time, the show offers an alternative philosophy regarding the outsider. That this stranger is a Muslim man, who is not only embraced in his person but in his faith, signals a dramatic shift from the alt-right politics of the prepper-survivalist that the show previously valorized. Moreover, it is this act of kindness and faith that will lead to Carl's death as he gets bitten by walkers when helping Siddiq fend off an attack. Yet, rather than depict this fate as a result of a bad choice, it's represented as the outcome of a good one. Because he must find a place to hide Siddiq from his father, Carl locates a tunnel system of sewers under Alexandria that will facilitate the group's escape and survival. In the episode "Honor," Carl faces Negan in the final showdown and assumes a Christ-like posture by offering his own death as a sacrifice to save both communities. When Rick finds out Carl has brought Siddiq back, he asks Carl pointedly, "Did you know he was a doctor? Is that why you brought him back?" But refusing this utilitarian reasoning, Carl explains, "He wasn't going to make it alone. He needed us. That's why" (Darabont et al. 2017; 8:9).

Knowing he will ultimately die from the bite, Carl, before the escape, writes several letters, including ones to Rick and Negan, exhorting them to broker a peace. When Siddiq acknowledges that in saving him, he was honoring his mother and her teachings, Carl reminds him that he was honoring his own mother, too. Here the show offers a feminine pacific alternative to the hardline masculine code of vengeance and competitive survival usually endorsed on *TWD*. Siddiq tells Carl that he can never repay him for saving him, but "I can honor you by showing your people, your friends, your family that what you did wasn't for nothing. That it mattered, that it meant something, because it did." The racial and ethnic harmony represented in the friendship of Siddiq and Carl is reinforced in Carl's relationship with Michonne. Telling her to be strong for Rick, Judith, and herself, he notes, "You're my best friend, Michonne." "You're mine, too," she answers. "You're mine" (Darabont et al. 2017; 8:9).

In his last words, Carl reminds Rick that in the battle with Woodbury, Rick had "put away [his] gun" and offered sanctuary to The Governor's people so that Carl could grow up to be the man he is today. "What you did then, how you stopped the fighting. It was right. It still is. . . . I know you can't see it yet. How it could be. But I have . . . everybody living, helping everybody else live. If you can still be who you were. That's how it could be." Rick explains that all the conflict with other people was for Carl: "A father's job is to protect his son." Shaking his head, Carl corrects him: "Love. It's just to love" (Darabont et al. 2017; 8:9). Significant to the ultimate message, the scenes of Carl reminding Rick of the senselessness of his past brutality are juxtaposed with the violent efforts of Hilltop and the Kingdom, other members of Rick's coalition, to defend themselves against the Saviors. Morgan, who, since his mania of season 3, had embraced life and its defense only when necessary, has, in the face of the evil, torturous actions of the Saviors, reverted to the killing machine he embodied in season 3. Even though Gavin is surrendering and begging for mercy, Morgan is determined to kill him. Ezekiel tells him to "relent" and adds, "Ending him is the coward's way. We've won. We don't have to kill him," and Carol reminds him that it was Morgan who told her that they "can be better than them." But Morgan, in an echo of his "clearing" days, simply says, "I have to" (Darabont et al. 2017; 8:9).

By advocating the putting aside of hatred and the ceasing of animosity, it's the peaceful, cooperative message of Carl that the show wants to foreground now, not the vindictive violence embodied by Negan and, by association, brought out in Rick and Morgan. In his final minutes, Carl's conciliatory message echoes beyond the show to the partisan divide in America. "It's gotta stop, Michonne. It's not supposed to be like this. I know it can be better" (Darabont et al. 2017; 8:9). As a result of Carl's dying wish, Rick doesn't kill Negan when he captures him but instead imprisons him in Alexandria, where he will eventually redeem himself by killing Alpha, the leader of the Whisperers.

RECOGNIZING WHITENESS

Fiske argues that the way social and cultural messages in popular entertainment circulate in discourse "is never determined by the nature of the experience itself, but always by the social power to give it one set of meanings rather than another" ([1996] 2016; 4). As I've argued throughout this book, entertainment media productions in the Obama-to-Trump era do not merely reflect the racial tumult of this period, but, alongside news and social media narratives, help construct and contest it. The racist invective circulating in discourses of the political Right was bolstered by the media's framing of immigration as a demographic crisis, gun control as a curtailing of American freedom, and racially motivated police violence as a justified response to the perception of Blackness as a threat. The prevailing social power from 2008–2016, then, was not, as its critics claimed, a Black space or even a "postracial" space; it was clearly a white space, a space where white people's desire for recognition and visibility were targeted by a media marketplace. Invested in commodifying whiteness as a newly diverse identity, media outlets produced and profited from white identity politics, while at the same time, journalists, writers, "producers," and consumers engaged in collaborative forms of race-making facilitated by a networked mediascape. The social meanings that issued from this social power, as exemplified by, but not limited to, three profitable and long-running SF franchises, *The Planet of the Apes, The Walking Dead,* and *Star Trek,* contributed to the racially divisive messaging of the Obama-to-Trump era. However, as I have shown here, the same discursive structures facilitated the resistance of large swaths of Americans to the tyrannical dictator-like workings of the Trump administration. Black filmmakers like Peele and Coogler and the white creative teams behind *War for the Planet of the Apes* and seasons 7–10 of *TWD* tapped into that social power to produce social meanings that contested the prevailing politics of the time.

NOTES

INTRODUCTION: MEDIA EVENTS, "PANDEMIC TV," AND THE RUSE OF THE POSTRACIAL

1. When asked at a press briefing whether he would consider pardoning Maldonado-Passage, who, according to his husband, is a "really big Trump supporter" and is currently serving a twenty-two-year sentence for hiring a hit man to kill Baskin, Trump, after acknowledging he knew nothing of the case, said, "I'll take a look" (Al-Arshani 2020).

2. Produsage is the creation of shared content "in a networked, participatory environment which breaks down the boundaries between producers and consumers and instead enables all participants to be users as well as producers of information and knowledge" (http://produsage.org/produsage; Bruns 2008).

3. While *Tiger King* is billed as a documentary and *Waco* is based on a true story, the dramatic scripts, as well as the editing and framing of the narratives, follow generic conventions of fictional programming.

4. I use this linkage as a way of recognizing that radical white nationalist movements resurfaced in the Obama era and were mainstreamed through political constituencies like the Tea Party during Obama's tenure as president. The visibility of extreme right-wing positions in the mainstream and in media in 2008–2012 helped to legitimize a radicalized vocal movement on the right which facilitated a white reception of Trump's toxic political brand.

5. For an interesting analysis of these paratexts and fans' engagement with them, see Freeman 2019.

6. This is not to say that the producers (writers, directors, editors) of these fictional texts deliberately reinforce prevailing ideologies but rather to recognize that these texts don't exist in isolation from the social context in which they're produced. The meanings of cinematic narratives, which is to say our interpretation of their meanings, change when viewed in relation to the media events surrounding them.

7. *Watchmen* was adapted from the 1995 graphic novel of Alan Moore/Dave Gibbons by white writer/director Damon Lindelof but makes racial persecution central to the narrative, including an extensive depiction of the Tulsa Massacre of 1921. *Ma* is also the product of a white creative team, and while the film doesn't deal with race or racism overtly, the kind of othering experienced by people of color in white spaces is made visible through the casting of Octavia Spencer in the titular role and impacts the depiction of the ostracization and bullying that the character experiences as a teenager.

CHAPTER 1. WHITE IDENTITY POLITICS

1. Trump was acquitted by the Senate on February 13, 2021, in a vote of 57–43.

2. Duke is referring to Black Lives Matter and an anti-fascist group on the left.

3. Of course, whites who support Trump might readily identify other issues like gun control, taxes, or abortion as their key issues. The emphasis I'm attributing to racial identity need not obscure these other motivators; however, because Trump's appeals to white identity politics are so overt, white voters who don't actively support a racist agenda do so tacitly in their support of him. "Ultimately, many white voters are simply attached to what Trump represents. 'These voters are very much about the idea that the status quo isn't a problem and that we should make America great again back when we didn't have to worry about PC culture... Because when you're in power, why would you give it up?'" (Cineas and North 2020).

4. There is plenty of data demonstrating how right-wing media outlets like Fox News and Breitbart peddled anti-Obama, anti-Black, anti-immigration stories leading up to the 2008 election and throughout the tenure of Obama's presidency and helped to cultivate out-group hostility among whites. See mediamatters.org for a list of these. But I'm also interested in how mainstream reporting—major networks, national newspapers, etc.—also framed these issues.

5. Apparently, "What separates a 'show starring Black people' from a 'Black show' is that the latter contains the intrinsic cultural DNA of the Black experience" (Schilling 2016).

6. Quite notably, season 17 of *Grey's Anatomy*, which ran from November 2020 to June 2021, moves away from colorblind discourse. Several episodes in this season, which was filmed during the COVID-19 lockdowns and in the aftermath of the death of George Floyd, explore the racial disparities of the pandemic and include storylines about BLM protests and racial profiling.

7. A 2013 Pew Research study concluded that in 2010, Black men were "six times more likely to be incarcerated in federal, state, and local jails" (Gao 2014).

8. Replacement Theory is a white nationalist conspiracy theory that was popularized in the 2011 book *Le Grand Remplacement* by French author Renaud Camus. The theory refers to the belief that white Europeans are slowly being "replaced" culturally and demographically by non-white people. The theory has also been embraced by Americans on the alt-right and is believed to have motivated mass shooters like Dylann Roof, who murdered nine African Americans in June 2015 while attending a bible study at Emanuel African Methodist Episcopal Church in Charleston, South Carolina, and Brenton Tarrant, who murdered fifty-one Muslims in two separate attacks on mosques in New Zealand in March 2019. See Bowles 2019; Darby 2019.

9. Counter discourses contest power formations, as my analysis of Peele's and Coogler's films demonstrates.

10. For an analysis of how the "emptiness" of whiteness produces a desire among whites in settler postcolonial societies to be racially marked, see Ingram 1999 and Ingram 2001.

11. For a representative sample of these, see Smarsh 2016; Cohn 2016; Walsh 2016; Illing 2016.

12. Trump made this comment during a presidential debate with Joe Biden on September 29, 2020, when he was asked to denounce white supremacy.

13. President Biden revoked Trump's Executive Order 13950, "Combatting Race and Sex Stereotyping" on January 20, 2021, and instituted Executive Order 13985, "Advancing Racial Equity and Support for Underserved Communities."

14. The debate over Critical Race Theory (CRT) emerged out of the reporting done by Nikole Hannah-Jones for the *New York Times' 1619 Project*, the intention of which was "to reframe the country's history by placing the consequences of slavery and the contributions of

Black Americans at the very center of our national narrative" (Hannah-Jones 2019). Legislators in several states attempted to ban the teaching of CRT in schools and, more problematically, any examination of racial inequality or white privilege. As of June 2021, legislation to ban the teaching of CRT (broadly defined) has been proposed in twenty-two states and signed into law in five of them: Idaho, Iowa, Oklahoma, Texas, and Tennessee. See Char, Smith, and Tambe 2021.

15. The scarcity of broadcast frequencies in the mid-twentieth century prompted government regulation of the airwaves to ensure that the public was exposed to social, cultural, and political issues. The Fairness Doctrine (1949) required radio and television broadcasters to discuss issues of public importance and provide adequate expression of contrasting viewpoints. The FCC, under the Reagan administration, rolled back provisions and eventually repealed the Fairness Doctrine in 1987, stating that the doctrine "hurt the public interest and violated free speech rights guaranteed by the First Amendment." The Democratic-controlled Congress attempted to block the FCC ruling by passing the Fairness in Broadcasting Act of 1987, but Reagan vetoed the bill. While the doctrine only applied to free-to-air broadcasters and not cable outlets, it paved the way for a more partisan, politicized broadcasting market in which cable outlets like Fox flourished.

16. Interestingly, researchers at the University of Pennsylvania have found that these armchair activists constitute a "critical periphery in social protests" and can extend the life of social movements as a result of the volume of circulation across multiple networked communities.

17. Trump, of course, set himself up as the ultimate arbiter of these distinctions, frequently pronouncing stories unfavorable to him as products of the "fake news media" and even shouting "fake news" at reporters who asked him pointed questions at press briefings.

18. Obviously, many Klan members were brazen in their racism and were often protected by their community members in positions of authority. However, they knew that there was always the possibility, at least in the twentieth century, they could be arrested for murder and other acts of domestic terrorism.

CHAPTER 2. WE'RE ALL INFECTED

1. For a more general discussion of the white response to demographic change, see Outten et al. 2012.

2. Debates in Congress over health care had taken place since the 1990s, when the Clintons proposed universal health care coverage.

3. James Simpson's 2015 book *The Red-Green Axis: Refugees, Immigration and the Agenda to Erase America* is one particularly inflammatory example of this line of thinking.

4. Trump has repeatedly made derogatory comments about immigrants from non-white countries. In January 2018, seeking to limit immigration from "shithole countries" in Africa and Haiti, Trump suggested that the US should encourage immigrants from Norway. In the context of a meeting discussing recipients of US visas in 2017, Trump purportedly stated that Haitians "all have AIDS" and Nigerians, if admitted to the US, would never "go back to their huts" (Shear and Davis 2017).

5. This is not to suggest that immigrants to the US have always been welcomed. European immigrants in the eighteenth century and Irish and Chinese immigrants in the nineteenth century faced racial and ethnic discrimination and sparked nativist movements among the US populace.

6. Miller, particularly, has long been linked to white nationalist groups and, as leaked emails of his reveal, considers legal immigration and refugee resettlement as an Obama administration plot to displace America's white population. See Wilson 2019.

7. Steven Pokornowski (2013) suggests that the "violent history of racism, colonialism, and empire" undergirds historical and contemporary zombie representations.

CHAPTER 3. SIMIAN FLU OR EBOLA REDUX

1. Instead of using approved WHO testing kits, the agency insisted on using its own kits, many of which were faulty and produced incorrect results. Hospitals were required to use the CDC tests, which could only be sent to CDC-approved labs, creating a delay in reporting and making contact tracing impossible. In order to stem the bottleneck, the CDC restricted testing to those arriving from China or to those exposed to an infected person, actions which obscured the growing infection rate among the US populace. See Sandler 2020.

2. Both Fox and Warner Bros. were interested in adapting Preston's book for the big screen. The Fox production *Crisis in the Hot Zone*, helmed by Ridley Scott and starring Robert Redford and Jodie Foster, was ultimately scrapped, but Petersen's film, which diverged significantly from Preston's book, went on to be a box office hit. See Schweitzer 2018, 22.

3. The H_1N_1 virus, popularly known as "swine flu," was a much more consequential epidemic for Obama. The first reported case occurred on April 21, 2009, a few weeks after which Obama declared a "public health emergency." Approximately sixty million Americans were infected with the virus and, of those, thirteen thousand died. The pandemic's timing and origin (it wasn't close to an election cycle and originated in North America) couldn't provide Republicans with the same metaphorical connection to Obama that the Ebola virus would provide.

4. Trump has repeatedly called Obama "stupid," "not very smart," "the most ignorant president in history," and "clueless," and declared that "he knows less" than he did when taking office. In 2011, Trump questioned how Obama had been accepted into Columbia University and Harvard Law School. He repeatedly called on Obama to release his transcripts, claiming that Obama was a "terrible student" despite the fact that Obama graduated magna cum laude from Harvard Law and was the first Black president of its prestigious *Law Review* (Conway 2016; Reilly 2019). A significant part of Trump's success with the "people" is his capacity to successfully tap into and exploit long-standing, albeit discredited, views about race and racial difference, including beliefs about race and intelligence.

5. In Pierre Boulle's original novel, *La Planète des Singes* (1963), the ape/human hierarchy does not function as an allegory for race relations; Boulle's primary concern was to understand what separates human beings from animals and how human superiority could be asserted and maintained in the face of a challenge to it (Greene 33). Rupert Wyatt's 2011 reboot, *Rise of the Planet of the Apes*, foregrounds some of these original themes, locating them within particular issues of concern to twenty-first century audiences. Issues relating to the ethics of bioengineering and big pharma, and the extent to which we should utilize animals as test subjects in human drug trials, are opened for examination. To that end, the film also explores the question of species boundaries and what constitutes the difference between the human and the animal.

6. David Denby calls *Rise* "shrewd, coherent, and fully felt" and a "needling rebuke to human vanity" (https://www.newyorker.com/magazine/2011/09/05/noble-creatures). Roger Ebert sees *Rise* as a "traditional hero's journey ... surprisingly intimate and wrenching," and describes *Dawn* as a "messy, often sad sequel" exploring the aftermath of revolution, wherein

the "tribe's survival must be purchased at the cost of its soul" (https://www.rogerebert.com/reviews/dawn-of-the-planet-of-the-apes-2014). The *New York Times*' A. O. Scott suggests that while *Dawn* "paints a darker, scarier picture of the future," it ultimately champions "tolerance and cooperation" (https://www.nytimes.com/2014/07/11/movies/review-dawn-of-the-planet-of-the-apes-continues-the-saga.html). While most mainstream media critics see *Rise* and *Dawn* as transcending the racial politics of the earlier franchise, many bloggers have addressed the racial politics of the film directly. For a small sample of these, see Goodkind 2011; Smith 2011; Bowen 2017; and Sarkeesian 2017.

7. There is not a great deal of consensus on these numbers. Geneticists and archaeologists differ in their assessment methods, but the most consistent figures suggest the two populations split between five and eight million years ago. "Generation times in wild chimpanzees and gorillas suggest earlier divergence times in great ape and human evolution." (*Proceedings of the National Academy of Science of the United States of America*. 109 no. 39. 2012. http://www.pnas.org/content/109/39/15716.full).

8. Here again there is some disagreement as to whether there was a single migration forty thousand to eighty thousand years ago or a multiple dispersal, with the first occurring one hundred twenty thousand to one hundred thirty thousand years ago to Australasia and Southeast Asia, and a second migration from Africa during the later period. See Tucci and Akey 2016; Zimmer 2016.

9. In the 1968 movie *Planet of the Apes*, Bright Eyes is the name Kim Hunter's Zira, the ape scientist, gives to Charlton Heston's George Taylor when he is captured after his spaceship crash-lands on the apes' planet, the future Earth (Wilson, Serling, and Boulle 1968).

10. On May 26, 2020, Trump moved away from the Ebola story and began attacking Obama and Biden for their handling of the H1N1 epidemic. See Blitzer 2020.

11. Greene argues that the image of the destroyed statue suggests that "the voyage into outer space leads not to 'the final frontier' as *Star Trek* was then promising, but rather to a wasteland, a societal graveyard where the wages of the sins committed on the earlier American 'frontiers' have been paid in full" (Greene 1998, 54).

12. Twentieth-century examples of this kind of pseudo-science include Herrnstein and Murray 1994; Rushton 1995; Sarich and Miele 2004; and Wade 2014.

13. In 1776, using an original research sample of sixty skulls and then later two hundred human skulls, German physician and naturalist Johann Friedrich Blumenbach (1752–1840) was one of the first to speculate that human variation in phenotype could be attributed to differences in physical skeletal form, particularly differences among crania. Blumenbach postulated the existence of five races: Caucasian (white), Mongolian (East and Central Asian), Malay (Southeast Asian and Pacific Islanders), Ethiopian (sub-Saharan African), and the American (American Indian). Unlike others who would use his work to support theories of polygenism, the belief that different races descended from different species, Blumenbach supported a monogenic approach theorizing that all races shared a common ancestor but were subject to "degeneration" (from a Caucasian standard) as a result of environmental changes and migration. He considered that such degeneration could be reversed, however, with appropriate environmental controls. See Harris (1968) 2001, 84.

14. For more on Morton and the development of scientific racism in nineteenth-century America, see Stanton 1960 and Fabian 2010.

15. For the original critique of Gould, see Lewis et al. 2011. For more context on the issue, see Kaplan et al. 2015.

CHAPTER 4. WHEN THE LOOTING STARTS, THE SHOOTING STARTS

1. On June 25, 2021, Chauvin was sentenced to twenty-two-and-a-half years in prison.

2. On June 3, in the midst of a rapidly changing political and social environment, Minneapolis prosecutors added an additional charge of second-degree murder to Chauvin and charged the other three officers, Thomas Lane, J. A. Kueng, and Tou Thao, with second-degree aiding and abetting felony murder and second-degree aiding and abetting manslaughter.

3. On March 3, 2022, Hankison was found not guilty of three counts of felony wanton endangerment.

4. On January 7, 2022, both Travis and Gregory McMichael were sentenced to life in prison without the possibility of parole. The McMichaels' neighbor, William Bryan, who recorded the fatal shooting of Arbery, was sentenced to life in prison with the possibility of parole.

5. My thanks to "Auntie" Ken Roemer for identifying the instrument used in the score of this scene.

6. The killing of Black nineteen-year-old Timothy Thomas by police on April 7, 2001, led to rioting in the city of Cincinnati and was the largest scale racial uprising since 1992; however, the Rodney King event has had a lasting effect on the nation's psyche in a way that other racial protests, prior to #BLM, have not.

7. This is not to imply that this kind of police brutality is new—African Americans have historically suffered abuses and death at the hands of police, but rather to acknowledge its more recent visibility to the white population because of the ubiquity of cell phones.

8. An investigation of the incident by the Department of Justice, published on March 4, 2015, supported Wilson's version of events based on DNA evidence and found that witness statements suggesting Brown was raising his hands to surrender were "inaccurate because they are inconsistent with the physical and forensic evidence" and that others were "materially inconsistent" with prior statements by the same witnesses. See Department of Justice 2015.

9. Obviously, Muslim communities were differently impacted by the anti-Islam rhetoric circulating after 9/11 and suffered hate crimes and legislation restricting their liberties.

CHAPTER 5. "ANIMALS" WITH GUNS

1. An editorial in the *New York Times* suggested that the gunman who shot Giffords was incited by Palin's PAC. The *Times* later retracted this statement. https://www.nytimes.com/2017/06/14/opinion/steve-scalise-congress-shot-alexandria-virginia.html?_r=0.

CHAPTER 6. BIOENGINEERED MONSTERS

1. See chapter 1.

2. Urban Dictionary defines racial fatigue as "tired of hearing about racial this and racial that." https://www.urbandictionary.com/define.php?term=Racial%20fatigue.

3. The plot to kill Khan is somewhat complicated by Admiral Marcus's subplot to sacrifice Kirk and his crew to the mission so as to avoid detection of his involvement in "weaponizing" Khan.

4. N.W.A.'s song "Fuck da Police" functions in a similarly strategic way in Jordan Peele's *Us* discussed in chapter 8.

5. Jaylah is played by the Algerian actress Sofia Boutella. The alien whitewashing of Boutella's brown skin has interesting implications for the larger race issues traversing the film. Jaylah is

marked as "other" not by her skin but by her identification with Edison's protest music. However, unlike Edison, she is rescued by the crew and finds a home with them, suggesting that her form of rebelliousness will be contained.

6. "What is Bioengineering?" https://bioeng.berkeley.edu/about-us/what-is-bioengineering. Accessed May 2017.

CHAPTER 7. OF CHIMERAS AND MEN

1. "In the Antilles, the young Negro identifies himself de facto with Tarzan against the Negroes. This is much more difficult for him in a European theater, for the rest of the audience, which is white, automatically identifies him with the savages on the screen" (Fanon ([1968] 1970, 108).

2. In *Battle for the Planet of the Apes*, Caesar finds a recording of an interview with his father, Cornelius, from 1972. When asked how apes first acquired the power of speech, Cornelius responds, "They learned how to refuse. On a historic day, an ape spoke a word which had been spoken to him time and again without number by humans. He said 'no!'" (Boulle and Dehn 1973).

3. See forum about Wade's book titled *American Renaissance: Nicholas Wade Attacks the Regime* on neo-Nazi website Stormfront. https://www.stormfront.org/forum/t1027136/.

CHAPTER 8. BLACK HORROR

1. In July 2019, Trump made headlines again for telling four congressional women of color to go back to the "corrupt" countries they came from "whose governments are a complete and total catastrophe." The fact that only one of the four is actually foreign-born—Ilhan Omar immigrated to the US from Somalia when she was twelve—seems to make no difference to the scores of Republicans who supported Trump's sentiments and chanted "send her back" at one of Trump's rallies. This divisiveness is part and parcel of Trump's America, where "there's a massive partisan divide in what people see as racist. Only 45 percent of Republicans found telling minorities to "go back where they came from" to be a racist statement, which starkly contrasts with the 85 percent of Democrats who think that way. See Catherine Kim, "New Polling Indicates Republicans Actually Like Trump More Following Racist Tweet Controversy." https://www.vox.com/2019/7/17/20697721/trump-racist-tweet-polling.

2. The particular brand of progressive whiteness exhibited by the Armitage family represents a form of "postracial" Americanness familiar to, if not actually embraced by, white viewers of the film.

3. For an in-depth analysis of Black representation in film, see Guerrero 1993; Bogle 2015; hooks 1992; Entman and Rojecki 2000; Sexton 2017.

4. "The Lived Experience of the Black Man" is the title of chapter 5 of Fanon's *Black Skin, White Masks* (1968) 1970.

5. Technically, Chris is a "final boy." While these do exist in horror, they are much less common than the "final girl." In any case, the reversal of girl to boy here is consistent with the other categorical reversals Peele employs in *Get Out*.

6. Even though Red's story elicits sympathy, affective identification with her family is not possible when they assume the conventional role of sadistic aggressor.

7. See Plantinga 2009; Hanich 2010; and Ndalianis 2012.

8. According to Carroll, slasher films like *Halloween* and *Saw* don't qualify as horror, but rather belong to the genre of action/suspense or "tales of terror."

9. Obviously, I'm not implying that heroism is white, nor am I suggesting that spectators of other races view Chris's actions as white; rather, I'm suggesting that the racial grammar of Hollywood film rarely, if ever, codes heroism as anything other than white. Because whiteness presumes its own dominance and mastery, the white viewer is incapable of seeing Chris's heroism as anything other than white. See Wilderson 2010.

10. See DiAngelo 2018.

CONCLUSION. MEDIA MATTERS

1. For a detailed account of the raid of bin Laden's compound in Pakistan, see http://www.cbsnews.com/news/seals-first-hand-account-of-bin-laden-killing/.

2. The comparisons of Caesar and Moses are many, both in the original franchise and in the reboot. In *Escape from the Planet of the Apes* (1971), Caesar's parents defied the order that all baby apes be killed by hiding him in a circus, where he was later adopted. In the current film, Caesar liberates the apes from slavery and leads them to the promised land, where, like Moses, he dies upon arrival.

REFERENCES

ABC News. 2020. "Transcript: Trump to Mobilize Federal Resources to Stop Violence, Restore Security." June 1, 2020. https://abcnews.go.com/Politics/transcript-trump-mobilize-federal-resources-stop-violence-restore/story?id=71008802.

Abdul-Jabbar, Kareem. 2020. "Don't Understand the Protests? What You're Seeing Is People Pushed to the Edge." *Los Angeles Times*, May 30, 2020. https://www.latimes.com/opinion/story/2020-05-30/dont-understand-the-protests-what-youre-seeing-is-people-pushed-to-the-edge.

Abrajano, Marisa, and Zoltan Hajnal. 2015. *White Backlash, Immigration, Racism, and American Politics*. Princeton, NJ: Princeton University Press.

Abrajano Marisa, and Zoltan Hajnal. 2017. "Media Framing and Partisan Identity: The Case of Immigration Coverage and White Micropartisanship." *Journal of Race, Ethnicity and Politics* 2: 5–34.

Abrams, J. J., director. 2013. *Star Trek Into Darkness*. Paramount. 131 min. DVD.

Abrams, J. J., director. 2015. *Star Wars: Episode VII—The Force Awakens*. Walt Disney Studios. 138 min.

Abrams, Natalie. 2013. "*The Walking Dead*'s Michael Rooker 'Relieved' by Merle's Fate." *TV Guide*, March 26, 2013. https://www.tvguide.com/news/walking-dead-michael-rooker-merle-death-1063201/.

Adams, Chanel. 2016. "Jeffrey Dean Morgan Slams Donald Trump's Immigration Policy." *Inquisitr*, October 14, 2016. https://www.inquisitr.com/3592746/jeffrey-dean-morgan-slams-donald-trumps-immigration-policy/.

Adams, Char, Allan Smith, and Assdit Tambe. 2021. "Map: See Which States Have Passed Critical Race Theory Bills." NBC News, June 17, 2021. https://www.nbcnews.com/news/nbcblk/map-see-which-states-have-passed-critical-race-theory-bills-n1271215.

Agamben, Giorgio. 1998. *Homo Sacer: Sovereign Power and Bare Life*. Stanford: Stanford University Press.

Ahmed, Sarah. [2004] 2014. *The Cultural Politics of Emotion*. 2nd edition. New York and London: Routledge.

Al-Arshani, Sarah. 2020. "A Reporter Asked Trump If He'd Pardon Joe Exotic from 'Tiger King,' and Trump Said He'd Look into It." *Insider*, April 8, 2020. https://www.businessinsider.com/trump-said-hed-look-into-pardoning-joe-exotic-tiger-king-2020-4.

Alexander, Michelle. [2010] 2012. *The New Jim Crow: Mass Incarceration in the Age of Colorblindness*. Second edition with a foreword by Cornel West. New York: The New Press.

Allam, Hannah. "'Us vs. Them' In a Pandemic: Researchers Warn Divisions Could Get Dangerous." *NPR*, May 15, 2020. https://www.npr.org/sections/coronavirus-live-updates/2020/05/15/857165715/us-vs-them-in-a-pandemic-researchers-warn-divisions-could-get-dangerous.

Allen, Harry. 1995. "Telling Time: On Spike, Strike and the 'Reality' of *Clockers*," *Village Voice*, October 3, 1995.

Alsultany, Evelyn. 2012. *Arabs and Muslims in the Media: Race and Representation after 9/11*. New York: New York University Press.

Alsultany, Evelyn. 2013. "Arabs and Muslims in the Media after 9/11: Representational Strategies for a 'Postrace' Era." *American Quarterly* 65, no. 1: 161–69.

AMC Networks. 2012. "9 Million Viewers Tune-In to 'The Walking Dead' Season 2 Finale Making it the Highest Rated Episode in Series History with a 5.8 HH Rating." Press release. March 19, 2012. https://www.amcnetworks.com/press-releases/9-million-viewers-tune-in-to-the-walking-dead-season-2-finale-making-it-the-highest-rated-episode-in-series-history-with-a-5-8-hh-rating/.

Andersen, Gregers, and Esben Bjerggaard Nielsen. 2018. "Biopolitics in the Anthropocene: On the Invention of Future Biopolitics in *Snowpiercer*, *Elysium*, and *Interstelllar*." *Journal of Popular Culture* 51, no. 3: 615–34. https://onlinelibrary.wiley.com/doi/pdf/10.1111/jpcu.12689.

Anderson, Carol. 2017. *White Rage: The Unspoken Truth of Our Racial Divide*. New York: Bloomsbury.

Anderson, Reynaldo, and Charles E. Jones. 2016. "Introduction: The Rise of Astro-Blackness." In *Afrofuturism 2.0: The Rise of Astro-Blackness*, edited by Reynaldo Anderson and Charles E. Jones, vii–xviii. Lanham, MD: Lexington.

Andreeva, Nellie. 2015. "Pilots 2015: The Year of Ethnic Castings." *Deadline*, March 24, 2015. https://deadline.com/2015/03/tv-pilots-ethnic-casting-trend-backlash-1201386511/.

Andrejevic, Mark. 2011. "The Work That Affective Economics Does." *Cultural Studies* 25, nos. 4–5 (July-September): 604–20. http://doi.org/10.1080/09502386.2011.600551.

Ashurst, Sam. 2014. "Exploring Dawn of the Planet of the Apes' Political Message." Video. *GamesRadar*, July 16, 2014. https://www.gamesradar.com/exploring-dawn-of-the-planet-of-the-apes-political-message/.

Babb, Valerie. 2020. "The Past Is Never Past: The Call and Response between Marvel's *Black Panther* and Early Black Speculative Fiction." *African American Review* 53, no. 2. (Summer): 95–109. https://doi.org/10.1353/afa.2020.0015.

Baker, Peter, Maggie Haberman, Katie Rogers, Zolan Kanno-Youngs, and Katie Benner. 2020. "How Trump's Idea for a Photo Op Led to Havoc in a Park." *New York Times*, June 2, 2020, updated September 17, 2020. https://www.nytimes.com/2020/06/02/us/politics/trump-walk-lafayette-square.html.

Balter, Michael. 2014. "Geneticists Decry Book on Race and Evolution." *Science*, August 8, 2014. https://www.science.org/content/article/geneticists-decry-book-race-and-evolution-rev2.

Banet-Weiser, Sarah. 2012. *Authentic: The Politics of Ambivalence in a Brand Culture*. New York: New York University Press.

Banks, Chloe. 2018. "Disciplining Black Activism: Post-racial Rhetoric, Public Memory and Decorum in News Media Framing of the Black Lives Matter Movement." *Continuum: Journal of Media & Cultural Studies* 32, no. 6: 709–20.

Barry, Dan, and Sheera Frenkel. 2021. "'Be There. Will Be Wild!': Trump All but Circled the Date." *New York Times*, January 6, 2021, last updated July 27, 2021. https://www.nytimes.com/2021/01/06/us/politics/capitol-mob-trump-supporters.html.

Bazelon, Emily. 2017. "What Is Steve Bannon and Jeff Sessions' Shared Vision for Remaking America?" Interview by Terry Gross, NPR (*Fresh Air*), March 9, 2017. http://www.npr.org/2017/03/09/519415023/what-is-steve-bannon-and-jeff-sessions-shared-vision-for-remaking-america.

Beauchamp, Zack. 2017. "White Riot: How Racism and Immigration Gave Us Trump, Brexit, and a Whole New Kind of Politics." *Vox*, January 20, 2017. https://www.vox.com/2016/9/19/12933072/far-right-white-riot-trump-brexit.

Beckett, Lois. 2018. "Pittsburgh Shooting: Suspect Railed Against Jews and Muslims on Site Used by 'Alt-Right.'" *The Guardian* (US edition), October 27, 2018. https://www.theguardian.com/us-news/2018/oct/27/pittsburgh-shooting-suspect-antisemitism.

Beckwith, Ryan Teague. 2016. "Read Trump's Acceptance Speech at the Republican Convention." *Time*, July 21, 2016. https://time.com/4418493/republican-convention-donald-trump-transcript/.

Belcher, Cornell. 2016. *A Black Man in the White House: Barack Obama and the Triggering of America's Racial-Aversion Crisis*. Healdsberg, CA: Walter Street Press.

Beltran, Cristina. 2021. "To Understand Trump's Support, We Must Think in Terms of Multiracial Whiteness." 2021. *Washington Post*, January 15, 2021. https://www.washingtonpost.com/opinions/2021/01/15/understand-trumps-support-we-must-think-terms-multiracial-whiteness/.

Benedictus, Leo. 2013. "How Skittles Became a Symbol of Trayvon Martin's Innocence." *The Guardian* (US edition), July15, 2013. https://www.theguardian.com/world/shortcuts/2013/jul/15/skittles-trayvon-martin-zimmerman-acquittal.

Benkler, Yochai, Robert Faris, Hal Roberts, and Ethan Zuckerman. 2017. "Study: Breitbart-Led Right-Wing Media Ecosystem Altered Broader Media Agenda." *Columbia Journalism Review*, March 3, 2017. https://www.cjr.org/analysis/breitbart-media-trump-harvard-study.php.

Bergengruen, Vera. 2021. "'Our First Martyr.' How Ashli Babbitt Is Being Turned into a Far-Right Recruiting Tool." *Time*, January 10, 2021. https://time.com/5928249/ashli-babbitt-capitol-extremism/.

Berman, Mark, and Wesley Lowery. 2015. "The 12 Key Highlights from the DOJ's Scathing Ferguson Report." *Washington Post*, March 4, 2015. https://www.washingtonpost.com/news/post-nation/wp/2015/03/04/the-12-key-highlights-from-the-dojs-scathing-ferguson-report/.

Bernardi, Daniel. 1999. *Star Trek and History: Race-ing Toward a White Future*. New Brunswick, NJ: Rutgers University Press. https://hdl-handle-net.ezproxy.uta.edu/2027/heb.08268.

Bernstein, Joseph. 2015. "I Spent Two Weeks Tracking a Secret Teen white Supremacist Messaging Group." *BuzzFeed News*, July 9, 2015. https://www.buzzfeednews.com/article/josephbernstein/white-supremacy-lmfao-lol.

Berry, Lorraine. 2013. "'Walking Dead': Still a White Patriarchy." *Salon*, April 1, 2013. https://www.salon.com/2013/04/01/walking_dead_still_a_white_patriarchy/.

Bertoni, Steven. 2016. "Exclusive Interview: How Jared Kushner Won Trump the White House." *Forbes*, November 22, 2016. https://www.forbes.com/sites/stevenbertoni/2016/11/22/exclusive-interview-how-jared-kushner-won-trump-the-white-house/?sh=17e0aeb43af6.

Bishop, Bryan, and Nick Statt. 2016. "The Walking Dead Quitter's Club: Goodbye for Real." *Verge*, October 24, 2016. https://www.theverge.com/2016/10/24/13378876/the-walking-dead-season-7-premiere-recap-review-end-of-quitters-club.

Bishop, Kyle. 2009. "Dead Man Still Walking." *Journal of Popular Film and Television*. 37, no. 1: 16–25.

Bishop Kyle. 2010. *American Zombie Gothic: The Rise and Fall (and Rise) of* The Walking Dead *in Popular Culture*. Jefferson, NC: McFarland.

Bishop, Kyle. 2015. *How Zombies Conquered Popular Culture: The Multifarious Walking Dead in the 21st Century*. Jefferson, NC: McFarland.

Bittle, Jake. 2020. "The Right's Reign on the Air Waves." *New Republic*, June 1, 2020. https://newrepublic.com/article/157926/rights-reign-air-waves.

Blacula (Mark Harris). 2018. "The State of Black Horror: Get Out and Beyond," June 18, 2018. http://www.Blackhorrormovies.com/the-state-of-Black-horror/.

Blake, John. 2016. "What Black America Won't Miss about Obama." CNN, July 1, 2016. https://www.cnn.com/2016/06/30/politics/why-Black-america-may-be-relieved-to-see-obama-go/index.html.

Blatter, Emily. 2016. "Mark Levin: Obama Is 'Soft' on Terrorism." *CNS News*, June 20, 2016. http://www.cnsnews.com/commentary/emily-blatter/mark-levin-obama-soft-terrorism.

Blitzer, Ronn. "Trump Hits Biden Over Swine Flu, as Dem's Campaign Hammers Coronavirus Response." Fox News, May 26, 2020. https://www.foxnews.com/politics/trump-hits-biden-over-swine-flu-as-dems-campaign-hammers-coronavirus-response.

Blomkamp, Neill, director. 2013. *Elysium*. TriStar Pictures. 1 hr., 49 min. DVD.

Bloodsworth-Lugo, M. K., and C. R. Lugo-Lugo. 2010. *Containing (Un)American Bodies: Race, Sexuality, and Post-9/11 Constructions of Citizenship*. Amsterdam: Rodopi Press.

Bloodsworth-Lugo, Mary K., and Carmen R. Lugo-Lugo. 2011. "Post-9/11 Discourse of Threat and Constructions of Terror in the Age of Obama." *Altre Modernità* (September–November): 261–78.

Bogle, Donald. 2015. *Tom, Coons, Mulattoes, Mammies, and Bucks: An Interpretive History of Blacks in American Films*. New York: Bloomsbury Academic (US).

Bolnick, Deborah. 2008. "Individual Ancestry Inference and the Reification of Race as a Biological Phenomenon." In Koenig 2008, 70–85.

Bonilla-Silva, Eduardo. 2003. "'New Racism,' Color-Blind Racism, and the Future of Whiteness in America." In *White Out: The Continuing Significance of Racism*, edited by Ashley Doane and Eduardo Bonilla-Silva, 271–84. New York: Routledge.

Bonilla-Silva, Eduardo. 2012. "The Invisible Weight of Whiteness: The Racial Grammar of Everyday Life in Contemporary America." *Ethnic and Racial Studies* 35, no. 2: 173–94. https://doi.org/10.1080/01419870.2011.613997.

Bonilla-Silva, Eduardo. 2022. *Racism without Racists: Color-Blind Racism and the Persistence of Racial Inequality in America*. Sixth ed. Durham, NC: Duke University Press.

Bonilla-Silva, Eduardo, and Austin Ashe. 2014. "The End of Racism? Colorblind Racism and Popular Media." In Nilsen and Turner 2014, 57–79.

Booth, Robert. 2015. "Organisms and Human Bodies as Contagions in the Post-Apocalyptic State." In Gurr 2015, 17–30.

Bould, Mark. 2007. "The Ships Landed Long Ago: Afrofuturism and Black SF." *Science Fiction Studies* 34, no. 2: 177–86.

Boulle, Pierre, Paul Dehn, writers. 1972. *Conquest of the Planet of the Apes*. Directed by J. Lee Thompson. Twentieth Century Fox. 88 min. DVD.

Boulle, Pierre, Paul Dehn, and John William Corrington, writers. 1973. *Battle for the Planet of the Apes*. Directed by J. Lee Thompson. Twentieth Century Fox. 93 min. DVD.

Bowden, Mark. "'Idiot,' 'Yahoo,' 'Original Gorilla': How Lincoln Was Dissed in His Day." *Atlantic*, June 2013. https://www.theatlantic.com/magazine/archive/2013/06/abraham-lincoln-is-an-idiot/309304/.

Bowen, Sesali. 2017. "Why Some People Think *Planet of the Apes* Is Racist." *Refinery* 29, July 11, 2017. https://www.refinery29.com/en-us/2017/07/163146/planet-of-the-apes-racism-skin-color-stereotypes.

Bowles, Nellie. 2019. "'Replacement Theory,' a Racist, Sexist Doctrine, Spreads in Far-Right Circles." *New York Times*, March 18, 2019. https://www.nytimes.com/2019/03/18/technology/replacement-theory.html.

Bradley, Bill. 2016. "*Walking Dead* Star Michael Cudlitz Compares Donald Trump to Negan." *HuffPost*, August 22, 2016. https://www.huffpost.com/entry/walking-dead-star-michael-cudlitz-compares-donald-trump-to-negan_n_57bae271e4b00d9c3a187f38.

Brantley-Jones, Kiara, Abby Cruz, and Meredith Deliso. 2021. "'Extraordinary Dichotomy' in Police Response to Black Lives Matter Protest, Capitol Chaos: D.C. Attorney General." ABC News, January 8, 2021. https://abcnews.go.com/US/extraordinary-dichotomy-police-response-black-lives-matter-protests/story?id=75118567.

Breznican, Anthony. 2017. "How *Black Panther* Solves the Problem of M'Baku." *Entertainment Weekly*, July 13, 2017. https://ew.com/movies/2017/07/13/black-panther-mbaku-man-ape-issue/.

Brooks, David. 2016. "Dignity and Sadness in the Working Class." *New York Times*, Sept 20, 2016. https://www.nytimes.com/2016/09/20/opinion/dignity-and-sadness-in-the-working-class.html?mcubz=3.

Brooks, Kinitra. 2014. "The Importance of Neglected Intersections: Race and Gender in Contemporary Zombie Texts and Theories." *African American Review* 47, no. 4: 461–75.

Brooks, Kinitra D. 2019. "*Us* Makes Us Look in the Mirror—What If We Don't Like What We See?" *Elle.com*. March 29, 2019. https://www.elle.com/culture/movies-tv/a26988747/us-movie-review-horror-tropes/.

Browning, Lexi, and Lindsey Bever. 2016. "'Ape in Heels': W.Va. Mayor Resigns Amid Controversy Over Racist Comments about Michelle Obama." *Washington Post*, November 16, 2016. https://www.washingtonpost.com/news/post-nation/wp/2016/11/14/ape-in-heels-w-va-officials-under-fire-after-comments-about-michelle-obama/.

Brueck, Hilary. "Doomsday Preppers Are Thinning Out across the U.S., and It May Be Because President Trump Quiets Their Fears." *Insider*, August 26, 2019. https://www.businessinsider.com/what-are-doomsday-preppers-why-are-they-right-wing-2019-8?op=1.

Bruns, Axel. 2008. *Blogs, Wikipedia, Second Life, and Beyond: From Production to Produsage*. Lausanne, CH: Peter Lang.

Burgin, Xavier, director. 2019. *Horror Noire: A History of Black Horror*. Stage 3 Productions. 83 min.

Bush, G. W. 2006. "President Bush's State of the Union Address." Transcript of speech delivered to Congress, January 31, 2006. http://www.washingtonpost.com/wp-dyn/content/article/2006/01/31/AR2006013101468.html.

Caffrey, Jane. 2013. "Hollywood's African-American Film Renaissance." CNN, updated October 20, 2013. https://www.cnn.com/2013/10/18/showbiz/movies/african-american-film-renaissance/index.html.

Campbell, Damian. 2017. "Obama's Ticking Time Bomb Has You in Its Sites." *Concerned Patriot*, January 20, 2017. https://concernedpatriot.com/obamas-ticking-time-bomb/.

Canavan, Gerry. 2010. "We Are the Walking Dead." *Extrapolation* 51, no. 3: 431–53.

Caplan, Arthur L. 2002. "Revulsion Is Not Enough." Book Review. *American Journal of Bioethics*, 2, no. 3 (summer): 57–61.

Carrington, Andre. 2016. *Speculative Blackness: The Future of Race in Science Fiction*. Minneapolis: University of Minnesota Press.

Carroll, Noel. 1990. *The Philosophy of Horror or Paradoxes of the Heart*. New York: Routledge.

Caulfield, A. J. 2021. "Why People Stopped Watching the Walking Dead." *Looper*, updated June 4, 2021. https://www.looper.com/112759/people-stopped-watching-walking-dead/.

CDC. 2020. "Pandemic Influenza." Last reviewed May 12, 2020. https://www.cdc.gov/flu/pandemic-resources/index.htm.

Center for Security Policy. 2010. "Center Files National Security-Focused Amicus Brief in Support of Arizona Law SB-1070." *Center for Security Policy*, September 3, 2010.

Chang, Ailsa. 2019. "Jordan Peele Looked into the Mirror and Saw the Evil Inside 'Us.'" NPR (*All Things Considered*), March 22, 2019. https://www.npr.org/2019/03/22/705875221/jordan-peele-looked-into-the-mirror-and-saw-the-evil-inside-us.

Chang, Justin. 2017. "'War for the Planet of the Apes' Offers a Masterful Vision of Humanity's Many Forms." Review of *War for the Planet of the Apes* directed by Matt Reeves. NPR (*Fresh Air*), July 13, 2017. https://www.npr.org/2017/07/13/537024887/war-for-the-planet-of-the-apes-offers-a-masterful-vision-of-humanitys-many-forms.

Chason, Rachel, and Samantha Schmidt. 2021. "Lafayette Square, Capitol Rallies Met Starkly Different Policing Response." *Washington Post*. January 14, 2021. https://www.washingtonpost.com/dc-md-va/interactive/2021/blm-protest-capitol-riot-police-comparison/?request-id=9061f79c-2131-46e4-b095-fdc691266749&pml=1.

Chavez, Nicole. 2021. "Rioters Breached U.S. Capitol Security on Wednesday. This Was the Police Response When It Was Black Protestors on D.C. Streets Last Year." CNN. Last updated January 10, 2021. https://www.cnn.com/2021/02/08/politics/trump-january-6-speech-transcript/index.html.

Cherry, Brigid. 2009. *Horror*. London and New York: Routledge.

Chia, Jessica. 2017. "Brawls Erupt as Torch-Wielding White Supremacists March through University of Virginia Campus." *New York Daily News*. August 12, 2017. https://www.nydailynews.com/news/national/white-nationalists-march-uva-torches-article-1.3404681.

Christie, Ron. 2017. "How the Media and Obama Made Ferguson Worse." *Daily Beast*, March 12, 2015, updated April 14, 2017. http://www.thedailybeast.com/how-the-media-and-obama-made-ferguson-even-worse.

Cineas, Fabiola, and Anna North. 2020. "We Need to Talk about the White People Who Voted for Donald Trump." *Vox*, November 7, 2020. https://www.vox.com/2020/11/7/21551364/white-trump-voters-2020.

Cinelinx. 2012. "TV Review: The Walking Dead—'Beside the Dying Fire.'" Accessed June 27, 2019. https://www.cinelinx.com/movie-reviews/beside-the-dying-fire-review/.

Clover, Carol. 1992. *Men, Women, and Chain Saws: Gender in the Modern Horror Film*. Princeton: Princeton University Press.

CNN. 2010. "CNN Poll: Most Important Issue Facing the Country," n.d. https://www.cnn.com/ELECTION/2010/the.issues/.

Coates, Ta-Nehisi. 2018. *We Were Eight Years in Power: An American Tragedy*. New York: One World Publishing.

Cobb, Jelani. 2018. "*Black Panther* and the Invention of Africa," *New Yorker*, February 18, 2018. https://www.newyorker.com/news/daily-comment/black-panther-and-the-invention-of-africa.

Cohn, Nate. 2016. "Why Trump Won: Working-Class Whites." New York Times, Nov. 9, 2016. https://www.nytimes.com/2016/11/10/upshot/why-trump-won-working-class-whites.html.

Coleman, Robin Means. 2011. *Horror Noire: Black in American Horror Films from the 1890s to Present*. New York: Routledge.

Collins, K. Austin. "Race Is the Past and Future of Horror Movies." *Ringer*, October 31, 2016. https://www.theringer.com/2016/10/31/16039122/race-is-the-past-and-future-of-horror-movies-17f561d72918.

Conway, Madeline. 2016. "9 of the Nastiest Things Trump Said about Obama." *Politico*, November 10, 2016. https://www.politico.com/story/2016/11/9-ways-trump-insulted-obama-231184.

Coogler, Ryan, director. 2018. *Black Panther*. Marvel Studios. 134 mins. DVD.

Coop, Graham, Michael B. Eisen, Rasmus Nielsen, Molly Przeworski, and Noah Rosenberg. 2014. Letter to the Editor, *New York Times*, August 8, 2014. https://www.nytimes.com/2014/08/10/books/review/letters-a-troublesome-inheritance.html.

Coors, Marilyn, Jacqueline J. Glover, Eric T. Juengst, and James M. Sikela. 2010. "The Ethics of Using Transgenic Non-Human Primates to Study What Makes Us Human." *Nature Reviews Genetics* 11: 658–62. https://doi.org/10.1038/nrg2864.

Couldry, Nick, Andreas Hepp, and Friedrich Krotz, eds. 2010. *Media Events in a Global Age*. London: Routledge.

Courtney, Susan. 2005. *Hollywood Fantasies of Miscegenation: Spectacular Narratives of Gender and Race, 1903–1967*. Princeton University Press.

Crenshaw, Kimberlé W. 2012. "From Private Violence to Mass Incarceration: Thinking Intersectionally about Women, Race, and Social Control." *UCLA Law Review* 59 (August): 1418–72.

Crucchiola, Jordan. 2017. "Get Out Proves the Vitality of Horror in the Trump Era." *Vulture*, February 24, 2017. https://www.vulture.com/2017/02/get-out-proves-horror-will-be-vital-in-the-donald-trump-era.html.

Crucchiola, Jordan, and Bilge Ebiri. 2020. "The 79 Best Pandemic Movies to Binge in Quarantine." *Vulture*. Last updated April 6, 2020. https://www.vulture.com/2020/04/best-pandemic-movies-on-netflix-hulu-prime-and-more.html.

D'Angelo, Paul, and Jim A. Kuypers, eds. 2010. *Doing News Framing Analysis: Empirical and Theoretical Perspectives*. London and New York: Routledge.

Darabont, Frank, Robert Kirkman, and Tony Moore, writers. 2010. *The Walking Dead*. Season 1, episode 1, "Days Gone Bye." Directed by Frank Darabont, featuring Andrew Lincoln, Jon Bernthal, and Sarah Wayne Callies. Aired October 31, 2010, on AMC. https://www.netflix.com/watch/70210887?trackId=14170286.

Darabont, Frank, Robert Kirkman, and Tony Moore, writers. 2010. *The Walking Dead*. Season 1, episode 2, "Guts." Directed by Michelle MacLaren, featuring Andrew Lincoln, Jon Bernthal, and Sarah Wayne Callies. Aired Nov 7, 2010. https://www.netflix.com/watch/70210888?trackId=14170286.

Darabont, Frank, Robert Kirkman, and Tony Moore, writers. 2010. *The Walking Dead*. Season 1, episode 6, "TS-19." Directed by Guy Ferland, featuring Andrew Lincoln, Jon Bernthal, and Sarah Wayne Callies. Aired December 5, 2010, on AMC. https://www.netflix.com/watch/70210892?trackId=200257859.

Darabont, Frank, Robert Kirkman, and Tony Moore, writers. 2012. *The Walking Dead*. Season 2, episode 4, "Cherokee Rose." Directed by Billy Gierhart, featuring Andrew Lincoln, Jon Bernthal, and Sarah Wayne Callies. Aired November 6, 2011, on AMC. https://www.netflix.com/watch/70248464?trackId=200257859.

Darabont, Frank, Robert Kirkman, and Tony Moore, writers. 2011. *The Walking Dead*. Season 2, episode 5, "Chupacabra." Directed by Guy Ferland, featuring Andrew Lincoln, Jon Bernthal, and Sarah Wayne Callies. Aired November 13, 2011, on AMC.

Darabont, Frank, Robert Kirkman, and Tony Moore, writers. 2012. *The Walking Dead*. Season 2, episode 8, "Nebraska." Directed by Clark Johnson, featuring Andrew Lincoln, Jon Bernthal, and Sarah Wayne Callies. Aired February 12, 2012, on AMC. https://www.netflix.com/watch/70248468?trackId=200257859.

Darabont, Frank, Robert Kirkman, and Tony Moore, writers. 2012. *The Walking Dead*. Season 2, episode 10, "18 Miles Out." Directed by Ernest R. Dickerson, Andrew Lincoln, Jon Bernthal, and Sarah Wayne Callies. Aired February 26, 2012, on AMC. https://www.netflix.com/watch/70248470?trackId=200257859.

Darabont, Frank, Robert Kirkman, and Tony Moore, writers. 2012. *The Walking Dead*. Season 2, episode 11, "Judge, Jury, Executioner." Directed by Frank Darabont, featuring Andrew Lincoln, Jon Bernthal, and Sarah Wayne Callies. Aired March 4, 2012, on AMC. https://www.netflix.com/watch/70248471?trackId=14170286.

Darabont, Frank, Robert Kirkman, and Tony Moore, writers. 2012. *The Walking Dead*. Season 3, episode 3, "Walk with Me." Directed by Guy Ferland, featuring Andrew Lincoln, Sarah Wayne Callies, and Laurie Holden. Aired October 28, 2012, on AMC. https://www.netflix.com/watch/70260049?trackId=200257859.

Darabont, Frank, Robert Kirkman, and Tony Moore, writers. 2012. *The Walking Dead*. Season 3, episode 5, "Say the Word." Directed by Greg Nicotero, featuring Andrew Lincoln, Sarah Wayne Callies, and Laurie Holden. Aired November 11, 2012, on AMC. https://www.netflix.com/watch/70260051?trackId=200257859.

Darabont, Frank, Robert Kirkman, and Tony Moore, writers. 2012. *The Walking Dead*. Season 3, episode 8, "Made to Suffer." Directed by Billy Gierhart, featuring Andrew Lincoln, Sarah Wayne Callies, and Laurie Holden. Aired December 2, 2012, on AMC. https://www.netflix.com/watch/70260054?trackId=200257859.

Darabont, Frank, Robert Kirkman, and Tony Moore, writers. 2013. *The Walking Dead*. Season 3, episode 12, "Clear." Directed by Tricia Brock, featuring Andrew Lincoln, Sarah Wayne Callies, and Laurie Holden. Aired March 3, 2013, on AMC. https://www.netflix.com/watch/70260058?trackId=200257859.

Darabont, Frank, Robert Kirkman, and Tony Moore, writers. 2013. *The Walking Dead*. Season 3, episode 14, "Prey." Directed by Stefan Schwartz, featuring Andrew Lincoln, Sarah Wayne Callies, and Laurie Holden. Aired March 17, 2013, on AMC. https://www.netflix.com/watch/70260060?trackId=200257859.

Darabont, Frank, Robert Kirkman, and Tony Moore, writers. 2013. *The Walking Dead*. Season 3, episode 15, "This Sorrowful Life." Directed by Greg Nicotero, featuring Andrew Lincoln, Sarah Wayne Callies, and Laurie Holden. Aired March 24, 2013, on AMC. https://www.netflix.com/watch/70260061?trackId=200257859.

Darabont, Frank, Robert Kirkman, and Tony Moore, writers. 2013. *The Walking Dead*. Season 3, episode 16, "Welcome to the Tombs." Directed by Ernest R. Dickerson, featuring Andrew

Lincoln, Sarah Wayne Callies, and Laurie Holden. Aired March 31, 2013, on AMC. https://www.netflix.com/watch/70260062?trackId=200257859.

Darabont, Frank, Robert Kirkman, and Tony Moore, writers. 2013. *The Walking Dead*. Season 4, episode 1, "30 Days Without an Accident." Directed by Greg Nicotero, featuring Andrew Lincoln, Norman Reedus, and Steven Yeun. Aired October 13, 2013, on AMC. https://www.netflix.com/watch/70297524?trackId=255824129.

Darabont, Frank, Robert Kirkman, and Tony Moore, writers. 2013. *The Walking Dead*. Season 4, episode 2, "Infected." Directed by Guy Ferland, featuring Andrew Lincoln, Norman Reedus, and Steven Yeun. Aired October 20, 2013, on AMC. https://www.netflix.com/watch/70297525?trackId=200257859.

Darabont, Frank, Robert Kirkman, and Tony Moore, writers. 2013. *The Walking Dead*. Season 4, episode 3, "Isolation." Directed by Daniel Sackheim, featuring Andrew Lincoln, Norman Reedus, and Steven Yeun. Aired October 27, 2013, on AMC. https://www.netflix.com/watch/70297526?trackId=200257859.

Darabont, Frank, Robert Kirkman, and Tony Moore, writers. 2014. *The Walking Dead*. Season 5, episode 2, "Strangers." Directed by David Boyd, featuring Andrew Lincoln, Norman Reedus, and Steven Yeun. Aired October 19, 2014, on AMC. https://www.netflix.com/watch/80010528?trackId=200257859.

Darabont, Frank, Robert Kirkman, and Tony Moore, writers. 2015. *The Walking Dead*. Season 5, episode 12, "Remember." Directed by Greg Nicotero, featuring Andrew Lincoln, Norman Reedus, and Steven Yeun. Aired March 1, 2015, on AMC. https://www.netflix.com/watch/80010538?trackId=200257859.

Darabont, Frank, Robert Kirkman, and Tony Moore, writers. 2015. *The Walking Dead*. Season 5, episode 13, "Forget." Directed by David Boyd, featuring Andrew Lincoln, Norman Reedus, and Steven Yeun. Aired March 8, 2015, on AMC. https://www.netflix.com/watch/80010539?trackId=200257859.

Darabont, Frank, Robert Kirkman, and Tony Moore, writers. 2015. *The Walking Dead*. Season 6, episode 2, "JSS." Directed by Jennifer Lynch, featuring Andrew Lincoln, Norman Reedus, and Steven Yeun. Aired October 18, 2015, on AMC. https://www.netflix.com/watch/80031919?trackId=254743534.

Darabont, Frank, Robert Kirkman, and Tony Moore, writers. 2015. *The Walking Dead*. Season 6, episode 4, "Here's Not Here." Directed by Stephen Williams, featuring Andrew Lincoln, Norman Reedus, and Lauren Cohan. Aired November 1, 2015, on AMC. https://www.netflix.com/watch/80031921?trackId=200257859.

Darabont, Frank, Robert Kirkman, and Tony Moore, writers. 2016. *The Walking Dead*. Season 6, episode 16, "Last Day on Earth." Directed by Greg Nicotero, featuring Andrew Lincoln, Norman Reedus, and Steven Yeun. Aired April 3, 2016. https://www.netflix.com/watch/80031933?trackId=14170289.

Darabont, Frank, Robert Kirkman, and Tony Moore, writers. 2016. *The Walking Dead*. Season 7, episode 1, "The Day Will Come When You Won't Be." Directed by Greg Nicotero, featuring Andrew Lincoln, Norman Reedus, and Steven Yeun. Aired October 23, 2016. https://www.netflix.com/watch/80202475?trackId=14170289.

Darabont, Frank, Robert Kirkman, and Tony Moore, writers. 2016. *The Walking Dead*. Season 7, episode 2, "The Well." Directed by Greg Nicotero, featuring Andrew Lincoln, Norman Reedus, and Lauren Cohan. Aired October 30, 2016. https://www.netflix.com/watch/80202476?trackId=200257859.

Darabont, Frank, Robert Kirkman, and Tony Moore, writers. 2016. *The Walking Dead*. Season 7, episode 3, "The Cell." Directed by Alrick Riley, featuring Andrew Lincoln, Norman Reedus, and Lauren Cohan. Aired November 6, 2016. https://www.netflix.com/watch/80202477?trackId=14277283.

Darabont, Frank, Robert Kirkman, and Tony Moore, writers. 2017. *The Walking Dead*. Season 8, episode 1, "Mercy." Directed by Greg Nicotero, featuring Andrew Lincoln, Norman Reedus, and Lauren Cohan. Aired October 22, 2017. https://www.netflix.com/watch/81022952?trackId=200257859.

Darabont, Frank, Robert Kirkman, and Tony Moore, writers. 2017. *The Walking Dead*. Season 8, episode 6, "The King, the Widow and Rick." Directed by John Polson, featuring Andrew Lincoln, Norman Reedus, and Lauren Cohan. Aired November 26, 2017. https://www.netflix.com/watch/81022957?trackId=14277283.

Darabont, Frank, Robert Kirkman, and Tony Moore, writers. 2018. *The Walking Dead*. Season 8, episode 9, "Honor." Directed by Greg Nicotero, featuring Andrew Lincoln, Norman Reedus, and Lauren Cohan. Aired February 25, 2018. https://www.netflix.com/watch/81022960?trackId=155573558.

Darabont, Frank, Robert Kirkman, and Tony Moore, writers. 2019. *The Walking Dead*. Season 10, episode 2, "We Are the End of the World." Directed by Greg Nicotero, featuring Norman Reedus, Danai Gurira, and Melissa McBride. Aired October 13, 2019. https://www.netflix.com/watch/81071680?trackId=254743534.

Darabont, Frank, Robert Kirkman, and Tony Moore, writers. 2019. *The Walking Dead*. Season 10, episode 3, "Ghosts." Directed by David Boyd, featuring Norman Reedus, Daphne Gurira, and Melissa McBride. Aired October 20, 2019. https://www.netflix.com/watch/81071681?trackId=14170289.

Darabont, Frank, Robert Kirkman, and Tony Moore, writers. 2020. *The Walking Dead*. Season 10, episode 11, "Morning Star." Directed by Michael E. Satrazemis, featuring Norman Reedus, Daphne Gurira, and Melissa McBride. Aired March 8, 2020. https://www.netflix.com/watch/81071689?trackId=200257859.

Darby, Luke. 2019. "How the 'White Replacement' Conspiracy Theory Spread Around the Globe." *GQ*. June 21, 2019. https://www.gq.com/story/white-replacement-conspiracy-theory.

Davis, Bradford William. 2016. "Why the Black Image Is Dominating Contemporary Film." *IndieWire*, October 17, 2016.

DeCook, Julia R. 2018. "Memes and Symbolic Violence: #Proudboys and the Use of Memes for Propaganda and the Construction of Collective Identity." *Learning, Media, and Technology* 43, no. 4: 485–504. https://doi.org/10.1080/17439884.2018.1544149.

Department of Justice. 2015. "Department of Justice Report Regarding the Criminal Investigation into the Shooting Death of Michael Brown by Ferguson, Missouri Police Officer Darren Wilson." March 4, 2015. https://www.justice.gov/sites/default/files/opa/press-releases/attachments/2015/03/04/doj_report_on_shooting_of_michael_brown_1.pdf.

DePinto, Jennifer, Fred Backus, Anthony Salvanto, and Kabir Khanna. 2020. "Americans' Views Shift on Racial Discrimination—CBS News Poll." CBS News, June 4, 2020. https://www.cbsnews.com/news/racial-discrimination-americans-views-shift-cbs-news-poll/.

DeVega, Chauncey. 2015. "Donald Trump's 'Death Wish' Fantasies: Guns, White Vigilantism, and the Right's Toxic Masculinity." *Salon*, October 6, 2015. https://www.salon.com/2015/10/06/donald_trumps_death_wish_fantasies_guns_white_vigilantism_and_the_rights_toxic_masculinity/.

DiAngelo, Robin. 2018. *White Fragility: Why It's So Hard for White People to Talk about Racism.* Boston: Beacon Press.

Diaz, Evelyn. 2016. "Here's What Caused Fox to Shut Down Comments on Its Article about Malia's Harvard Plans." *BET*, May 4, 2016. https://www.bet.com/article/ffn52x/fox-shuts-down-comments-on-article-about-malia-obama.

Diehl, Laura. 2013. "American Germ Culture: Richard Matheson, Octavia Butler, and the (Political) Science of Individuality." *Cultural Critique* 85 (Fall): 84–121. https://doi.org/10.5749/culturalcritique.85.2013.0084.

DiFazio, Joe. 2018. "How Much Does the NRA Spend on Lobbying? Gun Group Had Record Year in 2017." *Newsweek*, May 1, 2018. https://www.newsweek.com/last-year-nra-spent-record-sum-lobbying-907203.

Doane, Ashley (Woody). 2014. "Shades of Colorblindness: Rethinking Racial Ideology in the United States." In Nilsen and Turner 2014, 15–38.

Douglass, Patrice, and Frank Wilderson. 2013. "The Violence of Presence: Metaphysics in a Blackened World." *Black Scholar* 43, no. 4: 117–23. Published online November 10, 2015. https://doi.org/10.5816/blackscholar.43.4.0117.

Downing, John, and Charles Husband. 2005. *Representing Race: Racisms, Ethnicity and the Media.* London: Sage.

Dreher, Tanja. 2020. "Racism and Media: A Response from Australia During the Global Pandemic." *Ethnic and Racial Studies* 43, no. 13: 2363–71. https://doi.org/10.1080/01419870.2020.1784452.

Dreisbach, Jim and Tim Mak. 2021. "Yes, Capitol Rioters Were Armed. Here Are the Weapons Prosecutors Say They Used." NPR (*Morning Edition*), March 19, 2021. https://www.npr.org/2021/03/19/977879589/yes-capitol-rioters-were-armed-here-are-the-weapons-prosecutors-say-they-used.

Dsouza, Arnold. 2020. "NASCAR's Bubba Wallace Booed, Crashes as Confederate Flags Fly Around Racetrack." *RepublicWorld*, July 20, 2020. https://www.republicworld.com/sports-news/other-sports/bubba-wallace-booed-crashes-as-confederate-flags-fly-around-racetrack.html.

Du Bois, W. E. B. (1903) 2016. *The Souls of Black Folk.* N.p: Dover Publications.

Due, Tananarive. 2019. "Jordan Peele's Us. Black Horror Comes Out of the Shadows." *Medium*, March 24, 2019. https://medium.com/@tanadue/jordan-peeles-us-black-horror-comes-out-of-the-shadows-787c9ad4865b.

Dunaway, Dustin. 2018. "Arête of Violence: Hypermasculinity as Power Currency in the Post-Apocalyptic Political Economy." In *The Politics of Race, Gender and Sexuality in* The Walking Dead: *Essays on the Television Series and Comics*, edited by Elizabeth Erwin and Dawn Keetley, 11–21. Jefferson, NC: McFarland.

Dupre, John. 2008. "What Genes Are and Why There Are No Genes for Race." In *Revisiting Race in a Genomic Age*, edited by Barbara A. Koening, Sandra Soo-Jin Lee, and Sarah S. Richardson, 39–55. New Brunswick, NJ: Rutgers University Press.

Dyer, Richard. 1997. *White.* London and New York: Routledge.

Easley, Jason. 2016. "Jake Tapper Drops a Reality Bomb on Paul Ryan: Millions Are Terrified of Trump's Presidency." *PoliticusUSA*, November 13, 2016. https://www.politicususa.com/2016/11/13/jake-tapper-drops-reality-bomb-paul-ryan-millions-terrified-trumps-presidency.html.

Eels, Josh. 2018. "Ryan Coogler: Why I Needed to Make 'Black Panther.'" *Rolling Stone*, February 26, 2018. https://www.rollingstone.com/movies/movie-features/ryan-coogler-why-i-needed-to-make-black-panther-203737/.

Egan, Lauren. 2020. "Trump Calls Coronavirus Democrats' 'New Hoax.'" NBC News, last updated February 28, 2020. https://www.nbcnews.com/politics/donald-trump/trump-calls-coronavirus-democrats-new-hoax-n1145721.

Ehrenfreund, Max. 2015. "What Social Science Tells Us about Racism in the Republican Party." *Washington Post*, December 11, 2015. https://www.washingtonpost.com/news/wonk/wp/2015/12/11/what-social-science-tells-us-about-racism-in-the-republican-party/.

Ehrenfreund, Max. 2016. "Americans Now Think It's Okay to Say What They Really Think about Race." *Washington Post*, June 17, 2016. https://www.washingtonpost.com/news/wonk/wp/2016/06/17/americans-now-think-its-okay-to-say-what-they-really-think-about-race/.

Entman, Robert. 2007. "Framing Bias: Media in the Distribution of Power." *Journal of Communication* 57: 163–73.

Entman Robert M., and Andrew Rojecki. 2000. *The Black Image in the White Mind*. Chicago: University of Chicago Press.

Erigha, Maryann. 2016. "Do African Americans Direct Science Fiction or Blockbuster Franchise Movies? Race, Genre, and Contemporary Hollywood." *Journal of Black Studies* 47, no. 6: 550–69.

Erigha, Maryann. 2019. *The Hollywood Jim Crow: The Racial Politics of the Movie Industry*. New York: New York University Press.

Eshun, Kodwo. 2003. "Further Considerations on Afrofuturism." *CR: The New Centennial Review* 3, no. 2: 287–302.

Evans, Elizabeth. 2020. *Understanding Engagement in Transmedia Culture*. Abingdon, Ox and New York: Routledge.

Fabian, Ann. 2010. *The Skull Collectors*. Chicago: The University of Chicago Press.

Fanon, Frantz. (1968) 1970. *Black Skin, White Masks*. Translated by Charles Lam Markmann. London: Paladin.

Faramelli, Anthony. 2019. "Liberation On and Off Screen: *Black Panther* and Black Liberation Theory." *Space, Place, and Identities Onscreen* 43, no. 2 (September). https://doi.org/10.3998/fc.13761232.0043.202.

Fawaz, Ramzi. 2011. "Where No X-Man Has Gone Before." *American Literature* 83, no. 11: 355–88. https://doi.org/10.1215/00029831-1266090.

Fawaz, Ramzi. 2016. *The New Mutants: Superheroes and the Radical Imagination of American Comics*. New York: New York University Press.

Fazekas, Angie. 2020. "Alpha/Beta/Omega: Racialized Narratives and Fandom's Investment in Whiteness." In *Fandom, Now in Color: A Collection of Voices*, edited by Rukmini Pande, 95–108. Iowa City: Iowa University Press.

Feagin, Joe R. 2013. *The White Racial Frame: Centuries of Racial Framing and Counter-Framing*. 2nd ed. New York: Routledge.

Fernandez, Manny. 2015. "Conspiracy Theories Over Jade Helm Training Exercise Get Some Traction in Texas." *New York Times*, May 6, 2015. https://www.nytimes.com/2015/05/07/us/conspiracy-theories-over-jade-helm-get-some-traction-in-texas.html.

Fiske, John. (1996) 2016. *Media Matters: Race and Gender in U.S. Politics*. 2nd ed. with a new introduction by Black Hawk Hancock. New York: Routledge.

Fiske, John. 2013. "Moments of Television: Neither the Text nor the Audience." In *Remote Control: Television, Audiences, and Cultural Power*, edited by Ellen Seiter, Hans Borchers, Gabriele Kreutzner, Eva-Maria Warth, 56–78. New York: Routledge.

Fitts, Alexis Sobel. 2014. "Michael Brown Shooting and the Crimes Journalists Choose as Newsworthy." *Columbia Journalism Review*, August 28, 2014. https://archives.cjr.org/minority_reports/michael_brown_ferguson_media.php.

Fleetwood, Nicole. 2011. *Troubling Vision: Performance, Visuality, and Blackness*. Chicago: University of Chicago Press.

Ford, Rebecca, and Borys Kit. 2016. "Hollywood's Casting Blitz: It's All about Diversity in the Wake of #OscarSoWhite." *Hollywood Reporter*, March 2, 2016. https://www.hollywoodreporter.com/movies/movie-news/oscarssowhite-spurs-diversity-casting-boom-872005/#!

Fowler, Matt. "*The Walking Dead*: 'Last Day on Earth' Review." *IGN*, updated May 2, 2017. https://www.ign.com/articles/2016/04/04/the-walking-dead-last-day-on-earth-review.

Fox, Andrew. 2016. "The Media Event as Enhanced News Story: How User-Generated Content Determines the News Agenda." In *Global Perspectives on Media Events in Contemporary Society*, edited by Andrew Fox, 17–27. N.p.: IGI Global. DOI: 10.4018/978-1-4666-9967-0.ch002.

France, Lisa Respers. 2016. "Why the Beyoncé Controversy Is Bigger than You Think." CNN, February 24, 2016. https://www.cnn.com/2016/02/23/entertainment/beyonce-controversy-feat/index.html.

Frankenberg, Ruth. 1993. *White Women, Race Matters*. Minneapolis, MN: University of Minnesota Press.

Freeman, Matthew. 2019. *The World of* The Walking Dead. New York: Routledge. https://www-taylorfrancis-com.ezproxy.uta.edu/books/mono/10.4324/9780203731147/world-walking-dead-matthew-freeman.

French, David. 2015. "In the Zombie World, Only the Conservative Survive." *National Review*, October 3, 2015. https://www.nationalreview.com/2015/10/walking-dead-zombie-fiction-conservative/.

Freud, Sigmund. [1919] 2010. "The Uncanny." In *The Norton Anthology of Theory and Criticism*, edited by Vincent Leitch, 824–41. New York: W. W. Norton.

Fukuyama, Francis. 2003. *Our Posthuman Future: Consequences of the Biotechnology Revolution*. New York: Picador.

Gao, George. 2014. "Chart of the Week: The Black-White Gap in Incarceration Rates." Pew Research Center, July 18, 2014. https://www.pewresearch.org/fact-tank/2014/07/18/chart-of-the-week-the-Black-white-gap-in-incarceration-rates/.

Gates, Racquel, and Kristen J. Warner. 2018. "*Wakanda Forever*: The Pleasures, the Politics, and the Problems." *Film Quarterly* "Quorum," March 9, 2018. https://filmquarterly.org/2018/03/09/wakanda-forever-the-pleasures-the-politics-and-the-problems/.

Gencarella, Stephen Olbrys. 2016. "Thunder without Rain: Fascist Masculinity in AMC's *The Walking Dead*." *Horror Studies* 7, no. 1: 125–46.

Gillborn, David. 2006. "Rethinking White Supremacy: Who Counts in 'WhiteWorld.'" *Ethnicities* 6, no. 3: 318–40. http://doi.org/10.1177/1468796806068323.

Gillespie, Michael Boyce. 2016. *Film Blackness: American Cinema and the Idea of Black Film*. Durham, NC: Duke University Press.

Glasgow, Joshua. 2009. *A Theory of Race*. New York: Routledge.

Goff, Phillip Atiba, Jennifer L. Eberhardt, Melissa J. Williams, and Matthew Christian Jackson. 2008. "Not Yet Human: Implicit Knowledge, Historical Dehumanization, and Contemporary Consequences." *Journal of Personality and Social Psychology* 94, no. 2: 292–306.

Goffman, Erving. 1974. *Frame Analysis: An Essay on the Organization of Experience*. Cambridge, MA. Harvard University Press.

GoldDerby. 2017. "Jordan Peele (Get Out) on How White Audiences Have Responded to the Film." November 17, 2017. https://www.youtube.com/watch?v=qHtQIlLUT5Y.

Goldberg, David Theo. 2015. *Are We All Postracial Yet?* Cambridge: Polity Press.

Goldman, Eric. 2012. "*The Walking Dead*: 'Beside the Dying Fire' Review." *IGN*, updated March 19, 2012. https://www.ign.com/articles/2012/03/19/the-walking-dead-beside-the-dying-fire-review.

Goodkind. 2011. "Enlightened Racism in Rise of the Planet of the Apes." *Paracinema*, December 19, 2011. https://paracinema.net/2011/12/enlightened-racism-in-rise-of-the-planet-of-the-apes/.

Goodwyn, Wade. 2015. "Texas Governor Deploys State Guard to Stave off Obama Takeover." *NPR*, May 2, 2015. https://www.npr.org/sections/itsallpolitics/2015/05/02/403865824/texas-governor-deploys-state-guard-to-stave-off-obama-takeover.

Göttlich, Udo. 2010. "Media Event Culture and Lifestyle Management: Observations on the Influence of Media Events on Everyday Culture." In Couldry et al. 2010, 172–83.

Gould, Stephen J. 1981. *The Mismeasure of Man*. New York: W. W. Norton.

Graham, David A. "Trump Says Democrats Want Immigrants to 'Infest' the U.S." *Atlantic*, June 19, 2018. https://www.theatlantic.com/politics/archive/2018/06/trump-immigrants-infest/563159/.

Graham, Shawn. 2012. "How *The Walking Dead* Satiates Its Voracious Fans with Interactive Digital Content." *Fast Company*, April 3, 2012. https://www.fastcompany.com/1827124/how-walking-dead-satiates-its-voracious-fans-interactive-digital-content.

Gray, Herman. 1995. *Watching Race: Television and the Struggle for "Blackness."* Minneapolis, MN: University of Minnesota Press.

Gray, Herman. 2013. "Subject(ed) to Recognition." *American Quarterly* 65, no. 4: 771–98. http://www.jstor.org/stable/43822990.

Gray, Jonathan. 2007. "The News: You Gotta Love It." In *Fandom: Identities and Communities in a Mediated World*, edited by Jonathan Gray, Cornel Sandvoss, and C. Lee Harrington, 75–87. New York: New York University Press.

Gray, Jonathan. 2010. *Show Sold Separately: Promos, Spoilers, and Other Media Paratexts*. New York: New York University Press. https://hdl-handle-net.ezproxy.uta.edu/2027/heb.31973.

Gray, Jonathan, Cornel Sandvoss, and C. Lee Harrington, eds. 2007. *Fandom: Identities and Communities in a Mediated World*. New York: New York University Press.

Greely, Henry T. (2011) 2013. "Human/Nonhuman Chimeras: Assessing the Issues." In *The Oxford Handbook of Animal Ethics*, edited by T. L. Beauchamp, and R. G. Frey, 671–98. Reprint. Oxford: Oxford University Press.

Green, Emma. 2020. "The McCloskeys' Unsubtle Message to White America." *Atlantic*, August 25, 2020. https://www.theatlantic.com/politics/archive/2020/08/mccloskeys-trump-suburbs-rnc/615655/.

Greene, Eric. 1998. *Planet of the Apes as American Myth: Race, Politics, and Popular Culture*. Wesleyan Press.

Gregory, Todd, Salvatore Colleluori, and Daniel Angster. 2014. "Report: New York City Television Stations Give Lopsided Coverage to Black Crime." *MediaMatters*, August 22, 2014. https://

www.mediamatters.org/nbc/report-new-york-city-television-stations-give-lopsided-coverage-black-crime.

Griffin, Robert, and Ruy Teixeira. 2017. "The Story of Trump's Appeal: A Portrait of Trump Voters." Democracy Fund Voter Study Group, June 2017. https://www.voterstudygroup.org/publication/story-of-trumps-appeal.

Griggs, Brandon. 2015. "Internet Trolls Call New 'Star Wars' Movie 'Anti-White.'" CNN, October 21, 2015. http://www.cnn.com/2015/10/20/entertainment/star-wars-trailer-boycott-anti-white-feat/index.html.

Gruttadaro, Andrew. 2016. "No POC Deserved to Be Nominated for an Oscar This Year (But That's Not the Point)." http://uk.complex.com/pop-culture/2016/01/oscars-so-white-2016.

Grynbaum, Michael. 2020. "How Right-Wing Pundits Are Covering Coronavirus." *New York Times*, March 11, 2020. https://www.nytimes.com/2020/03/11/us/politics/coronavirus-conservative-media.html.

Guerrero, Ed. 1993. *Framing Blackness: The African American Image in Film*. Philadelphia: Temple University Press.

Guerrero, Lisa, and David J. Leonard. 2012. "Playing Dead: The Trayvoning Meme and the Mocking of Black Death." *NewBlackMan (In Exile): The Digital Home for Mark Anthony Neal* (blog). May 29, 2012. https://www.newblackmaninexile.net/2012/05/playing-dead-trayvoning-meme-mocking-of.html.

Guhl, Jakob, and Jacob Davey. 2020. "A Safe Space to Hate: White Supremacist Mobilisation on Telegram." London: ISD Global. https://www.isdglobal.org/wp-content/uploads/2020/06/A-Safe-Space-to-Hate2.pdf.

Gupta, Arun. 2018. "Why Young Men of Color Are Joining White-Supremacist Groups." *Daily Beast*, September 4, 2018. Updated September 6, 2018. https://www.thedailybeast.com/why-young-men-of-color-are-joining-white-supremacist-groups.

Gurr, Barbara, ed. 2015. *Race, Gender, and Sexuality in Post-Apocalyptic TV and Film*. London: Palgrave MacMillan.

Guthrie, Ricardo. 2019. "Redefining the Colonial: An Afrofuturist Analysis of *Wakanda* and Speculative Fiction." *Journal of Future Studies* 24, no. 2: 15–28. https://doi.org/10.6531/JFS.201912_24(2).0003.

Hafner, Josh. 2016. "'Deal from Strength or Get Crushed,' Kids Sing in Bizarre Trump Anthem." *USA Today*, January 14, 2016. https://www.usatoday.com/story/news/politics/onpolitics/2016/01/14/deal-strength-get-crushed-kids-sing-bizarre-trump-anthem/78804652/.

Hagler, Jamal. "8 Facts You Should Know about the Criminal Justice System and People of Color." *Center for American Progress*, May 28, 2015. https://www.americanprogress.org/article/8-facts-you-should-know-about-the-criminal-justice-system-and-people-of-color/.

Hall, Stuart. [1980] 2004. "Encoding/Decoding." In *Culture, Media, Language: Working Papers in Cultural Studies, 1972–79*, edited by Stuart Hall, Dorothy Hobson, Andrew Lowe, and Paul Willis, 117–27. London: Routledge. https://www-taylorfrancis-com.ezproxy.uta.edu/books/edit/10.4324/9780203381182/culture-media-language-stuart-hall-doothy-hobson-andrew-lowe-paul-willis.

Hall, Stuart. [1981] 2019. "Notes on Deconstructing 'The Popular.'" In *Essential Essays, Volume 1: Foundations of Cultural Studies*, edited by Stuart Hall and David Morley, 347–61. Durham: Duke University Press. https://ebookcentral.proquest.com/lib/utarl/reader.action?docID=5609562.

Hall, Stuart, Chas Critcher, Tony Jefferson, John Clarke, and Brian Roberts. 1978. *Policing the Crisis: Mugging, the State, and Law and Order*. New York: Holmes and Meier Publishers, Inc.

Hannich, Julian. 2010. *Cinematic Emotion in Horror Films and Thrillers*. Abingdon, Oxon and New York: Routledge, 2010.

Hannah-Jones, Nikole. 2019. "Our Democracy's Founding Ideals Were False When They Were Written. Black Americans Have Fought to Make Them True." *New York Times Magazine*, August 14, 2019. https://www.nytimes.com/interactive/2019/08/14/magazine/black-history-american-democracy.html.

Harper, Phillip Brian. 1998. "Extra-Special Effects: Televisual Representation and the Claims of 'The Black Experience.'" In *Living Color: Race and Television in the United States*, edited by Sasha Torres, 62–81. Durham: Duke University Press.

Harris, Geraldine. 2012. "A Return to Form? Postmasculinist Television Drama and Tragic Heroes in the Wake of *The Sopranos*." *New Review of Film and Television Studies* 10: 443–63.

Harris, Marvin. (1968) 2001. *The Rise of Anthropological Theory: A History of Theories of Culture*. Lanham, Md: Altamira Press.

Harris, Sam. 2017. "Forbidden Knowledge." *Making Sense* (Podcast). Episode 73, April 23, 2017. https://www.samharris.org/podcasts/making-sense-episodes/73-forbidden-knowledge.

Harsin, Jayson and Mark Hayward. 2013. "Stuart Hall's 'Deconstructing the Popular': Reconsiderations 30 Years Later." *Communication, Culture, and Critique* 6: 201–7.

Hartman, Margaret. 2013. "Post-Newton, States Passed More Gun-Rights Laws, Not Restrictions." *Intelligencer*, April 4, 2013. https://nymag.com/intelligencer/2013/04/post-newtown-states-loosen-gun-restrictions.html.

Hartman, Saidiya. 1997. *Scenes of Subjection: Terror, Slavery, and Self-Making in Nineteenth-Century America*. New York: Oxford University Press.

Hartman, Saidiya, and Frank Wilderson. 2003. "The Position of the Unthought." Qui Parle 13, no. 2: 183–201.

Hasan, Zaki. "Exclusive Interview: *Rise of the Planet of the Apes* Writers Amanda Silver and Rick Jaffa." *HuffPost*, August 7, 2011, updated December 6, 2017. https://www.huffpost.com/entry/exclusive-interview-rise-_b_925944.

Hawley, George. 2017. "The Long History of White Nationalism in America." *Literary Hub*, August 16, 2017. https://lithub.com/the-long-history-of-white-nationalism-in-america/.

Hay, James. 2011. "'Popular Culture' in a Critique of the New Political Reason." *Cultural Studies* 25, nos. 4–5, 659–84. http://doi.org/10.1080/09502386.2011.600554.

Haynes, Chris, S. Karthick Ramakrishnan, and Jennifer Merolla. 2016. *Framing Immigrants: News Coverage, Public Opinion, and Policy*. New York: Russell Sage Foundation.

Hayward, John. 2013. "Obama's Race-Baiting." Breitbart, July 19, 2013. https://www.breitbart.com/blog/2013/07/19/obama-s-race-baiting/.

Hearn, Alison. 2008. "'Meat, Mask, Burden': Probing the Contours of the Branded 'Self.'" *Journal of Consumer Culture*, 8, no. 2: 197–217. https://doi.org/10.1177/1469540508090086.

Henderson, Alex. 2020. "Rush Limbaugh Says Trump's Coronavirus Task Force Is Part of the 'Deep State,' Can't Be Trusted." *Salon*. March 28, 2020. https://www.salon.com/2020/03/28/rush-limbaugh-says-trumps-coronavirus-task-force-is-part-of-the-deep-state-cant-be-trusted-_partner/.

Hepp, Andreas, and Nick Couldry. 2010. "Introduction: Media Events in Globalized Media Cultures." In Couldry et al. 2010, 1–20.

Herndon, Astead W. 2019. "How 'White Guilt' in the Age of Trump Shapes the Democratic Primary." *New York Times*, updated October 14, 2019. https://www.nytimes.com/2019/10/13/us/politics/democratic-candidates-racism.html.

Herrnstein, Richard J., and Charles Murray. 1994. *The Bell Curve*. New York: Free Press.

Hersko, Tyler. 2020. "'Tiger King' Had 34 Million Viewers within 10 Days of Launch, Fox to Air Special." April 8, 2020. https://www.indiewire.com/2020/04/tiger-king-netflix-viewership-fox-special-1202223808/.

History on the Net. "The Coon Caricature: Blacks as Monkeys." Last modified July 20, 2012. https://www.historyonthenet.com/authentichistory/diversity/african/3-coon/6-monkey/.

Ho, Helen. 2016. "The Model Minority in the Zombie Apocalypse: Asian-American Manhood on AMC's *The Walking Dead*." *Journal of Popular Culture* 49, no. 1: 57–76.

Hogan, Ron. 2012. "*The Walking Dead* Season 2 Episode 13 Review: Beside the Dying Fire." *Den of Geek*, March 19, 2012. https://www.denofgeek.com/tv/the-walking-dead-season-2-episode-13-review-beside-the-dying-fire/.

hooks, bell. 1992. *Black Looks: Race and Representation*. Cambridge: South End Press.

HuffPost. 2010. "Glenn Beck Compares Obama's America to 'Planet of the Apes.'" August 7, 2010. https://www.huffpost.com/entry/glenn-beck-compares-obama_n_674591.

Hughey, Matthew W. 2009. "Cinethetic Racism: White Redemption and Black Stereotypes in 'Magical Negro' Films." *Social Problems* 56, no. 3, pp. 543–77.

Hulse, Carl, and Kate Zernike. 2011. "Bloodshed Puts New Focus in Vitriol in Politics." *New York Times*, January 8, 2011. https://www.nytimes.com/2011/01/09/us/politics/09capital.html.

Huver, Scott. 2017. "No, *The Walking Dead*'s Negan Isn't an Allusion to Donald Trump." *Vulture*, March 19, 2017. https://www.vulture.com/2017/03/no-the-walking-deads-negan-isnt-an-allusion-to-trump.html.

Ibanez, Ray. 2011. "The Guns of *The Walking Dead*." *Armory Blog: Gun News, Reviews and Opinion* (blog), December 11, 2011. https://www.armoryblog.com/firearms/the-guns-of-the-walking-dead/.

Igielnik, Ruth, Scott Keeter, and Hannah Hartig. 2021. "Behind Biden's 2020 Victory." Pew Research Center, June 30, 2021. https://www.pewresearch.org/politics/2021/06/30/behind-bidens-2020-victory/?org=982&lvl=100&ite=8768&lea=1873968&ctr=0&par=1&trk=.

Ignatiev, Noel. 1995. *How the Irish Became White*. New York and London: Routledge.

Illing, Sean. 2016. "Why So Many People Voted to 'Make America Great Again.'" *Vox*, updated November 9, 2016. https://www.vox.com/2016/9/29/12930730/donald-trump-2016-elections-mark-lilla-revolution-fascism-europe.

Ingram, Penelope. 1999. "Can the Settler Speak? Appropriating Subaltern Silence in Janet Frame's *The Carpathians*." *Cultural Critique* 41 (Winter): 79–107. https://doi.org/10.2307/1354521.

Ingram, Penelope. 2001. "Racializing Babylon: Settler Whiteness and the 'New Racism.'" *New Literary History* 32, no. 1: 157–76.

Isom, Deena A., Toniqua C. Mikell, and Hunter M. Boehme. 2021. "White America, Threat to the Status Quo, and Affiliation with the Alt-Right: A Qualitative Approach." *Sociological Spectrum* 41, no. 3: 213–28. https://doi.org/10.1080/02732173.2021.1885531.

Izzo, David Garrett. 2015. "Introduction." In *Movies in the Age of Obama: The Era of Post-Racial and Neo-Racist Cinema*, edited by David Garrett Izzo, vii–xii. Lanham, MD: Rowman and Littlefield.

Jackson, Zakiyyah Iman. 2020. *becoming human: Matter and Meaning in an Antiblack World*. New York: New York University Press.
Jagernauth, Kevin. 2016. "Academy Pledges to Double Women and Minority Members by 2020." *IndieWire*. January 22, 2016. http://www.indiewire.com/2016/01/Academy-pledges-to-double-women-and-minority-members-by-2020-88234/.
James. Edward. (1990) 2014. "Yellow, Black, Metal, and Tentacled: The Race Question in American Science Fiction." In *Black and Brown Planets: The Politics of Race in Science Fiction*, edited by Isiah Lavender III, 199–222. Jackson, MS: University Press of Mississippi.
James, Frank. "Portraying Obama as Chimp Not Like Showing Bush as One." *NPR*, April 27, 2011. https://www.npr.org/sections/itsallpolitics/2011/04/27/135771740/portraying-obama-as-a-chimp-not-the-same-as-showing-bush-as-one.
Jardina, Ashley. 2019. *White Identity Politics*. Cambridge: Cambridge University Press.
Jarvis, Michael. 2018. "Anger Translator: Jordan Peele's *Get Out*." *Science Fiction Film and Television* 11, no. 1: 97–109.
Jeffries, Stuart. 2016. "*The Walking Dead* Season Seven Premiere: The Day Will Come When You Won't Be." *The Guardian* (US edition), October 24, 2016. https://www.theguardian.com/tv-and-radio/2016/oct/24/the-walking-dead-season-seven-premiere-the-day-will-come-when-you-wont-be.
Jenkins, Henry. 2006. *Convergence Culture: Where Old and New Media Collide*. NYU Press.
Jenkins, Henry. 2011. "Transmedia 202: Further Reflections." *Confessions of an ACA-Fan* (blog). July 31, 2011. http://henryjenkins.org/blog/2011/08/defining_transmedia_further_re.html.
Jenkins, Henry. (1992) 2013. *Textual Poachers: Television Fans and Participatory Culture*. New York: Routledge.
Jenn, 2013. "*The Walking Dead*'s Ongoing Black Man Problem." *Nerds of Color* (blog), October 29, 2013. https://thenerdsofcolor.org/2013/10/29/the-walking-deads-ongoing-Black-man-problem/.
Jionde, Elexus. 2018. "The Curious Case of T-Dog: A Magical Negro?" In *The Politics of Race, Gender, and Sexuality in The Walking Dead: Essays on the Television Series and Comics*, edited by Elizabeth Erwin, and Dawn Keetley, 21–30. Jefferson, NC: McFarland.
Johnson, Dominique Deidre. 2015. "Misogynoir and Antiblack Racism: What *The Walking Dead* Teaches Us about the Limits of Speculative Fiction Fandom." *Journal of Fandom Studies* 3, no. 3: 259–75. http://doi.org//10.1386/jfs.3.3.259_1.
Johnson, Jessica. 2018. "The Self-Radicalization of White Men: 'Fake News' and the Affective Networking of Paranoia." *Communication Culture & Critique* 11: 100–115.
Johnson, Paul Elliott. 2017. "Walter White(ness) Lashes Out: *Breaking Bad* and Male Victimage." *Critical Studies in Media Communication* 34, no. 1. Published online October 18, 2016. https://doi.org/10.1080/15295036.2016.1238101.
Johnson, Tre. 2018. "Black Superheroes Matter: Why a *Black Panther* Movie Is Revolutionary." *Rolling Stone*, February 16, 2018. https://www.rollingstone.com/movies/movie-news/black-superheroes-matter-why-a-black-panther-movie-is-revolutionary-198678/.
Jones, Nicholas, Rachel Marks, Roberto Ramirez, and Merarys Ríos-Vargas. 2021. "2020 Census Illuminates Racial and Ethnic Composition of the Country." United States Census Bureau, August 12, 2021. https://www.census.gov/library/stories/2021/08/improved-race-ethnicity-measures-reveal-united-states-population-much-more-multiracial.html.

Joseph, Ralina L. 2011. "Imagining Obama: Reading Overtly and Inferentially Racist Images of Our 44th President, 2007–2008." *Communication Studies* 62, no. 4: 389–405.

Joseph, Ralina, L. 2018. *Postracial Resistance: Black Women, Media, and the Use of Strategic Ambiguity.* New York: New York University Press.

Kallis, Aristotle. 2015. "A Thin Red Line? Far Right and Mainstream in a Relational Perspective." In *The European Far Right: Historical and Contemporary Perspectives*, edited by G. Charalambous. Oslo: Prio.

Kaplan, Jonathan Michael, Massimo Pigliucci, and Joshua Alexander Banta. 2015. "Gould on Morton, Redux: What Can the Debate Reveal about the Limits of Data?" *Studies in History and Philosophy of Science: Part C: Studies in History and Philosophy of Biological and Biomedical Sciences* 52 (August).

Karlin, Susan. 2011a. "Michael Rooker on the Return of Merle Dixon." *Michael Rooker Online*, November 10, 2011. https://michaelrookeronline.com/hands-up-for-michael-rooker.

Karlin, Susan. 2011b. "How One *Walking Dead* Actor's Racist Maniac Makes for Must-See TV." *Fast Company*, November 21, 2011. https://www.fastcompany.com/1795779/how-one-walking-dead-actors-racist-maniac-makes-must-see-tv.

Karpowics et al. 2004. "It Is Ethical to Transplant Human Stem Cells into Nonhuman Embryos." *Nature Medicine* 10, no. 4: 331–35.

Kaufmann, Eric. 2019. *White Shift: Populism, Immigration, and the Future of White Majorities.* New York: Abrams Press.

Keeley, Matt. 2020. "Trump Says Antifa and Radical-Left Criminals Are Behind Violence, Vows to Stop Mobs." *Newsweek*, May 30, 2020. https://www.newsweek.com/trump-says-antifa-radical-left-criminals-are-behind-violence-vows-stop-mobs-1507620.

Keetley, Dawn. 2014a. "Human Choice and Zombie Consciousness." In *We're All Infected: Essays on AMC's* The Walking Dead *and the Fate of the Human*, edited by Dawn Keetley, 156–72. Jefferson, NC: McFarland.

Keetley, Dawn. 2014b. "Introduction." In *We're All Infected: Essays on AMC's* The Walking Dead *and the Fate of the Human*, edited by Dawn Keetley, 3–25. Jefferson, NC: McFarland.

Keetley, Dawn. 2018. "Afterword: From Identity Politics to Tribalism." In *The Politics of Race, Gender and Sexuality in* The Walking Dead: *Essays on the Television Series and Comics*, edited by Elizabeth Erwin and Dawn Keetley, 155–64. Jefferson, NC: McFarland.

Kellner, Douglas. 2010. *Cinema Wars.* Oxford: Wiley Blackwell. https://onlinelibrary.wiley.com/doi/book/10.1002/9781444314809.

Kellner, Douglas, and Michael Ryan. 1988. *Camera Politica: The Politics and Ideology of Contemporary Hollywood Film.* Bloomington: Indiana University Press.

Kelly, Casey Ryan. 2016. "The Man-pocalpyse: *Doomsday Preppers* and the Rituals of Apocalyptic Manhood." *Text and Performance Quarterly*, 36, nos. 2–3: 95–114. https://doi-org.ezproxy.uta.edu/10.1080/10462937.2016.1158415.

Kelly, Casey Ryan. 2020. *Apocalypse Man: The Death Drive and the Rhetoric of White Masculine Victimhood.* Columbus, OH: The Ohio State University Press.

Khetpal, Vishai. 2014. "Ferguson, and the Media That Divides Us." *HuffPost*, Dec 4, 2014, updated February 3, 2015. https://www.huffpost.com/entry/ferguson-and-the-media-th_b_6259226.

King, C. Richard. 2014. "Watching TV with White Supremacists." In Nilsen and Turner 2014, 219–36.

King, James. 2016. "White Supremacists Talk of 'Race War' After Dallas Police Shootings." *Vocativ*, July 8, 2016. https://www.vocativ.com/338228/white-supremacists-dallas-police-shootings-police/.

Knowles, Eric, D., and Kaiping Peng. 2005. "White Selves: Conceptualizing and Measuring a Dominant-Group Identity," *Journal of Personality and Social Psychology*. 89, no. 2: 223–41.

Knowles, Eric D., Brian S. Lowery, Elizabeth Shulman, and Rebecca L. Schaumberg. 2013. "Race, Ideology, and the Tea Party: A Longitudinal Study." *Plos One*, June 25, 2013. https://doi.org/10.1371/journal.pone.0067110.

Knowles, Eric D., and Linda R. Tropp. 2016. "Donald Trump and the Rise of White Identity Politics." *The Conversation*, October 28, 2016. https://theconversation.com/donald-trump-and-the-rise-of-white-identity-in-politics-67037.

Koenig, Barbara A., Sandra Soo-Jin Lee, and Sarah S. Richardson. 2008. "Introduction: Race and Genetics in a Genomic Age." In Koenig et al. 2008, 1–17.

Koenig, Barbara A., Sandra Soo-Jin Lee, and Sarah S. Richardson, editors. 2008. *Revisiting Race in a Genomic Age*. New Brunswick, NJ: Rutgers University Press.

Kohn, Eric. 2017. "Jordan Peele Challenges Golden Globes Classifying *Get Out* as a Comedy: 'What Are You Laughing At?'" *IndieWire*, November 15, 2017. https://www.indiewire.com/2017/11/jordan-peele-response-get-out-golden-globes-comedy-1201897841/.

Kristol, William, and Eric Cohen. 2002. *The Future Is Now: America Confronts the New Genetics*. New York: Rowman and Littlefield.

Krogstad, Jens Manuel. 2020. "Americans Broadly Support Legal Status for Immigrants Brought to the U.S. Illegally as Children." Pew Research Center, June 17, 2020. https://www.pewresearch.org/fact-tank/2020/06/17/americans-broadly-support-legal-status-for-immigrants-brought-to-the-u-s-illegally-as-children/.

Krugman, Paul. 2020. "How Zombies Ate the GOP's Soul." *New York Times*, February 3, 2020. https://www.nytimes.com/2020/02/03/opinion/republican-party-trump.html.

Kube, Courtney, and Rich Schapiro. "Pentagon Chief Esper Reverses Decision to Send Some Troops Home from D.C. Amid Protests." NBC News, June 3, 2020. https://www.nbcnews.com/news/us-news/bucking-trump-pentagon-chief-esper-says-no-need-military-response-n1223456.

Kunyosying, Kom, and Carter Soles. 2018. "The Hyperreal Hillbilly: Horror, Melodrama and Backwoods White Protagonists." In *The Politics of Race, Gender and Sexuality in* The Walking Dead: *Essays on the Television Series and Comics*, edited by Elizabeth Erwin and Dawn Keetley, 31–42. Jefferson, NC: McFarland.

Kunzelman, Michael. 2017. "Trump Comments Please, Anger, Then Please Hate Group Leaders." *Chicago Tribune*, August 15, 2017. https://www.chicagotribune.com/nation-world/ct-trump-angers-white-nationalists-20170815-story.html.

Kurtz, Howard. 2015. "How a False Media Narrative Made Ferguson Worse." Fox News, December 20, 2015. http://www.foxnews.com/politics/2014/11/26/how-false-media-narrative-made-ferguson-worse.html.

Lahut, Jake. 2020. "Trump in 2014 Said Obama Was 'a Psycho' Not to Immediately Cancel Flights into the U.S. Amid Ebola Outbreak in West Africa." *Insider*, February 25, 2020. https://www.businessinsider.com/trump-called-obama-a-psycho-in-2014-over-ebola-outbreak-2020-2?op=1.

Lang, Nico. 2014. "5 Reasons Why *The Walking Dead* Is the Biggest Show on TV." *Daily Dot*, October 15, 2014, updated May 30, 2021. https://www.dailydot.com/via/why-walking-dead-biggest-show-television/.

Lane, Kimberly, Yaschica Williams, Andrea N. Hunt, and Amber Paulk. 2020. "The Framing of Race: Trayvon Martin and the Black Lives Matter Movement." *Journal of Black Studies* 51, no. 8: 790–812.
Lauro, Sarah Juliet, and Karen Embry. 2008. "A Zombie Manifesto: The Nonhuman Condition in the Era of Advanced Capitalism." *Boundary 2* 35, no. 1: 85–108.
Lavender, Isiah, III. 2011. *Race in American Science Fiction*. Bloomington: Indiana University Press.
Lavender, Isiah, III. 2019. "Jordan Peele's Get Out (2017) and Ryan Coogler's *Black Panther* (2018)." In *Sci-Fi: A Companion*, edited by Jack Fennell. New York: Peter Lang.
Lavin, Melissa F., and Brian M. Lowe. "Cops and Zombies: Hierarchy and Social Location in *The Walking Dead*." In Gurr 2015, 113–24.
LeBron, Christopher. 2018. "*Black Panther* Is Not the Movie We Deserve." *Boston Review*, February 17, 2018. https://bostonreview.net/articles/christopher-lebron-black-panther/.
Lee, Michelle Ye Hee. 2017a. "The Bogus Claim That a Map of Crosshairs by Sarah Palin's PAC incited Rep. Gabby Giffords's Shooting." *Washington Post*, June 15, 2017. https://www.washingtonpost.com/news/fact-checker/wp/2017/06/15/the-bogus-claim-that-a-map-of-crosshairs-by-sarah-palins-pac-incited-rep-gabby-giffordss-shooting/.
Lee, Michelle Ye Hee. 2017b. "Was Former Arizona Sheriff Joe Arpaio's Criminal Conviction an Obama 'Political Witch Hunt.'" *Washington Post*, August 30, 2017. https://www.washingtonpost.com/news/fact-checker/wp/2017/08/30/was-former-arizona-sheriff-joe-arpaios-criminal-conviction-an-obama-political-witch-hunt/.
Lee, Paula Young. 2015. "Spare Us Your French Flag Filter: The Self-Indulgent Social Media Performance Doesn't Help Anyone." *Salon*, November 16, 2015. https://www.salon.com/2015/11/16/facebooks_pointless_french_flag_filter_the_self_indulgent_social_media_performance_that_doesnt_help_anyone/.
Leech-Steffens, Lauren. 2013. Answer to "Answer to *Star Trek Into Darkness* (2013 movie): Am I the Only Person Bothered by the Whitewashing?" *Quora*, December 8, 2013. https://www.quora.com/Star-Trek-Into-Darkness-2013-movie-Am-I-the-only-person-really-bothered-by-the-whitewashing?share=1.
Lemonick, Michael D. 2014. "*Planet of the Apes*: That Couldn't Happen . . . Right?" *Time*, July 11, 2014. https://time.com/2977183/planet-of-the-apes-science/.
Levina, Marina. *Pandemics and the Media*. 2015. New York: Peter Lang.
Lewis, Jason E., David DeGusta, Marc R. Meyer, Janet M. Monge, Alan E. Mann, and Ralph L. Holloway. 2011. "The Mismeasure of Science: Stephen Jay Gould versus Samuel George Morton on Skulls and Bias." *Plos Biology* 9, no. 6 (June). https://doi.org/10.1371/journal.pbio.1001071.
Lichtblau, Eric. 2017. "Sessions Indicates Justice Department Will Stop Monitoring Troubled Police Agencies." *New York Times*, February 28, 2017. https://www.nytimes.com/2017/02/28/us/politics/jeff-sessions-crime.html.
Lieberman, David. 2017. "*Walking Dead* Tames Some Gruesome Scenes Following Viewer Protests." *Deadline*, January 18, 2017. https://deadline.com/2017/01/walking-deal-tamed-violence-viewer-protest-amc-1201888731/.
Lin, Justin, director. 2016. *Star Trek Beyond*. Paramount. 122 mins. DVD.
Linneman, Travis. 2014. "*The Walking Dead* and Killing State: Zombification and the Normalization of Police Violence." *Theoretical Criminology* 18, no. 4: 506–27.
Lipsitz, George. 1990. *Time Passages: Collective Memory and American Popular Culture*. Minneapolis: University of Minnesota Press.

Lipsitz, George. 1998. "Genre Anxiety and Racial Representation." In *Refiguring American Film Genres: Theory and History*, edited by Nick Browne, 208–32. Oakland: University of California Press.

Lipsitz, George. 1998. *The Possessive Investment in Whiteness: How White People Profit from Identity Politics*, 2nd ed. Philadelphia: Temple University Press.

Liptak, Kevin, and Kristen Holmes. 2020. "Trump Calls Black Lives Matter a 'Symbol of Hate' as He Digs in on Race." CNN, July 1, 2020. https://www.cnn.com/2020/07/01/politics/donald-trump-black-lives-matter-confederate-race/index.html.

López, Gustavo, and Jens Manuel Krogstad. 2017. "Key Facts about Unauthorized Immigrants Enrolled in DACA." Pew Research Center, September 25, 2017. https://www.pewresearch.org/fact-tank/2017/09/25/key-facts-about-unauthorized-immigrants-enrolled-in-daca/.

Los Angeles Times. 2016. "Donald Trump's Complete Convention Speech, Annotated." July 21, 2016. https://www.latimes.com/politics/la-na-pol-donald-trump-convention-speech-transcript-20160721-snap-htmlstory.html.

Lott, Eric. 2017. *Black Mirror: The Cultural Contradictions of American Racism*. Cambridge, MA: Belknap Press.

Lotz, Amanda. 2018. *We Now Disrupt This Broadcast: How Cable Transformed Television and the Internet Revolutionized It All*. Cambridge, MA. MIT Press.

Loza, Susana. 2017. *Speculative Imperialisms: Monstrosity and Masquerade in Postracial Times*. Lanham, MD: Lexington Books.

Lynch, Tim. 2016. "The 'War on Cops': Flawed Logic and Fantasy." *Newsweek*, July 31, 2016. https://www.newsweek.com/war-cops-flawed-logic-fantasy-485546.

Maas, Jennifer. 2020. "*Outbreak* Is Netflix's 9th Most Popular Overall Title in the U.S. Right Now." *The Wrap*, March 14, 2020. https://www.thewrap.com/outbreak-movie-top-10-netflix-titles-movies-pandemic-tv-series-coronavirus/.

Maidy, Alex. 2016. "The Unpopular Opinion: *Star Trek Into Darkness*." *JoBlo*, May 5, 2016. https://www.joblo.com/the-unpopular-opinion-star-trek-into-darkness-752-02/.

McCarty, Andrew C. 2013. "The Obama Administration's Race-Baiting Campaign." *National Review*, July 20, 2013. https://www.nationalreview.com/2013/07/obama-administrations-race-baiting-campaign-andrew-c-mccarthy/.

McCollum, Victoria, ed. 2019. *Make America Hate Again: Trump-Era Horror and the Politics of Fear*. New York: Routledge.

McCormack, David. 2015. "Univision Sacks Emmy-Winning Host after He Says Michelle Obama 'Looks Like She's Part of the Cast of *Planet of the Apes*.'" *Daily Mail*, March 12, 2015, updated March 14, 2015. https://www.dailymail.co.uk/news/article-2992012/Univision-Sacks-Emmy-winning-host-says-Michelle-Obama-looks-like-s-cast-Planet-Apes.html.

McGreal, Chris. 2020. "'I Wanted to Take Action': Behind the 'Wall of Moms' Protecting Portland's Protesters." *The Guardian* (US edition), July 21, 2020. https://www.theguardian.com/us-news/2020/jul/21/trump-federal-agents-portland-protests-moms.

Marcotte, Amanda. 2021. "'Planned in Plain Sight': Why Donald Trump Makes No Attempt to Hide His Insurrectionist Plots." *Salon*, June 8, 2021. https://www.salon.com/2021/06/08/planned-in-plain-sight-why-donald-trump-makes-no-attempt-to-hide-his-insurrectionist-plots/?scrolla=5eb6d68b7fedc32c19ef33b4.

Massie, Christopher. 2014. "*The New York Times* Criticized for Michael Brown Profile." *Columbia Journalism Review*, August 25, 2014. https://archives.cjr.org/the_kicker/new_york_times_michael_brown_no_angel.php.

Mauer, Marc and Ryan S. King. 2007. "Uneven Justice: State Rates of Incarceration by Race and Ethnicity." *The Sentencing Project*, July 2007. https://www.sentencingproject.org/wp-content/uploads/2016/01/Uneven-Justice-State-Rates-of-Incarceration-by-Race-and-Ethnicity.pdf.

Mercer, Kobena. 2007. *Welcome to The Jungle: New Positions in Black Cultural Studies*. London and New York: Routledge.

Meta. 2021. "Using Facebook Profile Frames to Inspire Action." *Facebook* (blog), January 29, 2021, updated February 18, 2022. https://www.facebook.com/gpa/blog/using-facebook-profile-frames-to-inspire-action.

Metcalfe, Keith. 2013. Answer to "*Star Trek Into Darkness* (2013 movie): Am I the Only Person Really Bothered by the Whitewashing?" *Quora*, December 8, 2013. https://www.quora.com/Star-Trek-Into-Darkness-2013-movie-Am-I-the-only-person-really-bothered-by-the-whitewashing?share=1.

Meyer, Nicholas, director. 1982. *Star Trek II: The Wrath of Khan*. Paramount. 113 min.

Miller, John L. 2011. "Sorry, Bam: Lincoln Had It Way Worse." *New York Post*, August 17, 2011. https://nypost.com/2011/08/17/sorry-bam-lincoln-had-it-way-worse/.

Mills, Charles. 1997. *The Racial Contract*. Ithaca: Cornell University Press.

Mills, Michael F. 2021. "Obamageddon: Fear, the Far Right, and the Rise of 'Doomsday' Prepping in Obama's America." *Journal of American Studies* 55, no. 2: 336–65. https://doi.org/10.1017/S0021875819000501.

Montoya-Galvez, Camilo. 2019. "New Pictures Show 'Dangerous Overcrowding' at Border Patrol Facilities in Texas." CBS News, July 2, 2019. https://www.cbsnews.com/news/dhs-inspector-general-report-reveals-squalid-conditions-at-migrant-detention-centers/.

Morais, Betsy. "The Science of 'Planet of the Apes': Could Simians Get Scary Smart?" *Atlantic*, August 5, 2011. https://time.com/2977183/planet-of-the-apes-science/.

Moreno, J. Edward. 2020. "DC Mayor Blasts 'Gross' Trump Tweet Threatening 'Vicious Dogs' at White House." *The Hill*, May 30, 2020. https://thehill.com/homenews/news/500273-dc-mayor-blasts-gross-trump-tweet-warning-about-vicious-dogs-at-white-house/.

Morley, Dave. 1980. "Texts, Readers, Subjects." In *Culture, Media, Language: Working Papers in Cultural Studies*, 1972–79, edited by Stuart Hall, Dorothy Hobson, Andrew Lowe, and Paul Willis, 154–65. London: Routledge.

Moreman, Christopher M. and Cory James Rushton, eds. 2011. *Race, Oppression and the Zombie: Essays on Cross-Cultural Appropriation of the Caribbean Tradition*. Jefferson: McFarland.

Morrison, Toni. 1992. *Playing in the Dark: Whiteness and the Literary Imagination*. Cambridge, Ma.: Harvard University Press.

Movieclips Trailers. 2013. "*Dawn of the Planet of the Apes* Official PSA—Simian Flu (2014)." December 18, 2013. Promotional Video, 0.30. https://www.youtube.com/watch?v=NRPkO_hKxUk.

Mukherjee, Roopali, Sarah Banet-Weiser, and Herman Gray, eds. 2019. *Racism Postrace*. Durham: Duke University Press.

Mulvaney James. 2015. "Enough with the French Flag Logo." CNN, November 18, 2015. https://www.cnn.com/2015/11/17/opinions/mulvaney-facebook-french-flag/.

Musser, Amber Jamilla. 2014. *Sensational Flesh: Race, Power, and Masochism*. New York: New York University Press.

Nakamura, Lisa and Peter Chow-White. 2012. *Race after the Internet*. New York: Routledge.

Nama, Adilifu. 2008. *Black Space: Imagining Race in Science Fiction Film*. Austin: University of Texas Press.

Nama, Adilifu. 2011. *Superblack: American Pop Culture and Black Superheroes*. Austin: University of Texas Press.

Narea, Nicole. 2020. "Fox News's Dangerous Decision to Downplay the Threat of Coronavirus." *Vox*, March 13, 2020. https://www.vox.com/2020/3/13/21178188/fox-news-coronavirus-sean-hannity-trump-response.

Ndalianis, Angela. 2012. *The Horror Sensorium: Media and the Senses*. Jefferson, NC: McFarland.

Neiwert, David. 2018. *Alt-America: The Rise of the Radical Right in the Age of Trump*. London and New York: Verso.

Nelson, Alondra. 2008. "The Factness of Diaspora: The Social Sources of Genetic Genealogy." In Koenig et al. 2008, 253–69.

Nelson, Alondra. 2016. *The Social Life of DNA: Race, Reparations, and Reconciliation after the Genome*. Boston: Beacon Press.

Nelson, Louis. 2016. "Trump: 'I Am the Law and Order Candidate.'" *Politico*, July 11, 2016. https://www.politico.com/story/2016/07/trump-law-order-candidate-225372.

Newkirk, Vann R. II. 2018. "The Provocation and Power of *Black Panther*." *Atlantic*, February 14, 2018. https://www.theatlantic.com/entertainment/archive/2018/02/the-provocation-and-power-of-black-panther/553226/.

NewsOne. 2015. "Winning! Fox's 'Empire' Smashes 23-Year Ratings Record." February 9, 2015. https://newsone.com/3090152/empire-ratings-breaks-23-year-record/.

New York Times. 2017. "The Hate He Dares Not Speak Of." August 13, 2017. https://www.nytimes.com/2017/08/13/opinion/trump-charlottesville-hate-stormer.html?mcubz=3.

New York Times. 2020. "Seattle Mayor Defies Trump." June 11, 2020, updated June 12, 2020. https://www.nytimes.com/2020/06/11/us/george-floyd-protests.html?action=click&pgtype=Article&state=default&module=styln-george-floyd&variant=show&region=TOP_BANNER&context=storylines_menu.

Nilsen, Sarah. 2014. "'Some People Just Hide in Plain Sight': Historicizing Racism in *Mad Men*." In Nilsen and Turner 2014, 191–218.

Nilsen, Sarah and Sarah E. Turner, eds. 2014. *The Colorblind Screen: Television in Post-Racial America*. New York: New York University Press.

Noble, Safiya. 2014. "Teaching Trayvon: Race, Media, and the Politics of Spectacle." *The Black Scholar* 44, no. 1: 12–29.

Norman, Greg. 2019. "Families of Americans Killed by Illegal Immigrants Take Issue with Claim Trump Is 'Manufacturing a Crisis.'" Fox News, January 9, 2019. https://www.foxnews.com/us/families-of-americans-killed-by-illegal-immigrants-take-odds-with-schumer-and-pelosi-words-that-trump-is-manufacturing-a-crisis-to-get-border-wall.

Norton, Michael I., and Samuel R. Sommers. 2011. "Whites See Racism as a Zero-Sum Game That They Are Now Losing." *Perspectives on Psychological Science* 6, no. 3: 215–18.

Nowrasteh, Alex. 2018. "USCIS Report Shows that DACA Arrest Rate Is Below That of Other U.S. Residents." *CATO at Liberty* (blog), CATO Institute, June 19, 2018. https://www.cato.org/blog/uscis-report-shows-daca-arrest-rate-below-other-us-residents.

NPR. 2016. "Pat Buchanan on Why He Shares Trump's Ideas on Foreign Policy." Interview by Rachel Martin. *Morning Edition*, May 5, 2016. https://www.npr.org/2016/05/05/476844409/pat-buchanan-on-why-he-shares-trump-s-ideas-on-foreign-policy.

NPR. 2017. "Get Out Sprang from an Effort to Master Fear, Says Director Jordan Peele." Interview by Terry Gross. *Fresh Air*, March 15, 2017. https://www.npr.org/sections/codeswitch/2017/03/15/520130162/get-out-sprung-from-an-effort-to-master-fear-says-director-jordan-peele.

NPR. 2021. "The Capitol Siege: The Cases Behind the Biggest Criminal Investigation in U.S. History." *All Things Considered*, March 5, 2021. Updated May 13, 2022. https://www.npr.org/2021/02/09/965472049/the-capitol-siege-the-arrested-and-their-stories.

NRA. 2012. "NRA: Full Statement by Wayne LaPierre in Response to Newtown Shootings." *The Guardian* (US edition), December 21, 2012. https://www.theguardian.com/world/2012/dec/21/nra-full-statement-lapierre-newtown.

Nygaard, Taylor and Jorie Lagerwey. 2020. *Horrible White People: Gender, Genre, and Television's Precarious Whiteness*. New York: New York University Press. Kindle.

O'Connor, Mike. 2012. "Liberals in Space: The 1960s Politics of Star Trek." *The Sixties* 5, no. 2: 185–203. http://doi.org/10.1080/17541328.2012.721584.

O'Kane, Sean. "Day 1 in Trump's America." *Medium*, Nov 9, 2016. https://medium.com/@seanokane/day-1-in-trumps-america-9e4d58381001#.p8hp57srx.

Oliver, J. Eric, and Tali Mendelberg. 2000. "Reconsidering the Environmental Determinants of White Racial Attitudes," *American Journal of Political Science* 44, no. 3: 574–89.

Oliver, J. Eric, and Wendy M. Rahn. 2016. "Rise of the Trumpenvolk: Populism in the 2016 Election." *The Annals of the American Academy of Political and Social Science* 667, no. 1 (September): 189–206. http://dx.doi.org/10.1177/0002716216662639.

Olsson, Anna S., and Peter Sandøe. 2010. "'What's Wrong with My Monkey?' Ethical Perspectives on Germline Trangenesis in Marmosets." *Transgenic Res* 19, no. 2 (April): 181–86. https://doi.org/10.1007/s11248-009-9316-6.

Omi, Michael, and Howard Winant. 2014. *Racial Formation in the Unites States*. 3rd ed. New York: Routledge.

Ortega, Frank J., and Joe R. Feagin. 2016. In *The Routledge Companion to Media and Race*, edited by Christopher P. Campbell, 19–30. New York: Routledge.

Osnos, Evan. 2015. "The Fearful and the Frustrated." *New Yorker*, August 24, 2015. https://www.newyorker.com/magazine/2015/08/31/the-fearful-and-the-frustrated.

Otterson, Joe. 2016. "*Walking Dead* Fan Theory Suggests Walter White Caused Zombie Apocalypse" (video). *The Wrap*, November 3, 2016. https://www.thewrap.com/walking-dead-fan-theory-breaking-bad-walter-white/.

Ouellette, Laurie, and Sarah Banet-Weiser. 2018. "Special Issue: Media and the Extreme Right Editor's Introduction." *Communication, Culture, & Critique* 11: 1–6.

Outten, Robert, Michael Schmitt, Daniel A. Miller, and Amber L. Garcia. 2012. "Feeling Threatened about the Future: Whites' Emotional Reactions to Anticipated Ethnic Demographic Changes." *Personality and Social Psychology Bulletin* 38, no. 1:14–25.

Packer, George. 2016. "How Donald Trump Appeals to the White Working Class." *New Yorker*, May 8, 2016. https://www.newyorker.com/magazine/2016/05/16/how-donald-trump-appeals-to-the-white-working-class.

Palacios-Gonzalez, César. 2015a. "Ethical Aspects of Creating Human-Nonhuman Chimeras Capable of Human Gamete Production and Human Pregnancy." *Monash Bioethics Review* 33, nos. 2–3: 181–202. https://doi.org/10.1007/s40592-015-0031-1.

Palacios-González, César. 2015b. "Human Dignity and the Creation of Human-Nonhuman Chimeras," *Medicine, Health Care, and Philosophy* 18 (May): 487–99. https://doi.org/10.1007/s11019-015-9644-7.

Papacharissi, Zizi. 2015. "Toward New Journalism(s): Affective News, Hybridity, and Liminal Spaces." *Journalism Studies* 16, no. 1: 27–40.

Parker, Ashley, Josh Dawsey, and Rebecca Tan. 2020. "Inside the Push to Tear-Gas Protestors Ahead of a Trump Photo-Op." *Washington Post*, June 1, 2020. https://www.washingtonpost.com/politics/inside-the-push-to-tear-gas-protesters-ahead-of-a-trump-photo-op/2020/06/01/4b0f7b50-a46c-11ea-bb20-ebf0921f3bbd_story.html.

Paugh, Ileana Johnson. "The True Story of Ebola in Reston, Virginia." *Canada Free Press*, August 5, 2014. https://canadafreepress.com/article/the-true-story-of-ebola-in-reston-virginia.

PBS News Hour. 2017. "Get Out Dials Up the Scary Side of Race in America." Transcript of interview with Jordan Peele by Jeffrey Brown. March 6, 2017. https://www.pbs.org/newshour/show/get-dials-scary-side-race-america.

Peele, Jordan, director. 2017. *Get Out*. Universal Pictures, 104 min. DVD.

Peele, Jordan. 2019. *Us*. Universal Pictures, 116 min. DVD.

Pew Research Center. 2020. "Public's Mood Turns Grim; Trump Trails Biden on Most Personal Traits, Major Issues." June 30, 2020. https://www.pewresearch.org/politics/2020/06/30/publics-mood-turns-grim-trump-trails-biden-on-most-personal-traits-major-issues/.

Phelan, Jo C., Bruce G. Link, Sarah Zelner, and Lawrence H. Yang. 2014. "Direct-to-Consumer Racial Admixture Tests and Beliefs about Essential Racial Differences." *Social Psychology Quarterly* 77, no. 3: 296–318.

Phillips, Michael. 2017. "Jordan Peele's 'Social Thriller' Launches a Directorial Career." *Chicago Tribune*, February 24, 2017. https://www.chicagotribune.com/entertainment/movies/ct-jordan-peele-get-out-interview-20170224-column.html.

Phillips, Whitney. 2012. "The House the Fox Built: Anonymous, Spectacle, and Cycles of Amplification." *Television and New Media* 14, no. 6: 494–509.

Phillips, Whitney. 2016. *This Is Why We Can't Have Nice Things: Mapping the Relationship Between Online Trolling and Mainstream Culture*. Cambridge: MIT Press.

Phillips, Whitney. 2018. "The Oxygen of Amplification. Better Practice for Reporting on Extremists, Antagonists, and Manipulators Online." *Data & Society*, May 22, 2018.

Pilkington, Ed. 2008. "Obama Angers Midwest Voters with Guns and Religion Remark." *The Guardian* (US edition), April 14, 2008. https://www.theguardian.com/world/2008/apr/14/barackobama.uselections2008.

Planet of the Apes. 2014. "*Dawn of the Planet of the Apes*: Prepare for Dawn." June 13, 2014. Promotional video, 1:46. https://www.youtube.com/watch?v=eb8B-bAr_WE.

Plantinga, Carl. 2009. *Moving Viewers: American Film and the Spectator's Experience*. Oakland: University of California Press.

Plaut, Victoria C. 2010. "Diversity Science: Why and How Difference Makes a Difference." *Psychological Inquiry* 21, no. 2 (April–June): 77–99. http://www.jstor.org/stable/25704854.

Pokornowski, Steven. 2013. "Insecure Lives: Zombies, Global Health, and the Totalitarianism of Generalization." *Literature and Medicine* 31, no. 2 (Fall): 216–34.

Pokornowski, Steven. 2016. "Vulnerable Life: Zombies, Global Biopolitics, and the Reproduction of Structural Violence." *Humanities* 5, no. 71: 1–22. http://doi.org/10.3390/h5030071.

Porter, Rick. 2016. "Sunday Cable Ratings: 'Walking Dead' Down but Stays on Top, 'Real Housewives of Atlanta' Returns Lower." *TV by the Numbers* (blog), November 8, 2016. Accessed July 27, 2019.

PRRI. 2020. "In Trump Era, Increasing Polarization on Immigration, but Common Ground Remains for Path to Citizenship, Opposing Family Separation." Press Release, December 3, 2020. https://www.prri.org/press-release/in-trump-era-increasing-polarization-on-im migration-but-common-ground-remains-for-path-to-citizenship-opposing-family-sep aration/.

Redmond, Sean. 2006. "The Science Fiction of Whiteness." *Scope* 6: 1–21. https://www.nottingham .ac.uk/scope/documents/2006/october-2006/redmond.pdf.

Ray. 2011. "The Guns of The Walking Dead." *Armory Blog: Gun News, Reviews and Opinion* (blog), December 11, 2011. https://www.armoryblog.com/firearms/the-guns-of-the-walking-dead/

Reed, Robert. 2017. "Obama's Economic Legacy: Big Bailouts That Worked." *Chicago Tribune*, January 10, 2017. https://www.chicagotribune.com/business/ct-obama-economy-robert -reed-110-biz-20170109-column.html.

Reeve, Elspeth. 2016. "Alt-right Trolls Are Getting 23andme Genetic Tests to 'Prove' Their Whiteness." *Vice News*, October 8, 2016. https://news.vice.com/story/alt-right-trolls-are-getting -23andme-genetic-tests-to-prove-their-whiteness?cl=fp.

Reeves, Matt, director. 2014. *Dawn of the Planet of the Apes*. Twentieth Century Fox, 130 min. DVD.

Reeves, Matt, director. 2017. *War for the Planet of the Apes*. Twentieth Century Fox, 140 min. DVD.

Reilly, Katie. 2019. "Donald Trump Criticized Obama's Grades. But His Lawyer Threatened Trump's Alma Maters Not to Release His Own Grades." *Time*, February 27, 2019. https:// time.com/5540152/donald-trump-michael-cohen-academic-records/.

Respers, Lisa. 2013. "'The Butler' Reflects America's Racial Conversations." CNN, August 20, 2013. https://www.cnn.com/2013/08/19/showbiz/movies/the-butler-race/index.html.

Reyes, Xavier Aldana. 2012. "Beyond Psychoanalysis: Post-Millennial Horror Film and Affect Theory." *Horror Studies* 3, no. 2: 243–61.

Reyes, Xavier Aldana. 2016. *Horror Film and Affect: Towards a Corporeal Model of Viewership*. New York: Routledge.

Roberts, Dorothy. 2011. *Fatal Invention: How Science, Politics, and Big Business Re-create Race in the Twenty-First Century*. New York: The New Press.

Robert, Jason, and Françoise Baylis. 2003. "Crossing Species Boundaries." *American Journal of Bioethics* 3, no. 2: 1–13. https://doi.org/10.1057/9781137349088_10.

Robles, Frances. 2015. "Dylann Roof Photos and a Manifesto Are Posted on Website." *New York Times*, June 20, 2015. https://www.nytimes.com/2015/06/21/us/dylann-storm-roof-photos -website-charleston-church-shooting.html.

Roddenberry, Gene, creator. 1967. *Star Trek: The Original Series*, "Space Seed." Directed by Marc Daniels, featuring William Shatner, Leonard Nimoy, and Ricardo Montalbán. Aired February 16, 1967.

Roddenberry, Gene, creator. 1968. *Star Trek: The Original Series*, "Plato's Stepchildren." Directed by David Alexander, featuring William Shatner, Leonard Nimoy, and De Forest Kelley. Aired November 22, 1968.

Roe, Phoenix. "5 Ways *The Walking Dead*'s Negan Is Trump." *Odyssey*, February 12, 2017. https://www.theodysseyonline.com/5-similarities-between-the-walking-deads-negan-and-our-president.

Roediger, David R. (1991) 2007. *The Wages of Whiteness*. New edition with an introduction by Kathleen Cleaver. New York: Verso.

Roose, Kevin. 2020. "What if Facebook Is the Real 'Silent Majority'?" *New York Times*, August 27, 2020. https://www.nytimes.com/2020/08/27/technology/what-if-facebook-is-the-real-silent-majority.html.

Rose, Steve. 2016. "Black Films Matter—How African American Cinema Fought Back Against Hollywood." *The Guardian* (US edition), October 13, 2016. https://www.theguardian.com/film/2016/oct/13/do-the-right-thing-how-black-cinema-rose-again.

Ross, Dalton. 2017. "*The Walking Dead* Producers Claim They Did Not Tone Down Violence Due to Backlash." *Entertainment Weekly*, January 23, 2017. https://ew.com/tv/2017/01/23/walking-dead-violence-season-7-producers/.

Ross, Janell. 2015. "Are Race Relations Really Worse Under President Obama?" *Washington Post*, August 4, 2015. https://www.washingtonpost.com/news/the-fix/wp/2015/08/04/are-race-relations-really-worse-under-president-obama/?utm_term=.57039b827ff3.

Ross, Marlon B. 2004. *Manning the Race: Reforming Black Men in the Jim Crow Era*. New York and London: New York University Press.

Rothstein, Edward. 2009. "The U.S.S. *Enterprise*, in Strange New World of Museum." *New York Times*, May 29, 2009. http://www.nytimes.com/2009/05/30/arts/design/30star.html.

Rotten Tomatoes. 2016. Review of Last Day on Earth: *The Walking Dead* Season 6. N.d. https://www.rottentomatoes.com/tv/the_walking_dead/s06/e16.

Rovin, Jeff. 1987. *The Encyclopedia of Supervillains*. New York: Facts on File.

Rupar, Aaron. 2020a. "Trump Is Facing a Coronavirus Threat. Let's Look Back at How He Talked about Ebola." *Vox*, February 26, 2020. https://www.vox.com/2020/2/26/21154253/trump-ebola-tweets-coronavirus.

Rupar, Aaron, 2020b. "Why Trump's Efforts to Blame Obama for the Coronavirus Make Absolutely No Sense." *Vox*, April 20, 2020. https://www.vox.com/2020/4/20/21227903/trump-blames-obama-coronavirus.

Rushton, J. Philippe. 1995. *Race, Evolution, and Behavior*. New Brunswick: Transaction Publishers.

Russonello, Giovanni. 2016. "Race Relations Are at Lowest Point in Obama Presidency, Poll Finds." *New York Times*, July 13, 2016. https://www.nytimes.com/2016/07/14/us/most-americans-hold-grim-view-of-race-relations-poll-finds.html.

Ryzik, Melena. 2016. "J. J. Abrams Takes Steps to Lift Diversity in Filmmaking." *New York Times*, March 3, 2016. http://www.nytimes.com/2016/03/03/movies/jj-abrams-takes-steps-to-lift-diversity-in-filmmaking.html.

Sacks, Ethan. 2013. "*Star Trek Into Darkness* Political Themes Stir Up Controversy." *New York Daily News*, May 22, 2013. http://www.nydailynews.com/entertainment/tv-movies/star-trek-darkness-political-themes-stir-controversy-article-1.1351740.

Saha, Anamik. 2018. *Race and the Cultural Industries*. Cambridge: Polity Press.

Sammy, Marisa. 2013. "*Star Trek*: Into Whiteness." *Racebending.com*, May 9, 2013. http://www.racebending.com/v4/featured/star-trek-whiteness/.

Sandler, Rachel. 2020. "How the CDC Botched Its Initial Coronavirus Response with Faulty Tests." *Forbes*, March 2, 2020. https://www.forbes.com/sites/rachelsandler/2020/03/02/how-the-cdc-botched-its-initial-coronavirus-response-with-faulty-tests/?sh=348fe18670ef.

Sarich, Vincent, and Frank Miele. 2004. *(Race): The Reality of Human Differences.* Boulder: Westview Press.

Sarkeesian, Anita. 2017. "Masculinity, Rage, and Racism: Some Thoughts on *War for the Planet of the Apes*." *Feminist Frequency* (blog), July 18, 2017. https://feministfrequency.com/2017/07/18/masculinity-rage-and-racism-some-thoughts-on-war-for-the-planet-of-the-apes/.

Schiappa, Edward. 2008. *Beyond Representational Correctness: Rethinking Criticism of Popular Media.* Albany: SUNY Press.

Schilling, Dave. 2016. "Empire's State of Mind: The New TV Shows Highlighting African Americans." *The Guardian* (US edition), January 22, 2016. https://www.theguardian.com/tv-and-radio/2016/jan/22/tv-show-empire-donald-glover-atlanta-shots-fired-african-american.

Schweitzer, Dahlia. 2018. *Going Viral: Zombies, Viruses, and the End of the World.* New Brunswick: Rutgers University Press.

Scott, A. O. 2012. "The Black, the White and the Angry." Review of *Django Unchained*, directed by Quentin Tarantino. *New York Times*, December 24, 2012. https://www.nytimes.com/2012/12/25/movies/quentin-tarantinos-django-unchained-stars-jamie-foxx.html.

Scott, A. O., and Manohla Dargis. 2013. "Movies in the Age of Obama." *New York Times*, January 16, 2013. https://www.nytimes.com/2013/01/20/movies/lincoln-django-unchained-and-an-obama-inflected-cinema.html.

Seeyle, Katharine Q., and Jeff Zeleny. 2008. "On the Defensive, Obama Calls His Words Ill-Chosen." *New York Times*, April 13, 2008. https://www.nytimes.com/2008/04/13/us/politics/13campaign.html.

Seigworth, Gregory, and Melissa Gregg. 2010. "An Inventory of Shimmers." In *The Affect Theory Reader*, edited by Seigworth and Gregg, 1–28. Durham: Duke University Press.

Seitz, Matt Zoller. 2014. "Dawn of the Planet of the Apes." Review of *Dawn of the Planet of the Apes*, directed by Matt Reeves. *RogerEbert.Com*, July 11, 2014. https://www.rogerebert.com/reviews/dawn-of-the-planet-of-the-apes-2014.

Serwer, Adam. 2018. "The Tragedy of Erik Killmonger." *The Atlantic*, February 21, 2018. https://www.theatlantic.com/entertainment/archive/2018/02/black-panther-erik-killmonger/553805/.

Sexton, Jared. 2011. "The Social Life of Social Death: On Afro-Pessimism and Black Optimism." *InTensions Journal* 5 (Fall/Winter): 1–47. https://www.yorku.ca/intent/issue5/articles/pdfs/jaredsextonarticle.pdf.

Sexton, Jared. 2016. "Afro-Pessimism: The Unclear Word." *Rhizomes* 29. https://doi.org/10.20415/rhiz/029.e02.

Sexton, Jared. 2017. *Black Masculinity and the Cinema of Policing.* Cham, Switzerland: Palgrave Macmillan.

Seymour, Gene. 2013. "Why 'The Butler' Is Groundbreaking." CNN, August 20, 2013. https://www.cnn.com/2013/08/19/opinion/seymour-the-butler/index.html.

Shabad, Rebecca. 2016. "Why More than 100 Gun Control Proposals in Congress Since 2011 Have Failed." CBS News, June 20, 2016. https://www.cbsnews.com/news/how-many-gun-control-proposals-have-been-offered-since-2011/.

Sharf, Zack. 2017. "*Get Out*: Jordan Peele Reveals the Real Meaning behind the Sunken Place." *IndieWire*, November 30, 2017. https://www.indiewire.com/2017/11/get-out-jordan-peele-explains-sunken-place-meaning-1201902567/.

Sharf, Zack. 2020. "Trevor Noah's Big *Tiger King* Lesson: Joe Exotic and Trump Are the Same Person." *IndieWire*, May 31, 2020. https://www.indiewire.com/2020/03/trevor-noah-tiger-king-joe-exotic-trump-1202221622/#!.

Sharma, Sanjay. 2013. "Black Twitter? Racial Hashtags, Networks and Contagion." *New Formations* 78 (Summer): 46–64. http://doi.org//10.3898/NEWF.78.02.2013.

Sharpe, Christina. 2016. *In the Wake: On Blackness and Being*. Durham, NC: Duke University Press.

Shaviro, Steven. 1993. *Cinematic Body*. Minneapolis: University of Minnesota Press.

Shear, Michael D. and Julie Hirschfield Davis. 2017. "Stoking Fears, Trump Defied Bureaucracy to Advance Immigration Agenda." *New York Times*, December 23, 2017. https://www.nytimes.com/2017/12/23/us/politics/trump-immigration.html?_r=0.

Sheffield, Matthew. 2017. "Trolling for a Race War: Neo-Nazis Are Trying to Bait Leftist 'Antifa' Activists into Violence—and Radicalize White People." *Salon*, April 27, 2017. https://www.salon.com/2017/04/27/trolling-for-a-race-war-neo-nazis-are-trying-to-bait-leftist-antifa-activists-into-violence-and-radicalize-white-people/.

Sheppard, Elena. 2017. "What the Alt-Right Wears and Why." *Nylon*, August 21, 2017. https://www.nylon.com/articles/alt-right-fashion-why.

Shohat, Ella and Robert Stam, eds. 2004. "Stereotype, Realism and the Struggle over Representation." In *Unthinking Eurocentrism: Multiculturalism and the Media*, edited by Ella Shohat and Robert Stam, 178–219. New York: Routledge.

Sides, John. 2017. "Race, Religion, and Immigration in 2016: How the Debate over American Identity Shaped an Election and What It Means for a Trump Presidency." Democracy Fund Voter Study Group, June 2017. https://www.voterstudygroup.org/publication/race-religion-immigration-2016.

Sim, Gerald. 2016. "Race and the Cinematic Machine." In *The Routledge Companion to Media and Race*, edited by Christopher P. Campbell, 87–95. New York: Routledge.

Sims, David. 2018. "What Chadwick Boseman and Lupita Nyong'o Learned about Wakanda." *The Atlantic*, February 28, 2018. https://www.theatlantic.com/entertainment/archive/2018/02/what-chadwick-boseman-and-lupita-nyongo-learned-about-wakanda/554474/.

Smarsh, Sarah. 2016. "Dangerous Idiots: How the Liberal Media Elite Failed Working-Class Americans." *The Guardian* (US edition), October 13, 2016. https://www.theguardian.com/media/2016/oct/13/liberal-media-bias-working-class-americans.

Smith, Allan. 2020. "Trump Attacks NASCAR and Bubba Wallace over Confederate Flag Banning, Noose Incident." NBC News, July 6, 2020. https://www.nbcnews.com/politics/donald-trump/trump-attacks-nascar-bubba-wallace-over-confederate-flag-banning-noose-n1232967.

Smith, David. 2020. "What Is 'Obamagate' and Why Is Trump So Worked Up about It?" *The Guardian* (US edition), May 11, 2020. https://www.theguardian.com/us-news/2020/may/12/what-is-obamagate-and-why-is-trump-so-worked-up-about-it.

Smith, Jamil. N.d. "The Revolutionary Power of Black Panther." *Time*, n.d. Accessed July 2020. https://time.com/black-panther/.

Smith, Mychal Denzel. "The Racial Politics Behind 'Planet of the Apes.'" *Grio*, August 5, 2011. https://thegrio.com/2011/08/05/the-racial-politics-behind-planet-of-the-apes/.

Southern Poverty Law Center. 2016. "Ten Days After: Harassment and Intimidation in the Aftermath of the Election." *SPLC: Southern Poverty Law Center Publication*, November 29, 2016. https://www.splcenter.org/20161129/ten-days-after-harassment-and-intimidation-aftermath-election.

Squires, Catherine. 2014, *The Post-Racial Mystique: Media and Race in the Twenty-First Century*. New York: New York University Press. Kindle.

Stanley, Alessandra. 2014. "Wrought in Rhimes's Image." *New York Times*, September 18, 2014. https://www.nytimes.com/2014/09/21/arts/television/viola-davis-plays-shonda-rhimess-latest-tough-heroine.html?_r=0.

Stanley-Becker, Isaac. 2020a. "Mask or No Mask? Face Coverings Become Tool in Partisan Combat." *Washington Post*, May 12, 2020. https://www.washingtonpost.com/politics/in-virus-response-riven-by-politics-masks-are-latest-rorschach-test/2020/05/12/698477d4-93e6-11ea-91d7-cf4423d47683_story.html.

Stanley-Becker, Isaac. 2020b. "White Instigators to Blame for Mayhem in Some Protests, Local Officials Say." *Washington Post*, June 1, 2020. https://www.washingtonpost.com/national/protests-white-instigators/2020/06/01/b916bd98-a426-11ea-bb20-ebf0921f3bbd_story.html.

Stanton, William. 1960. *The Leopard's Spots: Scientific Attitudes toward Race in America 1815–59*. Chicago and London: The University of Chicago Press.

Staples, Brent. "The Movie *Get Out* Is a Strong Antidote to the Myth of 'Postracial' America." *New York Times*, March 27, 2017. https://www.nytimes.com/2017/03/27/opinion/the-movie-get-out-is-a-strong-antidote-to-the-myth-of-postracial-america.html.

Stedman, Alex. 2014. "Leaked Sony Emails Reveal Jokes about Obama and Race." *Variety*, December 10, 2014. http://variety.com/2014/biz/news/leaked-sony-emails-reveal-jokes-about-obama-and-race-1201376676/.

Stein, Sam. 2016. "Donald Trump Suggest Obama May be Sympathetic to Islamic Terrorism." *HuffPost*, June 13, 2016. http://www.huffingtonpost.com/entry/trump-obama-isis-terrorism_us_575ea346e4b00f97fba8c1d7.

Stewart, Emily. 2020. "America's Growing Fake News Problem, in One Chart." *Vox*, December 22, 2020. https://www.vox.com/policy-and-politics/2020/12/22/22195488/fake-news-social-media-2020.

Stieb, Matt. 2019. "Everything We Know about the Inhumane Conditions at Migrant Detention Camps." *Intelligencer*, July 2, 2019. https://nymag.com/intelligencer/2019/07/the-inhumane-conditions-at-migrant-detention-camps.html.

St. John, Allen. "Walking Dead 703: Is Negan the Donald Trump of the Post-Apocalypse?" *Forbes*, November 6, 2016. https://www.forbes.com/sites/allenstjohn/2016/11/06/walking-dead-703-is-negan-the-donald-trump-of-the-post-apocalypse/?sh=5d4520c9155e.

Stout, Jeffrey. (1988) 2001. *Ethics after Babel: The Languages of Morals and Their Discontents*. Reprint with a new postscript by the author. Princeton: Princeton University Press.

Stratton, Jon. 2011. "Trouble with Zombies: Muselmanner, Bare Life, and Displaced People." *Somatechnics* 1, no. 1: 188–208.

Sumerau, J., and Sarah L. Jirek. 2015. "Post-Apocalyptic Inequalities: Race, Class, Gender, and Sexualities in *Firefly*." In Gurr 2015, 71–83.

Sussman, Dalia. 2015. "Negative View of U.S. Race Relations Grows, Poll Finds." *New York Times*, May 5, 2015. https://www.nytimes.com/2015/05/05/us/negative-view-of-us-race-relations-grows-poll-finds.html?_r=0.

Sutare, Patrick. 2020. "Bubba Wallace Ripped, Called Liar after FBI Probe Discovers 'Fake Noose.'" *International Business Times*, June 23, 2020. https://www.ibtimes.com/bubba-wallace-ripped-called-liar-after-fbi-probe-discovers-fake-noose-2999405.

Swaine, Jon, Oliver Laughland, Jamiles Larty, and Ciara McCarthy. 2015. "Young Black Men Killed by U.S. Police at Highest Rate in Year of 1,134 Deaths." *The Guardian* (US edition), December 31, 2015. https://www.theguardian.com/us-news/2015/dec/31/the-counted-police-killings-2015-young-black-men.

Tactical Editor. 2013. "Weapons of the Walking Dead." *Tactical Shit News* (blog), October 20, 2013. https://www.tacticalshit.com/weapons-walking-dead/.

Taibi, Catherine. 2015. "What's Not Working in Media's Coverage of Baltimore." *HuffPost*, April 28, 2015. https://www.huffpost.com/entry/baltimore-media-coverage_n_7164064.

Takacs, Stacy. 2012. *Terrorism TV: Popular Entertainment in Post-9/11 America*. Lawrence: University of Kansas Press.

Taylor, Jessica. 2015. "Trump Calls for 'Total and Complete Shutdown of Muslims Entering' U.S." *NPR*, December 7, 2015. https://www.npr.org/2015/12/07/458836388/trump-calls-for-total-and-complete-shutdown-of-muslims-entering-u-s.

Tesler, Michael, and David O. Sears. 2010. *Obama's Race: The 2008 Election and the Dream of a Post-Racial America*. Chicago: Chicago University Press.

Tesler, Michael. 2016a. *Post-Racial or Most-Racial? Race and Politics in the Obama Era*. Chicago: University of Chicago Press.

Tesler, Michael. 2016b. "Trump Is the First Modern Republican to Win the Nomination Based on Racial Prejudice." *Washington Post*, August 1, 2016. https://www.washingtonpost.com/news/monkey-cage/wp/2016/08/01/trump-is-the-first-republican-in-modern-times-to-win-the-partys-nomination-on-anti-minority-sentiments/.

Thernstrom, Abigail. 2013. "Obama's Mistake on Trayvon Martin Case." *CNN*, July 15, 2013. https://www.cnn.com/2013/07/15/opinion/thernstrom-trayvon-martin-obama/index.html.

Thompson, Ginger. 2019. "Border Patrol Agent Calls Migrant Prison Camp a 'Scene from a Zombie Apocalypse.'" *Truthout*, July 19, 2019. https://truthout.org/articles/border-patrol-agent-calls-migrant-prison-camp-a-scene-from-a-zombie-apocalypse/.

Thrasher, Steven. 2017. "Why *Get Out* Is the Best Movie Ever Made about American Slavery." *Esquire*, March 1, 2017. https://www.esquire.com/entertainment/movies/a53515/get-out-jordan-peele-slavery/.

Titley, Gavan. 2019. *Racism and Media*. London: Sage Publications.

Totenberg, Nina. 2020. "Supreme Court Rules for DREAMers, against Trump." *NPR*, June 18, 2020. https://www.npr.org/2020/06/18/829858289/supreme-court-upholds-daca-in-blow-to-trump-administration.

Travers, Peter. 2013. Review of *12 Years a Slave*, directed by Steve McQueen. *Rolling Stone*, October 17, 2013. https://www.rollingstone.com/movies/movie-reviews/12-years-a-slave-113891/.

Trianni, Francesca. 2021. "Flags, Hate Symbols and Qanon Shirts." *Time*, January 11, 2021. https://time.com/5928627/symbols-capitol/.

Trivedi, Bijal P. "Introducing ANDi: The First Genetically Modified Monkey." Genome News Network, January 16, 2001. http://www.genomenewsnetwork.org/articles/01_01/ANDi.shtml.

Trump, Donald. 2020. "Donald Trump Mount Rushmore Speech Transcript at 4th of July Event." Rev Transcripts. July 3, 2020. https://www.rev.com/blog/transcripts/donald-trump-speech-transcript-at-mount-rushmore-4th-of-july-event.

Trump White House. 2018. "Remarks by President Trump and Members of the Angel Families on Immigration." Trump White House Archives, June 22, 2018. https://trumpwhitehouse.archives.gov/briefings-statements/remarks-president-trump-members-angel-families-immigration/.

Trump White House. 2019. "President Donald J. Trump's Address to the Nation on the Crisis at the Border." Trump White House Archives, January 8, 2019. https://trumpwhitehouse

.archives.gov/briefings-statements/president-donald-j-trumps-address-nation-crisis-border/.
Tucci, Serena, and Joshua M. Akey. 2016. "A Map of Human Wanderlust." *Nature* 538 (September): 179–80. https://www.nature.com/articles/nature19472.
Turner, Jacob, and Lisa G. Perks. 2019. "White Men Holding on for Dear Life and Taking It." *Sex Roles* 81: 655–69. https://doi.org/10.1007/s11199019-1009-x.
Turner, Sarah E. and Sarah Nilsen, eds. 2019. *The Myth of Colorblindness: Race and Ethnicity in American Cinema*. London: Palgrave Macmillan.
USA Today. 2013. "Democrats Reintroduce Assault Weapons Ban." January 24, 2013. https://www.usatoday.com/story/news/politics/2013/01/24/assault-weapons-ban-feinstein-democrats/1861493/.
US House of Representatives. 2019. "Child Separations by the Trump Administration." Staff Report Committee on Oversight and Reform, July 2019. https://oversight.house.gov/sites/democrats.oversight.house.gov/files/2019-07-2019.%20Immigrant%20Child%20Separations-%20Staff%20Report.pdf.
Verhoeven, Beatrice. 2017. "Jordan Peele Reveals His Alternate *Get Out* Ending." *The Wrap*, March 3, 2017. https://www.thewrap.com/jordan-peele-reveals-alternate-get-out-ending/.
Verstraete, Ginette. 2011. "The Politics of Convergence." *Cultural Studies* 25, nos. 4–5 (July-September): 534–47. http://doi.org/10.1080/09502386.2011.600544.
Vigna, S. Della, and E. Kaplan. 2007. "The Fox News Effect: Media Bias and Voting." *Quarterly Journal of Economics* 122, no. 3: 1187–234.
Voltaire. (1772) 2009. *Les Lettres D'Amabed*, translated by L'Abbé Tamponet. Kessinger Publishing.
Wade, Nicholas. 2014. *A Troublesome Inheritance: Genes, Race, and Human History*. London and New York: Penguin.
Wald, Priscilla. 2008. *Contagious: Cultures, Carriers, and the Outbreak Narrative*. Durham: Duke University Press.
Walker, Chris. 2020. "Portland's Wall of Moms Joined by Dads with Leaf Blowers against Trump's Police." *Truthout*, July 21, 2020. https://truthout.org/articles/portlands-wall-of-moms-joined-by-dads-with-leaf-blowers-against-trumps-police/.
Wall Street Journal. 2009. "Why the Elderly Are Right to Worry When the Government Rations Medical Care." August 14, 2009. https://www.wsj.com/articles/SB10001424052970203863204574344900152168372.
Wallace, Carvell. 2018. "Why *Black Panther* Is a Defining Moment for Black America." *New York Times Magazine*, February 12, 2018. https://www.nytimes.com/2018/02/12/magazine/why-black-panther-is-a-defining-moment-for-black-america.html.
Walsh, Joan. 2016. "Can the Democrats Win Back White Working-Class Voters?" Nation, September 6, 2016. https://www.thenation.com/article/archive/can-the-democrats-win-back-white-working-class-voters/.
Wang, Amy B. 2017. "One Group Loved Trump's Remarks about Charlottesville: White Supremacists." *Washington Post*, August 13, 2017. https://www.washingtonpost.com/news/post-nation/wp/2017/08/13/one-group-loved-trumps-remarks-about-charlottesville-white-supremacists/.
Ward, Alex. 2020. "The Unmarked Federal Agents Arresting People in Portland, Explained." *Vox*, July 20, 2020. https://www.vox.com/2020/7/20/21328387/portland-protests-unmarked-arrest-trump-wold.

Warner, Kristen. 2015. "ABC's *Scandal* and Black Women's Fandom." In *Cupcakes, Pinterest, and Ladyporn: Feminized Popular Culture in the Early Twenty-First Century*, edited by Elana Levine, 32–50. Champaign: University of Illinois Press.

Warren, Calvin. 2018. *Ontological Terror: Blackness, Nihilism, and Emancipation*. Durham, NC: Duke University Press.

Washington Post. 2013. "President Obama's Remarks on Trayvon Martin" (full transcript). July 19, 2013. https://www.washingtonpost.com/politics/president-obamas-remarks-on-trayvon-martin-full-transcript/2013/07/19/5e33ebea-f09a-11e2-a1f9-ea873b7e0424_story.html.

Washington Post. 2015. "Full Text: Donald Trump Announces a Presidential Bid." June 16, 2015. https://www.washingtonpost.com/news/post-politics/wp/2015/06/16/full-text-donald-trump-announces-a-presidential-bid/.

Watson, Kathryn. 2020. "A Timeline of What Trump Has Said on Coronavirus." CBS News, last updated April 3, 2020. https://www.cbsnews.com/news/timeline-president-donald-trump-changing-statements-on-coronavirus/.

Watts, Eric King. 2017. "Postracial Fantasies, Blackness, and Zombies." *Communication and Critical/Cultural Studies* 14, no. 4: 317–33. http://dx.doi.org/10.1080/14791420.2017.1338742.

Watts, Eric King. 2018. "'Zombies Are Real.' Fantasies, Conspiracies, and the Post-Truth Wars." *Philosophy and Rhetoric* 51, no. 4, 441–70.

Wayne, Michael. 2014a. "Ambivalent Anti-heroes and Racist Rednecks on Basic Cable: Post-race Ideology and White Masculinities on FX." *Journal of Popular Television* 2, no. 2: 205–25.

Wayne, Michael. 2014b. "Mitigating Colorblind Racism in the Postnetwork Era: Class-Inflected Masculinities in *The Shield*, *Sons of Anarchy*, and *Justified*." *Communication Review* 17: 183–201.

Weheliye, Alexander. 2014. *Habeus Viscus: Racializing Assemblages, Biopolitics, and Black Feminist Theories of the Human*. Durham, Duke University Press.

Weissert, Will, and Jonathan Lemire. 2020. "Face Masks Make a Political Statement in Era of Coronavirus." AP, May 7, 2020. https://apnews.com/article/virus-outbreak-donald-trump-ap-top-news-politics-health-7dce310db6e85b31d735e81d0af6769c.

White, Khadijah Costley. 2018. *The Branding of Right-Wing Activism: The News Media and the Tea Party*. Oxford: Oxford University Press.

Wilderson, Frank III. 2010. *Red, White, and Black: Cinema and the Structure of U.S. Antagonisms*. Durham, NC: Duke University Press.

Wilderson, Frank B. III, Samira Spatzek, and Paula von Gleich. 2016. "'The Inside-Outside of Civil Society': An Interview with Frank B. Wilderson III." *Black Studies Papers* 2, no. 1: 4–22.

Williams, Johnny E. 2015. "Talking about Race without Talking about Race: Color Blindness in Genomics." *American Behavioral Scientist* 59, no. 11: 1496–1517. https://doi.org/10.1177/0002764215568987.

Williams, Linda. 1991. "Film Bodies: Gender, Genre, and Excess." *Film Quarterly* 44, no. 4: 2–13.

Wilson, Christopher. 2020. "McConnell Puts Blame for 2020 Coronavirus Failure on Barack Obama, in Office 2009–2017." Yahoo! News, May 12, 2020. https://news.yahoo.com/coronavirus-trump-mcconnell-blame-obama-pandemic-140217286.html.

Wilson, Jason. 2016. "What Preppers and Survivalists Tell Us about America's Apocalyptic Readiness." *The Guardian* (US edition), February 10, 2016. https://www.theguardian.com/us-news/2016/feb/10/preppers-survivalists-survivalcon-expo-nuclear-bomb-republicans-mormons.

Wilson, Jason. 2019. "Leaked Emails Reveal Trump Aide Stephen Miller's White Nationalist Views." *The Guardian* (US edition), November 14, 2019. https://www.theguardian.com/us-news/2019/nov/14/stephen-miller-leaked-emails-white-nationalism-trump.

Wilson, Michael, Rod Serling, and Pierre Boulle, writers. 1968. *Planet of the Apes*. Directed by Franklin J, Schaffer, featuring Charlton Heston, Roddy McDowall, and Kim Hunter. Twentieth Century Fox, 112 min. DVD.

Winddance Twine, France, and Charles Gallagher. 2008. "The Future of Whiteness: A Map of the 'Third Wave.'" *Ethnic and Racial Studies* 31, no. 1: 4–24. http://dx.doi.org/10.1080/01419870701538836.

Winders, Jamie. 2016. "Immigration and the 2016 Election." *Southeastern Geographer* 56, no. 3 (Fall): 291–96.

Winkler, Adam. 2011. *Gunfight: The Battle over the Right to Bear Arms in America*. New York: W. W. Norton.

Winter, Aaron. 2017. "Charlottesville, Far-Right Rallies, Racism and Relating to Power," *Open-Democracy*, August 17, 2017. https://www.opendemocracy.net/en/charlottesville-far-right-rallies-racism-and-relating-to-power/.

Wise, Tim. 2010. *Colorblind: The Rise of Post-Racial Politics and the Retreat from Racial Equity*. San Francisco: City Lights Books.

Wofford, Taylor. 2015. "Donald Trump Retweets Racist Propaganda." *Newsweek*, November 23, 2015. https://www.newsweek.com/donald-trump-racist-retweet-twitter-397567.

Wolf, Cam. 2017. "The New Uniform of White Supremacy." *GQ*, August 27, 2017. https://www.gq.com/story/uniform-of-white-supremacy.

Wolfe, Cary. 1999. "Faux Post-Humanism, or Animal Rights, Neocolonialism, and Michael Crichton's *Congo*." *Arizona Quarterly* 55, no. 2 (summer): 115–53.

Worldometer. n.d. "COVID-19 Coronavirus Pandemic." Accessed July 6, 2021. https://www.worldometers.info/coronavirus/#countries.

Wuthnow, Robert. 2018. "Robert Wuthnow on *The Left Behind*." Princeton University Press, January 12, 2018. https://press.princeton.edu/ideas/robert-wuthnow-on-the-left-behind.

Wyatt, Rupert, director. 2011. *Rise of the Planet of the Apes*. Twentieth Century Fox, 105 min. DVD.

Yang, Yueqi. "'Bizarre' that Face Masks Are a Partisan Issue, NIH Chief Says." *Bloomberg*, July 19, 2020. https://www.bloomberg.com/news/articles/2020-07-19/-bizarre-that-face-masks-are-a-partisan-issue-nih-chief-says.

Yo, Zushi. 2016. "Scarlett Johansson in *Ghost in the Shell*: Why Hollywood Whitewashing Isn't Always Racist." *New Statesman*, May 18, 2016. https://www.newstatesman.com/culture/observations/2016/05/Scarlett-Johansson-ghost-shell-whitewashing-racist.

Yuen, Nancy Wang. 2016. *Reel Inequality: Hollywood Actors and Racism*. New Brunswick, NJ. Rutgers University Press.

Yuhas, Alan. 2013. "The Walking Dead Is All about Blood, Gore—and Gun Control." *The Guardian* (US edition), April 1, 2013. https://www.theguardian.com/commentisfree/2013/apr/01/walking-dead-blood-gore-gun-control-background-checks.

Zapotosky, Matt. 2020. "Trump Threatens Military Action to Quell Protests, and the Law Would Let Him Do It." *Washington Post*, June 1, 2020. https://www.washingtonpost.com/national-security/can-trump-use-military-to-stop-protests-insurrection-act/2020/06/01/c3724380-a46b-11ea-b473-04905b1af82b_story.html.

Zimmer, Carl. 2016. "A Single Migration from Africa Populated the World, Studies Find." *New York Times*, September 21, 2016. https://www.nytimes.com/2016/09/22/science/ancient-dna-human-history.html?action=click&contentCollection=Science&module=RelatedCoverage&region=EndOfArticle&pgtype=article.

INDEX

Abrajano, Marisa, 75–76, 83, 146
Affordable Care Act (ACA), and Republican opposition to, 78–79
Africa, as metaphor for contagion, 102, 105–6
African Americans: and ape imagery, 111–24, 147–49, 153; as biothreat, 102; excessive policing of, 25, 139, 145–46; and intelligence of, 119, 123–24, 213, 296; myth of exceptionalism, 25; purported criminality of, 42, 44, 84, 130, 143, 145–47, 153, 187, 256; representation in Reagan era, 36, 43–44; visibility in the media, 39–43, 206–8
Afrofuturism, 259, 291, 296–302
Afropessimism, 268, 307; and The Void, 291–92, 302, 306
Agamben, Georgio, 100; *bios* and *zoē*, 86
Ahmed, Sarah, 264, 274
Alexander, Michelle, 153, 242–43
alt-right: and Capitol riots, ix, 28–30, 33, 35, 61, 65, 71, 182; "Unite the Right" rally, ix, 29–32, 60–65, 69, 182, 319, 328; genetic testing and, 249; social media and, 43, 57–61, 66, 68–73
AMC network: and "Story Sync," 16, 99, 165; white niche marketing of, 99–100
America, and myth of "postracial," 9–13, 18, 34, 36, 102, 110, 120
"Angel" families, 95
animality: and association with Black people, 25, 127–54, 234, 240, 242, 258, 264,
299, 302–8; as SF trope, 14, 15, 20, 23, 24, 258
ape imagery, and the Obamas, 111–12, 114, 149–51
Arbery, Ahmaud, ix, 129
Arizona SB 1070, 89
Arpaio, Joe, 89
audience: political branding of, 4, 50, 55, 58, 66–67, 70, 309; as produsers, 16–17, 54, 58, 60, 61, 72, 147–48, 309, 330

Banet-Weiser, Sarah, 52, 53, 67, 309
Beck, Glenn, 55, 111, 149
Bell Curve, 124, 213
bioengineering: and chimeras, 116, 136, 122, 227, 230–34; and eugenics, 26, 212–13; and fears about empowering minorities, 110, 122, 204–5, 211–13, 216, 224, 225–34, 251
bios and *zoē*, 86
Bishop, Kyle, 87, 90, 97
Black Lives Matter, 16, 18, 23, 43, 48, 62, 65, 71, 332n, 336n; and Freddie Gray, 144–45; and George Floyd, 22, 29, 157–58; and media, 12, 24, 33, 54, 55, 143, 144–45; and Trayvon Martin, 42, 130, 143, 206; and Trump, 30, 256
Black Panther, 21, 22, 26, 290–308; Afrofuturism of, 22, 259, 291, 296–97, 299–302; ontological becoming and, 299, 302, 305, 306
BlacKkKlansman, 21, 257, 261
Blacks. *See* African Americans

Blind Side, The, 40
BLM. *See* Black Lives Matter
Blumenbach, Johann, 122, 123, 247, 335n
Bolnick, Deborah, 249, 250
Bonilla-Silva, Eduardo, 20, 32, 42, 45, 48, 130; white habitus, 51–52
Bowers, Robert, 60, 61
Breaking Bad, 98, 99, 100, 101
Breitbart, 34, 57, 58, 66, 150, 332n
Brown, Michael, 25, 42, 130, 136, 138, 139, 144, 189, 206, 244, 285; and Darren Wilson, 138–39, 145, 189, 206; Ferguson uprising and, 134–36, 139, 141, 144, 146, 147, 150, 151, 153, 244
Bruns, Axel, and produsage, 54, 331n
Buchanan, Pat, 84, 151
Burgin, Xavier, 267

Calhoun, John C., 123
Canavan, Gerry, 87, 90, 159
Capitol Riots, ix, 28–30, 33, 35, 61, 65, 71, 182
Carrol, Noel, 264, 271, 277–79, 338n
Center for Disease Control (CDC): and appearance in *TWD*, 91, 92, 101; and contagion narratives, 101; and COVID-19 response, 3, 101, 106, 334n
Charlottesville, Virginia. *See* "Unite the Right" rally
Clinton, Hillary: and James Comey, 46; and Obama, 149, 160; and Trump, 58, 65, 66, 317
Clover, Carol, 263, 264, 271; and "final girl" trope, 272–74, 286
Coates, Ta-Nehisi, on Trump, 38, 49
Coleman, Robin Means, 265–67
colorblind casting, 41, 45
colorblindness, and racism, 9, 20, 21, 24, 36, 37, 110, 143, 155, 179, 207, 310
Complex TV, 165
Conquest of the Planet of the Apes (1972), 16, 109, 118, 227; and *Dawn of the Planet of the Apes,* 153, 227, 234, 244; and *Rise of the Planet of the Apes,* 119, 137, 234, 238, 240, 244
conspiracy theories, and alt-right, 31, 60, 68, 85, 167–68, 332n

contagion: as metaphor for foreign/racial other, 4, 25, 75–124; as SF trope, 14–15, 20, 23–25
Contagion (2011), 4, 102
convergence: of media, 5–7, 69; Jenkins and, 34, 54, 57; and production of race narratives, 8, 12, 18, 24, 35
Coogler, Ryan, 14, 21, 22, 23, 26, 258, 259, 294–96, 303–6
Courtney, Susan, 52, 207
COVID-19 (coronavirus), ix, 101; death tolls and, 3, 4; lockdowns and, 28, 62, 104, 127; masking and, 5, 71; as media event, 4, 6, 8; racial disparities and, 332n; Trump's handling of, 3, 104, 107, 256

DACA, 12, 23, 24, 75, 85, 91, 94–95
Daniels, Lee: *The Butler,* 40, 41; *Empire,* 41
Dawn of the Planet of the Apes (2014): and contagion discourse, 101–21; and race riot imagery, 25, 130, 131–54
DeCook, Julia, 59, 69–70, 147
Democratic Party: and cloning, 229; on gun control, 155, 160–62, 168; and immigration, 76, 82, 337n; and purported "softness" on terrorism, 106; representation in *The Walking Dead,* 195–96; and Trump, 3, 28, 30, 95; and white "left-behind" narratives, 45–46; and white voters, 77, 84
Django Unchained (2012), 40
Doane, Ashley "Woody," 36–37
Dobbs, Lou, and immigration, 83
dog whistle racism, 9, 105, 154, 189
doomsday preppers, 25, 161; rise of during Obama presidency, 167–68; and *The Walking Dead,* 156
DREAM Act, 89, 94–95
Due, Tananarive, 260, 266, 267

Eberhardt, Jennifer, 112, 153
Ebola: and association in media with Obama and Africa, 102, 104–7, 114, 115, 334n, 335n; *Outbreak* and, 102, 105, 115
Elysium (2013), ACA and theme of immigration in, 78–81
Erigha, Maryann, 22, 257

Fairness Doctrine (1949), 52, 333n
fake news: and produsage, 56; and Trump, 333n
fandom: and alt-right movements, 67–68, 165; and political brand identification, 34, 66–67; and Shondaland shows, 41–42; and *Star Trek* franchise, 13, 209, 213–15; strategic use in politics and racial movements, 34; and *The Walking Dead*, 16, 98, 99, 101, 155, 156, 164, 165, 176, 181, 182, 184, 192, 311–16; and whiteness, 16, 68, 155, 176, 182, 257
Fanon, Frantz, 237, 264, 268, 283, 337n
Fawaz, Ramzi, 290, 292–93, 294, 296, 302
Feagin, Joe R., 34, 51–53, 130
Ferguson uprising. See Brown, Michael
Fields, James Alex, 60, 63
Fiske, John: and media event, 6; on role of audience, 54; and social and political discourse of media, 7, 35, 107, 310, 330
Fleetwood, Nicole, 258–59
Floyd, George: and charging of Derek Chauvin, 128, 336n; protests after murder of, ix, 29, 42, 127; and Trump response to protests, 127–28, 157
Fox News: and COVID-19 reporting, 3; and relation to alt-right online trolling, 58–59, 66
franchises, and paratexts of, 6, 15–16, 20, 147
Frankenberg, Ruth, 36, 44
Fruitvale Station (2013), 22, 40, 261

Garner, Eric, 25, 42, 127, 138, 261, 285
genetic testing: and purported racial differences, 248–51; use by alt-right and, 249
gerrymandering, 3
Get Out (2017), 260–68; parodic miscegenation in, 26, 273; white fetishization of Black bodies in, 258–59, 262, 268, 271, 286–88, 310; white liberals/progressives in, 264, 280, 281, 282, 285, 286, 287
Giffords, Gabby: and shooting of, 161–62, 163; and Palin, 162, 336n
Gillespie, Michael Boyce, 258
Goff, Phillip, 112, 153
Goffman, Erving, 53

Goldberg, David Theo, 9, 49
Gould, Stephen Jay, 113, 124, 335n
Gray, Freddie, 130; and Baltimore protests, 134, 135, 141, 142, 144, 151, 153, 206, 244; media coverage of, 144–46
Gray, Herman, 7, 21, 22, 23, 35, 147, 198; on race and new media technologies, 44, 52, 129, 309; on representations of race in 1980s, 10, 36, 43
Gray, Jonathan, 15, 67, 101, 108, 109, 114
Great Replacement Theory, 39; immigration and, 83, 206; white genocide and, 84–85, 100
Greene, Eric: and civil rights movements, 109; on "planet of the apes" as sign of racial apocalypse, 110, 147, 149; and race in original *Planet of the Apes* franchise, 108, 120–21, 150, 151–52, 153–54, 227, 228, 235, 239, 242, 244, 334n, 335n; and Watts riots, 137
gun control: and NRA, 161; and Sandy Hook, 161, 174; and Second Amendment, 5, 12, 330

Hall, Stuart: audience agency, 53–54, 69, 71, 72, 83, 98; and media framing, 6, 39, 72; and *Policing the Crisis*, 35–36, 129–30
Hanich, Julian, 283, 287, 337n
Harris, Sam, and Murray interview, 124
Hartman, Saidiya, 261–62, 268–71, 275, 276, 282, 299
Help, The (2011), 40
hillbillies: as marginalized form of whiteness, 192; in *The Walking Dead*, 165, 179, 181, 192
H1N1 virus, and the Obama administration, 101, 102, 115, 334n, 335n
horror, affective possibilities of Black, 257–89
Horror Noire (book), 265
Horror Noire (documentary), 266, 267
human genome: and bioengineering, 212, 228; and chimeras, 230, 232; fears about cloning, 229; mapping of, 121; use in reifying race, 121–22, 247, 250–51

If Beale Street Could Talk (2018), 21, 257, 261
immigration: and media coverage of, 33, 38, 75–76, 83, 97, 309, 330; Tea Party opposition to, 85, 256; Trump voters and, 76, 90; white backlash against, 32, 43, 45, 46, 75. *See also* DACA; DREAM Act; Great Replacement Theory
imperiled whiteness: feeling among whites, 8, 10, 23, 34–39, 43–52, 70–72, 78; as programming cycle, 17–19, 22, 24, 179; speculative fiction and, 13, 16–17, 23, 88, 310, 327
in-group identity, and whites, 17, 31–35, 45, 50, 123. *See also* Jardina, Ashley

Jackson, Zakiyyah, 22, 298–307
January 6 riots. *See* Capitol Riots
Jardina, Ashley, 11, 31–38, 43, 47, 50; on American identity as white, 34; on perception of anti-white discrimination, 43, 51; Trump voters and white identity, 47; white in-group favoritism, 17, 31, 32, 35, 36, 50. *See also* in-group identity; out-group hostility
Jenkins, Henry: and fandom, 67, 214–15; and media convergence, 5, 34, 54, 57; and produsage, 60; and transmedia, 57, 67

Kaufmann, Eric: and partisan media, 53, 85; and white antipathy to immigrants, 32–33, 47, 83, 85; on white ethnic pride, 11, 38, 44, 45; and white Trump voters, 38, 46
Kellner, Douglas: and Hollywood and political ideologies, 108, 110, 152, 321; and media spectacle, 143, 145, 146
Kelly, Casey Ryan: and doomsday preppers, 167; and gun use by white men, 155–56, 162, 163, 170, 173; and toxic white masculinity, 30, 180
King, Rodney, and riots, 43, 120, 137, 138
Ku Klux Klan, and David Duke, 30

Latino/a/x people. *See* immigration
Levina, Marina, 102, 105, 107
Limbaugh, Rush, 3, 33, 37

Lipsitz, George, 8, 35; on genre, 263; and white identity, 48, 50, 271
Lotz, Amanda, 99
Loza, Susana, 130, 237

Mad Men, 99–100
Martin, Trayvon: and media framing of, 130, 143–44; Obama's comments on death of, 42, 150; social media practice of "Trayvoning" and, 144, 148
masculinity: and alt-right, 50, 70; Black, in *The Walking Dead*, 150, 170–74, 185–91, 237; in *Breaking Bad*, 98–100; in *Mad Men*, 100; white, in *The Walking Dead*, 25, 88, 90, 99–100, 155–99, 329
McCloskey, Mark and Patricia, 62, 65
media: agenda-setting of, 11, 33, 39, 53, 66; "always-on" nature of, 12, 24, 55; framing by, 11, 33, 39, 53–54, 83, 97, 129, 309, 330; partisan nature of, 52–60; and race-making, 12, 14, 24, 51–52, 68–72, 143, 145, 146, 330. *See also* produsage
memes: use by alt-right, 12, 69; fandom and, 42; of Obama, 147, 148; outrage and, 59; Pepe the Frog, 66; social and political messaging of, 56, 59
Metz, Christian, 271
Mittell, Jason, 165–66
monstrosity, and SF trope, 14, 15, 18, 20, 23, 24, 203–51
Morton, Samuel, 122–23, 249
MSNBC, 53
Murray, Charles, 124, 213

Nelson, Alondra, 124, 249
neo Nazis: and presence on social media, 60–61, 147; and support for Trump, 11, 29–35, 43, 45, 49, 84, 250, 311; and targeting of Obama, 43, 49, 147, 149; and "Unite the Right" rally, 29–32, 63, 65; on *The Walking Dead*, 192–93, 318, 319; in *War for the Planet of the Apes*, 323, 327
networks: broadcast, 99, 333n; cable, 53, 99; decentralization of, 52; digital ecology of, 56
Nygaard, Taylor, and Jorie Lagerwey, *Horrible White People*, 17–18, 36, 110

Oath Keepers, 30, 32
Obama, Barack: and ape imagery, 111–12, 114, 149–51; on Martin's death, 42, 150; Trump's statements about, 106, 334n; white backlash against, 49, 71, 120, 208
Obamacare. *See* Affordable Care Act
Omi, Michael, and Howard Winant, 84, 109, 250–51; colorblindness, 10, 48, 207; dog whistle racism, 154; racial rearticulation, 48–49, 110, 154, 213
Outbreak (1995), 102, 115; and coronavirus pandemic, 4, 104, 105
out-group hostility, and whites, 11, 17, 23, 33, 35, 45, 50, 67, 123, 332n. *See also* Jardina, Ashley

Palin, Sarah: and ACA "death panels," 79; and Giffords, 162
"Pandemic TV," 3–9
Papacharissi, Zizi, 12, 39, 56–60
paratexts, 6; and *Planet of the Apes* franchise, 15–16, 101, 147; and *Star Trek* franchise, 15–16, 214; and *The Walking Dead*, 16, 20, 165
Peele, Jordan, 14, 21, 23, 26, 258, 259, 260–89; on *Get Out*, 257, 260, 263, 267; on *Us*, 262
Phillips, Whitney, 11–12, 56–59, 66
Planet of the Apes: and Obama meme, 111, 114, 147–50; as racist concept, 110, 147, 149
Planet of the Apes (1968). *See* Greene, Eric
Plantinga, Carl, 280, 286, 337n
Pokornowski, Steven, 82, 87, 169, 334n
police violence: toward Black people, 18, 25, 42–43, 114, 115, 127–31, 137–53, 179, 206, 222, 261, 285, 330, 336n. *See also* Brown, Michael; Floyd, George; Gray, Freddie; Rice, Tamir; Taylor, Breonna
postracial resistance, 14–15, 21–23, 26, 255–308; and Ralina Joseph, 14, 21
postracialism: and colorblindness in media, 13–15, 17, 20, 24, 34, 36, 39–40, 72, 110; cultivation of white identity in response to, 34–39, 72, 78; myth of, 9–20, 23, 24
preppers. *See* doomsday preppers
produsage, 7, 12, 17, 34, 54, 56, 58, 72, 309, 330, 331n; and alt-right, 58, 60, 61, 148

Proud Boys: and role in Capitol Riots, 29, 30; Western Chauvinism, 60, 68; and white identity, 32, 50

QAnon: role in Capitol Riots, 29, 30, 55

racism: and colorblindness, 9, 20, 21, 24, 36, 37, 110, 143, 155, 179, 207, 310; dog whistle, 9, 154; scientific, 121–24, 224, 225, 250–51, 335n. *See also* police violence
Reagan, Ronald, 36, 43, 44, 52, 333n
redlining, 18, 31
Republican Party: and Obama, 38, 78, 79, 81, 106–7, 111–12, 150; and race, 49, 65, 75, 83–84; and views on immigration, 47, 75–76, 83, 85; and *The Walking Dead*, 89, 194; and white "left behind" narrative, 10, 37, 46, 47, 48, 180, 197. *See also* bioengineering; gun control
Reyes, Xavier Aldana, 263–64, 271–84, 288–89
Rhimes, Shonda, 41–42
Rice, Tamir, 25, 140, 261
Rise of the Planet of the Apes (2011): and fears about bioengineering, 227–51; and white fears about African American empowerment, 101–24
Roof, Dylann, 60, 61, 332n

Schweitzer, Dahlia, 3, 87, 88, 96, 101, 105–7, 334n
Second Amendment, 5, 12, 160–62, 168; Trump and, 129, 255; *The Walking Dead* and, 155–58, 160; whiteness and, 168, 169. *See also* doomsday preppers; gun control
Sexton, Jared, 144, 149–50
Sharpe, Christina, 298
Shaviro, Steven, 282, 288
social media: activism on, 52–56; and Black Twitter, 68; fake news and Trump, 58, 65; as forum for exploring white identity, 39, 43–44, 51, 57, 58–61, 68–72, 309–10, 330; impact on mainstream media news, 12, 56–60; as site of self-branding, 70; trolling and meme culture, 12, 56–61, 66, 68–69, 148; use of hashtags in, 55

speculative fiction (SF): Black authors of, 14, 21; infection narratives of, 97; marginalization of Black directors in, 257; as political and social allegory, 15, 17, 20, 257, 310; progressive possibilities of, 21, 23, 26, 258–59, 290, 297–302; racism of, 13, 15, 17, 18–19, 44, 82–83, 96–97, 208, 224, 290, 310; whitewashing and, 18, 208

Squires, Catherine, 9, 10, 20

Star Trek: The Original Series, race and, 13, 15–16, 205, 209, 223

Star Trek Beyond (2016), 25, 216–26

Star Trek II: The Wrath of Khan (1982), and Ricardo Montalbán, 204, 210–14, 224

Star Trek Into Darkness (2013), 25, 204–6, 209–16, 221, 223–26; representation of terrorism, 215–16; whitewashing Khan in, 209–15

Star Wars: The Force Awakens (2015), and white genocide claims, 204

"Stop the Steal" rally, 28, 29, 61

Straight Outta Compton (2015), 261

Tarrio, Enrique, 68

Taylor, Breonna, 128

Tea Party, 49, 55, 85, 150, 168, 256, 331n; opposition to ACA, 79

Tiger King, 5–8; Joe Exotic and Trump, 5, 331n

Titley, Gavan, 9, 12, 20, 55, 57, 61, 72, 144

transmedia, 7, 8, 11, 15, 17, 20, 22; convergence, 8, 24; and Jenkins, 57–58; role in articulating race, 20, 22, 23, 45, 66–69; use by alt-right, 56–58

Trump, Donald: Capitol Riots and, 28–30; comparison to *The Walking Dead*'s Negan, 316–17; family separation policy, 85–86; fandom and, 34, 67–68; impeachment of, 28, 332n; "shithole countries" comment by, 105, 333n; statements about Mexicans, 75, 77, 84; statements about Obama, 106, 107, 334n; on the "Unite the Right" rally, 29–30; white identity and support for, 24, 28–38, 43–47, 51, 65–72; white voters and, 35, 40, 46–47, 50–51, 65, 76–77, 84–85, 107, 129, 168, 197, 332n

12 Years a Slave, 40

"Unite the Right" rally, 29, 30, 31, 32, 37, 61, 62, 63, 64, 65, 69, 182, 319, 328

United States. *See* America

Us (2019), 21, 22, 26, 258, 262–89

Voting Rights Act, 42

Waco (2018), 5–8

Wade, Nicholas, 247–50

Walking Dead, The: Alpha, 159, 163, 318–20; Daryl, 175–76, 180, 183, 184, 186–89, 192–99; fan response to gratuitous violence in, 312, 314; guns in, 155–99; Merle, 16, 93, 175–85, 192–99; Michonne, 16, 93, 172–74, 175–76, 180, 182–85, 191, 192, 198, 329, 330; microtargeting viewers by Trump campaign, 90; Negan, 27, 159, 160, 163, 175, 311–18; "Story Sync" platform and, 16, 99, 165; white masculinity in, 25, 88, 90, 99–100, 155–99, 329; zombies and, 25, 88–98, 158–99

Wallace, Bubba, 113

War for the Planet of the Apes (2017), 108, 116, 311, 321–30

Warner, Kristin, 42, 45

Warren, Calvin, 299–300

Watts riots, 127, 137, 139–40, 152, 244

Weheliye, Alexander, 169–70

white identity politics, 9–12, 28–72. *See also* Jardina, Ashley; Kaufmann, Eric

white men: and doomsday preppers, 25, 161, 167–68; and left-behind narrative, 10, 37, 46, 47, 48, 180, 197; perceived victimization of, 48, 130; radicalization on social media, 11–12, 39, 43–44, 51, 57, 58–61, 68–72, 309–10, 330

white nationalism, 9, 16, 22, 23, 30, 65–68, 325. *See also* alt-right; neo-Nazis; outgroup hostility: and whites; white men: and radicalization on social media

white racial frame, 51–72, 130. *See also* Feagin, Joe R.

whiteness: as Americanness, 34; commodification by media, 9, 11, 38, 50, 198; as "imperiled," 8, 10, 23, 34–39, 43–52, 70–72, 78; multiracial expression in alt-right groups, 68; as performance, 11, 34, 58–72, 160; purported genocide of, 60, 78, 85, 96, 100, 204, 208; as racial frame, 51–72, 130; as unmarked/marked, 36, 44, 332n; working class, 8, 45–46, 49, 51, 77, 80, 88, 90, 141, 160, 166, 169, 175, 179–81, 192–98, 208

whitewashing, in *Star Trek Into Darkness*, 203–6, 209–16

Wilderson, Frank, 106, 141, 260, 268–71, 288, 297–307, 338n

Williams, Johnny, 121, 122, 250

Wolverine Watchmen, and Gretchen Whitmer, 62, 65

Zimmerman, George, 143–44, 206

zoê, immigrant as, 86

Zoltan, Hajnal, 75

zombies: as bare life, 86, 87, 90; Haitian roots of, 87; as immigrant, 85–88, 94, 96, 100, 156; and 9/11, 87; and "Pandemic TV" cycle, 4, 6; in *The Walking Dead*, 25, 88–98, 158–99

ABOUT THE AUTHOR

Photo credit: © Cedrick May

Penelope Ingram is a Distinguished Teaching Professor and an associate professor in the Department of English at the University of Texas at Arlington. She is the author of *The Signifying Body: Toward an Ethics of Sexual and Racial Difference* and has published widely in race, gender, and cultural studies.